EDUCATION
OF THE
GIFTED

MERLE R. SUMPTION
PROFESSOR OF EDUCATIONAL ADMINISTRATION
UNIVERSITY OF ILLINOIS

and
EVELYN M. LUECKING
ASSOCIATE PROFESSOR OF EDUCATION
BALL STATE TEACHERS COLLEGE

THE RONALD PRESS COMPANY · NEW YORK

Library of Congress Catalog Card Number: 60–7767
PRINTED IN THE UNITED STATES OF AMERICA

Preface

The education of all boys and girls in American schools today is being questioned and evaluated. In such a period of examining practices developed for the education of all youth, it is only natural that the possibilities for, and practices of, teaching gifted youth so that they may more fully develop their potential should also come under scrutiny. The vital problem of educating gifted boys and girls is being studied in many areas by school and lay people. Much literature has been and is being published to help schools and communities analyze the problem and choose wisely, among the various possible programs, the one which in their combined judgment appears most promising for the gifted youngsters of their own community.

As yet, there are few school systems in this country that have planned and are conducting comprehensive programs for the education of the gifted. The number so organized has been estimated as less than 5 per cent of the total number of school systems in the United States. This book is written for the purpose of bringing together and interpreting the major research findings with regard to understanding and educating the gifted and to show its use in everyday school programs. It discusses the roles and responsibilities of the various professional workers, the parents, the community, and the general public. The authors believe that the best program for the education of the gifted will develop only as community and school investigate the many facets of the problem and decide upon the program best suited to their particular needs and resources.

The book has grown from the experience of the authors in working with gifted children in the classroom, with teachers and supervisors striving to develop and improve programs for educating the gifted, and with principals and superintendents responsible for the administration of such programs. It embodies their experiences in working with both school and community in solving educational problems. It promotes no particular viewpoint but rather attempts to present objectively the information presently available as to the advantages and disadvantages of the various kinds of educational organizations and practices in educating the gifted. It points out the need for and the uses of various types of educational facilities and materials designed to foster optimum educational development of the gifted.

The book is designed for teachers in service as well as for those students who are preparing to teach. Every teacher is a teacher of gifted children whether he wills it or not; gifted children may appear in any classroom at any time. The concepts developed for understanding the gifted youngster as he is should prove especially helpful to teachers in regular classrooms who may have had no previous study in the area but are confronted with the task of teaching some gifted children every year. The overview of problems in administering programs of education of the gifted, although possibly of primary interest to superintendents and principals, should aid both teachers and parents as well in seeing the problem in a larger perspective as it relates to the over-all school program. The chapters presenting organizational patterns and indicating the kinds of experiences helpful to the gifted at all levels of education from preschool through college should also help teachers to develop a clearer understanding of the entire process of education as it relates to the gifted and assist them in determining which methods and procedures seem to be best suited to their own students.

This book gives a brief history of the attitudes toward, and theories of, education for the gifted and reviews educational practices throughout the country. It presents methods, formal and informal, that may be used by teachers and parents in identifying giftedness. Documented information from accepted research applicable to the education of the gifted is presented in order to help the reader build a consistent and accurate picture of the gifted. Various forms of acceleration, enrichment, and instructional grouping are discussed objectively. There is a detailed analysis of the personal and professional qualifications deemed desirable for the teachers of the gifted.

It is hoped that this comprehensive presentation of research and theory, of organization and procedures, and of practices and personnel will make some contribution to the development of solidly based and well thought out programs for the education of the gifted.

The authors gratefully acknowledge the valuable assistance of Professors Glenn Blair, Norman Gronlund, and T. Ernest Newland of the University of Illinois and Laura Schroeder of Ball State Teachers College in reading and criticizing the manuscript. Thanks are due as well to Mrs. Therese Jowasky and Mrs. Rhea Cabin for their assistance in preparing the manuscript. The authors also take this opportunity to express appreciation to the authors and publishers who generously gave permission to quote.

MERLE R. SUMPTION
EVELYN M. LUECKING

February, 1960

Contents

CHAPTER   PAGE

1 THE NATURE OF GIFTEDNESS 3

2 A HISTORICAL OVERVIEW 21

3 IDENTIFICATION OF THE GIFTED CHILD . . . 41

4 RESEARCH ON THE GIFTED 64

5 GUIDANCE OF THE GIFTED 108

6 ADMINISTRATION OF EDUCATION FOR THE GIFTED . 157

7 PRESENT ORGANIZATION AND PRACTICE . . . 184

8 TEACHERS FOR THE GIFTED 233

9 THE ROLE OF THE COMMUNITY 258

10 THE PRESCHOOL PROGRAM 290

11 THE ELEMENTARY-SCHOOL PROGRAM . . . 333

12 THE SECONDARY-SCHOOL PROGRAM 386

13 THE COLLEGE PROGRAM 442

    NAME INDEX 477

    SUBJECT INDEX 479

vii

EDUCATION
OF THE
GIFTED

1

The Nature of
Giftedness

Who are the gifted? What is giftedness? In what terms
should it be defined? These questions have been raised many
times and answered in many ways. All or almost all students
of the gifted are agreed in general on the broad meanings of
the terms. However, there are many kinds of definitions,
varieties of concepts, and differences in degree of inclusive-
ness of definitions.

The extremes in point of view are well represented, on the
one hand by the psychologist who says that the term "gifted"
is properly applied only to those who possess I.Q.'s of 140 or
above and on the other by the teacher who says, "All my
children are gifted—in one way or another." Neither position
is completely defensible. The most valid definition lies somewhere between, probably closer to that of the psychologist
than to that of the teacher quoted.

Early students in the field placed the greatest if not the
sole emphasis on innate capacity in defining giftedness. A
person was said to be gifted if it could be determined that
his mental capability was great. According to this definition
a person might go through life without rising above mediocrity with respect to performance in real-life situations and
yet be gifted. The term "real-life situations" is used here to
exclude performance in formal test situations. Of course, the
problem of determining innate capacity is a difficult one.
Only by some type of performance either in test or real-life

situations can any valid measure of capacity be obtained. Therefore, it is only natural that emphasis has shifted to the performance aspect as an essential factor in identifying giftedness. Society is naturally most interested in what the individual does, rather than what he has the potential to do; what he contributes, rather than what he has the capacity to contribute. Most present definitions of giftedness place emphasis upon the demonstration of ability as well as inherent capacity.

Thus, the concept of giftedness has taken on a developmental aspect. It is dynamic in nature, a continuously unfolding process. It is founded, however, upon the firm basis of a superior quality central nervous system capable of keen perception, accurate observation, and a high order of mental abstraction. Favorable conditions induce growth and realization accompanied by the power to organize experiences into complex patterns and relate them one to another. This concept recognizes the influence of environment on the development of intelligence as well as on other personality traits.

TYPES OF DEFINITIONS OF GIFTEDNESS

Giftedness has many definitions, but in general they all fall into one or another of the following classifications:

1. The objective definition
2. The descriptive definition
3. The comparative definition
4. A combination of two or three of the foregoing

Giftedness is usually objectively defined by reference to a score made on an intelligence test or similar instrument of measurement. For example, Lewis Terman, one of the foremost authorities on the gifted, used the score of 140 on the Stanford-Binet intelligence test as the lower limit for his gifted group. Leta Hollingworth and others have defined the gifted child as one having an I.Q. of 130 or above. Others have used 120, 125, and even 110 as cutoff points on the I.Q. scale. The standardized achievement test, the aptitude test, and similar instruments of measurement are other forms of tests which provide some objective measure of ability.

The descriptive definition is much more inclusive. For example, Witty defines the gifted child as one "whose performance, in a potentially valuable line of human activity, is consistently remarkable."[1] R. J. Havighurst has said that "gifted children are those individuals from kindergarten through high-school age who show unusual promise in some socially useful area and whose talent might be stimulated." Other descriptive definitions emphasize achievement, extraordinary curiosity, creative thinking, unusual ability to understand abstractions, exceptional breadth of interest, artistic ability, and even advanced physical and social maturity.

Definitions such as that of Witty are based upon performance. It may be assumed that in most cases the type of performance described is possible only because the individual possesses superior abstract intelligence. However, possible exceptions may be noted, principally in the creative arts. For example, some children who display remarkable ability in the graphic arts such as drawing and painting, are, *as far as can be determined by tests*, possessed of only average abstract intelligence. Those who excel in such creative arts as musical composition and poetry writing will be found to possess both abstract intelligence and creative imagination.

A number of definitions of the gifted are based on comparisons. Of course, to a certain extent all definitions contain at least an implied comparison. The intelligence test score is calculated on a comparative basis. When one speaks of extraordinary curiosity, unusual achievement, or exceptional breadth of interest, there is an implied comparison with the average child of the age group.

However, some definitions, such as "a gifted child is one who is able to show consistent superiority in academic achievement over the majority of his fellows in his age group," make direct comparisons. Other such definitions designate class rank, or academic rating which is so outstand-

[1] National Society for the Study of Education, *Education for the Gifted* (Chicago: University of Chicago Press, 1958), p. 62.

ing that it sets the student apart from other students, as criteria of giftedness. Some definitions are combinations of two or three of the general types noted.

A DEFINITION OF GIFTEDNESS

In seeking a usable and readily understood definition of the gifted the student should recognize that superior intellectual ability is the most common characteristic of giftedness. This type of ability makes possible the high order of abstract thinking which is prerequisite to outstanding performance in the vast majority of the areas of human endeavor. The possible exceptions lie in the field of creative arts where persons of exceptional talent are sometimes found to possess only average intellectual ability *as far as existing tests can determine.* It is entirely possible that a facet of intelligence yet unmeasured is present to a high degree in persons who excel in creative ability. For want of a better name it might be called creative imagination.

Therefore an acceptable definition of the gifted must recognize that present tests of mental ability may be incomplete or incapable of measuring the total spectrum of intelligence. If such is the case then the I.Q. must be ruled out as the sole determinant of the degree of giftedness. On the other hand, to adopt a definition such as "consistently remarkable performance in a potentially valuable line of human activity," which is admittedly ex post facto in nature, opens the door to a wide variety of interpretations. While the I.Q. test is too exclusive, the "remarkable performance" concept appears to be too inclusive.

For purposes of this text the gifted are defined as *those who possess a superior central nervous system characterized by the potential to perform tasks requiring a comparatively high degree of intellectual abstraction or creative imagination or both.*

Such a definition recognizes the I.Q. test as well as other tests as valuable instruments in measuring certain phases of giftedness; yet it allows for the probability that all phases are not presently measured. The definition makes potential the prerequisite, and performance the evidence, of giftedness. Giftedness, so defined, is dynamic in nature since it is manifested in the ability to perform tasks the nature of which change with the growth and development of the individual. It excludes those whose superior performance in real-life situations is due solely to personality factors such as persistence, charm, aggressiveness, and similar characteristics. Unlike Witty's definition, it might include the mastermind of a criminal syndicate as well as the statesman or inventor. It includes those whose potential has not been released. It excludes those who are merely skillful, or highly imitative, or merely possess extraordinary physical coordination.

It defines giftedness in terms of intelligence and imagination, in terms of general ability rather than specific types or kinds of ability. Such a definition might be called a definition of intellectual ability, which, in fact, it is, if the term "intellectual" is broadly defined to include both mental abstraction and creative imagination. With such a concept of giftedness extraordinary performance in science, mechanics, arts, social leadership, or academic pursuits is a result of a happy combination of intellectual giftedness with interest, perseverance, and other similar personality traits. When such a combination exists in a favorable environment the chances for outstanding performance are greatly enhanced. On the other hand, an individual possessing such a combination of characteristics could conceivably accomplish little or nothing if imprisoned, or marooned on a desert island.

The difference between this definition and definitions accepting performance as the sole criterion of giftedness is the limiting of performance to the role of evidence pointing to a high order of intellectual abstraction or creative imagination. For example, leadership performance characterized by charm, cheerfulness, aggressiveness, persistence, courage, personal magnetism, and similar qualities does not necessarily denote the gifted leader. Such characteristics do not produce gifted social leadership unless they are accompanied by superior intellectual ability.

Two types of criteria may be employed in determining giftedness. One is performance on formal tests such as intelligence tests which are used as instruments to measure capacity in what may be called the abstract form. Consistently high performance on such tests is evidence of giftedness although the individual tested may not have expressed this ability in any real-life situation performance. On the other hand, failure to score high on such tests should not be regarded as conclusive evidence of non-giftedness. Low test performance may be due to lack of motivation or actual rejection of the tests. A second criterion is that of real-life situation performance revealed in academic work, creative activity, scientific investigation and the like. Consistently superior work in school due to ability to grasp concepts quickly, to see complicated relationships, to draw generalizations accurately, and to master complex patterns of thinking has great validity as evidence of giftedness. When a good academic record is due largely to ability to memorize, to aggressiveness, industriousness and persistence, it is dubious evidence. On the other hand, low academic standing should not be regarded as incontrovertible evidence of lack of giftedness since factors such as ill health or lack of motivation may be involved.

The composition of a poem or an opera, or the creation of a work of art such as a beautiful painting, is substantial evidence of giftedness. Likewise, explorations in the field of science which lead to the discovery of previously unknown scientific truth are solid evidence. Performance in social leadership characterized by broad vision, conceptualization on a high level, and ability to organize also may be considered weighty evidence. These are all types of evidence exhibited in real life situations, available from observation and requiring no formal testing.

Thus giftedness as it is defined in this text assumes a superior central nervous system which reveals itself by extraordinary performance either in test or in real-life situations. The question as to whether such a superior central nervous system is inherent or is acquired is not debated here since it is not germane to the definition. Suffice it to say the dynamic concept of intelligence to which the authors subscribe regards the growth and development of the central nervous system as a fact of life. It is quite reasonable to assume that an individual seriously handicapped by distinctly unfavorable environment in early life might show a significant improvement in test ability when placed in a favorable environment. Whether the central nervous system was superior at birth or whether it developed superiority under favorable conditions is a matter of conjecture. It is not known whether superiority existed and favorable environment permitted it to reveal itself or whether superiority was acquired as the forces of a favorable environment came into play. On the other hand, one can only guess at the number of gifted children whose potential has never been even remotely realized because of unfavorable environmental factors.

How much can an extremely favorable environment affect intelligence? It no doubt has an appreciable effect, just as a very unfavorable environment exerts an opposite influence. However, the question of whether environment can make the difference between mediocrity and superiority is one which is subject to various interpretations and need not be discussed here.

The definition adopted permits no single measuring stick for giftedness. Although the intelligence test is an important instrument of measurement it is by no means all-inclusive. As has been indicated, creative imagination is one facet of giftedness which has thus far escaped objective measurement. Perhaps there are others which have escaped even identification.

Under this definition of the gifted any estimate of numbers is of necessity purely arbitrary. However, a reasonable approximation based on test results and observation would probably be somewhere between 5 and 10 per cent of the general population at each age level. Thus in a group of typical children entering the first grade one or two in twenty might be expected to be gifted. This percentage would tend to vary somewhat from community to community as factors of heredity and environment exert their influence.

Included within this group is the extremely gifted individual, often referred to as a genius. Only about .1 per cent or one in a thousand merits this classification.

Specific Characteristics

There are many characteristics which singly or in combinations appear in those who are gifted in terms of this definition. These characteristics include:

1. Ability to form concepts
2. Ability to do creative thinking
3. A wide variety of interests
4. An active imagination
5. Extraordinary insight
6. Intellectual curiosity or desire to know
7. Originality in thinking
8. Power to generalize
9. Power to do inductive as well as deductive thinking
10. Ability to improvise
11. Sensitivity to problem situations
12. Fluency of ideas
13. An extensive vocabulary
14. Ability to visualize objects in several dimensions
15. Ability to memorize rapidly
16. Ability to retain and recall information
17. A relatively long span of attention

POTENTIAL AND PERFORMANCE

Potential, whether the result of heredity or of environment or both, is the basic concept of giftedness. To the extent that a child's potential is the result of heredity it is fixed; to the extent that it is affected by environment, it is flexible.

While society is most interested in performance, the psychologist is just as much interested in potential. He is challenged to discover potential wherever it may be. He has devised tests of various types designed to unveil hidden capacity. The educator, too, is interested in potential because he seeks both to develop it and to release it in the form of performance. The greater potential of the gifted promises greater performance once it is discovered, developed, and released into beneficial avenues of endeavor.

This concept of giftedness offers a challenge to psychologists and educators to seek out and release potentials which in the case of the gifted promise performance of rare excellence. Observation, measurement, and study of performance serve to help them identify potential and guide its expression into avenues of greatest benefit to the individual and society as a whole.

The potential of the gifted individual may find expression in one or more of a variety of general ways. This expression is referred to in this text as a manifestation of giftedness. These manifestations are performance abilities which can be fairly easily observed and in most cases objectively measured.

MANIFESTATIONS OF GIFTEDNESS

Giftedness manifests itself in a variety of ways. In its manifestations it is not infrequently confused with skills, attitudes, and certain behavior patterns. The more common types of manifestations are discussed below.

Academic Ability

The gifted, as defined in this text, are usually academically talented. They possess the intellectual ability necessary to exceptional achievement in the academic field. They are able to deal with abstract concepts and through depth of insight can form generalizations which escape most of their fellows. They have the ability to relate experiences in various combinations and to draw inferences from these relationships.

They have the ability to succeed in schoolwork, to advance in the educational program more rapidly than the average student. They do not always do so, of course, because of the many other factors which are involved in the achievement of outstanding scholarship. They sometimes fail because of lack of interest or challenge, or opportunity.

Nevertheless, they possess the ability to succeed academically; the rapidity with which the gifted are able to learn is perhaps their outstanding characteristic. Terman and Oden[2] state with reference to pupils in grades 3 through 8 that:

> It is a conservative estimate that more than half of the children with IQ's of 135 or above had already mastered the school curriculum to a point two full grades beyond the one in which they were enrolled, and some of them as much as three or four grades beyond.

Creative Ability

Creative ability is defined in a number of ways, but the common element in all definitions is the production of something new. There are, no doubt, a variety of creative processes all having a common element or elements. The type of personality, the cultural environment, and even the specific situation may affect the nature of the creative process. G. Wallas[3] describes the creative process as a four-stage development:

1. A period of preparation
2. A period of incubation
3. An illumination
4. A period of verification

Although this analysis of the creative process is helpful, it is merely descriptive and gives no clue to the mystery of the moment of insight, "illumination."

Creative ability, like academic ability, is a general ability which is basic to success in many types of endeavor. It is demonstrated in art, music, dramatics, poetry, social relations, and science. Many gifted persons possess creative ability of a high order. Creativity is based on an active imagination which is one of the common characteristics of the gifted person. However, it should not be assumed that all gifted people have exceptional creative ability. Some possess intelligence of a high order and yet do not display creative

---

[2] L. M. Terman and Melita H. Oden, *The Gifted Child Grows Up* (Stanford, Calif.: Stanford University Press, 1947), p. 28.

[3] G. Wallas, *The Art of Thought* (New York: Harcourt, Brace & Co., 1926), p. 80.

talent. Whether or not creative ability lies dormant in such people because it has not been stimulated to expression is an open question. Although creative thinking is prerequisite to creativity, it does not follow that all creative thinking results in creative expression.

The ability to create finds expression in many fields. The playwright who creates a drama, the artist who paints a portrait, the statesman who makes a major contribution to a cooperative plan among nations, and the physical scientist who develops a space rocket, are all exercising creative ability. The various interests which they have determine to a large extent the type of expression each will seek for his creative ability.

Creative ability is not easy to identify in children and even more difficult to measure. Paul Witty has suggested the use of films to promote creative expression as well as to identify those with extraordinary creative ability.[4] Close observation of performance will help in discovering creative talent, but offers only a very gross yardstick for this type of ability. J. P. Guilford of the University of Southern California suggests some leads toward measurement of creative ability in his analysis of what he terms the "structure of intellect." He regards creative ability as a function of divergent thinking which means thinking in varied directions. Thus versatility of intellectual response may be an important factor in creative ability.[5]

Leadership Ability

The ability to lead others, to aid and guide a group in achieving desired goals, is one of the common expressions of giftedness. Leadership assumes varied characteristics. In one case it is characterized by exhortation, in another, persuasion, and in yet another, behind-the-scenes guidance. It is

---

[4] Paul Witty, "The Use of Films in Stimulating Creative Expression and in Identifying Talented Pupils," *Elementary English*, XXXIII (1956), 340-44.

[5] J. P. Guilford, *Creative Intelligence and Education* (Los Angeles: California Educational Research and Guidance Association in conjunction with the Los Angeles County Supt. of Schools Office, Division of Research and Guidance, 1958).

manifested in many fields of human endeavor including business and industry, professional organizations, labor unions, and civic organizations, as well as in local, state, and federal government. Wise leadership of whatever type and in whatever field involves the ability to make reasonably accurate assessments of future developments. This in turn requires a high order of mental ability capable of interpreting past experiences and relating them to the future.

However, superior intelligence, important as it is, is only one of the factors which is commonly associated with the successful leader. Among other characteristics are forcefulness, aggressiveness, persistence, tactfulness, courage, loyalty, personal magnetism, a cooperative attitude, strength of character, resourcefulness, and "ability to get along with people." If the gifted individual does not have or acquire some of these traits he is not likely to exercise much if any leadership. On the other hand, a person possessing many of the traits of leadership listed above is not likely to become a wise and successful leader if he does not possess superior intelligence.

Society may in general expect to secure high-quality leadership only from those who are gifted in terms of the definition adopted in this text, namely, "marked superiority in intellectual abstraction or creative imagination or both," and in addition possess certain complementary traits such as those listed above. These additional traits make it possible for the gifted person to effectively exert his influence in dealing with people and thus acquire and exercise a position of leadership.

In some cases an individual may possess the complementary traits to such a high degree that he actually exerts leadership of the kind which may not achieve the most desirable results. Certain combinations of traits which do not include intellectual ability and creative imagination may produce a social leader. However, the quality of his leadership and the net results are likely to be inferior. In other words, some social leadership is and probably always will be exercised by individuals of only average intelligence who possess

combinations of personality traits which gain acceptance
for them as leaders. However, this fact in nowise obviates the
need for, and importance of, leadership by the intellectually
gifted. It is from this group that the most effective, the most
rewarding, and the highest type of socially conscious, responsible leadership may be expected.

Scientific Ability

The value and importance of scientific ability have been
generally recognized for a long time. Now it assumes even
greater value and importance as the growing rivalry in the
development of scientific weapons and the conquest of space
poses serious problems in national survival.

Scientific ability is difficult to define, since it is probably
a compound of attitudes and inclinations and other abilities. It is closely related to creative ability and is most productive when combined with it. Quantitative reasoning
ability and power to do inductive as well as deductive thinking may be said to characterize scientific ability. The ability
to be impartial, objective, and accurate along with a tendency to weigh evidence carefully, characterizes the scientific
mind. Usually scientific ability includes verbal ability as well
as the ability to calculate and to deal with symbols in a
variety of relationships.

Paul Brandwein in his book *The Gifted Student as Future
Scientist*[6] advances the theory that scientific ability is dependent on three factors which he terms the genetic, the
predisposing, and the activating factors. The genetic factor
probably has its primary basis in heredity and is closely related to general abstract intelligence potential. It also includes well-developed neuromuscular control and adequate
eye function. The characteristics of what he terms the predisposing factor include persistence and "questing," which
may be defined as a seeking for new knowledge motivated
by dissatisfaction with existing explanations. The activating
factor is the presence of certain favorable environmental

---

[6] Paul F. Brandwein, *The Gifted Student as Future Scientist* (New York:
Harcourt, Brace & Co., 1955), pp. 9-12.

conditions which "trigger" action. Examples include contact with an inspirational teacher, access to a scientific laboratory and opportunity for advanced training in science, or simply a general social or political atmosphere which places great value on scientific achievement.

Personal traits which are consistent with a high order of scientific ability include originality, curiosity, ingenuity, and persistence. When the gifted child with scientific ability possesses these personality characteristics, and is favored by an environment which both stimulates his interest in science and provides the opportunity for experimentation, genuine achievement may be confidently anticipated.

Artistic Ability

The expression of artistic ability takes many forms. It may appear in music, painting, poetry, drawing, sculpture, architecture, or on the stage. It usually requires a variety of abilities in creating, relating, and arranging symbols, forms, patterns, colors, and sounds in such a way as to make them aesthetically pleasing or inspiring.

Many people exhibit artistic ability early in life. Others wait until they are in their teens and in a few cases until middle age or even later.

Artistic performance as an expression of the gifted individual is sometimes confused with skill in imitation. Although most people with exceptional artistic ability possess superior general intelligence, some make only average scores on I.Q. tests. However, such individuals possess creative ability which only those with unusual powers of imagination enjoy. It seems reasonable to assume that the great artists of all ages were people who combined high intelligence and creative imagination with other favorable personality traits in an environment which created or nurtured an interest in art and stimulated artistic achievement. Environment may stimulate achievement in various ways. In some cases, handicaps spur the gifted to greater accomplishment. Milton in his blindness and "Beethoven, deaf, who heard great melodies" are cases in point. In other cases it is the advantage of favorable circumstances such as an artistic family background which provides the motivation for achievement in art.

Creativity is probably the distinguishing characteristic of most gifted performances in the field of art. Exceptional skill in imitation or in duplication of the efforts of others in itself does not suggest giftedness. It is in the creation of the painting that the gift of artistic ability is revealed. The gift of poetry lies in the creation of verbal images which are challenging, or pleasing, or inspiring. In music, probably the greatest recognition and certainly the most lasting is given to those who compose great music. Even those who excel in interpreting music may exercise creative ability in their expression of the works of others.

Norman Meier[7] suggests six components of artistic ability: (1) manual skills, (2) drive, (3) general intelligence, (4) keen perception, (5) creative imagination, and (6) aesthetic judgment. The first is largely a product of physiological coordination, the second is a nonintellectual personality trait, and the other four are intellectual characteristics common to the gifted as defined in this text.

In short, those gifted in the artistic field are usually possessed of superior general intelligence as well as a richly creative imagination. Their performances rise above the level of skillful imitation or faithful reproduction of sounds and symbols. Their artistic efforts are characterized by originality, ingenuity, and depth of insight.

Mechanical Ability

The gifted, more frequently than is sometimes assumed, express themselves in mechanical performance. Individuals with a combination of high mental ability and creative imagination together with the inclination to work along mechanical lines produce the complicated machines we have today. The inventors of such machines as the cotton gin, the steam engine, the telephone, the airplane, and the electronic

[7] Norman C. Meier, *Art in Human Affairs* (New York: McGraw-Hill Book Co., 1942), pp. 127-29.

computer no doubt possessed this combination of traits to a high degree.

A clear distinction should be made between the gifted whose performance is along mechanical lines and the person who possesses mechanical skills. The latter has manipulative skill and by reason of strong interest and close attention is able to perform complicated mechanical tasks. The skilled mechanic is not necessarily intellectually gifted. However, an intellectually gifted person may in some cases work for a time as a mechanic and then move on to a more creative type of work or to a supervisory position if appropriate personality traits are present. An individual with average intelligence whose aptitude and interest make him a good garage mechanic or machine operator makes a genuine contribution to society. However, no matter how skillful he may become he should not be confused with the gifted individual whose intellectual ability and mechanical interest make possible a type of performance which goes beyond manipulative aptitude and skill. Such an individual makes his contribution largely on the theoretical level, in the solution of mechanical problems and the creation of machines, or in the discovery of more effective mechanical processes.

Mechanical aptitude tests, particularly those which include problems of spatial relationships, visual perception of mechanical patterns, and matching configurations, are sometimes useful in differentiating between the skilled and the gifted. Likewise the intelligence test is revealing. Actual performance is probably the best indicator since "the proof of the pudding is in the eating." However, the observer must be able to differentiate between gifted performance and simple mechanical skill which at times yields a performance which seems beyond that attainable by the average person. In early childhood the distinction is probably best made by application of the criterion of creativity. Does the child actually create mechanical devices or does he simply manipulate mechanical objects with skill? The answer to this question will give a fairly reliable guide to differentiation.

Other Abilities

Social competence, ability in human relations, and motor ability are sometimes regarded as avenues of expression of giftedness. Social competence and ability in human relations are closely related and are based on unusual sensitivity to and understanding of the attitudes, interests, and motivations of others. Such abilities are likely to be found in those who exert leadership.

Motor ability and physical coordination in all probability belong in the skill class. A champion boxer or an expert tumbler has developed extraordinary skill in muscular coordination and timing of body movements. Such ability is founded upon favorable body structure, muscular development, and quick reactions, and is not causally related to giftedness as defined in this text. Hence, motor skill or ability would not qualify as a distinctive avenue of expression of the gifted person. This is not to say that giftedness as sometimes defined does not include highly developed motor ability. However, it does mean that this type of performance is not a direct expression of giftedness as defined here.

SELECTED READINGS

ABRAHAM, WILLARD. *Common Sense About Gifted Children.* New York: Harper and Brothers, 1958. 268 pp. Chapter 2.
   Definitions of giftedness are discussed and devices for discovering gifted children are given.

DEHAAN, ROBERT F., and HAVIGHURST, ROBERT J. *Educating Gifted Children.* Chicago: University of Chicago Press, 1957. 276 pp. Chapter 1.
   A definition of giftedness is established, the relationship between giftedness and talent is discussed, and two case studies are analyzed in terms of the definition of giftedness adopted.

NATIONAL SOCIETY FOR THE STUDY OF EDUCATION. *Education for the Gifted.* Chicago: University of Chicago Press, 1958. 420 pp. Chapters 3 and 4.
   Chapter 3 presents Witty's broad definition of giftedness, lists of characteristic behaviors by which gifted and talented children may be recognized, and concrete examples by which specific gifted children have been identified. Chapter 4 shows Strang's discussion of concepts of giftedness. Group characteristics as well as individual differences are indicated, and the kinds of conditions conducive to the development and the stifling of talent and giftedness are explored.

TERMAN, LEWIS M., and ODEN, MELITA H. *The Gifted Child Grows Up.*
(*Genetic Studies of Genius,* Vol. IV.) Stanford, Calif.: Stanford University Press, 1947. 448 pp.

This is the report of twenty-five years of research made by Terman and his associates of a group of superior children selected in 1921.
Data collected in 1936, 1940, and 1945 are presented and analyzed to indicate the development of the nearly fifteen hundred subjects studied in terms of mental and physical traits.

WITTY, PAUL (ed.). *The Gifted Child.* Boston: D. C. Heath & Company, 1951. 338 pp. Chapters 2 through 5.

Chapter 2 discusses the identification of gifted children in terms of concepts of giftedness, influences upon the gifted, and specific methods of identifying them. Chapter 3 summarizes briefly the research of Terman and his associates; characteristics of the gifted group are presented, and proposals are made for the education of gifted children in general. Chapter 4 relates the contributions made by Leta S. Hollingworth to the study and education of gifted children. Chapter 5 presents some generalizations that can be made about gifted children, based on the research of Terman, Hollingworth, and the Counseling Center for Gifted Children at New York University.

2

A Historical Overview

A brief history of education of the gifted in Western civilization is presented in order to give the reader a perspective for viewing present practices in the field. It is interesting to note that the education of superior children has been recognized as an important problem for centuries. The reluctance of society to provide special educational opportunities for the gifted is evident in the history of almost every nationality group and social culture. However, there are strong indications that this attitude is undergoing a change both in the Americas and Europe and that in the future society will provide greater educational opportunities for the gifted and in return secure the benefits of greater utilization of their abilities.

EARLY HISTORY IN WESTERN CULTURE

In its broadest sense the special education of gifted children is probably as old as the race of man. In all likelihood the early cave dwellers recognized the superiority of particular children and utilized their quickness in learning to teach them the more intricate methods of hunting and fishing.

In ancient Athens, somewhat more than twenty-three hundred years ago, Plato speculated upon ways of determining which children were gifted, in order to educate them for leadership in the state. His plan of discovery consisted mainly in testing their ability to detect deceit, recognize superstitions, and profit by "trial and error" learning. Crude as the method may appear today, it was a long forward step that twenty-three hundred years later reappeared in a more refined and elaborate form as a series of mental tests devised by the French psychologists Binet and Simon.

Plato's thesis was that citizens of a republic should be trained to do that for which they were best fitted. He advocated that the young men who gave evidence by the various tests that they were possessed of unusual mental ability, be separated from those of average intelligence and given a specialized type of education. This education would include the mastery of science, philosophy, and metaphysics. From this group the future leaders of the state were to come. Plato believed that the Greek democracy could hope to remain pre-eminent only as long as it provided the best educational opportunities for those of its youths who were to become its future leaders.

He made provision also, in his plan, for two other classes. One class included children of average intelligence who were to be trained in music and gymnastics. These were to be the merchants, tradesmen, and warriors. The other class included children of lesser ability who were to be trained as artisans and laborers.

The Romans, who flourished in powerful magnificence for more than five hundred years after the downfall of the Greeks, adopted parts of Plato's plan for the special education of the different classes of human resources. It was, of course, assumed in the selection of superior children for special education that Romans were physically and mentally superior to the various other races and nationalities of the empire. The families of noble birth imported Greek teachers—sometimes men of rank who had been enslaved—and installed them in their homes as tutors of their children. Sons of noble Romans were specially trained for leadership in war, law, oratory, and government.

Perhaps the most notable effort in the education of the superior, following the disintegration of the Roman Empire, was that of Suleiman the Magnificent, in the sixteenth century. He sent emissaries throughout the Turkish Empire with instructions to examine and select the fairest, strongest, and most intelligent youth of the Christian population (human tribute levied by the conquerors) for special education and for upbringing in the Mohammedan faith. These "talent scouts" went about over the Empire at regular intervals, and after vigorous selection presented to the Sultan the finest and brightest youths they could find. Then there followed an intensive educational program designed to develop leaders in war, religion, art, and science. It is noteworthy that under the leadership of Suleiman and his successors, the Ottoman Empire developed into a great power which at one time threatened to conquer all Europe. This Turkish example is perhaps as near as one may come to illustrate, from history, the effectiveness of training the superior child in accomplishing desired goals.

During the seventeenth, eighteenth, and the major portion of the nineteenth century, organized training of superior children was almost nonexistent. A few highly intelligent children were privately tutored, and some astounding accomplishments of gifted children are recorded. Karl Witte was able to read French, German, Italian, Latin, and Greek at the age of nine. His tutor had him ready for college at the age most children are learning to read. He received the doctor of philosophy degree from the University of Leipzig at the age of fourteen. Lord Kelvin, who was tutored by his father, was prepared to enter college at the age of ten years. He won considerable distinction at the University of Glasgow before he was twelve. Many such cases might be noted, but they are isolated instances in this period characterized by an educational philosophy that insisted upon the equality of all men. Hobbes, Jacotot, and the French Encyclopedists, concurring with Leibnitz, asserted that all native intelligences are equal and differences come about through training.

This educational philosophy had its roots in the psychology of the time. Johann F. Herbart, a German philosopher, considered the mind as an apperceptive mass. Experience played upon it and made it whatever it became. John Locke spoke of the human mind as a blank tablet on which experience writes. Thus controlled experience or training or education was the only thing to be considered. The mind was passive and relatively unimportant in the creation of the personality. Still later John Watson, the behaviorist, went so far as to say that he could take any well-formed, healthy body and make of it what he pleased—"a rich man, poor man, beggar man, thief, doctor, lawyer, merchant, or chief."

It is not difficult to see that under the existing philosophy and educational psychology of those times, special education of gifted children had little or no place. The emphasis on equality led naturally to a standardized school curriculum. Superior children, except when privately educated, partook of the same training as all others. This educational theory fitted in so well with the political theories in America after the Revolution, that it had no trouble establishing itself in the educational structure of the American Republic.

DIFFERENCES IN MENTAL ABILITY

In America educators were slow to recognize mental differences, and the traditional school curriculum failed to make any provision for such differences. The school was fashioned for the average pupil, and those who varied from the norm were more or less forced into the educational channel which was provided for the average pupil.

The first group of children, in terms of intelligence, to attract the attention of educators was the group having low mental ability. Long before intelligence testing was introduced, teachers realized that some children were unable to meet school requirements as they were then set up; but even noticeable inability to perform the mental abstractions required in school did not secure special attention for over a century. Lack of interest, laziness, and general perversity were often ascribed to children of low mental ability to explain their failure in school.

The problem increased as the scope of education widened. More children came to school as a result of compulsory-attendance laws. The schools soon discovered that in extending educational facilities to larger and more unselected groups of children, they were receiving more slow learners.

Gradually teachers began to realize that many failing pupils lacked sufficient mental ability to keep pace with normal children. With the advent of intelligence testing early in the twentieth century, this point of view gained wider recognition. In fact, it was for the extreme of the retarded group, the feeble-minded, that intelligence testing was first devised. Special classes for the mentally retarded were organized. In many schools individual instruction was inaugurated to meet the needs of these duller children. Thus the measurement of intelligence became one means of breaking down the so-called "lock-step system" in education. Children with inferior mental equipment were recognized as handicapped and as requiring educational opportunities that differed from those offered to average children.

The recognition which these children received was owing, no doubt, to the fact that their presence disturbed the orderly and uniform progress of pupils through the curriculum of the traditional school. It is axiomatic that the group which causes most difficulty receives the first attention.

At the same time, teachers readily recognized that there were some pupils of exceptional ability. Intelligence tests later confirmed this fact and established some basis of comparison. However, the bright children as a rule caused little disturbance in the uniform school program as they could easily master the required work. In most cases, they adapted themselves to the pace of the average pupil and, in consequence, most teachers felt that all was well. Occasionally a pupil of superior intelligence became a problem because of his dissatisfaction with routine drill. His expressions of annoyance and frustration were usually treated as pure misbehavior and he was punished repeatedly without any inquiry regarding the cause of his behavior.

Under these conditions, it can be readily seen why there was little attempt to establish special provisions for gifted students in the early schools in the United States. The advent of the intelligence test served not only to delineate the low intelligence group, but also pointed quite clearly to the existence of a group of comparable numbers at the other end of the scale. The objective measurement furnished by the tests became an important factor in the early progress made in identifying gifted children.

EARLY ATTEMPTS TO ACCOMMODATE THE GIFTED

The earliest attempt to make some systematic provision for gifted children in the American educational system was probably that of William T. Harris in St. Louis about 1867. His efforts to care for superior children consisted mainly in introducing a greater flexibility in the grading and promotional system of his schools.

Bentley[1] divides the history of special education of gifted children into three epochs. The first, extending from 1867 to 1899, may be described as the period of flexible promotions. Out of this period came the epoch of acceleration extending from 1900 to 1919. In this era the emphasis on hastening the gifted child through his school program led to the question of the importance of maturity. Was the physical, social, and emotional maturity of the child being given sufficient consideration? The third epoch, that of enrichment, beginning about 1920, stressed the importance of breadth and depth in the curriculum.

Flexible Promotion

Superintendent Harris' plan involved first semiannual, later quarterly, and finally five-week-period promotions. In 1886, the Elizabeth, New Jersey, schools adopted a multiple-track system whereby pupils were placed in sections and allowed to advance at whatever speed they were capable of making. This allowed the superior children to advance more

[1] John Edward Bentley, *Superior Children* (New York: W. W. Norton & Company, Inc., 1937), pp. 192-93.

rapidly than they otherwise could have done. The Cambridge plan, originated in 1891, is known as the double-track plan. By this plan a pupil could cover the first six grades in four years, if he pursued the accelerated track, or he could take the other track and devote the entire six years to the first six grades. Special teachers often tutored the brighter pupils in the program.

In California, the Santa Barbara schools in 1898 organized a plan for the education of exceptional children which involved a variation of courses but equality of progress. The children were divided into three groups: one group was given minimum essentials; the second group was given the regular course, which covered not only basic work but elaborated it and gave it more intensive attention; the third group, consisting of the pupils above the average, was given even more intensive training than the second group. The Santa Barbara plan, somewhat modified and changed, is still in operation. The third group is now provided with an enriched course of study as well as an intensive one. However, the plan is not considered entirely satisfactory for gifted children because this third group generally contains many pupils of little better than average mental ability.

The Batavia, New York, plan, instituted by Dr. John Kennedy, made provision for individual instruction of pupils during school time. Each class had two teachers. One teacher instructed the class as a whole; the other was free to give individual instruction as it was needed. In 1928 the Batavia schools abandoned the double-teacher plan, and now assign individual children to special or atypical classes.

The San Francisco plan made use of individual instruction by allowing gifted children to work out assignments under teacher direction and report individually to the different teachers involved. They received assistance only when they ran into difficulty and reported it to the teacher in charge of the project. The plan was flexible and allowed superior children to proceed through the grades at an accelerated rate.

Various adaptations of the multiple-track plan were instituted in large cities during the last two decades of the nineteenth century. However, only a small proportion of gifted students were affected.

Acceleration

Probably the first organized classes specifically designed for rapid advancement purposes were those established in New York City in 1900. These classes were the forerunners of the present special-progress classes which permit pupils to complete three years' work in two.

McDonald[2] gives 1901 as the date of the establishment of the first special school for gifted children in the United States. It was known as a "preparatory school" and was located at Worcester, Massachusetts. Children from all over the city were selected and brought to the school for special instruction under outstanding teachers. These superior children did the regular work of the grades and, although they were in only grades seven, eight, and nine, were given work in high school subjects, such as Latin, French, German, and algebra. In order to obtain admission to this school, pupils had to be in good health and possess high scholastic standing. The principal objective was to accelerate the progress of the children. In 1936, according to Bentley,[3] there were a number of these preparatory schools or centers in Worcester. They have operated as indicated above for more than a generation but in recent years have been incorporated in new junior high schools. At the present time only one remains as an independent school and it is assumed that in time this too will be absorbed in a junior high school.

In 1902 Baltimore established similar schools for bright children. In the same year Stuyvesant High School in New York City opened its doors to boys with marked superiority in mechanics, mathematics, and science.

The standardization and incorporation of intelligence tests in the "tool kit" of the educator early in the twentieth century gave impetus to the acceleration movement. When a child demonstrated by test his ability to learn more quickly

[2] Robert Alexander Fyfe McDonald, *Adjustment of School Organization to Various Population Groups* (New York: Teachers College, Columbia University, 1915), p. 99.

[3] Bentley, *op. cit.*, p. 206.

than his fellows it was considered advisable to give him the opportunity to forge ahead. In addition to rapid-progress classes and special schools individualized instruction was employed to achieve acceleration. Such individualized instruction was designed to permit the superior child to progress at his own pace from grade to grade and yet remain for the most part in the regular classroom.

Just as the practice of flexible promotion carried over into the period of emphasis on acceleration, so has the idea of acceleration persisted far into the third epoch.

Enrichment

The year 1920 roughly marks the beginning of what Bentley calls the third epoch in the special education of gifted children in the public schools of the United States. This is the period characterized by the idea of enrichment rather than acceleration. As the third decade of the twentieth century opened, three city school systems in different parts of the country inaugurated plans for educating gifted children, based on the idea of enrichment. They were Los Angeles, California, Rochester, New York, and Cleveland, Ohio.

An experimental class for gifted children was established in Los Angeles during the school year 1915-16. For four years various methods of teaching and administration were tried. However, by 1920 the principle of enrichment was adopted as basic to the program, and several special classes were set up on this basis. The teacher of the experimental class became supervisor of these Opportunity classes, as they were called. The classes now enroll pupils who are selected mainly on the basis of their intelligence quotient. The standard for admission to these Opportunity classes is an intelligence quotient of 125; this limit is not rigidly applied, as some pupils with a lesser rating are admitted. They must, however, have shown marked success in academic achievement.

The Opportunity classrooms are "workshops in which children experience purposefully." Individual research projects are carried out and reported to the class. Often long discussions follow.

The Los Angeles program includes creative music, original poetry, plays, pageants, school papers, and many other things. Pupil activity is fostered and pupil initiative is encouraged. A modern language is studied in all classes where a capable teacher is available. The aim is to provide a differentiated program of enriched subject matter, together with suitable methods of instruction for gifted children.

By 1927-28 there were fifteen such classes; the next year two more were added. A total of 510 pupils were enrolled in these seventeen classes.[4] Twenty-one Opportunity classes enrolling 630 pupils were reported in 1937.[5]

Reports made on research incidental to the program indicate that pupils in these classes, when promoted to high school, do better work than children of like intelligence who have not participated in the enriched curriculum offered by the Opportunity classes. In one study 284 gifted pupils from the Opportunity classes were compared with 381 gifted pupils of the regular school. When compared on the basis of high-school records the Opportunity group was found to have made (1) more A and B marks in high school; (2) a higher average on grade points for all marks; and (3) fewer failing marks than the control group. No follow-up studies of these children after high school have been reported.

Rochester, New York, adopted a plan involving special classes in school centers in 1920. Two classes were organized in September of that year. Pupils having an intelligence quotient of 120 or above were eligible for these classes. The classes were begun at the fifth-grade level; their main purpose was enrichment, but pupils were not held back if they could advance more rapidly than a grade a year. No attempt was made to hold these classes to rigid requirements of a course of study. Reported experiments indicated that (1) these classes did better when the same teacher was retained; and (2) pupils from these classes did better than others from the regular grades when they entered the junior high school.

---

[4] Division of Psychology and Educational Research of the Los Angeles Public Schools. *Third Yearbook: School Publication 185* (Los Angeles, 1929), pp. 23-43.

[5] Bentley, *op. cit.*, p. 209.

Bentley[6] reported in 1937 that the Rochester schools had disbanded these classes for superior children. The lack of proved techniques for teaching bright children and the difficulties of transportation were given as the reasons for discontinuing the program. Lack of interest by parents also played a part in the abandonment of the project. However, in 1956 a program for "very bright" children was re-established upon the recommendations of a group of teachers appointed to study the situation.

In Cleveland, Ohio the first special class for the gifted based on the idea of enrichment was inaugurated in October, 1921, after almost a year of planning and preparation. It consisted of twenty-five bright pupils selected from the fourth, fifth, and sixth grades. The following year five more enrichment classes were established. By 1927 fourteen elementary and two junior high schools offered such classes. Bright children from nearby schools without "Major Work classes," as these enriched classes were called, were permitted to transfer to schools having such classes.

The Major Work program was designed to give gifted children an enriched curriculum consisting of wider and more varied experiences, new contacts, challenging opportunities to learn, and room for growth within ever broadening horizons. Drill and repetition gave way to creative effort in prose, poetry, painting, and music. Typing, foreign languages, and science laboratory work were offered to pupils in the elementary-school classes. Field trips to banks, dairies, department stores, and airports were integral parts of the Major Work program.

The Cleveland school system has not only retained its Major Work program over the years but has constantly sought to improve it. Several evaluation studies of the program have been made and each has served to vindicate the judgment of those who have been responsible for the establishment and conduct of the program. The present program, although strengthened and expanded over the years, has steadfastly retained the original concept of enriched experience as opposed to rapid progress.

[6] *Ibid.*, p. 207.

Early in this period New York City organized special classes in selected elementary schools which were designed to offer an enriched program to bright children. It was in this period, also, that the school systems of Winnetka, Illinois, and Dalton, Massachusetts, introduced programs which permitted bright children to work on special projects in the regular classroom with teacher guidance. While the early enrichment programs were characterized, for the most part, by grouping of pupils in special classes, it was not long until attempts to secure enrichment in the regular classroom appeared. This trend toward individualized enrichment appeared in the 1930's and carried over until about 1950. While the extent and effectiveness of such enrichment may be open to serious question, there is little doubt that it represented a dominant motif until the mid-century point was reached.

There were, it was estimated, one and one-half million children with intelligence quotients of 120 and upward, and less than 1 per cent was enrolled in special classes, according to the White House Conference Report of 1931.[7] According to Heck,[8] in 1930 there were only four cities of ten thousand or more population reporting schools for the gifted. Only thirty cities reported either schools or classes or both, despite the fact that 96.6 per cent of the 762 cities of that size in the United States reported. These thirty cities reported a total of 3,883 pupils enrolled in 135 classes. Cleveland, Los Angeles, and Worcester, Massachusetts, led in the number of pupils enrolled; they had 518, 450, and 440 respectively at that time.

A rather complete study of educational provisions for the gifted in Ohio in 1951 showed that only about 2 per cent of Ohio schools had special classes for the gifted while 9 per cent reported enrichment in the regular classroom.[9]

[7] White House Conference on Child Health and Protection: Committee on Special Classes. *Special Education: The Handicapped and the Gifted* (New York: D. Appleton-Century Company, Inc., 1931), pp. 548-49.

[8] Arch O. Heck, "Special Schools and Classes in Cities of 10,000 Population and More in the United States" (U.S. Office of Education Bulletin No. 7 [Washington, D.C., 1930]), pp. 20-21.

[9] Ohio Commission on Children and Youth. *The Status of the Gifted in Ohio* (Columbus, Ohio: Ohio Department of Education, 1951).

EDUCATION OF THE GIFTED AT MID-TWENTIETH CENTURY

In Europe

Few objective data concerning the extent of provisions made for gifted children in Europe are available. Although most European countries have consistently attempted to select and provide for superior children in recent years, with the exception of Russia their efforts have been rather scattered and in most cases quite limited.

France, Belgium, and Switzerland have shown considerable interest in the discovery and training of their gifted. From 1917 until the advent of the Hitler regime, Germany experimented with the education of "children who show promise." Special schools and classes for superior children were formed on the basis of psychological tests. The city of Hamburg was prominent in these efforts. Petzoldt, a German educator and philosopher of the period, consistently advocated special training for superior youth.

France, where the intelligence test of Binet and Simon made its appearance, regularly grants scholarships on the basis of mental tests. Belgium has a foundation for the gifted and has attempted to meet the needs of poor children of high intelligence by grants of financial aid. Great Britain provides endowments that enable superior youths to pursue advanced work in colleges and universities.

It is in Russia, however, that we find the most extensive and probably the most productive efforts exerted. In the early days of the Soviet Socialist Republics the most promising youths were heavily indoctrinated in Communism with physical science, mathematics, and languages only incidental in the educational program; but in recent years the picture has changed. Although it is the goal of the educational program to make good Communist leaders, it is now recognized that physics, chemistry, and mathematics are essential—in fact, vital—to Soviet aspirations. Before World War II the Komsomol organizations sought to enroll only enthusiastic Communist agitators; after the War these or-

ganizations sought outstanding students, particularly potential leaders in science and the arts.

At the present, there are numerous programs and even
some schools which are designed exclusively for the exceptionally bright youth and those who are artistically gifted.

The programs which are carried on in conjunction with
the regular school curriculum consist largely of small selected
groups of gifted children receiving advanced work and enriched opportunities in special classes, many of which meet
before and after regular school hours. Teachers are usually
drawn from the regular staff or in some cases from a nearby
university. Most of the schools for the gifted are located in
the larger cities, are sponsored by a university, and make
use of university laboratories and other facilities under the
direction of university faculty members. Some of these
schools have eleven-year programs which are specially designed to serve the artistically gifted. Both the schools for
exceptionally bright children and those for the artistically
gifted are characterized by small classes, excellent laboratory
facilities, and high-quality instruction.

Aside from Russia, it is probably accurate to say that European countries are for the most part subsidizing the education of gifted children in the regular schools, rather than
offering them a special type of education. Exceptions should
be noted, however, in some cities of both East and West Germany as well as what was formerly Austria, where enriched
curricula and special grouping of the gifted are being practiced to a considerable extent.

In the United States

At mid-century there is no general agreement concerning
the best plan for the education of gifted children. Although
many schools recognize the desirability of segregation and
enrichment, many others are reluctant to abandon the idea
of acceleration. Some adopt a compromise plan involving
both enrichment and acceleration. Others believe that individual instruction is the answer to the problem. Many educators consider the basic problem in educating gifted chil-

dren to be one of developing methods and techniques for their instruction. The solution of this problem might well determine best administrative procedure and practices. The few studies in the field of the education of the gifted have failed to shed much light on this phase of the problem.

It is apparent that the public schools of the United States have hardly made a beginning in the special education of superior children. One reason undoubtedly is the fact that comparatively few schoolmen have realized the potential value of such a program in the development of a progressive, democratic state.

In 1953, the "Talented Youth Project" was established by the Horace Mann–Lincoln Institute of School Experimentation of New York City. The project was aimed toward helping schools to improve provisions for developing the potential of talented youth for outstanding achievement. Its announced purposes are to conduct studies of the nature of talent and its role in our culture; to experiment in modifying educational procedures and provisions to meet the needs of talented youth; and to summarize and interpret research which will aid schools in planning to better serve them. Major efforts have been directed toward the study of the effects of administrative and instructional modifications, achievement of talented pupils, the attitude of peers toward them, and the development of a guide for self-appraisal of secondary-school programs for the talented. Although much of the work of the project is done in New York, it is national in scope with current studies in Norfolk County, Virginia, Denver, Colorado, and Evanston, Illinois.

Current school programs for the gifted include one in Portland, Oregon, which is of the seminar type; one in Brockton, Massachusetts, of the "special class" type emphasizing careful selection; and another in East Meadow, New York, characterized by limited acceleration, usually in the lower grades.

Among large cities which have devoted considerable attention to the problem of educating gifted children in the public schools, the following are prominent:

Baltimore, Maryland   Los Angeles, California
Cleveland, Ohio   New York, New York
Houston, Texas   Pittsburgh, Pennsylvania
Indianapolis, Indiana   San Francisco, California
Long Beach, California

On a statewide basis California, Illinois, Ohio, North Carolina, and New York have exerted special efforts to encourage research on the gifted, establish provisions for their education, and promote desirable educational practices. A study of special provisions for the education of the gifted in the elementary schools of the state of New York in 1956 indicated increased attention to the gifted.[10] A similar study also including secondary schools was launched in Illinois in 1959. A number of other states are appropriating funds for study of the problem of educating the gifted and subsidizing those local school districts which offer special education for these children. Such subsidization is usually limited to paying the excess cost as is the case in connection with the education of the handicapped.

Among institutions of higher learning devoting time to research or offering courses in the education of the gifted are Boston University, George Peabody College, Hunter College, Kent State University, Northwestern University, Pennsylvania State University, San Francisco State College, Stanford University, Teachers College (Columbia University), and the University of Illinois.

Over 300 colleges and universities are participating in what is known as the Advanced Placement Program in cooperation with over 700 secondary schools. In this program basic college courses are offered to bright high-school students who are then eligible to take special examinations, which, if passed, exempt them from freshman classes. Thus a bright secondary student participating in this program may anticipate completing college in three years.

---

[10] *A Study of Current Practices in the Education of Gifted Children in the Elementary Schools of New York State* (Albany, New York: Division of Elementary Education, N.Y. State Department of Education, 1956).

The following statement issued in 1958 by the Educational Policies Commission reflects the general concern with the problem.

American leaders in public life or in private occupations come not from one class or one economic level; they rise from every section of the people and possess widely varied talents. The country needs an educational system which attracts leaders from every source and provides for the talented without divorcing them from the greater society.

Gifted pupils should be identified early and given opportunities to challenge their powers and develop their talents to the fullest. They should be motivated to high achievement and should have a sense of responsibility for the wise and socially profitable employment of their abilities. It is extremely important that a larger proportion of these young people seek higher education.

In making plans for the education of the gifted, it is important to realize that giftedness may be difficult to recognize. Far more is involved than merely testing verbal abilities and equating them with intelligence. Talents lie in many areas and are of many types. Pupils who rank low by one set of standards may rank high by another. Wide and flexible programs are needed to identify talents and to plan for them that combination of general studies which will develop them as good citizens and advanced courses which will develop their talents to the fullest.

In high schools, courses of study should be designed to allow the abler students to carry heavier loads in balanced programs which include mathematics, science, and languages, together with English, social studies, and humanities. Also, care should be taken to give talented students the opportunity to satisfy their wide intellectual and cultural interests and their specific occupational interests. Courses for these students can be provided in such a way that they are not held back by the less able. This can be done and is being done in comprehensive high schools without prejudice to the democratic school spirit or to the status of students who progress at varying rates of speed and varying depths of scholarship.

Advanced courses, however, should not be imposed on students who lack the required talent. To do so would deprive the latter of the educational program which will benefit them and consequently the nation. National welfare demands not only the education of the outstandingly able but also the best possible education of all students. America requires trained talents of every type.[11]

[11] Educational Policies Commission, *The Contemporary Challenge to American Education* (Washington, D.C.: National Education Association, 1958), p. 9.

In February, 1958, the National Education Association with the aid of a grant from the Carnegie Corporation of New York sponsored a conference of some two hundred outstanding educators and laymen who had special interest and knowledge in the education of the gifted. Dr. James B. Conant, former president of Harvard University, acted as chairman of the two-and-one-half-day meeting. The proceedings are reported by the National Education Association in the publication entitled, "The Identification and Education of the Academically Talented Student in the American Secondary School."[12]

THE BEGINNING OF A NEW ERA

The invasion of space represented by the launching of the Russian-made satellite in late 1957 provided a major impetus to the movement for discovering and educating the gifted. For the first time the public became acutely conscious of the fact that the United States was behind the Soviets in certain aspects, at least, of scientific accomplishment. Wherein had they excelled? Obviously in the development of scientific ability. Certainly in America, the land of opportunity, there had been no dearth of opportunity for scientists to work. It was not opportunity which was lacking but rather a conscious purposeful program of searching out youth of exceptional ability with an interest in science and providing them with the type of education which would insure the full development of their ability in the scientific field.

Although such a need obviously exists and has existed in other fields, such as law and medicine, it took a spectacular scientific achievement to make the public seriously concerned with the need. People quickly realized that in stern competition for international supremacy a failure on our part to keep abreast of scientific advances could well be fatal to us as a nation.

[12] National Education Association, *The Identification and Education of the Academically Talented Student in the American Secondary School* (Washington, D.C.: The Association, 1958).

Although considerable clamor was raised in criticism of our system of public education, the more sober thinkers realized that the remedy lay not in revolutionizing the school by revamping the curriculum for all but by giving adequate attention to those with superior intellectual ability. It was obvious to them that perhaps fewer than 10 per cent of students had the requisite ability to make notable contributions to scientific knowledge in any form. The problem then was to find these youths and provide them with a suitable program. To require all students to take advanced mathematics, physics, chemistry, and the like would be sheer folly in view of the diverse interests and abilities of the student population.

Although some far-sighted educators had urged and supported special education for the gifted many had opposed it on the plea that it was "undemocratic," that it would create snobs, that all should be treated alike, and similar sentiments. Many opposed grouping of the gifted on the grounds that average and dull children profited by being with bright ones in learning situations. However, since the inauguration of the "space age" in 1957 and the demand for the development of young scientists, most of the critics of special education for the gifted have withdrawn their objections in the light of recent events. It has become abundantly clear that our educational practice cannot be geared solely to our national aspirations but must serve us in an international context if we are to remain a free people.

In view of the foregoing it appears that education of the gifted is about to enter a new era of rapid development. It appears likely that the emphasis on scientific achievement will bring increased provisions and vastly improved education for the gifted not only in the field of science but in all fields. Society will benefit immeasurably if such is the case.

SELECTED READINGS

CALIFORNIA ELEMENTARY SCHOOL ADMINISTRATORS ASSOCIATION. *The Gifted Child in the Elementary School* (26th Yearbook). Sacramento: The Association, 1954. 174 pp.

This volume describes in some detail several programs for gifted children being carried on in the elementary schools of California.

EDUCATIONAL POLICIES COMMISSION. *Education of the Gifted.* Washington, D.C.: National Education Association, 1950. 88 pp.

The responsibility of society to capitalize upon the rich resources of talent possessed by gifted children and youth is stressed, and suggestions are made for educational opportunities to be provided in elementary, secondary, and higher education of the gifted.

HALL, THEODORE. *Gifted Children.* New York: The World Publishing Company, 1956. 90 pp.

Mr. Hall tells in an informal, easy style the story of the Major Work program in Cleveland, Ohio. He takes the reader into the classroom and gives him a clear picture of education of the gifted in action.

HAVIGHURST, ROBERT J., STIVERS, EUGENE, and DeHAAN, ROBERT F. *A Survey of the Education of Gifted Children.* Chicago: University of Chicago Press, 1955. 114 pp.

Seventy pages of summary descriptions of programs for gifted boys and girls are included in the survey, which also discusses briefly some criteria for good programs, discovery and motivation of gifted children, the possible uses of resources in the community, and the choice of better methods of teaching gifted children.

HOLLINGWORTH, LETA STETTER. *Gifted Children: Their Nature and Nurture.* New York: The Macmillan Co., 1926. 374 pp.

This is one of the first studies of gifted children using research methods and a scientific approach. It discusses the psychology of gifted children and the necessity for good education to facilitate their optimum development.

NATIONAL SOCIETY FOR THE STUDY OF EDUCATION. *Education for the Gifted.* Chicago: University of Chicago Press, 1958. 420 pp.

This yearbook takes the point of view that it is highly desirable to adapt curriculum and methods to the capabilities and interests of the gifted in elementary and secondary schools, and colleges. The gifted individual is discussed, and ways of educating him are presented and analyzed. Examples of programs in operation are described.

PASSOW, A. HARRY, GOLDBERG, MIRIAM, TANNENBAUM, ABRAHAM J., and FRENCH, WILL. *Planning for Talented Youth.* New York: Bureau of Publications, Teachers College, Columbia University, 1955. 84 pp.

The pamphlet presents a framework of basic considerations which schools ought to bear in mind as they develop programs for their gifted and talented pupils. The problems involved are discussed under the topics of philosophical bases, identification, school provisions, and evaluation of the program.

ROBERTS, HELEN ERSKINE. *Current Trends in the Education of the Gifted.* Sacramento: California State Department of Education, 1954. 61 pp.

This volume describes briefly current practices in meeting the educational needs of the gifted in a number of elementary and secondary schools throughout the United States.

3

Identification of
the Gifted Child

Every youngster gives to his parents and his teachers a continuous flow of signals by which he expresses himself as a person and by which they are expected to understand and recognize him. Those skilled in interpreting these signals can usually determine whether or not a child is gifted, and can formulate programs designed to help him achieve his maximum potential in ways that are good and satisfying to both him and the society in which he lives. The earlier this identification of giftedness can be made, the better it will be for the child's subsequent progress. A child whose entire educative career is directed toward helping him develop his potential fully and realize his obligations to use his talents for the good of himself and his fellow man can go farther faster and with more beneficial results than the youngster whose giftedness for some reason is not recognized until he has reached, for example, his junior year in high school.

For some years teachers have been familiar with, or at least have paid lip service to, the concept of readiness as applied to individuals in various learning situations. Unfortunately, some teachers have given readiness its widest application only when dealing with slow learners. They have been quite willing to wait until a child was "ready" to learn to read or to grasp concepts involved in using number skills thoughtfully. This concept should apply equally to those youngsters who are "ready" earlier than the usual age ac-

41

cepted for beginning instruction in reading, number work, and the like. Gifted youngsters may be ready at age three or four to comprehend skills average children start learning at six or seven; they should not be penalized by being made to wait because they have not reached some arbitrary chronological age established as a convenient beginning point for studying a certain skill.

Though a gifted youngster should be encouraged to master skills and basic fundamentals as soon as he is able, it must be remembered that he is a child, that his giftedness may lie in one of many directions and that he may require more help in some areas of learning than in others. Teachers should neither push him to exploitation of his gifts nor force him into adult status at an unnecessarily early age. As a child he has needs for love and affection, for successful achievement of worthwhile tasks, for responsible participation in his group, be it family, Sunday-school class, nursery school, neighborhood play group, or school class group. He needs time to look around him and to explore his world, to receive and clarify sensory impressions, to exercise his wonder and curiosity, to digest and assimilate his experiences. Being gifted, he will absorb much more from these impressions and experiences and make of them a richer background of understanding than can ordinarily endowed people. Recognition of a child's giftedness carries responsibility that must rest squarely upon those who work and live most closely with him, but before they can fulfill these obligations, they must learn to interpret the signals they receive from the child's desires, attitudes, and behavior.

INFORMAL METHODS

It must be recognized at the outset that any citing of characteristics common to gifted children is true of them only as a group. Within the group there will be many deviations from the expected pattern. For example, gifted children as a whole tend to be physically larger and stronger than children of average intelligence at the same chronological age; this does not negate the possibility of finding some gifted children who seem small and weak for their ages. Children classified as gifted are not bunched at one point on a scale of physical fitness; they are of many shapes and sizes and form a continuum as does any group of people gathered on the basis of one like characteristic and then analyzed in terms of another. On the whole, as a group, gifted children tend to be larger and stronger and more healthy than their average contemporaries. Locating a few youngsters who are not larger or stronger or healthier does not disqualify the generalization presented here. The same caution must be kept in mind regardless of the specific characteristic being discussed; while it will be true of a group of the gifted, it may not be equally true of every individual member of that group.

Parental Observations

The parent is in the best position to observe the desires, attitudes and behavior of the preschool child. In some cases the parent is the only person in such a position. Observations by nurses, governesses, older brothers and sisters, and relatives living in the home may occasionally prove of value but are probably best interpreted by the parent if an attitude of objectivity can be maintained. However, no source of information should be neglected in the attempt to diagnose giftedness in early childhood.

Areas in which giftedness tends to exhibit itself early in the life of the child include ability to control and direct bodily effort in meaningful ways such as balancing, grasping, crawling, and walking. Language facility is another early indicator; a sense of time, a capacity to wonder about the environment are others. Mechanical ingenuity and general inventiveness often show up early in life; so do musical talent, artistic ability and creative imagination. Each of these are talent areas in which giftedness may be identified.

Gifted children as a group tend to begin walking and talking earlier than youngsters of average intelligence ordinarily do. They begin to fit words together into meaningful phrases and sentences at an earlier age than other youngsters manage this language achievement. Once they have grasped this skill, they ask questions about everything they see around them, and most of the time they listen to the replies. They are asking for information, not merely exercising a newly developed trick to secure their parents' attention as may seem the case with other youngsters. A gifted child who has received an adequate response to a question incorporates that information into his knowledge, and later his questions on that subject show understanding and use of it, as he advances to a higher level of seeking information.

Examples of such questions might be: "Where did yesterday go?" "Where is tomorrow?" "Why does the sun come up in the morning?" "What makes rain?" "Do sparrows get cold in winter without shoes on?" "Where does lightning come from?" As the youngster's experiences broaden from his immediate home environment during his preschool years, he sees more and more events and objects to study, observe, think about, work into an organized fund of information, and to add to his growing store of knowledge. His questions reveal an inquisitive mind, a desire to understand, an almost insatiable curiosity, and, perhaps, even the possession of a strong drive to learn.

As early as the age of two years a child may show unusual skill with his hands. He may build block towers that consistently stand very high, indicating good eye-hand coordination and excellent muscle control combined with ability to visualize space and form relationships. This may be the forerunner of mechanical ability of a high order.

In his play a preschool child may exhibit characteristics of creative ability. Ingenuity in creating what he needs for certain play or games from what he has is one way in which he may show greater than normal creative imagination. Blocks are many things to different children. They can be used to create buildings, fences, cities, farms, bridges, trains, castles —almost anything a child needs in his play can be made from unstructured toys such as blocks. This play may be the child's way of experimenting with concepts he is developing, of trying to arrange his environment as he would like it to be, and of coming to terms with it, as it is.

Every mother knows the fascination her kitchen utensils hold for her youngster. A very young child can play contentedly with lids from her pots or with her juice strainer; even empty cereal boxes sometimes seem to be preferred to more expensive toys, which lie neglected. The possibilities for creativity with the kitchen equipment are much greater. One mother reported that her three-year-old boy would play for an hour at a time with a bread board, a chopping board, and one of his own small wooden boats; the two boards were Manhattan and Staten Islands between which his boat plied its way as one of the many Staten Island ferries, accompanied by a complete story worked out by the child as he grew more and more absorbed in his creation.

This use of materials in ways other than those for which they were intended by the manufacturer seems characteristic of gifted youngsters. A further step involves adding something of the child's own invention to the article, as in the case of the youngster who crayoned action pictures on successive paper towels, and by manipulating an old broom handle and a rolling pin produced quite creditable "moving pictures" which he presented before his friends.

Most adults are familiar with the somewhat indiscriminate banging that may occur when a youngster in a high chair or seated at a table has a spoon, but as yet no food to eat. Banging on different objects within reach will create tones of varying pitch and resonance. A musically talented youngster gives some indication of his superior ability by hearing these differences, and consciously attempting to reproduce simple melodies he has heard and remembered. He may even attempt to experiment with some tunes of his own.

Mechanical ingenuity, creative effort, language facility, and musical talent have been mentioned as examples of abilities that appear early in youngsters. Another area in which a child may exhibit his talent at an early age is art. Such early indications depend to some extent upon the degree to which he is supplied with materials suited to his use and allowed to experiment with them in a place in the home which neither he nor his mother is greatly concerned about keeping clean.

Each of these talent areas can and often does appear quite early in a youngster's life. An alert parent can catch the clues the child supplies as he goes about his daily program, and can make plans to help develop these talents. A parent who is not attuned to the possible creativity a youngster is showing but reacts first to the mess, the noise, and the wasted paper towels, will take some effective steps to thwart and squelch further expressions of creativity by his child. A boy scout leader or a Sunday-school teacher may also show by his reactions that he holds cleanliness to be of greater value than experimentation or expressions of creativity. Such negative attitudes toward learning opportunities are unfortunate and should be guarded against by parents, teachers and all others who work with children.

Before a child has learned to read he is almost entirely dependent upon the people with whom he associates for getting answers to his questions, for extending his environment through direct experience. Once he has mastered the skill of reading he finds a world of information and experience opening to him, and he can explore it by his own efforts.

About 50 per cent of gifted children have learned to read before they enter public school. Many cannot remember *not* knowing how to read. They asked questions about letters and words they saw in newspapers and magazines, on boxes, jars, and bottles in the kitchen, on advertisements posted in buses and store windows, and on billboards along the highways. They had an early interest in books and usually owned a good number from which parents read to them rather regularly. In fact, they "read" these books themselves to the extent that they had remembered the content on each page guided by some clue such as a picture. Actually they had probably gone through quite a thorough program of reading readiness though neither they nor their parents had called it that, and one day, with their ability to reason, draw conclusions, and put two and two together, combined with the insight into problems gifted children usually display, they began to read.

Recognition of the signals discussed thus far depends in large degree upon the parents or other adults in the preschool youngster's immediate environment. It is the wise parent who shares his observations with the youngster's first teacher so that from the child's entrance into kindergarten or first grade, home and school can work cooperatively in planning and carrying out as good an educational program as can be designed for the individual youngster concerned. These parent observations can help immensely when a teacher begins to work with a child. It is the fortunate youngster whose parents have received his signals and transmitted them to his first teacher.

Not all observations by parents can be accepted as fully reliable or valid guides to a youngster's intelligence. In a home where there is a whole family of superior intelligence, a gifted youngster may seem perfectly normal as he fits the pattern of expectations his parents hold for him. If there is an extremely superior older child, a gifted youngster of lesser intelligence may even seem slow as he does not measure up to the expectations held by the parents in light of their experiences with the older child.

Though research indicates that gifted youngsters usually issue from gifted parents, it is possible that a gifted child will come from a home where he is the only member of the family who indicates a degree of superiority. In cases such as these, parental observations may be based upon the fact that the child is different, that he does not share the interests of the family, that he does not play with the youngsters of his own age group in the neighborhood, or that he always has some individual project on hand which the family does not understand. Like the preceding observations of signals, these too should alert a teacher to the possibility of the child's superiority, though neither these nor any of the others should be accepted as infallible evidence of a child's standing in the scale of general intelligence.

Teacher Observations

Teachers' observations of children's activities and their subsequent judgments are another means of identifying the gifted. A teacher can see who uses reference materials to an outstanding degree both of quality and quantity. He can see who finishes assigned work rapidly and either finds another task to work at or becomes troublesome in the classroom. He can see the youngster who reads almost constantly, exhausting the supply of books in the classroom library in a few short weeks, and then requests help in the school library, or brings public library or personally owned books to school to have something to read or to work at during spare time.

The teacher can also locate the child who neglects his schoolwork to give his time and effort to other activities, and he investigates to find some probable causes. The work may simply be so easy for the child that, in his judgment, it is not worth his time; it may consist of several pages of exercises to be done to learn a skill which he has mastered with the first explanation and one page of practice work; it may involve some principle which he has not yet grasped, and like most of us, a gifted youngster, too, prefers to do what he knows he does well, and dislikes work that he is not quite as skilled in accomplishing. The analysis of probable causes of a child's behavior thus provides clues to the teacher as he plans work to be the best suited to that particular youngster and his stage of development.

A gifted child in a classroom where the teacher's approach is simply to assign a greater portion of the same kind of problem exercises to the faster students will soon learn that he gains little by finishing his regular assignment in a shorter period of time. He may react by working more slowly, by adding his own inventions to the assigned exercises to make them a more interesting task for him to complete, or perhaps by finishing rapidly so that his paper will please his teacher and then working on some other project while pretending to continue work on the assignment. The observing teacher may on occasion see a sixth-grade youngster who is reading a book on the theory of thermodynamics concealed inside his geography text while his classmates silently study the portion of the text he has already finished.

Sometimes when a gifted youngster has had an older brother or sister who attended the same school he enters, he has already read the preprimer, primers, first-grade and even second-grade books, of the basic reading series used by the teacher. He may reject repetition of these and, indeed, should not be expected to work through them slowly and profitlessly paragraph by paragraph and page by page in conjunction with the other youngsters in the classroom to which he is assigned. Once the teacher has satisfied himself that the child can read and is familiar with the skills developed in the series, he must turn to other books and other topics to help him progress at a speed at which he is thoroughly capable. This involves a high degree of individualization of instruction in reading rather than the three-group method so often found in the primary grades.

Teachers also can be deceived by signals a youngster furnishes, especially if they are seeking the false stereotype of a gifted child that still exists in many people's thinking. The main points to keep in mind while observing children's behavior in the classroom are that any one of them may show evidence of superiority in one or another activity, and that teachers should not let themselves be misled by certain preconceived ideas or even biases concerning what children "should" do in school.

Cleanliness in appearance and neatness in schoolwork are sometimes mistakenly regarded by teachers as evidence of mental superiority. Docility is often looked upon as an indicator of giftedness; a teacher may have a good feeling toward a youngster who strives to obey and do each task expected of him, and may endow such a child with a halo of superiority regardless of whether or not tests indicate that this is deserved. In some cases it may be the youngster who causes disturbances who is truly gifted.

In their own classroom teaching experience the authors have developed preference for the youngster who has a somewhat devilish spark in his eye; he at least has sufficient intelligence to be creative in what he does though his choice of activity may not always be a wise one. He is much easier to work with because of his overt actions; the withdrawn, docile, dreamy, silent, nonparticipating child presents a much more complex problem. Yet he, too, may be gifted.

There is the case of the youngster who absolutely refused to participate in any of the first-grade reading activities planned for him by his teacher. The teacher in desperation called the child's father for a conference, and learned that this boy was not a nonreader as he had feared, but a youngster who at home delighted in building model airplanes to add to his collection, and read the complicated diagrams and instructions with ease, as evidenced by the accurate construction of his completed models.

Interest in making collections is another characteristic giving early indication of giftedness in youngsters. They may possess at one time many collections of various items such as rocks, shells, bird feathers, arrowheads, coins, stamps, butterflies, postcards, wild flowers, gems, fossils—the list could go on and on. These are not collections that have been bought in a prelabeled set but items in which the youngster himself has developed an interest. He has made the collections and has organized and labeled his specimens in a usable and informative manner.

Age is a significant factor for teachers to keep in mind as they observe their classes with the purpose of identifying gifted students. In a school which follows a policy of extra or double promotion as well as retention of youngsters who seem incapable of making progress at the next higher grade level, it is often the youngest children who are among the brightest in the classroom. As they may well be smaller than their classmates, it may be from this situation that the stereotype of "small and weak" has grown up; these youngsters may of course exceed in both height and weight the measurements of their contemporaries of like chronological age.

The reactions which a child displays to disciplinary techniques used by both parents and teachers may be still another indication of giftedness although, as adults dealing with children, parents and teachers are not always able to accept these often irritating reactions as signs of intellectual giftedness. A gifted youngster begins to rebel against "because I said so" much earlier than his average contemporaries. He can understand well-founded and well-explained reasons for behaving in certain ways rather than others; he can also pierce through illogical reasoning quite as rapidly. Because adults may feel that their status is endangered by the child's responses or questions, they are sometimes more inclined to add restrictions rather than to allow the greater independence of action which the gifted youngster is seeking, and may be fully qualified to accept.

A further point in this area concerns the gifted child's earlier development of resentment toward physical punishment. He knows that such striking out at him is seldom based on a reasoned approach, and that often it may serve merely as a release for outraged adult feelings. Many youngsters show this reaction at early adolescence; the gifted child shows it early in childhood. This attitude may also be reflected in the gifted child's reactions with regard to social problems, as illustrated by the following anecdote. Following World War II, a father was explaining to his young son the reasons that the nations involved sent representatives to treaty conferences. He told how they all sat around a table and tried to decide what should be done about the problems, after the fighting had ceased. The child looked at his father and thoughtfully asked, "Why didn't they do that before they fought?"

There are some talents that depend upon mastery of a certain skill for their fullest expression, and creative writing is one of these. A child can and does show by rich imagery in his speech and by facile language development that he has the imagination, the ability to choose words that express exactly the meaning he wishes to convey and to state his thoughts and ideas in interesting and unique fashion. Yet, until he has learned to write for himself, this talent is a fleeting one and the pleasure of his speech forms is limited to those within earshot. Primary teachers sometimes write down the stories youngsters share with them and thus a record of the young child's ability may be kept. It is when he is able to write his stories for himself that he becomes most able to exploit his talent for creative expression.

FORMAL METHODS

Since parents and teachers are human beings and liable to errors of judgment, their conclusions based on observations such as have been described are not necessarily infallible evidence of giftedness. Fortunately, it is not necessary to depend upon observation alone in identifying gifted youngsters; many other methods are available for the teacher's use in this highly important task.

Throughout this chapter qualities related to originality of thought and expression, creative approaches to problems, insightful learning, and personal invention are stressed. None of the kinds of tests to be described purport to discover a youngster's ability in these areas; in fact, to achieve a high score a child had better respond in recognized ways in order to reach expected answers to the problems posed in these tests. For recognition of these very significant aspects of the ways in which gifted youngsters work, human judgment based upon thoughtful observation of many children over many years, and the ability to recognize and interpret creativity and originality as they appear in the everyday accomplishments of gifted children must be relied upon.

Teachers' Marks

Teachers' marks interpreted as records of a child's performance in academic subjects can be a source for identifying giftedness though it may not be the child whose record shows all A's who is the most superior. Teachers can check these records to discover what judgments other teachers have made of the quality of children's work, keeping in mind that a mere letter or number grade does not of itself indicate a youngster's potential. Teachers interpret grading differently. Some grade on the basis of how much a child has learned since entrance into the class, and this may involve a great deal of information, especially if he scored poorly at the beginning of the year. A superior child's progress may not be indicated nearly so well, as he may have been already well above the average of his class at the beginning of the year. Another teacher who grades individually may feel that a superior child has not worked as well or as much as he could have, and may reward his efforts with only a B. Though teachers should try not to be, some are influenced in grading by a child's behavior in the classroom, and use grades in retaliation against the child. Some tend to give higher grades to the youngsters who agree with them, and lower ones to the dissenters. Grades, then, as records of past school performance as judged by teachers, are one more source of information about a child, but they should not be relied on exclusively to decide whether a child may or may not be gifted.

Health Records

In a school which has the services of a nurse the personal health records for each youngster may be filed in her office. Examination of these combined with the youngster's record of past attendance will give some indication of the child's state of physical health, and may show superiority in this area. Many schools require complete physical and dental examinations of each child at stated intervals in order that the youngster's health may be adequately protected and conserved. A record of childhood illnesses, immunizations, and the examining physician's remarks are helpful to a teacher as he works with a youngster. These records can provide clues to the most effective ways of helping a child make progress in school; they can also sometimes help in explaining behavior that would otherwise be most puzzling.

Reports from speech and hearing therapists as well as oculists also should be available to the teacher. Sometimes the recommendations from such specialists are predicated on a different form of teaching than that which is practiced in the school. Particularly is this true when they imply that a teacher is inflexible in his classroom by requesting that a child be seated toward the front of the room where he may see, or near the teacher so he may hear. Today's classroom is not composed of permanently fixed positions. A teacher will need to keep the background of such recommendations in mind as he and his youngsters move about the classroom pursuing their varying tasks.

Test Scores

Ordinarily records are kept of all the standardized tests a child has taken since his entrance into school. These test scores should of course be dated and some indication must be given so the teacher knows whether they represent percentile scores, mental age equivalents, or grade-equivalent scores. Usually the names of the tests on which the scores were achieved are also part of this record.

These scores serve only as a guide to indicate what a child's performance was at a certain time on a particular test. They cannot be accepted as they stand without some further knowledge. Achievement test scores need to be compared with intelligence test scores so that teachers can determine whether a child seems to be working at the expected level. Individual scores need to be compared with those of an entire class group to discover the placement of the individual within that group. Scores also should be considered in the light of the youngster's age and grade placement at the time he achieved them. It is important to examine the test itself to see how many points a youngster may earn by answering a question, or lose by missing one. In some tests this may involve as much as a six-months' differential in a final grade-equivalent score.

It would seem important also to have available the actual test booklets, at least for the most recent tests the child has taken. If these are to be used diagnostically, teachers must be able to see where a child needs help. Standardized tests are not given solely to rate youngsters; they are an integral part of teaching to help determine in which area children need more help. This is *not* teaching for the test itself; this is discovering what reading skills a child seems to lack so that he can be helped to develop them, or whether he really understands percentage and can apply it in story problems, or what concepts in science some youngsters have not grasped.

Standardized Tests

INTELLIGENCE TESTS. Group tests of intelligence appear on the agenda of every school's testing program. Usually they are administered to every student at regular intervals; one such scheme is to schedule the tests for kindergarten (or first grade), third, sixth, and ninth grades. Such a pattern provides a method for discovering the degree of consistency in the performance of each student as he progresses through school, and obtaining up-to-date information about him.

These group tests are not infallible; no one can be positive that the scores derived from the tests are an accurate measure for each person tested. It is common knowledge that group tests tend to compress scores toward the middle; that is, gifted youngsters' scores tend to be lower on group tests than on individual tests, and slow youngsters' scores tend to be higher. A high score may be indicative of superior intelligence in the areas which the test includes, but arrangements should be made for an individual test in order to have the most accurate information about a particular child.

Much has been said and written about the unfair qualities of such group intelligence tests as those now in use. The older a child is, the more a test seems to be based upon his reading ability. It also assumes that he will have had certain experiences and will understand certain materials, and this may not be true of all children who take the tests. Youngsters from bilingual homes may be handicapped if their understanding or use of English is below the average, as may youngsters from homes which offer fewer cultural advantages. Gifted children from such homes can be identified, but possibly evidence other than their performance on group intelligence tests will be required.

Intelligence tests do help to predict a youngster's probable academic success, and this information is needed by teachers who attempt to develop programs designed to help each youngster progress as far and as rapidly as he is capable of doing. Parents, too, need to know what quality of work their youngsters can be expected to achieve as they participate actively in the planning and guidance involved. This is not to say that an actual score should be used in discussing intelligence; as has already been noted the specific digits are not the most important end result derived from a mental test. Rather it is the prognosis of the child's potential ability, and then the use made of that knowledge that are of greatest significance for the welfare of the student.

The number which is recorded on the child's record is derived by manipulating raw scores from as many as ten or twelve subtests, each of which purports to test ability in a certain area of intelligence. These include spatial relationships, numerical and quantitative reasoning, inference, memory, verbal accuracy and facility, and the like. Teachers should consider a child's score in each area to determine where his greatest strengths seem to be; the final numbers attached to his record are descriptive of general intelligence. It can be assumed that a youngster who makes a very high score on group tests is gifted; despite the imperfections of these tests, they are at present the most reliable single guide in identifying the gifted in groups with any degree of assurance.

If the faculty members of a school have decided on a minimum score that a child must make before he can enter into a special program for gifted students, they face the problem of deciding how to judge the borderline scores, what to do with youngsters who score 129 when the minimum for entrance into such programs has been set at 130. If decisions are made from an office in which children are seldom seen, this one is not difficult; the set standard must be adhered to just as the deadline dates of chronological age for entrance into school are followed. However, many teachers who work with youngsters directly every day are not convinced that the problem can be solved quite that simply. Several methods of identifying the gifted are essential, and no single measurement should be regarded as supplying the final answer.

ACHIEVEMENT TESTS. Though intelligence quotients do indicate a youngster's potential ability, the possession of a high I.Q. does not insure that achievement will automatically be outstanding too. To check a child's achievement level and to diagnose areas of strengths and weaknesses in an orderly and acceptable fashion the standardized achievement tests offer more reliability than do individual teacher-made tests or subjective observations of school performance.

Scores derived from achievement tests indicate a youngster's performance level in various school subjects. They show not what he is capable of achieving but what he actually accomplished at a specific time. These scores can then be compared with what a youngster of high intellectual ability is expected to be achieving, and parents and teachers can plan ways of helping individual children on the basis of this information. The diagnostic uses of such tests were described in a previous portion of this chapter, and need not be repeated at this time.

There are some drawbacks in the use of achievement tests to determine grade placement. A superior sixth-grade pupil can better show what he knows on a test designed for grades seven, eight, and nine, than he can on one prepared for grades four, five, and six, as the latter may actually not extend high enough to test his knowledge. Its top possible scores may be easily attainable for the superior sixth grader, and the advanced rather than the intermediate form of the test may be a wiser choice in his case.

Portions of some tests are based on an outdated philosophy of teaching and learning, and a youngster's score may look disturbingly low on them though he may be quite well in-

formed in the general area being tested. Literature is a case
in point. A test on literature that draws heavily from so-
called children's classics penalizes a youngster who reads
very widely among the many excellent current books available to boys and girls at the present time. This is a fast-
growing field and some tests have not kept abreast of its
developments. Few of today's children will, of their own
choice, select Anna Sewell's *Black Beauty* from the library
shelves, when they can read about Marguerite Henry's *Misty*
and *Sea-Star* or Walter Farley's *Black Stallion*.

Some achievement tests contain a section on study habits.
Here the youngster shows how well he can interpret data
from graphs, charts, maps, and the like, and how well he can
make use of reference materials. In determining the quality
of a youngster's study skills these portions are helpful. They
do not insure that he makes use of his knowledge in studying; here his personal motivation toward his schoolwork
enters the situation. A superior youngster can see whether
his scores on study skills are compatible with those on the
sections of the tests dealing with academic subjects. If he
possesses that inner drive to learn, and his school experiences
have fostered that attitude, he and his teacher can use this
information in planning ways of building a workable program for him.

APTITUDE TESTS. Aptitude tests provide another means by
which youngsters who possess certain talents or giftedness in
one area of living may be identified. Some of these are not so
familiar to classroom teachers as are intelligence and achievement tests, and the services of a person trained in the use of
aptitude tests may be helpful in interpreting them and making effective use of the information they provide.

An aptitude has been defined as a natural tendency or an
acquired inclination in some specific direction. General aptitude tests have heretofore been used almost exclusively at
the secondary school level in connection with the guidance
program for the purpose of helping a student determine the
particular kinds of work for which he seems best fitted. For a

student who is intellectually superior the results of aptitude tests tend to indicate that he could be successful in any of several areas. These tests do not give specific answers to vocational problems; their results are not so direct as to say that one student should be a file clerk and another should be a nuclear physicist. They show rather the general areas of earning a living in which a student has reasonable chances for achieving successful performance as an adult. The results require further interpretation in light of the interests, intelligence, and realistic expectations of the student, and of his parents.

Tests to indicate specific aptitudes such as talents in music, art, drama, creative writing, the dance, and mechanical skills, have been devised for locating gifted children. A child of high verbal facility may do quite well in an aptitude test involving creative writing, but this may not fit the direction of his interests. A youngster with a deep desire to follow the journalistic profession may learn from such an aptitude test that he will have to improve his knowledge and use of grammatical skills if he expects to reach his goal.

These tests can be supplemented in several ways. One involves the collecting of samples of the student's work, and having a panel of experts judge the quality they express. The judges must exercise caution in their appraisals so that imitation of adult standards is not accepted as creativity, nor conformity rated higher than originality.

Sometimes a youngster's predisposition toward a certain skill area combined with a deep concern and persistent attempts at development will enhance a talent to a degree not indicated by his earlier performance. In the best of today's schools, all youngsters are encouraged in developing creativity of expression and originality of thought, particularly in the primary grades. The youngster who continues to show these qualities after others seem to have lost their desire to be creative may well be the one who has talent and can continue to develop it because of his deep-seated desire, his personal motivation.

INTEREST INVENTORIES. Aptitude tests have sometimes been confused with interest inventories by both students and their parents. The results of aptitude tests indicate ability in certain fields; interest inventories merely indicate what a student thinks he would like. The latter have no significant value in determining his ability to follow through on his likes. When the results of an interest inventory show that a youngster seems interested in the field of medicine, and his latest intelligence quotient figures at 98, he may need some guidance in realizing that his interests and his ability do not seem compatible in this instance. For superior youngsters, an interest inventory can be helpful in showing a little more definitely than mere observation where their interests lie; it can also be used as an encouraging device to help keep interests broad, and to avoid too early, too narrow, or too hasty specialization.

SOCIOMETRIC TESTS. An even less formal group of devices for identifying talent are the sociometric "tests." These are not tests in the sense that there are predetermined right or wrong answers. As in the cases of the aptitude tests and the interest inventories, the results of these tests for the most part should be interpreted in relation to the individual who makes the responses. The compilation of data acquired in answer to such questions as, "Who are your best friends in this group?" and "With whom would you prefer to work in order to accomplish a worthwhile task?" can give teachers insight into (1), popularity or possibly leadership ability, and (2), the quality of judgment exercised by individuals in the class. Leadership ability may be associated with giftedness, though not necessarily. This information would offer the teacher one more bit of evidence to be considered together with all the other information he possesses about his youngsters in order to identify the gifted ones.

INTERPRETATION OF CUMULATIVE RECORDS. Cumulative records for each child are kept by most schools. From these records teachers can learn about the family background of the child, his past grades, the results of standardized tests, his health status, his personality traits, and similar information. These records have been compiled by human beings and as such are subject to human error and prejudice. Especially descriptive comments about the child written by his previous teachers should be viewed as personal judgments rather than objective fact. Merely in choosing which items to report a teacher may unwittingly exhibit personal bias or prejudice; surely his beliefs and attitudes influence not only what he says but also what he regards as significant in a child's development.

Factual items such as those revealing the family background can usually be accepted. The occupations of fathers and mothers represent valuable information because research seems to indicate that more gifted children come from families of professional, managerial, and skilled occupations than from those of unskilled labor. The education of the parents as well gives some indication of the kinds of experiences they may have provided for their children and thus the kind of growth environment in which they live. Even in an area such as this which seems to involve only straight factual information, errors can creep in, and teachers should check carefully to be sure only accurate statements are entered. There is the case reported by a teacher of the youngster who entered his mother's occupation as "lawyer" on his enrollment card; a quick question brought out the information that she worked as a secretary in a lawyer's office.

The cumulative record contains a wealth of information for an alert teacher to make effective use of as he becomes acquainted with each class of youngsters. Even such a seemingly unrelated item as the church a youngster attends may hold significance when interpreted in the light of community feeling toward that church as expressed to him by his peers. His placement in the family, his feelings toward brothers and sisters or to a new or expected baby in his family may offer clues as to the stability of his emotional nature. The information is there, but teachers must read and interpret it in terms of their knowledge of the youngster himself in order to make it most useful in working with boys and girls, and finding what data support their observations of the intellectual superiority of members of their classes, and possibly what data do not lend any help in this direction.

SELECTED READINGS

BAKER, HARRY J. *Introduction to Exceptional Children* (revised edition). New York: The Macmillan Co., 1953. 500 pp. Chapters 17 and 18.

Chapter 17 defines the rapid learning group in terms of the quantitative and qualitative differences in intelligence from the average, and suggests that curricular adaptations and improved methods of instruction are needed for their best progress. Chapter 18 deals with definition, characteristics, and the story of education of the gifted, drawing upon the Stanford studies and the Cleveland Major Work program.

BRANDWEIN, PAUL F. *The Gifted Student as Future Scientist*. New York: Harcourt, Brace & Co., 1955. 107 pp. Chapters 1 through 4.

All four chapters deal with identifying the future scientists among gifted high school students: Chapter 1 develops the hypothesis concerning certain factors necessary for success in scientific pursuits; Chapter 2 shows possibilities of self-identification by the students; Chapter 3 discusses some tests that can help in identification; and Chapter 4 points out some characteristic behaviors.

CUTTS, NORMA E., and MOSELEY, NICHOLAS. *Teaching the Bright and Gifted*. Englewood Cliffs, N.J.: Prentice-Hall, Inc., 1957. 268 pp. Chapter 2.

Systematic observation on the part of the teacher is presented as the principal method of discovering the bright children in a classroom; records and psychological services such as testing are discussed as necessary checks on teachers' judgment.

DEHAAN, ROBERT F., and HAVIGHURST, ROBERT J. *Educating Gifted Children*. Chicago: University of Chicago Press, 1957. 276 pp. Chapters 3 and 4.

Chapter 3 discusses tests and observation as ways of screening children for ability, listing specific tests and emphasizing the need for early identification. Chapter 4 presents a case study of a program for identifying gifted and talented children, based upon materials from Quincy, Illinois, and Portland, Oregon.

DEHAAN, ROBERT F., and KOUGH, JACK. *Identifying Students with Special Needs*. (Teacher's Guidance Handbook, Secondary School Edition, Vol. I.) Chicago: Science Research Associates, Inc., 1956. 94 pp.

In order to help teachers to work with the gifted and talented students in their classes, this booklet presents a series of check lists for teacher observation of students, and suggests some supplementary tests to substantiate that observation.

FRENCH, JOSEPH L. (ed.). *Educating the Gifted: A Book of Readings*. New York: Henry Holt & Co., Inc., 1959. 555 pp. Section 2.

This section considers the characteristics of gifted individuals through their lives as studied by authorities in the field, and originally presented as articles in professional journals.

GARRISON, KARL C., and FORCE, DEWEY, JR. *The Psychology of Exceptional Children* (3rd ed.). New York: The Ronald Press Company, 1959. 586 pp. Chapter 7.

Chapter 7 discusses physical and mental characteristics of the gifted, their range of interests, their abilities, and their problems.

KOUGH, JACK, and DEHAAN, ROBERT F. *Identifying Children with Special Needs.* (*Teacher's Guidance Handbook,* Elementary School Edition, Volume I.) Chicago: Science Research Associates, Inc., 1955. 91 pp.

Section 2 presents check lists to aid teachers in identifying the gifted and talented children in elementary-school classrooms; the handbook emphasizes that all children should be studied and observed in order to identify all who may benefit from further help.

NATIONAL SOCIETY FOR THE STUDY OF EDUCATION. *Education for the Gifted.* Chicago: University of Chicago Press, 1958. 420 pp. Chapters 3 and 9.

Chapter 3 discusses historic methods of identifying the gifted, and presents lists of behaviors by which the gifted may be recognized. It also gives specific examples of children's work which embody some of the characteristics of giftedness. Chapter 9 describes screening and selection procedures that may be used in identifying gifted children by testing and by observation, and offers examples of programs in operation.

4

Research on the Gifted

Research is a term that has come into more common usage among public school people as it has among the general public as the citizens of the nation have developed increased understanding of the need for scientific progress. Even the definitions of research given by present-day dictionaries include the idea of science: *The American College Dictionary* published by Random House in 1957 defines research as "diligent and systematic inquiry or investigation into a subject in order to discover facts and principles: *research in nuclear physics.*"

Research is invaluable; it is necessary to do research in order to establish bases on which to build programs; research is needed in education as it is in many other fields. Yet some of the information which is gathered and presented before the reading public in journals, newspapers, and books, with all the accompanying paraphernalia of charts, tables, and statistical terminology, is not research at all. Much of it contains excellent suggestions of possibilities that might be considered for use in school programs, but it cannot be transferred bodily from the place in which it was carried out originally to another area which may be operating under quite different conditions and in entirely different circumstances, with boys and girls who present different kinds of problems.

As descriptions of programs in operation, these articles may offer some help for students, public school teachers, and parents. Always they must be interpreted in terms of the situation in which the incidents occurred, the specific people involved, the goals toward which they were directing their work, and the assumptions with which they began. These descriptions are not research in the sense that they could be repeated in another time at another place with identical results. The conclusions given in such articles are not meant to be taken as laws or principles; the writers are not attempting to deceive those who read the material. It is expected that readers will use some judgment and realize that the outcomes given were results of specific circumstances, not that they will occur time and again no matter where the work is carried on. It is not logical to generalize haphazardly from specific presentations to situations that may be unrelated. As Ernest Newland, one of the leaders in research on the gifted, has stated, "Research findings always must be evaluated in terms of the population which has been studied, in terms of the situation in which the study was made, and in terms of the particular methodology employed at the time."[1]

Adults who work with boys and girls find that one of their greatest needs concerns developing ideas for things the youngsters can do, for suitable activities which will foster learning. One of the richest sources for such activities is of course the youngsters themselves. The teachers and other adult workers need to have supplemental suggestions, however, and these can often be gleaned from articles concerned with "how we did it in our school." Let us approach these with caution, realizing that an activity developed with some particular youngsters is not necessarily proven as to its worth with all youngsters who are studying the same topic or questions. Teachers must exercise their judgment as to the possible use of that idea with the boys and girls in their classrooms. No one should let himself fall into the trap of considering such suggestions to be the result of "research" merely because they have been accepted for publication in some medium of communication.

[1] T. E. Newland, "Implications of Research in the Area of the Gifted," *Exceptional Children*, XXV (January, 1959), 195-98.

There is one further type of article that often appears, and may be misleading to an unwary reader: this is the "I know a child who" type. Though students and teachers can verbalize quite plainly that one ought not to generalize from a few cases, they can unfortunately be influenced by reading about some real child who had certain experiences in a certain kind of a program or with a particular subject of study, whether the article is suggesting that the experiences are good or bad. Many teachers and parents know "a child who"; such knowledge of one case should not be accepted as indicative of results when many children are involved.

The discussion presented in this chapter leans heavily upon accepted research sources in the area of the gifted. Nowhere is a study cited that cannot be identified as a substantial research project. Evidence for each point is limited to standard references that explain studies developed according to acceptable research procedures, based on validated assumptions. The conclusions presented have been made within the confines of the data gathered by the experimenters; when the authors of these studies have given opinion, they have made completely clear to the reader that it is opinion and not proven fact.

The greater portion of the data presented is based upon the well-known investigations carried out by Lewis M. Terman and his associates at Stanford University; to date these results have been published in a five-volume series known as the *Genetic Studies of Genius*. Specifically these publications are: Volume I, *Mental and Physical Traits of a Thousand Gifted Children*, 1926; Volume II, *The Early Mental Traits of Three Hundred Geniuses*, 1926; Volume III, *The Promise of Youth*, 1930; Volume IV, *The Gifted Child Grows Up*, 1947; Volume V, *The Gifted Group at Mid-Life*, 1959. Numerous quotations from these studies appear in the chapter.

Other valuable research studies such as those carried on by Leta S. Hollingworth are quoted from and used in developing this material. All studies and investigations mentioned are listed at the end of the chapter.

MENTAL CHARACTERISTICS

Gifted human beings have, by definition, more intelligence than those people of average or lower competence. They can grasp ordinary concepts much more rapidly than average people, and they can comprehend subtleties of meaning in situations beyond the grasp of their less gifted fellows. They evidence insight which enables them to see clearly through the complexities to the core of problem situations, and they are able to devise more possible ways of solving the problem as well. What evidence is available from scientific studies to substantiate these statements?

Terman's continuing studies of the gifted over a period of thirty-five years dealt with the brightest four or five out of a thousand, those youngsters who scored at or above 140 I.Q. on the Stanford-Binet scale. Through working with siblings of the gifted and also some high-school pupils, the I.Q. level did include some youngsters who scored below 140; the main experimental group of 643 with which his original studies are concerned was limited to those children who tested at or above 140 I.Q.

Hollingworth's studies of the gifted in her early work were limited to those youngsters who "are so gifted that not more than one child in a hundred falls within their range. Thus we draw our line, and arbitrarily choose to mean by 'intellectually gifted' the most intelligent one per cent of the juvenile population."[2] This line separates for study children who score at or above 130 I.Q. on an individual intelligence test administered by a competent examiner. One of the many legends that has developed about gifted children and Leta Hollingworth is that her data are applicable only to children above 180 I.Q.; one of her books does deal with such highly gifted youngsters but that is not the only significant aspect of her work with the gifted.

[2] Leta S. Hollingworth. *Gifted Children: Their Nature and Nurture* (New York: The Macmillan Co., 1926), p. 43.

That gifted youngsters are far more educable than average youngsters is obvious. They can grasp more quickly the main thesis of their lessons; they are more alert to words and the meanings of words; they see relationships more rapidly; and they learn to read more easily and quickly than other youngsters. Terman found that nearly half of his gifted group had learned to read before they began attending school. Hollingworth[3] deduced from her studies that:

The gifted are omnivorous readers, but certain preferences are nevertheless characteristic of them as a group. For instance, they like dictionaries, encyclopedias, and atlases much more than average children ever do. They are more interested in such reading matter before they are ten years old than the average person ever is at any time during life. Frequently they compile encyclopedias and dictionaries for themselves.

The educability of these youngsters is further testified to by the fact that Terman found them as a group accelerated by 14 per cent of their age though their educational achievement as indicated by mastery of school subjects was more than 40 per cent of their age. Somehow, even in schools which make little or no provision for educating the gifted commensurate with their ability except whatever guidance can be offered by individually concerned teachers, gifted boys and girls do ordinarily absorb a great deal of information from their schoolwork, and supplement it with further study and interpretation of their own to the degree that their knowledge in many school subjects and other areas as well is far greater than that expected for average students. They seem to learn more from everything they experience, and this knowledge becomes theirs to use in further growth.

Another trait shown by groups of gifted youngsters is that they tend to hold their place in the scale of intelligence as they grow; they do not as a group burn out quickly nor regress to mediocre standards of intelligence, though this has long been accepted in the mythology that has surrounded the gifted. In discussing youngsters at Hunter College Ele-

3 *Ibid.*, p. 139.

mentary School who are participating in an ongoing experiment to test the stability of the intelligence quotient, Brumbaugh,[4] the principal of Hunter College Elementary School, has said, "Dr. Frank T. Wilson is re-testing this group as they reach adolescence and has found that they have maintained their place in the top one percentum, and are versatile, healthy, well adjusted individuals."

Lamson, in answering the question, "Do young bright children become intellectually mediocre when they reach high school?" cautiously concludes that:

> The question as to the constancy of intellectual status cannot be answered with complete adequacy and finality, because no norms are available for an unselected sample of the population of the age which the members of the Gifted Group had attained at the time of this study. Ranging in age from 13 years 8 months to 16 years 0 months, with a mean age of 15 years 0 months, 53.6 percent of the young gifted had already reached the top centile of *adults,* according to the best distribution of the latter available. This result suggests that the members of the Gifted Group are not growing toward mediocrity. The physical and mental immaturity of the group, however, render impossible any exact comparison with the adult population at this time.[5]

Terman's gifted group tended to retain their intellectual superiority as a whole, scoring each time within the top 1 or 2 per cent of the total population, at whatever age the members of the group were tested. Volume III, the 1927-28 follow-up, reported that the portrait of the group as a whole had changed in only minor respects. The group was still highly superior, testing largely within the top 1 or 2 per cent of the total population. The intelligence tests administered to the gifted group in 1940 indicated that the adults involved had continued to maintain a high level of intelligence, and still tested with the top 1 or 2 per cent of the population.

[4] Merle Elbert Frampton. *The Intellectually Gifted* (Reprinted from *Special Education for the Exceptional,* 3 vols., Merle E. Frampton and Elena D. Gall, eds. [Boston: Porter Sargent Publisher, 1956]), p. 11.

[5] Edna E. Lamson. *A Study of Young Gifted Children in Senior High School.* (Teachers College, Columbia University, Contributions to Education, No. 424. [New York: Bureau of Publications, Teachers College, Columbia University, 1930]), pp. 73-74.

There were some individual variations noticeable; the statements presented here have to do with the entire group of youngsters and adults tested in each case.

The 1950-52 test scores reported in Volume V show not only continued high standing, with most of the subjects remaining near the ninety-ninth percentile in mental ability, but also that there has been some increase in intelligence measured by the concept mastery test.

Hollingworth[6] has stated that "observation of such cases as those described in the foregoing chapters suggests that children of exceptionally high intelligence do not regress toward mediocrity as they mature but maintain their initial distinguished status."

And finally, to look at the matter of constancy of I.Q. from another angle, Catharine Cox concluded from her study of eminent men and women, reported in Volume II, that the people who achieve greatness are characterized by childhood behavior indicative of an unusually high I.Q., and that these gifted youngsters can be located and identified through the use of intelligence tests in childhood.

For many years in the past it was felt that nature operated in accordance with some sort of law of compensation; that people who were blind had extraordinarily keen hearing; that those who were deaf had unusually excellent sight; and that those who were gifted mentally would have some sort of physical disability. Much research has been done to disprove this false belief; it is known that people have the physical ability with which their heredity has endowed them, and which their mental powers have enabled them to use effectively. It is equally well known to those who have read and studied in the area that gifted people of any age tend to have excellent attributes of other kinds, physical, emotional, and social. The puny little bespectacled misfit is not the picture of the gifted child, in the main; he is the stereotype who unfortunately still lives on, without proof of his existence as typical.

[6] Leta S. Hollingworth. *Children Above 180 IQ* (Yonkers, N.Y.: World Book Co., 1942), p. 245.

In 1926 Leta Hollingworth[7] wrote:

Galton deduced from his studies that ability to rise above the average in achievement follows the same general laws of frequency as stature and weight. Most men are of medium ability. Diverging from them, on the one hand, are those of better than average ability, and, on the other hand, those of less than average ability. The farther a person diverges from medium ability, in either direction, the less frequently will those like him occur in the world.

Her own studies led her to conclude:

A person may consistently "do better" in some kinds of situations than in others. Nevertheless there is a positive correlation, however imperfect, among performances. If a person scores above average in one situation, he usually falls somewhere above average in meeting most other situations also. If he deviates from average in one perform-ance, he will probably deviate from average *in the same direction,* whatever he undertakes, but he will probably not deviate *equally far* from average in all he does.[8]

The remainder of this chapter will be devoted to discussion of those deviations from the average in terms of physical and emotional characteristics, character and personality traits, social adaptability and leadership ability, scholastic achievement, leisure-time activities, occupational and marital adjustment, and acceptance of civic responsibility. As attributes of gifted people are being discussed, it would be assumed that these deviations will be found above the norms, insofar as those have been established. Let it be understood again that we are talking in terms of groups of people; what is true for a group may not necessarily be true for each individual member of that group. There may even be a puny little be-spectacled misfit in the group, but he does not typify the characteristics of that group.

PHYSICAL CHARACTERISTICS

Mentally superior children have been found to be physi-cally superior as well, in health, physical strength, speed, and beauty. The facts as reported by competent investigators indicate this superiority in each area; the deviation from the

[7] Hollingworth, *Gifted Children, op. cit.,* p. 5.
[8] *Ibid.,* pp. 29-30.

norm is in the same direction as is the greater intelligence. Hollingworth[9] reports:

In 1924 Hollingworth and Taylor measured forty-five school children, who had previously been selected by mental tests, without regard to physique. They ranged from 135 IQ to 190 IQ with a median at 151 IQ. They were all between the ninth and eleventh birthdays. These children, having first been chosen by mental tests, were then measured for height in inches, and their measurements were carefully compared with those made previously by another investigator, Tirapegui, on children chosen by mental tests from the middle fifty percent of intellects, and from the lowest one percent, respectively. To form the three comparative groups, each gifted child was matched with a child testing between 90 and 110 IQ and with another testing below 65 IQ, keeping age, race, and sex as the bases of matching and paying no attention whatever to size. Thus differences in size due to age, race, and sex were eliminated. As the intelligence of each group had been prescribed before the physical measurements were taken, the only factor of interest allowed to vary as it would was the factor of physique. The comparison is, therefore, nearly ideal for its purpose, which is to determine how much, if at all, physique varies with intelligence. . . .

The gifted group has a median height of 52.9 inches, as compared with a median of 51.2 inches for the children of average intelligence, and of 49.6 inches for the very stupid.

When these same children were compared as to weight, it was found that the reported weights of gifted children were heavier than the norms for average children, and further, "The gifted group considerably exceeds the others in amount of weight per unit of height. They are not only heavier, but are *heavier for their height,* than average children. The gifted are very well nourished according to the weight-height coefficient."[10]

Terman reported in Volume I that as a group the gifted California children were above the standards for American children as a whole, and for other groups of California children in average standing height and weight. Each experimenter stresses that there is much overlapping between the groups compared. Though the conclusions given are scientifically justified and accurately stated, they do not make it

9 *Ibid.,* pp. 80-83.
10 *Ibid.,* p. 85.

possible to infer superior intellect for a given youngster who is tall, heavy, and well-fed for his age.

Thorough medical examinations of the Terman group of gifted youngsters in the 1921-22 study indicated very few cases of any defects or abnormalities. Only about 10 per cent of the youngsters showed somewhat defective hearing or poor vision. The examining physicians themselves agreed that the gifted children were physically superior to unselected children of corresponding age.

The follow-up studies of the Terman group depended upon the filling out of questionnaires on health as the expense involved in separate medical examinations for each subject precluded the repetition of those. In the 1927-28 follow-up studies:

According to reports from home and school, between 77 percent and 90 percent of the gifted boys and girls have good general health. Between 1 percent and 5 percent have poor health.[11]

In the 1940 study:

Ratings of "poor" or "very poor" were made by only 1.9 per cent of men and 3.7 percent of women. Ratings of "good" to "very good" were made by 90.9 percent of men and 83.7 percent of women.[12]

Terman and Oden[13] have written:

In conclusion, it may be said that the gifted group is probably at least equal or superior to the generality in respect to general health, height, weight, and freedom from serious defects. This is not surprising in view of the fact that medical examinations and anthropometrical measurements had demonstrated their clear superiority in childhood.

The continuing studies reported in Volume V bore out this conclusion. Judgments of personal health made in 1940, 1950, and 1955 showed that more than 90 per cent of the gifted men and 84 to 88 per cent of the gifted women consistently rated their general health as good or very good.

Perhaps another enlightening aspect of this presentation in general health is the mortality rate for Terman's group of

[11] *Genetic Studies of Genius,* Vol. III, p. 217.
[12] *Genetic Studies of Genius,* Vol. IV, p. 97.
[13] *Ibid.,* p. 98.

gifted, the largest group that has ever been followed from childhood to adult status. Terman and Oden[14] state:

Of 1,500 gifted subjects for whom we have information, 61 or 4.07 percent died between 1922 and 1940. The proportion was 4.14 percent for males and 3.98 percent for females. According to the life tables of Dublin and Lotka, based on mortality rate [in 1936] for the general white population, the expected mortality rate by age thirty for persons who were alive at age eleven was 5.37 for males and 4.68 for females, or a little above 5 percent for the sexes combined. Thus the proportion of deaths in our total group was only about four-fifths of the expectancy for the general white population of comparable age.

The 1955 figures reported in Volume V indicate that the mortality rate for the total group as well as for the sexes separately continued to be lower than the expectation. Also, accidental deaths have been fewer than the expected percentage for people of like age.

In addition to these data concerning height, weight, nutrition, and mortality rate, there are to be noted studies of strength and speed that were made by Hollingworth and Taylor, working with the same group of gifted youngsters referred to previously. In strength of grip, "these gifted children are as strong in the left hand and stronger in the right hand than average children and stronger in both hands than the stupid."[15] A tapping test used to determine relative speed led to the conclusion that "the gifted are swifter, as a group, than are their schoolmates of the same sex, race, and age, chosen without regard to intellect. They move more quickly and effectively, both with right hand and with left hand."[16]

Terman found similarly that the California gifted children excelled the children of a control group in Oak Park, Illinois, in four physical traits: arm span, width of shoulders, width of hips, and grip.

In concluding a discussion of the physical characteristics of gifted people, Hollingworth[17] wrote:

[14] Terman and Oden, "The Stanford Studies of the Gifted" in *The Gifted Child,* Paul Witty (ed.) (Boston: D. C. Heath & Company, 1951), pp. 26-27.
[15] Hollingworth, *Gifted Children, op. cit.,* p. 104.
[16] *Ibid.,* p. 106.
[17] Hollingworth, *Children Above 180 IQ, op. cit.,* p. 256.

It has been amply proved, by measurements, that highly intelligent children are tall, heavy, strong, healthy, and fine looking as a group, exceeding the generality of children in all these respects. This does not mean that every individual among the gifted is physically superior, but it does mean that a gifted child is more likely to have a fine body than is a child taken from the general population.

Likewise, Terman's investigation showed that the gifted group was, in childhood, physically superior to the various groups with whom comparisons were made.

EMOTIONAL CHARACTERISTICS

In the area of the emotional characteristics of gifted people there are stereotyped beliefs, as was noted earlier in discussing physical characteristics. Perhaps the most familiar is the statement that genius is akin to insanity. Though it has been demonstrated time and again that such a statement has no basis in fact, it persists and leads to misunderstanding of the emotional stability of gifted people as a group. Brumbaugh[18] (in Frampton), drawing from her knowledge of the field and her experience at Hunter College Elementary School, has written:

Mental health of the gifted is also better than that of unselected children. More wholesome social attitudes, less cheating on school examinations, and related personality traits are attributes of such children. Contrary to the belief of uninformed persons, intellectually gifted children boast less than their contemporaries and are not snobbish. The exceptions stand out in the same way that the misdeeds of the minister's child receive headlines, despite the thousands of children from clerical homes who behave in acceptable ways.

In the same publication Lorge[19] has written:

Whatever the reason, the stereotype of the "inferiority of superiority" prevailed. I need not remind you that the late Leta S. Hollingworth as well as Terman, found it necessary to prove the error of that stereotype. Again and yet again, they demonstrated that the intellectually gifted child is not doomed either to psychosis, or to neurosis, or to dementia. Again and again, their evidence proved that the gifted do make a significantly better adjustment, both personal and social, than any others in the population. Such adjustment joined to superior in-

[18] Frampton, *op. cit.*, p. 9.
[19] *Ibid.*, p. 24.

tellectual ability lead them to make genuine contributions by their ideas, by their inventions, and by their concerns for the general welfare.

Unfortunately, stereotypes, once magnified by print, are not removed either by scientific fact or by socially demonstrable practical outcomes.

Let us look at some of that evidence, and at some more recent studies as well.

In 1933 Hollingworth applied the Bernreuter Inventory of Personality to a group of fifty-five highly intelligent adolescents. They had an I.Q. range of 135 to 190, with a median at about 153; the average age was eighteen years, six months. She concluded, "The summary of results shows that the highly intelligent are less neurotic, more self-sufficient, and less submissive, as a group, than are the populations with which they are comparable. This divergence from the norm is found for both boys and girls of the highly intelligent group, but it is much more pronounced for boys."[20]

In the 1921-22 study, Terman[21] discovered that "indications of 'nervousness' are reported by the school for 13.3 per cent of gifted and for 16.1 per cent of control. Stuttering, including mild cases, is reported for 2.6 per cent of the gifted and for 3.4 per cent of control. Only two cases gave a history of chorea. 'Excessive timidity' and 'tendency to worry' were reported with about equal frequency in the gifted and control groups." The 1927-28 follow-up[22] of the gifted group found that "the gifted group shows little change with respect to the number showing a 'marked tendency to worry,' the proportion of boys being 8 per cent and that of girls 10 per cent. There is little difference between the gifted and the control groups in this tendency." Of all those rated in 1940 and 1945 very few indicated any serious maladjustment; even those few who had been hospitalized had recovered in a comparatively short time, and it was believed that their higher intelligence facilitated their more rapid re-

[20] Hollingworth, *Children Above 180 IQ, op. cit.*, p. 251.
[21] *Genetic Studies of Genius,* Vol. I, *op. cit.*, p. 212.
[22] *Genetic Studies of Genius,* Vol. III, p. 218.

covery. Comparable data for the general population were not available; the indication from Terman's data is that highly intelligent people are less prone to mental or nervous disorders, as a group, than are those of average or lower intelligence. If there is any truth to the statement that deviations from a norm tend to occur in the same direction, it would be expected that gifted people as a group would deviate from the norms for emotional stability in a positive direction.

Data collected in 1955 and reported in Volume V showed that about 9 per cent of both men and women in the gifted group had experienced some serious maladjustment, with approximately 3 per cent having been hospitalized at one time or another for treatment of the illness. These figures include only seven cases of prolonged hospitalization; as was true in 1940 and 1945, most of those who had been hospitalized responded favorably to treatment and were released in a short period of time.

Students of the incidence of mental illness in the general population of the United States predict that by age seventy-five, one of every ten people will have been hospitalized. The gifted group with an average age of forty-four years in 1955 has not reached that proportion.

CHARACTER AND PERSONALITY TRAITS

Volume I of Terman's research describes a battery of seven tests of character traits given to 532 children of the gifted group and 533 children of a control group. He deduced that "comparison of mean scores of the gifted and control groups by age shows a significant superiority of the gifted group for both sexes and at all ages. On the separate tests from 60 to 80 per cent of the gifted equal or exceed the mean of the control group. On the total score of tests one to seven, 85 per cent of the gifted equal or exceed the mean of the control group." And further: "The gifted child of nine years has reached a level of character development corresponding roughly to that of unselected children of fourteen years." He concluded that "although these tests do not make possible a very reliable comparison of individual children, they warrant the conclusion that in the traits which they measure the gifted group is decisively superior to the control group, and that this superiority is greater for girls than for boys."[23]

When teachers and parents rated these children on twenty-five traits, they agreed that the gifted excelled the unselected control groups in intellectual, volitional, emotional, moral, physical, and social traits; in the order of the degree of superiority indicated by the ratings. Mechanical ingenuity is the only trait on which the control group is rated higher than the gifted group. It can be seen that those traits having to do with character and personality are included, and that the gifted exceeded the control group in each. Later performance tests indicated that they were also to exceed the control group in mechanical ingenuity, though they were rated lower in that area by both teachers and parents.

The 1927-28 follow-up study gave similar results. The mean scores on the character traits tests were almost identical with those obtained by the gifted of the same age in 1921-22. The teachers' and parents' ratings were similar in the follow-up study of the character traits. Teachers and parents tended to rate the gifted boys and girls higher on the intellectual traits, and lower on the social traits. These ratings were higher than those made for the control children in each instance.

In 1930 Lamson reported teachers' judgments of a group of young bright children in respect to self-control, intelligence, personal appearance, conceit, sustained effort, general deportment, general quality of schoolwork, and popularity with schoolmates. She concluded, "In the eight traits studied, there is a significant difference between the scores of the Gifted Group and those of the Control Group with respect to intelligence, general quality of work, and sustained effort. The difference is in favor of the Gifted Group." The relationship between these traits and those more directly connected with character and personality traits seems notable.

[23] *Genetic Studies of Genius,* Vol. I, pp. 516-17.

Lightfoot[24] studied 104 children at Speyer School to discover what personality differences existed between the bright and the dull. Forty-eight of the youngsters were very bright, members of a Terman class; fifty-six were in a Binet class for relatively dull children. The I.Q. distributions showed a range of 130 to 200 with a median of 147 for the Terman group, and a range of 68 to 104 with a median of 88 for the Binet group. The Terman children ranged in age from ten years, one month to twelve years, ten months, with a median age of eleven years, three and a half months. The Binet children ranged from ten years, one month to thirteen years, five months, with a median of eleven years, eight months. To gather her data she used a study of home background, an interview for which a definite structure was prepared, a psychological test, ratings by the staff of the school on forty attributes of personality, a projective technique involving film excerpts followed by group discussion which was stenographically recorded, and the case study approach for which the data on each individual were compiled into one folder so that each might be rated by competent psychologists who were unacquainted with the youngsters.

The twenty personality variables checked were: achievement, affiliation, aggression, appearance, autonomy, cognizance, creativity, defendance, deference, dependence, dominance, emotionality, exhibition, placidity, play, protectiveness, recognition, rejection, retention, and seclusion. Lightfoot stated as a result of her investigation that:

The conclusion is reached here that there are significant differences between bright and dull children on various personality traits as measured in this investigation. Secondly, it is concluded that the various types of data (as secured by the several techniques used) yield evidence of such differences in varying degrees.

The differences noted in relation to the Terman Group, or bright children, have to do with variables of a positive, outgoing kind, while those which seem to characterize the Binet Group, or dull children,

[24] Georgia Frances Lightfoot, *Personality Characteristics of Bright and Dull Children* (Teachers College, Columbia University, Contributions to Education, No. 969 [New York: Bureau of Publications, Teachers College, Columbia University, 1951]).

are the converse, a negative, withdrawing kind. The findings of this study, then, appear to be in accord with those of leading investigators in this field whose opinions and observations were quoted earlier. The "independence," "originality," "creative imagination," "forcefulness," "warmth," "vitality," "superior social adjustment," "play activities," and "honors," of which Hollingworth, Terman, and Witty wrote in regard to the bright, find their counterparts in Autonomy, Creativity, Dominance, Affiliation, Protection, Play, Achievement, and so on. Similarly, the "shyness," "repression," and "apathy" "encountered rather more frequently among the slow-learning children" remarked on by Featherstone, are reported in this study by Dependence, Seclusion, Rejection, and Placidity.[25]

She noted also that:

The ability to make friends, friendly understanding, sympathy, and a desire to help both friends and members of the group who are not close friends, a more than average degree of playfulness, an inclination to initiate social contacts and better-than-average good looks and appearance of body and clothing form a pattern important in successful social adjustment. The children of the Terman Group apparently were characterized by this pattern to judge from the mean of the ratings assigned to them by those who were in daily contact with them.

An average display of leadership, some enjoyment of rivalry, alertness, interest and vigor, an average amount of dominance (equally often controlling others and being controlled), more than average assurance and self-reliance, supported by courage and the tendency to defend the self against physical aggression, are also attributed to the Terman Group.

The pattern of achievement, with much enjoyment from mastery of problems, industriousness, creativity—the mean lying at a point between "resourcefulness in modifying, recombining the ideas of others" and "occasionally displays definitely original ideas"—and a high degree of curiosity exemplified by a more than ordinary interest or desire to learn, is the most marked of all the patterns characterizing the Terman Group.[26]

In the same year (1951) Ausubel published a study of the extent to which prestige motivation affects the performance of gifted children. He hoped to identify the personality traits related to present academic and future vocational success, being particularly concerned with the relationship of performance in school and personal prestige. He agrees that:

[25] *Ibid.*, p. 62.
[26] *Ibid.*, p. 82.

The most definitive study in this area is that by Terman and Oden who made a differential analysis of the individuals occupying the upper and lower quartiles respectively on a scale of empirically determined adult success. Research data going back twenty-five years were available for their subjects. Among other findings were the facts that the successful group excelled the unsuccessful group in integration toward goals, perseverance and self-confidence, undertook more extra-curricular and leadership activity in school, and did superior work in high school. Yet the two groups were evenly matched in intelligence. They conclude that, "intellect and achievement are far from perfectly correlated."[27]

Seventy-nine sixth-grade children were the subjects of Ausubel's study. He prepared pages of addition material and pages involving the cancellation of a certain letter. The children also took the Maller Self-Marking Test for deceit; there were sociometric tests to determine social acceptance; and there were the interview technique, teachers' ratings, and objective background information from school records.

He expected to find "that in comparing a group of individuals with high difference scores to a group of individuals with low difference scores, (a) the mean degree of prestige motivation in the upper group should be higher, (b) the mean degree of intrinsic motivation in the upper group should be lower, and (c) variability in both prestige and intrinsic motivation should be less in the upper group."[28]

The results of the study bore out the expectations for it. The consistency shown by the upper and lower prestige groups is explained by Ausubel as follows:

The upper prestige group consistently scored higher than the lower group on all of the criteria of prestige motivation used in this study, but the significance of the differences varied greatly. Their acceleration and prestige scores were significantly higher. They enjoyed the competitive test situation more than the lower group, and reported more often that even in the anonymous situation they set up a silent self-imposed competition with neighboring pupils. The upper group children showed greater liking for a prestige subject such as arithmetic,

[27] David Paul Ausubel, *Prestige Motivation of Gifted Children* (Genetic Psychology Monograph, 1951, 43:53-117 [New York: Department of Psychology, Teachers College, Columbia University]), pp. 58-59.
[28] *Ibid.*, p. 63.

and their addition difference scores were much higher in proportion to their cancellation scores than was the case in the lower group. They received higher self-ratings, higher parental ratings, and higher teacher ratings on scholastic competitiveness. The academic aspirations of their parents for them as well as their estimates of these aspirations were slightly and very unreliably greater. Their relative academic standing as rated by present classroom teachers was higher. Other slight and unreliable differences in their favor include higher teacher ratings on motivational personality traits, higher sociometric standing, slightly higher grades in arithmetic reasoning, and more parent initiation of extra-curricular activity.

Although many of the above differences do not meet the conventional test of statistical significance, the fact that they are all consistently in the same direction adds considerably to their reliability.

Evidence of greater intrinsic motivation in the lower prestige group is much less striking, partly because of the availability of fewer criteria. None of the differences are significant statistically, but again they enjoy the advantage of invariable consistency. In explaining why they worked hard during the anonymous session, they mentioned more frequently "self-satisfaction" and "to raise the class average." They were rated by their teachers as being more cooperative, and they rated themselves as exhibiting less anxiety over examinations. In the language arts which enjoy less academic prestige than arithmetic, their reading achievement scores were higher.

The lower prestige group also showed greater variability in several respects. A very interesting suggestive difference was in the variability of the deceit scores. . . . This group also exhibited greater variability in achievement scores in arithmetic computation and unreliably greater variability in mean number of hours spent weekly on extra-curricular reading, mean number of hours spent weekly on art-music activities, and class grades in arithmetic reasoning. With respect to present academic class standing, they showed bimodal distribution in contrast to the approximately normal distribution of the upper group.

There is, thus, reasonably good evidence for believing that the prestige motivation difference score (when considered in relation to validating data) actually corresponds in fact to the factors of prestige and intrinsic motivation and their inter-relationships which had been postulated as accounting for its relative magnitude.[29]

Personality factors thus operate upon performance in academic work. Ausubel concludes that "prestige motivation, hence, is just a competitive aspect of level of aspiration; and level of aspiration can have no meaning apart from specific ego-involvement."

[29] *Ibid.*, pp. 99-100.

SOCIAL ADJUSTMENT AND LEADERSHIP

A tendency among gifted children toward social maladjustment is often cited by those opposing special programs for the gifted. They maintain that special provisions aggravate this tendency. They claim that with special programs the gifted would become snobbish and boastful; they would be unable to relate successfully to others; they would not participate in so-called normal activities for their ages; they would in short become even greater misfits than they by nature are. Let us look at some of the evidence in the matter.

In the 1921-22 study, according to the results of a free association test to determine intellectual, social, and activity interests, 84 per cent of Terman's gifted group equaled or excelled the mean of unselected children in social interest, and there was no significant difference between the scores of the gifted and the control in activity interest. Terman determined also that even though the gifted child was usually younger than his classmates, he had companionship in school to about the same degree as other youngsters, and that there seemed to be little difference in social adjustment. These data were further substantiated by similar results in the 1927-28 follow-up study.

Participation in various extracurricular activities can be taken as one kind of evidence of social adjustment. Terman found that "one or more offices or honors are recorded upon the Interest Blanks of 87 per cent of the boys and 96 per cent of the girls from whom blanks were received. The gifted subjects take part in a wide variety of extracurricular activities, and are as likely to gain recognition in any one of the several kinds of nonacademic acitvity as they are in scholarship."[30]

The portion of Keys' study that dealt with high-school students gave similar results. Keys wrote, "With respect to participation in student activities, the underage group equals or surpasses the equally gifted controls on virtually all comparisons. Their showing is strikingly superior on boys' athletic

[30] *Genetic Studies of Genius*, Vol. III, p. 132.

teams and honors won therein, though differences are in no
instance sufficient for reliability."[31] In discussing results of
the Bernreuter scale, Keys said, "Moreover, the age of com-
panions preferred by members of the different groups indicates the bright pupils accelerated from two to five semesters
to be better socially adjusted to their classmates than those
retained in groups of like chronological age. Pupils' self-
estimates of general happiness in high school show the
bright, and particularly the bright accelerated, to best advantage, with the underaged of merely average intelligence
ranking lowest."[32]

One of Lamson's guiding questions also dealt with participation in activities, and she concluded, "The participation of
the Gifted Group in extracurricular activities exceeds the
participation of the Control Group by approximately twenty-
five percent, when such participation is measured by the
average number of activities per member in the respective
groups. The young gifted have not been debarred from extracurricular participation because of immaturity."[33]

As the gifted of Terman's group attended college, the picture remained the same. He wrote, in Volume IV, that the
men and women of the gifted group on the whole participated to a greater extent in extracurricular activities than did
the generality of college students. The evidence then seems
to indicate that gifted children and adults have little or no
difficulty in becoming members of groups that they wish to
join, in relating themselves to others in some sort of group
situation. This seems to be an accurate picture of the typical
gifted individual. Knowing that he customarily has traits of
personality that are highly acceptable to others, the student
should expect this to be so, and not be deceived by the misleading statements quoted earlier, that are not supported by
the evidence.

[31] Noel Keys, The Underage Student in High School and College: Emotional and Social Adjustments (Berkeley, Calif.: University of California
Press, 1938), p. 243.
[32] Ibid., p. 255.
[33] Lamson, op. cit., p. 74.

Those extremely gifted students do appear to have more difficulty in social relationships than does the typical gifted person. Keys found that "the chances of leadership of this sort (elective office) in a high-school group averaging close to 105 I.Q. appear brightest for accelerates with I.Q.'s of from 120 to 140. In the present study, members of the experimental group were, by reason of their rapid promotion, more nearly on a par with their classmates in mental age than were the controls. This seems to have offset in social relations the disadvantage of disparity in chronological age. If so, acceleration is favorable to social as well as to educational adjustment."[34]

Leadership ability, which has been implied throughout this discussion of participation in social activities, is another of the desirable attributes of the typical gifted child, and of course it can be fostered and developed as the child grows. Sumption[35] found in his study of the Major Work program in Cleveland that it developed a sense of social responsibility among the participants to a greater extent than was the case in the regular school, and that Major Work experiences were superior to the regular school program in developing leadership. This superiority was indicated primarily in the number of positions of leadership held rather than in the incidence of leadership, although the Major Work groups were slightly superior in this respect also. His conclusions were based on the quantitative rather than the qualitative aspect of leadership.

Hollingworth writes:

In observing who are the popular leaders in various groups of children, it appears that the intelligence of the leader is related in a fairly predictable manner, other traits being favorable, to the intelligence of the led. Among children with a mean IQ of 100, the IQ of the leader is likely to fall between 115 and 130 IQ. That is, the leader is likely to be more intelligent, *but not too much more intelligent*, than the average of the group led. If there is in an ordinary group of children a child of about their own mean age, relatively large, handsome,

[34] Keys, *op. cit.*, p. 243.
[35] Merle R. Sumption, *Three Hundred Gifted Children* (Yonkers, N.Y.: World Book Co., 1941), p. 98.

amiable, courageous, generous, and strong, and of IQ between 115 and 120, such a child is likely to be a leader (due regard being had to social attitudes governing leadership as related to sex). Above 130 IQ, however, the chances of leadership among a group such as described, appear to decrease till, beyond IQ of 160, a child has very little chance of being a popular leader. In a group with a mean IQ at 130, however, a child of IQ as high as 160 may well lead, for such a group gives allegiance to a degree of insight above that which wins the average group, other traits being favorable.[36]

Thus there seems to be some relationship between the average intelligence of a group and the intelligence of the person whom they will choose to be a leader. Intelligence does not, however, appear to be the only determinant in such a situation. There are some gifted children who have traits of personality that would make them favorites with children of any age; other gifted children, like some average children, have personalities that would limit their participation with any group.

Social adjustment or adaptability, and leadership ability as well, are traits possessed by the typical gifted youngster. The fact, however, that not all gifted are alike cannot be neglected; they show ranges in intelligence, in physical characteristics, in emotional adjustment, in any quality to be discussed; the generalizations made in each instance are applicable to the typical gifted child, but there are those who may not be typical, and may thus deviate from the conclusions given here.

SCHOLASTIC ACHIEVEMENT

This is one area in which the gifted youngsters might logically be expected to exceed the control groups, and on the whole they do. It has already been stated that the average gifted child was accelerated in school by 14 per cent of his age, a conclusion from Terman's early studies. He found also that about 85 per cent of the gifted children were accelerated. None of the youngsters had, however, been accelerated to the grade indicated by subject matter mastery; this gap appears to widen as the child grows older.

[36] Hollingworth, *Gifted Children, op. cit.,* p. 131.

In 1921-22 the gifted youngsters in the Terman group took the Stanford Achievement Tests in reading, arithmetic, language usage, and spelling, plus a general information test. The gifted showed very great superiority over a group of unselected children in all areas tested. From this group of tests, Terman concluded that at any given age there was little correlation between educational accomplishment and the number of terms the gifted child had attended school. The conclusion as stated gives cause for consideration by people who work in schools and presumably are committed to help each child progress as far as he is able during the time he is within their particular jurisdiction.

School subjects preferred by gifted children are much more likely to be abstract; gifted children evidence much less interest in so-called practical subjects. Terman reported in Volume I that the gifted rated such subjects as literature, grammar, debating, and ancient history as very easy and the control group judged such subjects as sewing, drawing, painting, general science, singing, folk dancing, and penmanship very easy. He also found the average correlation between ease and preference to be .59.

A free association test devised to measure intellectual, social, and activity interest was also administered to the gifted and control children. Terman discovered that about 90 per cent of the gifted children equaled or exceeded the mean of the control children in intellectual interest, and that about 84 per cent of the gifted equaled or exceeded the mean of the control children in social interest. He also learned that with respect to activity interest, the gifted and the unselected groups did not differ significantly. The relationship of intellectual interest to achievement was found significant for all school subjects except spelling; it was greatest for arithmetic reasoning. The two other interest areas tested seemed to have little or no effect upon school achievement of the gifted or of the control children.

The 1927-28 follow-up study of Terman's gifted group reported that the most recent Stanford Achievement Test level of the gifted boys was in agreement with their present mean

I.Q., and the achievement level of the gifted girls was a little higher than their present I.Q.'s would indicate. Another and perhaps more significant finding was:

> On the Iowa High-School Content Examination (which included English, mathematics, science, and history) the mean scores of the high-school senior and college freshman gifted boys tend to be roughly 1.5 to 2 control S.D.'s [standard deviations] above the norm; those of the high-school senior and college freshman gifted girls roughly 1 to 1.5 control S.D.'s above the norm. Considering that high school students are selected, perhaps representing in the eleventh or twelfth grades chiefly the upper fifty percent of the generality of school children, the showing made by the gifted group on the Iowa High-School Content Examination must be regarded as extremely gratifying.[37]

Insofar as grades received in school subjects may be indicative of achievement in the eyes of the teachers, the grades received by the gifted in high school and college are important. Terman found that gifted pupils of both sexes averaged far above unselected high-school pupils, and received "A" grades four to eight times as often as the unselected high-school pupils in the same school studies; the girls received "A" in about 75 per cent of their subjects, and the boys in 45 per cent. In college the gifted group was also above the average scholastically even though the gifted subjects at Stanford were competing for grades with students whose level of ability was only slightly below their own and who were also nearly two years older than the gifted students.

Lamson's study indicated also the superiority of gifted children in senior high school. In comparing the gifted group with the general high-school population, she wrote:

> Whatever the angle from which the Gifted Group was compared with the Control Group of high school pupils with reference to comparative scholastic achievement, the record of achievement on the part of the Gifted Group was significantly superior to the achievement of the Control Group; and their achievement was superior in spite of the fact that their chronological age was, on the average, two years less than that of their Control Group.[38]

[37] *Genetic Studies of Genius*, Vol. III, p. 99.
[38] Lamson, *op. cit.*, p. 74.

The 1957 report of the Ford Foundation's Fund for the Advancement of Education bears out the same conclusions in respect to achievement at the college level. The report states:

It should probably come as no surprise that academically the Scholars as a group outperformed their classes as a whole by a wide margin. But offhand, one might expect the Comparison students to do better than the Scholars, in view of their advantage in age and high school preparation. This has not been the case. Year after year, a higher proportion of Scholars than Comparison students ranked in the top tenth, fifth, and third of their classes.[39]

Another way of assessing academic achievement is to look at the honors earned by the students involved. For the California group, it was found that of fifty-four members who graduated from Stanford, 30 per cent were elected to Phi Beta Kappa, and of fifty-eight who graduated from the University of California, 28 per cent were elected to the honor society, as compared with 10 per cent of all seniors who graduated from eligible departments. The percentage of the Terman group who graduated from Stanford with distinction or with great distinction was more than twice the percentage for the Stanford graduates as a whole. At many points throughout his study, Terman makes reference to the rigorous standards for admission to Stanford at the time the gifted California group began to attend college. It is well to keep this in mind in interpreting his conclusions as to grades and honors earned by the students.

Keys also found that young gifted students tend to surpass those of average age in the areas of grades and honors achieved. For the high-school group he reported: "In groups of equally high I.Q., scholarship honors and better study habits are found associated with acceleration rather than with normal progress, even though the nonaccelerated enjoy a pronounced advantage in mental as well as chronological age."[40] For the college group he found that "students enter-

[39] The Fund for the Advancement of Education, *They Went to College Early* (Evaluation Report No. 2 [New York: Fund for the Advancement of Education, 1957]), pp. 22-24.

[40] Keys, *op. cit.*, p. 242.

ing under sixteen and a half show a large and significant superiority over unselected groups on practically all points of distinction. Even in the freshman and sophomore years, their grade-point ratio is one-quarter point above the average of their classes. The number of scholarships awarded to them is more than three times, and the percentage graduating with honors, twice that of the control group. Four times as large a proportion of the young entrants were elected to Phi Beta Kappa; and 38 per cent became members of honor societies of all kinds, as compared with 16 per cent of the controls."[41]

There are other studies that indicate the academic superiority of gifted students as they attend high school and college. One concerned with young high-school graduates made by Moore is cited. Judging from comparative scores on state-wide achievement tests, she wrote: "At the time of graduation from high school the young groups make scores on the average about one-half sigma above the scores achieved by the statewide groups with equal training. The results of the comprehensive examinations given at the end of the sophomore and senior years in college show that the students who graduated from high school at the age of fifteen maintained their superiority as they progressed through college."[42] Moore went on to state that it is desirable for gifted students as young as fifteen or sixteen years to enter college, on the basis of her findings based on objective tests and college grades.

Volume IV of Terman's research studies pointed out that nearly 90 per cent of the gifted men and 86 per cent of the gifted women attended college. Of the total gifted group, 70 per cent of the men and 67 per cent of the women graduated from college. The gifted group was graduating from college mostly between 1930 and 1940 when less than 8 per cent of the California men and women of college age were graduat-

41 *Ibid.*, p. 184.
42 Margaret Whiteside Moore, *A Study of Young High School Graduates* (Teachers College, Columbia University, Contributions to Education, No. 583 [New York: Bureau of Publications, Teachers College, Columbia University, 1933]), p. 65.

ing. The number of present-day college graduates is 12 per cent of the population of college age; the gifted California group exceeded even this percentage of later years by a great proportion.

Terman reported:

The average grade in college, while superior, was not always as high as might have been expected from a group of such marked intellectual superiority. Of those graduating from college, 77.5 per cent of men and 82.5 per cent of women had average college grades of B or better. Graduating "with honors" were approximately 30 per cent of both men and women. Elected to Phi Beta Kappa or Sigma Xi or both were 27.7 per cent of men and 21.5 per cent of women. On the other hand, 53 or 7.7 per cent of the men who entered college flunked out. Only 10 or 2 per cent of the women were disqualified. Nearly half of the men who failed later finished college, and a number took graduate degrees, but only one woman who was disqualified finished college.[43]

This last cited statement brings up the point of inferior scholarship among some gifted people. Though the relationship between mental ability and school tasks has been shown to be positive, it is necessary to return to and emphasize the fact that such statements are based on evidence drawn from the scores of large groups of individuals, and do not necessarily characterize each individual within that group. On the whole, gifted students do well with their school subjects, as the studies cited indicate. There are some gifted students who are underachievers, who do not reach the potential of performance expected of them. Future studies may determine the causes for such underachievement and develop some possible remedies for those causes. The causes of poor schoolwork among gifted children are probably as numerous and varied as those related to low achievement of average children, and remedies for such situations may need to be developed for each individual youngster.

Volume V of *Genetic Studies of Genius* has completed the educational record of the gifted group up to 1955. By that year 56 per cent of the men and 33 per cent of the women had earned one or more graduate degrees. Fourteen per cent

[43] *Genetic Studies of Genius*, Vol. IV, p. 168.

of the gifted men and 4 per cent of the gifted women had earned doctor's degrees; these percentages are very much higher than the current 2 per cent of all college graduates who go on to take the doctorate.

Recognition of adult achievement on the part of the gifted group has grown considerably, according to comparative data of 1945 and 1955. Though Terman and Oden predicted that listings of the gifted group in *American Men of Science* might possibly be doubled by 1960, the facts reported in 1959 show that they have quadrupled; there were nineteen men so listed in 1945, and seventy men and seven women in 1955. Entries in *Who's Who in America* numbered five in 1945; in contrast to the cautious prediction that this number might be three or four times as great by 1970, Volume V reports thirty-one men and two women so recognized by 1955. This represents more than six times as many with fifteen years remaining before 1970.

LEISURE ACTIVITIES

There is fully as wide a range of interests among the gifted as may be found among other less well-endowed people. Gifted persons enjoy being with their friends and participating in activities; they also possess sufficient inner resources to enjoy being alone and to follow their own pursuits. Evidence has been amassed to indicate that the more highly gifted person encounters greater difficulty in being one of the group, probably because he himself is so far removed from average that there aren't many like him to form a congenial group. Lightfoot has said:

There emerges the portrait of the gifted child, so well limned by Leta Hollingworth and others; one who is well-disposed toward his fellows, who makes an effort to join the group, to be cooperative, to participate, but who at the same time has a mental life of his own which he enjoys, which perforce leaves him rather far removed from others. Quite understandably, there are times when he had rather read a book than meet people.[44]

[44] Lightfoot, *op. cit.*, p. 92.

Some highly gifted children develop an imaginary play-mate to accompany them in leisure time activities. This seems satisfying to the very highly gifted, as such a playmate can, of course, participate in the advanced activities that are gratifying to the child himself, as he directs the play. The child understands the greater complexities of older children's play and may even at times develop further ramifications of rules and procedures to make the play more interesting to him and, he believes, to the others. He has not the physical skills or stature required to be acceptable to the much older children—but their games are of much greater interest to him than the lower-level activities considered typical for his chronological age. Hollingworth has written:

These young children of extremely high intellectual acumen fail to be interested in "child's play" for the same reasons that in adulthood they will fail to patronize custard-pie movies or chute-the-chutes at amusement parks. It is futile, and probably wholly unsound psycho-logically, to strive to interest the child above 170 IQ in ring-around-the-rosy or blindman's buff. Many well-meaning persons speak of such efforts as "socializing the child," but it is probably not in this way that the very gifted can be socialized. The problem of how the play interests of these children can be realized is one that will depend largely on individual circumstances for solution. Often it can be solved only by the development of solitary play.[45]

Few extremely gifted individuals are likely to be enrolled in public schools. Evidence indicates that they are quite stable emotionally and able to accept and work with their strengths and possible unevennesses of abilities in differing areas. Because of these facts there are those persons who feel that public school people should confine themselves to study of and work with less highly gifted individuals who are more likely to be encountered in regular classes. This feeling seems to smack of equality of opportunity, defined as identi-cal opportunity for all youngsters. Someone has said that this is equivalent to providing all ten-year-old boys with the same size shoes; it would seem fully as logical. There seems no

[45] Hollingworth, *Children Above 180 IQ, op. cit.*, p. 275.

reason to conclude that teachers should, by their practices in classrooms, neglect extremely gifted youngsters merely because they are extremely gifted.

Data gathered from Terman's gifted group, at or above 140 I.Q., show the breadth of interests referred to previously, and that one and three-fourths times as many gifted children as control children made collections. More than twice as many made scientific collections. The gifted group indicated more enthusiasm about varied activities than did the control children. In a study based on ratings of ninety plays, games, and amusements, the gifted children showed greater interest in the activities that required thinking, and less preference than the control children for competitive activities. As a whole, the gifted tended to prefer activities that are popular with older children. There was actually little difference in the amount of experience with the plays and games studied, but much difference in kind. The gifted reported much more experience with games that involve intellectual activity. Information from home and school indicated that the gifted played alone slightly more than the control children; yet they were still playing with other children in out-of-school activities more than two hours a day. Terman also found that many children had had imaginary playmates in imaginary countries.

The 1921-22 California study devoted an entire chapter to the reading interests of the gifted and the control children. Terman found that according to parents' estimates, the gifted increased the number of hours of reading per week from six at age seven to twelve at age thirteen. The teachers' estimates indicated that 88 per cent of the gifted and 34 per cent of the control groups read more than the average child; none of the gifted and about one-third of the control group read less. When a record of books read was kept for two months, again the gifted indicated superiority in this area. Terman wrote that "the average gifted child of 7 read more books in the two months than the average of the control group for any age up to 15. The average of gifted children at 8 or 9 is three times that for the control group of the same age."[46] The range of books read by the gifted was considerably wider than the range of the control group; the gifted reported more nonfiction books read, such as science, history, travel, biography, and the like. They also read more folk tales, poetry, and drama, and fewer books classified as adventure and emotional fiction.

The 1927-28 follow-up study of Terman's gifted group showed a continuing preference for history, biography, and travel books, with the girls continuing their interest in fiction, poetry, and drama, and the boys in adventure and detective stories. At age thirteen for girls and age fourteen for boys it was reported that the number of hours of home study overtook the number of hours spent on general reading.

Volume III reported that both boys and girls of the gifted group tended to prefer reading when they were able to choose their own activities though they liked active games and sports also, rating them second on lists of preferred activities. Boys made more collections than girls, and made many more collections related to scientific interests than did the girls of the gifted group.

To summarize these statements before moving into adult leisure time interests, it can be seen that reading ranks as a highly preferred activity for gifted children and adolescents. It should be pointed out that these same youngsters expressed enjoyment in being with others, and in participating in active sports and games. However, the preference for soliary activities can be seen in the reading and the collecting nterests. The gifted do not shun their age-mates, in general; they participate in their activities although they do express a preference for playing with older children. Yet, there are times when they "had rather read a book." Since they scored so well on the general information test referred to earlier in this chapter, it may well be that this concentration on reading in various fields of interest is one of their enjoyable ways of learning, and adding to their store of knowledge.

Again, as adults these gifted subjects indicated wide interests. In Volume IV, it was reported that nearly two-thirds of

[46] *Genetic Studies of Genius,* Vol. I, p. 454.

the group reported active interest in two or more avocational pursuits, while one-third reported three or more.

Sports led in preferred activities with both men and women. In the area of reading, fiction was preferred. The specialized abilities noted in childhood seemed more often to lead to various avocational interests than to occupational activity. The data presented in the study were gathered when most of the gifted were between twenty-five and thirty-five years of age; the men were ordinarily involved in getting established in a business or profession, and many of the women were occupied with household duties and the care of children. The implication seems to be that a great deal of time necessarily had to be devoted to the establishment of most of the gifted subjects in vocations and in homes, with not too much time available for avocational pursuits. They were still reading, still engaged in sports activities, and enjoyed photography, music, and gardening. These activities were among those listed with high rank among the preferences given.

The 1955 data presented in Volume V showed a continuing diversity and breadth in the avocational interests reported by the gifted subjects. Those ranked highest by the men were sports, music, and gardening. Women ranked the same three as their preferences but in different order: music, gardening, and sports.

No information concerning the amount of reading or the time given to it was requested in 1955. Instead the subjects were asked what kind of reading they preferred, and many of them listed more than one kind. Fiction was mentioned by more than two-thirds of the group; biography, history, and travel were listed as preferences by 35 to 40 per cent. Fifteen per cent indicated nonfiction as a choice and another 15 per cent mentioned reading of a technical or scientific nature. Nearly every member of the gifted group mentioned a reading interest of one kind or another; more than one-fifth indicated continuing study with emphasis on reading in a variety of areas, either independently or with study groups.

OCCUPATIONAL ADJUSTMENT

Youngsters who are selected for study on the basis of high intelligence tend to prefer and to enter professional fields of occupation. Terman's 1927-28 follow-up study showed that more than half of the gifted boys and girls had decided upon a vocation. Over four-fifths of these planned to enter a professional field. A substantial proportion of the gifted had already had some paid employment.

The scores on interest and aptitude tests at that time indicated that the choices made by the youngsters tended to receive highest scores; their choices were solidly based, as a whole. Terman wrote: "Scores of the gifted boys on the Strong Test on vocations which they are 'most likely' to enter give 23 per cent of "A" ratings, 50 per cent of "B" ratings, and 27 per cent of "C" ratings. By chance alone we might expect only 5 or 6 per cent of "A" ratings, 25 per cent of "B" ratings, and 70 per cent of "C" ratings."[47]

In 1940, the revised edition of the Strong Vocational Interest Test was given to 627 of the gifted men. Volume IV reported:

Of the scores on the occupation in which the men were engaged, 64.7 per cent were A, 13.6 per cent were B plus, 11.6 per cent were B, and only 10.1 per cent were below B. From these figures it appears that not over 10 or 20 per cent of the gifted men are following a vocation which is markedly out of line with their interest patterns.[48]

Comparing the two sets of ratings it might also be concluded that as they matured, the group on the whole moved into their preferred occupations. Terman felt that the results showed that the Strong Test was a very valuable aid in the educational and vocational guidance of the gifted as few men can be successful if they score low on the occupation at which they are working.

About 71 per cent of the gifted men were working at jobs that were classified either as professional or as semiprofes-

[47] *Genetic Studies of Genius*, Vol. III, p. 147.
[48] *Ibid.*, p. 203.

sional and higher business occupations in 1940. This proportion can be compared with the 13.8 per cent of California men in general whose occupations were so classified. To break this down still further, 45 per cent of the gifted men were in the professional fields, as compared with 5.7 per cent of all California men. The ratios are, respectively, slightly more than five to one, and about eight to one. The frequency for the fathers of gifted men whose occupations also were classified as professional was about six times that of California men in general. Gifted women also reported a significantly high percentage employed in the professional fields, 61 per cent. Only 27.8 per cent of the employed women were teachers, mostly in colleges or secondary schools. Terman felt that the most notable thing about gifted women's choice of occupations was the relative infrequency with which they chose education as their field.

For this group of employed men and women, income was higher than that reported for the main body of college graduates of like age, whose earnings in turn were considerably greater than those reported for unselected men and women who had not graduated from college. Finally, it was shown that income was also related to the amount of education. The 70 per cent of gifted men who were college graduates had a median income of $216 per month; the 30 per cent who were not college graduates earned $170 per month.

As reported in Volume V, by 1955 fully 86 per cent of the gifted men worked at occupations classified as professional, semiprofessional, or higher business. There remained 45 per cent in the professions; the increase occurred in the semiprofessional and higher business fields from more than 25 per cent in 1940 to more than 40 per cent in 1955. For the remainder about 11 per cent were holding jobs classified in the small retail business, clerical, and skilled occupations group, about 2 per cent in agriculture and related occupations, and 1 per cent in semiskilled jobs. No gifted subject had a job that could be classified on the lowest level, slightly skilled or unskilled workers, though 13 per cent of the urban population of the country were so classed in 1955.

Less than half of the gifted women work outside their homes. The occupations reported by these gifted women were not classified according to the Minnesota Occupational Scale as were those of the men. The women's occupations were divided into three categories: 65.2 per cent professional, 32.1 per cent business, and the remainder in miscellaneous jobs.

Volume V indicates that the salaries earned by the gifted men far surpassed those of the greater number of men in like occupations. Figures for 1954 showed that for the main body of men employed in professional, semiprofessional, and managerial classifications as well as those who were self-employed, the median earned income was about $5,800. For the 86 per cent of gifted men whose occupations were classified as professional, semiprofessional, and higher business, the median earned income was $10,556. The comparison is admittedly an approximation in that the job classifications correspond only partially; however, the advantage goes, by a very wide margin, to the gifted men. The differences in the amount of income earned are sufficiently large to allow the cautious conclusion that the gifted men are above average in yearly earnings when they are compared to the greater number of men occupied in similar fields.

Thus, according to the two standards of income from, and interest in, one's work, the gifted men of the Terman study would seem to have made more than satisfactory adjustment to their chosen vocations.

Keys' study of underage and gifted students tends to bolster this conclusion. He found that "the percentage of underage men entering professional callings is greater than among the controls, and the proportion engaging in business strikingly smaller. Earnings during the first four years after leaving college averaged slightly less for the underaged, but higher in terms of chronological age attained."[49]

A study comparing twenty-year-old women graduates of the College of Education of Ohio State University with twenty-two-year-old women graduates of the same year also

[49] Keys, *op. cit.*, p. 203.

bears out these points. Pressey[50] reported that a greater number of the younger group went on with further education, held administrative positions, earned higher salaries, and received higher ratings by their principals or superintendents. Though Pressey was accenting the idea of acceleration, this particular study showed that the younger gifted women were more noticeably successful in their careers than were those of the older group.

Personality characteristics, as well as age, contribute in varying degree to success. Terman and Oden made further study of the gifted men of their group, selecting the most and least successful by the criterion of the extent to which the men had used their superior intelligence. These two groups were designated A and C. There were noticeable contrasts in their educational and vocational records. Significant differences were found in emotional stability, social adjustment, and some traits of personality. Physical health was the only trait rating of the 1921-22 study in which A's and C's averaged similarly. Terman and Oden concluded: "Everything considered, there is nothing in which the A and C groups present a greater contrast than in drive to achieve and in all-round social adjustment. Contrary to the theory that great achievement is usually associated with emotional tensions which border on the abnormal, in our gifted group superior success is associated with stability rather than instability, with absence rather than presence of disturbing conflicts—in short, with well-balanced temperament and freedom from excessive frustration."[51]

MARITAL ADJUSTMENT

Since the Stanford studies of the gifted have been going on continuously since 1921 when the subjects averaged eleven years of age, it was possible in both Volumes IV and

[50] Sidney L. Pressey, *Educational Acceleration: Appraisals and Basic Problems* (Columbus, Ohio: Ohio State University, Bureau of Educational Research Monographs, No. 31, [1949]), p. 73.

[51] Lewis M. Terman and Melita H. Oden. "The Stanford Studies of the Gifted," in Witty, *The Gifted Child, op. cit.,* pp. 35-37.

V to make some generalizations concerning marriage within that group of individuals.

By 1945, it was reported that the percentage of the gifted group who married was about the same as that of the general population, and that they tended to marry at about the same ages. Those in the gifted group who were college graduates tended to marry at an earlier age than those of the gifted who did not graduate from college.

By 1955, when the average age of the gifted subjects was about forty-four years, 93 per cent of the men and almost 90 per cent of the women were married. These percentages are about the same as those for the general population of like age. Superior intelligence did not operate as a deterrent to marriage among the gifted subjects of either sex.

The record of divorce by 1945 included 14.4 per cent of the men and 16.3 per cent of the women. In 1955, slightly more than one-fifth of the gifted subjects who had married reported a divorce. Estimates of the divorce rates for the population of the United States are between one-fourth and one-third of the marriages made. For the gifted group the rate to 1955 was less than that for the general population of the United States as a whole. At neither date was there any indication of relationship between divorce record and child-hood I.Q.; in both reports it was noticeable that the gifted college graduates had a much lower divorce rate than did the gifted nongraduates.

The gifted tended to select husbands and wives whose average intelligence was equal to that of college graduates in general. In traits of personality, also, ratings of the husbands and wives compared favorably with those of the gifted mates.

The 1945 data revealed that 384 of the children born to the gifted subjects had a mean I.Q. of 127.70 on the Stanford-Binet test. Terman found also that

The proportion of offspring who test below 80 IQ is no higher than the proportion in the generality who test below 70. This indicates a relatively low incidence of feeblemindedness and border-zone mentality among offspring of the gifted group. At the opposite extreme of the distribution, the proportion of offspring with IQ's of 150 or

higher is about twenty-eight times as great as that found for the unselected children on whom the 1937 revision of the Stanford-Binet
was based.[52]

Volume V reported that approximately 2,500 children had
been born to the gifted subjects by 1955. When 1,525 of
these offspring were tested, the mean I.Q. was 132.7. About
one-third of this group tested at or above 140 I.Q.; about 2
per cent tested below 100.

CIVIC RESPONSIBILITY

Viewing the acceptance and exercise of civic responsibility
largely as a function of adulthood it becomes necessary to
draw once again upon Terman's studies for the discussion.
Exercising one's opportunity to vote is certainly a basic civic
responsibility. In this connection, Terman found that the
gifted group excelled the general population in the percentage who voted regularly. Ninety-one per cent of the
gifted reported regular voting in national elections in 1940,
and the percentage in 1950 was about the same. Women exercised their franchise fully as regularly as did the men,
though this is not the case in the country as a whole. From
the findings of both 1940 and 1950 it can be concluded that
the gifted men and women act in accordance with their civic
obligations more seriously and more regularly than does the
general population.

Beyond these facts the only data relating to adult civic
responsibility presented in Volume IV dealt with participation of various kinds in the war efforts related to World War
II. Terman wrote: "In view of the fact that more than half
of the gifted men were above the age of thirty years when
America entered the war, it is noteworthy that the proportion enrolled in the armed forces (42.5 percent) exceeded
that for all males in the country aged eighteen to forty-four."
He further stated: "Like a majority of their fellow citizens,
both the men and the women of our group participated
wherever and whenever possible in various kinds of volunteer war work. Blood-bank donations were mentioned by a

large proportion. Other activities frequently mentioned had to do with civilian defense, ration-board work, the Red Cross, and the U.S.O."[53]

Comparable data from the general population for these volunteer activities were not available. It is safe to conclude that the members of the California gifted group surely contributed at the very least a proportionate share of their time to the civic responsibilities involved in the wartime effort.

In the years following World War II the gifted men and women have shown increased interest in civic participation at the community level. As is reported in Volume V, they are involved with a great variety of community activities such as youth organizations, civic improvement plans and projects, local health problems, and other such activities. The emphasis on working with youth organizations such as scouts and church groups may be attributable to the relative ages of the subjects and their offspring.

Up to 1955 several members of the group had been elected or appointed to responsible government positions. Volume V predicts a greater incidence of active political participation as the gifted group grows older.

Summary

A summary of Terman's research seems fully appropriate as a concluding section to this chapter. It seems to point up the more significant aspects about which data have been gathered and facts established as to the nature of the gifted. The research of Terman and associates has established:

1. That in physique and general health, children of high I.Q. are on the average superior to the total child population and that the mortality rate for the gifted group to the age of forty-four is lower than for the general population; however, it is not known how much of this is to be credited to superiority of home environment.

2. That the achievement quotients of gifted children in the pre-high-school grades average nearly as high as their I.Q.'s; and that, in most cases, achievement continues to be very

[53] *Genetic Studies of Genius,* Vol. IV, pp. 356-57.

superior in the high school, but on the college level a good many lose interest and make poor or mediocre records.

3. That versatility rather than one-sidedness is the rule with gifted children since their achievement quotients are usually high in all the school subjects.

4. That the typical gifted child is customarily held to a grade level two or three years below that to which his mastery of the curriculum would entitle him, and that school retardation (defined as grade placement below achievement) is almost universal among the gifted.

5. That gifted children who have been accelerated in school are as a group equal or superior to gifted nonaccelerates in both health and general adjustment, produce better school-work, extend their education further, marry at a somewhat earlier age, and show more success in their adult careers.

6. That in character and personality, shown by tests and trait ratings, gifted children average higher than the total child population; however, the degree of superiority is less for traits related to emotional stability and social adjustment than it is for intellectual and volitional traits.

7. That at middle age the gifted may be expected to show a normal incidence of serious personality maladjustment, insanity, delinquency, alcoholism, and homosexuality.

8. That, as a rule, highly gifted children (those having an I.Q. above 170) are more often accelerated in school, get better grades, and receive more schooling than do other members of the gifted group; that they are not appreciably more prone to serious maladjustment; and that vocationally they are more successful.

9. That the intellectual status of the gifted individual is in most cases maintained throughout his life.

10. That in vocational achievement the gifted group rates well above the average of college graduates, and that gifted men have many times the representation in the higher professions and more responsible business positions than is the case with a random group of corresponding age.

11. That in vocational success the gifted, like others, are greatly influenced by motivational factors and personality adjustment.

12. That the marital and sexual adjustment of the gifted is equal or superior to that of the general population.

13. That the procreation rate of the gifted group is probably below that necessary for the continuation of the stock from which the subjects come.

SELECTED READINGS

AUSUBEL, DAVID PAUL. *Prestige Motivation of Gifted Children.* (Genetic Psychology Monographs, No. 43.) New York: Department of Psychology, Teachers College, Columbia University, 1951. 64 pp.

The monograph describes a study of the extent to which prestige motivation affects the performance of gifted children, working in class with material unrelated to their schoolwork yet familiar in that it consisted of exercises akin to arithmetic and reading but not dependent upon degree of skill attained in those subjects.

FRAMPTON, MERLE ELBERT. *The Intellectually Gifted.* Reprinted from *Special Education for the Exceptional.* Ed. Merle E. Frampton and Elena D. Gall. 3 vols. Boston: Porter Sargent Publishers, 1956. 46 pp.

The pamphlet deals briefly with the topics of definition, promising programs and procedures, major issues, and social gains in education of the gifted. Each section is presented by a person recognized as an authority in the field.

FUND FOR THE ADVANCEMENT OF EDUCATION. *They Went to College Early.* (Evaluation Report No. 2.) New York: The Fund, 1957. 117 pp.

This is the second report made on the progress of students who were enabled to leave high school and enter college before their expected date of high-school graduation. The report compares the progress of the Fund Scholars with classmates of expected age and grade placement to 1957; it indicates the usual age-grade system as not the best way of advancing the education and development of gifted students in school.

HOLLINGWORTH, LETA STETTER. *Children Above 180 IQ.* Yonkers, N.Y.: World Book Co., 1942. 332 pp.

Complete case records of several extremely gifted children are given in this posthumous publication, as well as several chapters dealing with implications for the education of the gifted. The materials were taken from files, notes, and previously published items and observations of Leta Hollingworth; supplementary material was organized by the editor, Harry L. Hollingworth.

————. *Gifted Children: Their Nature and Nurture.* New York: The Macmillan Co., 1926. 374 pp.

This is one of the first publications on gifted children using research methods and a scientific approach. It discusses the psychology of gifted children, and the necessity for good education to facilitate their optimum development.

KEYS, NOEL. *The Underage Student in High School and College: Educational and Social Adjustment.* Berkeley, Calif.: University of California Press, 1938. 127 pp.

The favorable results of accelerated programs for the gifted are shown by comparison of the records of groups of students who entered the University of California under sixteen and one-half years of age with those of normal age-grade placement, and a group of high-school students who were accelerated from one to five semesters with classmates of expected age.

LAMSON, EDNA E. *A Study of Young Gifted Children in Senior High School.* (Contributions to Education, No. 424.) New York: Bureau of Publications, Teachers College, Columbia University, 1930. 117 pp.

The study deals with a group of gifted children who had been identified by Stanford-Binet tests before they were nine years old; it follows them through high school, comparing their achievements and adjustments with control groups and showing results favorable to the younger students.

LIGHTFOOT, GEORGIA FRANCES. *Personality Characteristics of Bright and Dull Children.* (Contributions to Education, No. 969.) New York: Bureau of Publications, Teachers College, Columbia University, 1951. 136 pp.

Based on research with 104 children of whom 48 were very bright and 56 were relatively dull, this study shows what personality traits are characteristic of children who differ noticeably in intelligence. The judgments made by qualified persons indicated that the bright children possessed the more favorable traits.

MOORE, MARGARET WHITESIDE. *A Study of Young High School Graduates.* (Contributions to Education, No. 583.) New York: Bureau of Publications, Teachers College, Columbia University, 1933. 78 pp.

An analysis of the data of the Carnegie Foundation's Pennsylvania Study is made; state-wide testing of high-school graduates was followed by tests in sophomore and senior years in college. The study analyzed the success of 308 young high-school graduates; it stresses the need for adequate guidance for gifted students.

PRESSEY, SIDNEY L. *Educational Acceleration: Appraisals and Basic Problems.* (Research Monograph No. 31.) Columbus, Ohio: Bureau of Educational Research, Ohio State University, 1949. 153 pp.

Gives descriptions and analyses of accelerated programs operated at Ohio State University during World War II and immediately afterward. It is concluded that not only is acceleration a feasible procedure in educating gifted college students but that it should be practiced much more widely than it is.

SUMPTION, MERLE R. *Three Hundred Gifted Children.* Yonkers, N.Y.: World Book Co., 1941. 235 pp. Chapters 4, 5, and 6.

The three chapters cited present and interpret the data collected in a follow-up study of two groups of gifted children who attended the Cleveland public schools. Comparisons are made between one group which attended Major Work classes and the other which did not.

TERMAN, LEWIS M., *et al. Mental and Physical Traits of a Thousand Gifted Children. (Genetic Studies of Genius,* Vol. I.) Stanford, Calif.: Stanford University Press, 1926. 648 pp.

This volume presents the first report on the nature of the gifted based on information gathered about a large group of gifted children.

When the facts concerning physical, mental, and personality traits had been collected, they were compared with those relating to children of average mental ability; in each case the gifted as a group equaled or exceeded the mean scores of unselected children.

Cox, CATHERINE M., *et al. The Early Mental Traits of Three Hundred Geniuses. (Genetic Studies of Genius,* Vol. II.) Stanford, Calif.: Stanford University Press, 1926. 842 pp.

Volume II describes the historimetric study of eminent men of history. Bibliographical materials were read by three judges who rated each eminent person as to probable I.Q. in childhood and as a young adult. It was established that those who made worthwhile contributions to society as adults were recognizable for intellectual superiority in their childhood.

BURKS, BARBARA S., JENSEN, DORTHA W., and TERMAN, LEWIS M. *The Promise of Youth. (Genetic Studies of Genius,* Vol. III.) Stanford, Calif.: Stanford University Press, 1930. 508 pp.

Volume III continues the investigations made in 1921-22 on the traits of the gifted children followed over a six-year period. The most significant finding was that the group as a whole exhibited so little change from the original picture; the statements concerning their physical, mental, and personality traits remained true according to the 1927-28 data.

TERMAN, LEWIS M., and ODEN, MELITA H. *The Gifted Child Grows Up: Twenty-Five Years Follow-up of a Superior Group. (Genetic Studies of Genius,* Vol. IV.) Stanford, Calif.: Stanford University Press, 1947. 448 pp.

Volume IV continues the reports of data gathered about the original group of superior children; the group remains superior in those aspects investigated during childhood, and demonstrates superiority in activities related to adulthood.

TERMAN, LEWIS M., and ODEN, MELITA H. *The Gifted Group at Mid-Life: Thirty-Five Years Follow-up of the Superior Child. (Genetic Studies of Genius,* Vol. V.) Stanford, Calif.: Stanford University Press, 1959. 187 pp.

Volume V adds data collected up to 1955; the gifted group as a whole have become vocationally successful and well-adjusted adults, while they have maintained the intellectual superiority demonstrated as children. They have surpassed the cautious predictions of possible adult achievement made by Terman in the 1947 report.

5

Guidance of the Gifted

A foundation of understanding with respect to the gifted as individuals is essential to good guidance. In this chapter, a brief look is taken at the gifted in terms of their general characteristics, individual differences, interests, personality traits, mental characteristics, motivation, and mental health. This is followed by an exploration of the purposes, problems, processes, and goals of effective guidance based in large part on the factors discussed in the early part of the chapter.

GENERAL CHARACTERISTICS

The general characteristics of the gifted group will depend to some extent on the concept of giftedness which is accepted. The broadest concept will include certain individuals whose remarkable performance may be due to extraordinary skill or talent in the sense of "a prominent facility for effective performance along certain lines." A somewhat narrower concept includes only general abstract intelligence and creative imagination. Perhaps the narrowest of all is the one which limits giftedness to abstract intelligence as measured by the I.Q.

Regardless of which concept one adopts it is apparent that giftedness exists in various degrees, has many facets, and develops progressively under favorable circumstances and is retarded under unfavorable environmental conditions.

Physical

The gifted as a group are above average in physical structure and general health. One essential feature which they possess is a nervous system of superior quality and, in most cases, a set of keen sensory organs. The central nervous system is, in a sense, the foundation upon which intelligence grows and develops. As it reacts to its environment it responds with vigor in searching out and relating new experiences, one to another. It builds patterns and concepts which become tools in seeking, finding, and assimilating new knowledge. Heredity places definite limitations on the number of gifted who appear in each age group.

Gifted are superior *as a group* to the norm in physical measurements such as height, weight, body development, and muscular energy. Physical defects are less frequent in the gifted group. Its health history compares favorably to that of the normal group. Maturation takes place at a more rapid rate. The gifted *in general* are stronger, have better coordination, are speedier, and exhibit quicker muscular reactions. Finally, mortality rates are lower among gifted children than they are among the members of the normal or dull groups.

Gifted are found to be evenly distributed between the two sexes. There is no difference in degree of intelligence; the differences are in kind and grow out of the different roles that society imposes on the sexes.

Cultural and Social

Gifted children in the United States are most frequently detected in racial groups which have contributed most to the economic, social, and educational development of the country. In terms of nationalities the English, German, French, and Scandinavian countries have probably made the most substantial contributions to the gifted group. However, it would be totally unwarranted to ascribe superiority to any race or nationality. Giftedness appears among all races and all nationalities and there is no basis for assuming that one race or nationality is superior in this respect to any other. It can only be said that under the present and pre-existing social climate in the United States certain racial and national groups have produced more gifted individuals in proportion to their total numbers than have others. However, this is not to say that under different social conditions a quite different situation might not exist, since those who are born in an environment which the predominant social opinion pronounces good have more of an opportunity to achieve their potential and to be recognized as gifted.

Just as gifted children come from all races and nationalities, so do they come from homes of all levels of culture and social prestige. However, it is not surprising to find that in proportion to the number of such homes more gifted come from homes in which the cultural and social level is high. More gifted come from homes of professional people in proportion to the numbers of such homes than from those of skilled laborers. Eminent people are more numerous among their relatives. Parents of the gifted are in general better educated than those of the non-gifted.

The gifted as a group excel the average in desirable social attributes. They tend to be self-confident, friendly, and possess a high degree of social sensitivity. They are able to sense the attitudes, feelings, and desires of members of their social group and act appropriately in the social situation in which they find themselves.

The general social development of the gifted person is in all probability more a function of his environment than of any other single factor. It is easier to gain social competency in an environment of social competency than in one of social incompetency.

The gifted provide leadership in all strata of society from the lowest to the highest social class. The gifted become leaders because they are able to perceive more clearly the goals and function of leadership in the group and are sensitive to the needs and interests of others. Their physical fitness, desirable personality traits, and breadth of interests serve to enhance their leadership potential.

The social ideals and standards of the gifted reflect a more highly developed social consciousness than is found in the general population. Their social preferences are, in general, more acceptable to society as a whole and they are markedly superior in trustworthiness, honesty, and dependability under conditions of social stress.

INDIVIDUAL DIFFERENCES AMONG THE GIFTED

The range of differences among gifted children is seldom fully recognized and sometimes even disregarded. For example, gifted children have an I.Q. range of over seventy-five points if we place the lower limit at 125. If we apply this range to the group below 125 its lower limit would reach into the moron class. Thus, it can be seen that the divergence is as great among gifted as between the moron and the bright child as measured by the intelligence quotient which represents our best single measure of intelligence.

It is the very small group at the upper end of the range (160-200 I.Q.) which presents most difficult problems in adjustment. This is readily understandable since these children are so far advanced mentally in comparison with the other members of their age group. Those in the lower range of the gifted group (125-160) typically make better personal adjustment since they are within what might be called the adaptive range. They are not so far removed from the average child but that, by virtue of their superior intelligence, they can make a reasonable adjustment to life with their physical, social, and emotional peers.

Although, *in general,* the gifted as a group rate very high in academic achievement, there is great variation among them in this respect also. Gifted students may be found among academic failures as well as class valedictorians. Not infrequently the superior child is unable to adapt himself to the dull routine and drill which is characteristic of many classrooms. He resents the necessity of conforming to classroom procedures which are geared to the average child in his age group. As a result he may lose interest or deliberately rebel against what he considers useless activity.

This kind of student usually reacts in one of three ways. He may simply withdraw from class activity and refuse to participate in class work. He may refuse to do written exercises, turn in blank examination papers, and in consequence fail the grade or subject. To him this action is justified since he sees no value in repeating what he already knows.

A second type expresses his nonconformity by deliberately making himself disagreeable. He intentionally gives wrong answers and often misleads his fellow students in order to annoy the teacher. He argues vigorously for the opposition without regard to the merits of the case. He, in a way, creates challenges by adopting a negative attitude on all issues and then attempting to prove that the teacher or the class or both are wrong. As can be readily seen, such performances are not likely to bring high academic ranking.

The third and most common of the three types is the pupil who tolerates or endures the regular class routine. He does just enough to insure he will not be bothered by the teacher, and turns his attention to matters outside the classroom. He "renders unto Caesar that which is Caesar's" and gives over his best efforts to an outside area or project which he feels merits them. He will rate, perhaps, average or below in the teacher's grade book, but seldom will he be a failure. He has learned to adapt himself to conditions as they are, but there is no challenge to learning for him in the regular classroom.

The majority of gifted children, of course, achieve high academic standing in contrast to the minority who are represented in the above classifications. However, it is important to recognize the variation among gifted with respect to academic achievement. It is particularly significant in planning for a program of special education for them.

The causes for the variation in academic achievement are largely due to differences in personality. Reactions to regular academic work are in a sense expressions of personality. Although the gifted as a group have certain personality traits which may be regarded as characteristic of them, there is great variation among individuals. On one end of the scale are found extremely extroverted personalities who express themselves in aggressive action, and on the other, the shy, retiring introverts who express themselves only in the mildest ways.

The range with respect to types of personality is no doubt as great among the gifted as among the average group. Both the all-round well-adjusted personality and the self-effacing, shy, bookworm type are found among gifted children. Some are dominant, aggressive and independent; others are submissive, retiring, and dependent. Some are highly emotional; others placid and unemotional. Some are cooperative and unselfish; others uncooperative and quite selfish.

The gifted group is remarkable for its wide variety of interests. The natural curiosity which is characteristic of the bright child leads to a breadth of interest which is far greater than that of the average child. The gifted individual usually has a wide variety of interests; the gifted group has an even wider variety of interests. In fact, intense and compelling interests are found among ten-year-old gifted children in such widely divergent areas as astrophysics, numismatics, and entomology. Often these interests may represent solid foundations upon which illustrious and valuable careers can be built.

On the physical side the range of difference among the gifted is equally great. Although research has indicated clearly that the majority of gifted are well-endowed physically, the puny, nearsighted bookworm can also be found among very bright children. In fact, in the early part of the century this caricature was accepted as typical of the gifted.

In summary it can be said that the gifted group differs widely among its members in intelligence, academic achievement, personality traits, interests, and physical endowments. The gifted differ among themselves as much or more than do those in the average or slow-learning groups. This wide divergence presents many problems in the education of the gifted as well as in their personal adjustment.

INTERESTS

What are the principal interests of the gifted? How do they differ in number, variety, nature, and intensity from those of the normal group? First of all, the breadth and variety of interests among the gifted is quite great. How much broader and more varied than those of the general population in comparable age groups is difficult to measure. Studies indicate that the difference is considerable.

One of the most common interests is reading. Gifted children learn to read at an early age and reading becomes one of the principal, if not *the principal,* sources of new knowledge. They love books and treasure them as valuable possessions. The natural curiosity of the gifted stimulates his reading interests. The printed page brings to him information about a vast world which he is hungry to know about. It is estimated that gifted children in their early years read twice as much as do typical children. A large percentage of these children are able to read before entering school. A number of cases of gifted children reading at the age of three years are on record; a few read even younger. The literary quality of their reading is generally superior. Biography, adventure in foreign lands, history, drama, science, poetry, and school and home life are favorite topics. Pulp magazines, particularly of the emotional type, rate low in popularity among the gifted.

Sometimes reading interest is so intense that it leads to neglect of outdoor activity or social experience. The gifted child often prefers to stay indoors by himself so that he may read more. A boy of ten who was spending the summer with his aunt and uncle while his parents were abroad set for himself the task of reading all the books in his uncle's library. The library being a rather large one, this was no small undertaking. Despite the fact that he was urged to play outside he was able to read over a hundred volumes in two and a half months. Such an intense interest, if not properly guided, can lead to introversion, shyness, and even an antisocial attitude.

Another popular interest among the gifted is collecting. Collections are made of coins, stamps, rocks, insects, and various other objects. These collections are usually carefully classified and kept in good order during the period of collection. Like other children the gifted tend to outgrow collections, although they persist in collecting longer than do typical children. Furthermore the interest which motivates the collecting often carries over and becomes the foundation for more advanced interests. For example, the collection of rocks may lead to a career in geology or the collection of insects may develop an interest in biological science. The careful classification and the recording of data about each piece in the collection appear to be more fully carried out among gifted collectors as compared to typical children. However, the most notable aspect of collecting as practiced by the gifted is the persistence which they exhibit in the activity. Often they develop and maintain collections over a period of many years.

In brief, the gifted in comparison to the typical child has greater interest in collections, has larger collections, does a superior job of classifying and recording and, last but not least, persists longer in this type of activity.

The gifted are as much interested in play activities as the normal group but their knowledge of games and play activities in general is greater. As a group they prefer games of skill as opposed to those of chance. Play which involves imagination is favored in early youth. Gifted children who have limited opportunity to play with other children often create imaginary playmates with whom they converse and play games. Such imagery usually is discarded when the child enters school or becomes a member of a play group. In cases where it persists due caution should be exercised to see that the child is at all times aware of the difference between fantasy and reality.

At an early age, the gifted child discovers many of the realities of life and death. His inquiring mind begins the search for answers to the fundamental questions of human existence. What is the purpose of life? How did life originate? What follows after death? Is there a heaven? a hell? The queries often loom large in the mind of the child as he seeks to understand the universe and his place in it. He speculates on what will become of him if his father or mother dies. He wonders why he was born to them rather than to another couple. In some cases he may question his relationship to his parents, even suggesting that his natural parents have given him in adoption. This type of speculation reflects the inquiring mind not satisfied with ready-made answers. It is this speculative interest which may later unfold some of the most sought-after secrets of nature. It is a type of interest which should be encouraged by frank answers and a willingness to face the facts of life.

There is a pronounced tendency among gifted children to be aware of and to have interest in moral and social issues at a comparatively early age. This interest is often intense and compelling. The bright child becomes increasingly aware of life and the world in which he lives as he gains greater knowledge of his environment. His concern also grows as he observes real or imaginary injustices in society. He is likely to be uncompromising in his stand on social and moral issues.

The issue of capital punishment is one which attracts the attention of the bright child early in life. He raises the question as to the right of the state to take human life when it is unable to make restoration if later the innocence of the accused is established. The folly of war and the terrible suffering and losses which follow in its wake attract his attention. He is concerned with ways and means whereby peace may be brought to the people of all nations. The United Nations may be a topic in his conversation with his elders when he is only eight or ten years old. It is not uncommon for him to read extensively about world politics and similar topics and propound questions which amaze his parents and teachers. Such an interest combined with desirable personality characteristics and favorable environmental conditions may lead to a career in the diplomatic service or in some other area of political or social leadership. This type of interest holds real promise for the development of competence which later in life may yield significant social gains.

Due to their natural curiosity the gifted develop special interests to a greater extent than do typical children. The intense interest in science shown by many gifted children is a good example of this tendency. Many bright children with a special interest in science build their own laboratories in the garage or basement at home. Considerable ingenuity is often shown in getting equipment together, installing it, and improvising a substitute when a needed piece of equipment is unavailable. Often every cent of spending money is invested in laboratory equipment. The compelling interest which the embryonic scientist has, may cause him to devote all his leisure time to work in his laboratory. He may be so interested in his work as to be oblivious of the passage of time. His interest brings long periods of intense concentration. He is spurred on by the desire to create something useful or unique. In high school he stays after school hours to work in the laboratory. He works for his own satisfaction rather than for teacher approval or academic credit. It is this type of scientific interest which can, if properly encouraged and guided, provide the creative chemists, physicists, and medical researchers of tomorrow.

Special interests such as painting, drawing, music, poetry, and astronomy, are quite common among the gifted and assert themselves at an early age. The literature is replete with examples of art productions which are quite remarkable when the age of the artist is considered. A little Chinese girl pianist, composing and playing very creditable musical scores at the age of five; a boy of seven creating a series of cartoons depicting current political issues; and another boy of eight painting a landscape which was judged best in competition with adult artists, are examples of young artists who perform remarkably for their age.

In comparison with typical children, the gifted have more interests and a greater breadth of interest. Furthermore, their interests are more conducive to activity which gives promise of social, moral, and scientific gains. Their interests are characterized by a greater intensity and persistence than are those of the normal group. Finally, these interests in many cases are the key to the future development of the gifted personality.

PERSONALITY TRAITS

What are the personality traits which are most common to the gifted? Which traits do they possess to a greater degree than do typical children? Which traits are least common among gifted? Which do they possess to a lesser degree than do typical children? The answers to these questions give some important insights into the gifted personality and provide valuable information for use in guidance.

Despite the claim that there is a paucity of research on some aspects of giftedness, few will deny that there is quite a respectable body of research data available on the personality aspect. It is treated at some length in Chapter 4.

From observation as well as the data assembled it is clear that certain personality traits are found almost universally among members of the gifted group. One of these is curiosity, the desire to discover, to acquire greater knowledge, to explore, to seek answers. Paul Brandwein, author of *The Gifted Student as Future Scientist,* calls it "questing." It is curiosity augmented by a drive to discover. It takes many forms and pursues many directions. It has a basis in dissatisfaction with ready-made answers, an unwillingness to accept things as they are without knowing why. The inquiring mind of the gifted child questions the basic assumptions which the typical individual accepts without a second thought.

Bright children are good listeners. They are curious to learn what others may have to tell. However, they listen only as long as something of significance is said. They hunger to know and are eager to listen, but not to unrewarding conversation. They retain a sense of wonder, a joy of discovery, much longer than does the average child. In fact, it is not unusual for them to regard their environment as an external challenge to strive unceasingly to unveil life's mysteries until life itself is gone.

A second common characteristic is originality. This trait is evident in many of the things bright children do both at home and in school. Originality is shown in poetry writing, musical composition, drawing, play activity, mechanical construction, and many other activities. Examples of excellent original poetry written by children under ten years of age are plentiful. Often the rules for standard games are revised or adjusted by bright children in order to improve them or make them more adaptable to existing situations.

One kindergarten teacher reported the case of one of her pupils who at the age of five constructed and brought to school an original creation which he termed a "movie projector." The materials of this masterpiece included a shoe box, a roll of paper toweling, a crank, and a flashlight. The child had cut a hole in one side of the box, inserted the roll of paper on a crank, and placed the flashlight inside so that it would shine directly on the aperture in the box. The toweling which had been decorated with drawings and lettering could be unrolled and rolled up by means of the crank and in the process the pictures and letters were plainly visible through the aperture in the box, illuminated by the flashlight behind them. The child had combined originality with mechanical inventiveness to produce a gadget which amused and delighted his fellow pupils.

Desire to excel is another common trait among bright children. Since they have certain inherent advantages over typical children it is natural that they should desire to do better than the average. In some cases the desire to excel becomes so intense that it produces tension and nervousness. Carried to extremes it may seriously affect mental health. The gifted, like their less able fellows, must learn to accept the fact that they cannot always excel. Nevertheless, the trait is a very desirable one and stimulates greater achievement. It should never be discouraged but rather guided in such a way that the child can accept failure to excel without remorse and recriminations, and try again.

Perseverance is another common trait. Difficult situations or tasks are regarded as challenges which the gifted child believes can be met if he perseveres. Perseverance is closely related to another very common trait, self-confidence. The bright child, because of his perception and mental ability, feels a certain superiority which tends to give him a sense of confidence in his own ability. In early life he finds he is able to do things which are not ordinarily expected of children of his age group. This discovery encourages him to believe in himself. When this trait becomes too prominent or induces boasting the child will be regarded as conceited, smart-aleck, or egotistical. He will become unpopular with both bright and dull children. Usually the bright child is able to avoid this, but occasionally it presents a real problem in guidance. Although early concepts of the gifted pictured them as conceited and boastful, careful research has indicated the inaccuracy of these concepts. While some are forward, domineering, and egotistical, these are in the very decided minority among the gifted.

Other common personality traits among the gifted are conscientiousness, a willingness to assume responsibility, a sense of humor, truthfulness, courtesy, cooperation, a sense of independence, and forcefulness. They have a tendency to be self-critical as well as an ability to penetrate the disguise of others who may seek to appear to be what they are not. On the other hand, they are quick to see merit in others. They are resourceful and versatile. They have a passion for truth, seeking it in themselves as well as in others.

The gifted possess all these common traits to a greater degree than do children in the average or dull group. They probably excel most in desire to know or curiosity, originality, desire to achieve, perseverance, independence, and resourcefulness. Most of these traits have their basis in the intellectual realm. These traits form a cluster which, combined with superior intelligence and physical vigor, produces a high incidence of leadership among the gifted.

On the other end of the scale, dependence as a personality trait is probably one of the most uncommon among the gifted group. Self-confident and resourceful, they do not readily seek help or protection. They do not adhere to their parents or seek their sympathy and intervention as much as do children in the normal group. In exceptional cases the bright child may seek the parents' sympathy not because he feels dependent but rather because he is quick to see that he may obtain privileges or advantages by such action.

Another uncommon trait is submissiveness. It is foreign to the gifted to be acquiescent, to accept orders without question. Closely related is their general lack of deference to accepted custom and tradition. They are unwilling to conform for the sake of conformity. Passiveness is another uncommon trait among the gifted. On the contrary, they are active, outgoing, and vital.

In general, this group of uncommon traits, when they are possessed by the gifted, are possessed to a lesser degree than is true in the case of the average or dull child.

Little difference can be ascertained between the gifted and the typical groups in many personality traits. In kindliness, sympathy, cheerfulness, generosity, desire for affection, and honesty, among others, there appear no significant differences.

MENTAL CHARACTERISTICS

It is in the intellectual traits that gifted children differ most markedly from typical children. This is to be expected, since general intelligence combined with creative imagination is the basis for their designation as gifted. Therefore, in seeking to understand these children it is necessary to analyze the facets of intellectual activity to see in what ways the gifted excel. What are the common characteristics of the superior mind?

One of the very important abilities of the superior mind is that of being able to form concepts. The ability to form concepts permits the mind to function on a higher plane and to develop intricate thought patterns which contribute to the ability to interpret experience effectively. The ability to form concepts is, of course, the basis of abstract thinking. It is in the realm of ideas that the gifted child stands out most markedly among his fellows.

He possesses what is sometimes referred to by Paul Brandwein in his book, *The Gifted Student as Future Scientist*, as the "joy of ideas." He seems actually to glow with anticipation when he is in pursuit of a new idea. There is a thrill of discovery, an excitement in perceiving a logical relationship between two or more discrete concepts. He enjoys exploring in the world of ideas. It is a realm which holds, for him, a strong attraction, one which offers an eternal challenge to intellectual achievement.

A second common characteristic displayed by the superior mind is that of creative imagination. Almost all of the gifted group have the ability to think creatively in some degree. It is quite true that imagination in itself may not lead to creativity if it serves only to amuse by developing mental fantasies. However, the dividing line between useless fantasy and creative imagining is, in some cases, a thin one.

The ability to think creatively often exhibits itself at an early age. It may express itself in poetry, art, music, science, or in a multitude of other human activities. It may be active in only one field of human endeavor, or in many. It is one of the two most distinctive mental characteristics of the gifted group.

Extraordinary insight is another characteristic of the group; it is quite closely related to conceptual ability and creative imagination. This is the ability which enables the individual to "see through" a problem situation. In the young child it may be exhibited when he perceives the relationship between lightning and thunder, between wind and waves, or between clouds and rain. It enables him to successfully traverse the puzzle maze and solve the word scrambles when he is a little older. Without insight, experience would be a poor as well as a dear teacher.

The power to generalize is probably a facet of conceptual ability. Valid generalizations require an accurate appraisal of data which in many cases are the result of isolated experiences. The ability to form valid generalizations which are developed only after accurate observation of a sufficient number of cases, is one of the prominent characteristics of the gifted. They seldom jump at conclusions but rather evaluate individual data carefully before generalizing. Their generalizations are likely to be carefully drawn so as to avoid overstatement.

Another mental ability which is difficult to separate from the foregoing is the power to reason inductively as well as deductively. Ability to improvise is another characteristic in this spectrum. It is exhibited early in life by the child who places the kitchen stool on a chair to enable him to reach the cookie jar. Later he may build a model airplane from cigar boxes and assorted materials available around the home. He may still later improvise a space ship which will permit man to explore the vast and unknown reaches of the universe.

Fluency of ideas is another characteristic common to the gifted. Not only do they have ideas, but they can express them. They tend to associate ideas in such a way as to enable them to move quickly from one idea to a related one.

They are also fluent with respect to words. A large and ready vocabulary is a characteristic of the very bright child. He adds to his vocabulary at every opportunity, constantly seeking the meaning of unfamiliar words. Often his parents and teachers are asked, "What does this word mean?" "How do you use it?" "What word is it like?" Extensive reading, which is usually one of his chief interests, keeps on building his vocabulary. His vocabulary is not only large but also contains words which are not commonly used by the child's age group. An eight-year-old youngster referring to an "alleged fact," a "tedious story," or a "voluntary effort," is illustrative of this characteristic. These unusual words appear in his themes and other written schoolwork and in his letters to relatives and friends, particularly when they are adults. They will be found in his diary and personal memoranda also.

The bright child characteristically has the ability to memorize rapidly and retain memorized material for later recall. In some cases he may seem to have a "photographic mind" which allows him to perceive a set of data or combination of numbers at a glance and recall them accurately months later. Often the bright child will recall the address of a friend of the family or his telephone number when both parents are unable to do so. One ten-year-old boy, who was an enthusiastic football fan and attended the home games of a large university team which had a roster of over sixty players, memorized the numbers of all the players together with their ages, weights, and class standing. When he and his parents attended the games they had little use for a program except in referring to the opposing team.

Another common and somewhat distinctive characteristic of the gifted is a comparatively long span of attention. Early in life a child's attention wanders from one thing to another quickly. Nothing seems to hold his interest very long. However, as he grows older his span of attention grows longer. He is not quite so hasty in discarding one item of interest and moving to another. His interest appears to deepen and his span of attention grows broader. In the case of the gifted child his natural curiosity and desire to know keep his mind at work on ideas or a problem situation longer than might be expected. His background of information enables him to analyze, establish relationships, and interpret the idea or problem situation. This, coupled with a mental vigor and intensity characteristic of the superior mind, produces a significantly longer span of attention. This vigor and intensity is particularly noteworthy since it seems to be one of the essential characteristics of high-level ability in science. It is both mental and physical in nature. It has its base in a superior central nervous system and exhibits itself in a hard-driving will to learn. It contributes to the long periods of concentrated effort which are so common among those who seek new truth in science or in any other field.

MOTIVATION

Why do some gifted individuals achieve much while others do not? What is it that makes one person develop his ability to its fullest while another leaves his undeveloped? Why do some attain much with only average ability and others little, with great ability? What is the cause of "underachievement"? What is the cause of "overachievement"? What forces work behind the scenes in the lives of people, making them strive to achieve?

The problem of motivation is particularly important in the education of the gifted since such great potential is involved. It is to this group that we look for leadership in politics, industry, education, science, and the arts. If its membership is to make a full contribution there must be adequate motivation. Superior ability combined with favorable environment does not necessarily result in maximum achievement. The hidden factor in the equation, motivation, can and often does determine the outcome. In general, motivation as a factor influencing achievement may be divided into two categories; namely, social motivation and individual motivation.

Social Motivation

When an individual in a social group fails to make the contribution of which he is capable, society as well as the individual is the loser. Such loss may be due to lack of motivation in the individual or it may be due to an unfavorable social atmosphere or to both.

Every society has its own set of values and applies its own standard of success. In the United States, high status is obtained largely by achievement in the business, amusement, industrial, education, political, or professional worlds. Within each of these categories there is a hierarchy of values which serves as a motivating force to the individual. Because of certain adolescent values which it maintains, society gives greater monetary rewards to successful television comics and popular singers than it does to successful teachers of science and medical research workers. Presidents of large corporations and labor unions receive higher salaries than do members of the United States Senate. Although monetary reward is only one of several contributors to high status, it is a powerful motivating force.

Another force which sometimes works against the full translation of ability into achievement is social pressure. Social pressure toward conformity is one device by which society controls its members. At the same time, society often penalizes itself by discouraging the gifted individual who is, in many respects, a nonconformist. The very fact that he is intellectually superior sets him off from the group. If he translates his ability into superior achievement he still further removes himself from his fellows and may often alienate others whose cooperation is essential to his continued success. Margaret Mead writes:

It becomes fashionable not to get better grades than others, not to be too good, not to go up too fast. These pressures for keeping on all fours with one's classmates, neighbors, business associates, which are increasing in American life, tend to be particularly felt in the school-age groups, especially in the case, of the child who shows intellectual or artistic gifts.[1]

The tendency to refer to the gifted student as an "egg-head," a "brain," or a "square," is common in American life. The advent of the so-called space age has considerably en-hanced the prestige of the scientific genius but this "break-through" is largely in the upper reaches of adult life. This respect for exceptional ability may in time penetrate the mores of the younger, particularly the student groups, but the impact at present is negligible. Thus, in a way, society defeats itself by ostracizing the individual who exhibits un-usual ability and by exerting powerful social pressures to insure conformity in those who show signs of standing out above the crowd.

It should be noted, however, that the nature and types of social pressure vary from one community to another. For ex-ample, in a community made up largely of factory workers, social pressure is often directed against higher education, and few secondary-school graduates enter college. On the other hand, in many residential suburbs, where most of the bread-winners are professional people, over 90 per cent of high-school graduates go to college. Social pressure in these two kinds of communities works in exactly opposite direc-tions. Even when ability is equal, Cole[2] found that in pro-portion to their respective numbers more than twice as many high-school graduates with fathers in the professions went to college in comparison with graduates whose fathers were semiskilled workers and farmers.

In many homes and communities there is little motivation for the superior youth to pursue his education beyond high

[1] Margaret Mead, "The Gifted Child in the American Culture of Today," *Journal of Teacher Education*, September, 1954, pp. 211-14.
[2] Charles C. Cole Jr. *Encouraging Scientific Talent: A Report of the National Science Foundation* (New York: College Entrance Examination Board, 1955).

school. This situation tends to rob society of valuable talent since most professional and scientific work requires college training. It is true that some turn to business and industry where the educational requirements are more elastic, but even in these areas those who work their way to the top without formal education are becoming rarer as time goes on. With notable exceptions the field of politics draws its leaders from among college-educated men and women.

Social motives include the desire to be recognized by others as a worthwhile person. Prestige comes in many forms. For one boy it may be top rank in his class, for another it may be "making" the football team. In either case achievement comes from a desire to be well-regarded, to be admired and respected by one's fellows.

The desire for the approbation of one person may be the driving force in achievement. One of the parents, a teacher, a guidance counselor, or a sweetheart, may be the person who stimulates achievement. For this one person who has become a symbol, the individual bends every effort to succeed. It may be love, respect, gratitude, or admiration which is accorded the person in question, but whatever it may be, it stimulates achievement.

Social motivation often lies behind high attainment in schoolwork. Many strive to become class valedictorians or salutatorians in order to gain prestige. The approval of the teacher, the parents, and the community are goals which many students strive to attain. It is often some teacher or adult friend who recognizes superior ability and is understanding and sympathetic. Such a person may be able to help a frustrated future scientist or statesman adjust to or change the conditions or attitudes which stymie his progress in school. The student then feels a sense of gratitude and obligation, and is motivated to high academic achievement in order to express that gratitude and discharge his obligation.

How do race, sex, and religion influence motivation to intellectual achievement? Since there is usually a close relationship between socioeconomic status and each of the foregoing, it is often difficult to draw clear-cut distinctions. No evidence has been presented to indicate any superiority in intellectual potential of one race over another, one sex over the other, or one religious affiliation over another. It is quite true that Negroes achieve distinction in fewer cases than members of the white race in proportion to their numbers in both the United States and in the world. However, when the environmental conditions which have surrounded the Negro for centuries are considered, such underachievement is to be expected. Since Negro children usually come from the lower socioeconomic strata of society they are not generally motivated toward intellectual achievements. Add to this the lack of educational traditions, the tendency for society to relegate Negroes to jobs which require little intellectual effort, and the many discriminatory social factors which have existed and still exist in our society, and there is little wonder that the achievement level of the race is low.

On the other hand, another minority group, the Jews, is characterized by a high level of achievement. Traditionally, the Jewish people have placed a high value on education. For centuries the Jewish rabbi has been the very epitome of learning. This respect for learning combined with a strong drive for socioeconomic status has given the members of this group a superior record of achievement when compared with most other groups.

In considering the two groups it can be readily seen that even though, as far as can be determined, there is little or no difference in intellectual potential, there is a wide divergence in conditions, which is reflected in the achievement records of the groups.

As far as can be determined, the male and female sex are equal in intellectual potential. In scholastic achievement girls tend to outrank boys. Among the gifted as a group Gowan[3] found that in school boys failed to achieve up to their ability to a much greater degree than did girls. However, in advanced training the male sex has a preponderance of repre-

[3] John Gowan, "The Underachieving Gifted Child . . . A Problem for Everyone," *Journal of the International Council for Exceptional Children,* Vol. XXI (1955).

sentatives. Although more girls attend college today than ever before they are still outnumbered by college men. Particularly is this true in graduating classes.

In general achievement in postschool life the male sex shows definite superiority. This can be explained by the fact that in our society the man is the breadwinner and the woman the homemaker. The man enters a profession or business or similar field in which he has broad opportunity to achieve. He is motivated by the need to provide for his family and to gain social status. The wife accepts the role of childbearing and family rearing, typically content to share the socioeconomic status gained by the husband. In short, in our society, despite the increase in the number of career women, by and large, it is the male sex which is motivated to achievement and is provided with the greatest opportunities to achieve.

Religion in itself probably has little effect on achievement in general. However, it should be noted that among those who have achieved eminence in the field of science most have been found to be affiliated with religious groups which have a minimum of dogma and encourage independent thought. Orthodoxy appears to be a negative influence in science motivation as reflected in the number of eminent scientists from the more unorthodox religious groups.[4]

Summarizing, it may be said that each society has inherent motivating forces which operate in relation to the gifted as well as the general population. These forces are largely determined by the set of values which the society adopts. In our own society monetary reward is a primary motivating force. The type of achievement which receives greatest financial reward is likely to be the one which is the object of greatest effort. A second important motivating force is social pressure. Pressures which force the individual to conform to the standards of society frequently work against outstanding achievement by the gifted; but in some situations they encourage advanced training which may lead to superior

[4] Harvey Lehman and Paul Witty, "Scientific Eminence and Church Membership," *Scientific Monthly*, XXXIII (1931), 544-49.

achievement. Sometimes the desire to win the approbation of an individual such as a teacher, a counselor, or an esteemed friend, motivates the gifted boy or girl to outstanding achievement. A tradition of learning fostered by a racial or national group can also produce powerful motivation. Among others, the desire for social status deserves special mention in this connection. Race, sex, and religion are not inherent distinctive motivating forces but do reflect socioeconomic motivation of various types.

Individual Motivation

Social motivation is a power in determining achievement. However, individual motivation occasionally is an even greater power. Some gifted individuals rise to great achievement from a social atmosphere which is distinctly unfavorable to achievement. Remarkable attainments have been recorded by individuals coming from the lowest social levels. Homes in which learning and occupational status were at the lowest levels have produced men of learning and great professional stature. On the other hand, the most favorable social and cultural conditions sometimes fail to motivate even the genius to superior achievement. A number of gifted children reared under seemingly ideal conditions have failed to achieve much either for themselves or for society. Much depends on the individual. He may rise above or sink beneath the level of achievement which might be predicted in view of his intellectual capacity and social environment.

There are, of course, physiological factors which affect performance of any type. Ill health in the form of heart trouble, diabetes, anemia and many other diseases may handicap the individual to such an extent that his achievement is limited or even negligible. Personality traits sometimes militate against achievement. The gifted child who becomes conceited, or is strongly aggressive, or extremely introverted may find it difficult to secure the full cooperation of his fellows and thus may handicap his achievement.

Recognizing that there are many physiological and personality traits which affect achievement, what motivates an individual to achieve? What gives the gifted or the average person the desire to excel? Why does one man work night and day to succeed while his neighbor has no interest in "getting ahead"?

The drive to achieve is a common, but by no means universal, characteristic of the gifted. Often it enables the superior child to overcome great physical handicaps and personality defects.

Individual motivation may arise out of a feeling of need for fulfillment. The gifted youth usually recognizes the potential which he possesses and it brings a desire to achieve. When this potential is combined with an intense interest in or concern with a specific field such as science or art, then motivation becomes compelling. Under such circumstances, failure to achieve would undoubtedly bring frustration and dissatisfaction.

Another primary factor is the desire for independence, to be able to do for oneself not only economically but socially, morally, and intellectually. Self-sufficiency is a goal which often serves to spur the superior youth to greater achievement.

Interest in itself may not stimulate achievement. However, when it is combined with such forces as desire for fulfillment, a desire to explore, and thirst for new knowledge, it serves to intensify the achievement drive. The desire to explore, the search for new knowledge, and the seeking of truth are common basic achievement drives among the gifted. Less frequently is the fear of failure a motivating force. However, it, like several other negative forces such as anxiety and guilt, does, in a few cases, motivate high achievement among the gifted. Sometimes a serious blow to the ego challenges the gifted individual to succeed in order to vindicate himself. A notable defeat in early life such as the loss of an election to the presidency of a high-school class or a failure to win a coveted scholastic award may result in a redoubled effort to succeed. Again, a significant defeat may plunge the superior youth into a state of despair and resignation. Early defeat may stimulate later victory, or it may establish a pattern of frustration which will persist through life.

In the final analysis, it must be admitted that we know little about the inner forces which spur a person to achieve. Much depends on the character and personality of the individual. Suffice it to say that those who possess a high degree of self-confidence, exceptional perseverance, and a healthy ego are most likely to be the ones who have the strongest individual motivation.

MENTAL HYGIENE

The great importance of mental hygiene has only comparatively recently been recognized in our society. The cause and effect of mental problems ranging from simple feelings of inferiority to serious psychoses are now the subject of widespread investigations. The importance of mental health among both young and old is widely recognized.

Good mental health is characterized by wholesome and satisfying relations with one's associates; freedom from unfounded fears, tensions, guilt and anxiety complexes; and the ability to meet, at least to one's own satisfaction, the demands of normal living. Good mental health is dependent to a great extent on accurate self-diagnosis, reasonably good physical health, and an emotional maturity which permits the individual to meet stresses, disappointments, and frustrations with relative calmness and equanimity.

Gifted children as a group are superior in mental health as well as in mental ability. Gifted children are generally superior to typical children in their age group in emotional maturity, adaptability, strength of character, and wholesomeness of social attitudes.

When poor mental health hinders or makes impossible the development of human ability both the individual and society loses. Undeveloped ability for the individual means lack of fulfillment, unrealized satisfactions; for society it means a lost contribution of indeterminate value, perhaps even the creation of a negative force against the march of human progress. With the gifted the stakes are exceedingly high.

While good mental health is important for everyone it is especially important for the gifted. The bright child is often subject to a variety of pressures simply because he is bright. His parents may expect a lot from him, show him off before friends, or exploit his abilities in other ways. In homes where parents are insecure themselves the opposite effect may be achieved through suppression, which may be just as bad for the child. His teacher in some cases may exhibit a tinge of jealousy in his dealings with him, thus creating feelings of insecurity or animosity in the child. His classmates may call him a "square," or "brain," a "super," an "egghead," or some similar name which reflects their jealousy or antagonism. Thus the gifted child has problems in mental hygiene because he is gifted just as the handicapped child has them because he is handicapped.

On the other hand there are superior children who have strong egos and parade their superiority before their fellows. These children quickly become unpopular and in some cases are almost completely cut off from companionship with those of their own age. This situation obviously leads to serious problems in mental hygiene.

Another common problem among the gifted is the adjustment of their academic ability and interests to the typical school program. In the classroom they are often forced to endure the detailed and tedious presentation of materials and methods with which they are long since familiar. They are frequently squelched by the teacher when they ask questions which go beyond the textual material. They are seldom encouraged to bring the fruits of their outside reading and experimentation to the classroom. The gifted student often hesitates to suggest that he knows another and perhaps a better way to perform the experiment which the teacher has just completed. His poem reflecting on the origin and destiny of man would probably not be gratefully received by the teacher or appreciated by the students. The typical classroom atmosphere presents many such frustrating situations for the bright child. He can easily develop feelings of insecurity, anxiety, lonely aloofness, and a variety of tensions.

Furthermore a limited curriculum works a greater hardship on the gifted than on the average child. The failure of a meager curriculum to challenge the gifted child may lead to serious maladjustments. He may feel that he is restricted in his search for knowledge not only by a sparse course of study but by inadequate laboratories and equipment. If accelerated in an attempt to overcome the handicaps of a limited curriculum the gifted child is faced with the possibility of developing a sense of inferiority in associating with an age group which is more mature physically, socially, and emotionally. Such feelings of inferiority are often accompanied by a feeling of "aloneness," since the youthful gifted student may find his social relations with older classmates inadequate and unsatisfying.

An unfavorable socioeconomic background is another frequent source of mental hygiene problems among the gifted. Feelings of resentment and bitterness grow out of the inability to attend college because of inadequate finances. The parents who explain to the gifted boy that his social level will necessitate his limiting his ambitions socially or vocationally may cause irreparable harm. As a result he may develop an antagonism against society which will not only create a personality problem but may also rob society of a worthwhile contribution. In fact, in extreme cases it may create an enemy of society who uses his superior ability to flout the law and impose upon his fellow men. Once an antagonism against the social order develops into a need or desire for revenge upon society the superior individual can be a much greater menace than is the average or dull social outcast.

While the gifted as a group are endowed with superior mental ability and physical vitality which enables them to cope with the emotional stress of modern life, many gifted individuals, particularly in early life, are besieged with personal and social problems which seriously affect their mental health. Maturity decreases the intensity of such problem situations; in childhood and youth the frustrations are harder for the youngster to bear. Fortunately, his intellectual ability gives him a superior capacity for self-analysis and self-diagnosis, which form the first essential steps toward good mental health. The gifted youth's own insights combined with adequate and effective counseling by parents, teachers, and school guidance workers can and should solve most of his problems of mental health.

TYPES OF GUIDANCE

The psychology of the gifted has been discussed in terms of their general characteristics, individual differences, interests, personality traits, mental characteristics, motivations, and mental health. Each of these areas has clear and direct implications for guidance and counseling. If the gifted are to make even a major part of the contribution of which they are capable they must have aid and advice from understanding parents, teachers, and counselors. It is true, of course, that many will succeed without such aid. The old adage "genius will out" applies in quite a few cases. However, there are probably many more cases in which genius does not "out" or falls far short of the degree of success possible because adequate guidance is lacking.

Guidance of the gifted should be designed to enable each individual to understand himself, his abilities, and interests; to develop himself to the fullest; and to relate himself to the highest life goals consistent with his abilities and interests and greatest social gains. Thus guidance is concerned primarily with three major areas in the individual's life: his personality, education, and vocation. Guidance is begun early in life, usually by the mother, and may continue throughout adult life with trusted friends and even professional counselors as advisers.

The practice of guidance other than that carried on in the home by parents and other older family members probably originated in the field of religion. Early in history man sought guidance from religious sources. For centuries he has counseled with his priest, his rabbi, or his minister. Not only is counsel sought on religious problems but also on moral, personal, and social problems. The development of mental hygiene has emphasized the need and value of proper guidance. Maladjustments in the lives of the gifted can take a heavy toll in human frustration and failure. Only skillful counseling can overcome many of such maladjustments. In the field of education, only within the last three or four decades has the concept of "knowing the child" been accepted as basic to the learning process. Educational guidance has become a major concern in the public schools in mid-twentieth century. Add to all these the fact that the rapid social change characteristic of the twentieth century presents the individual with a constantly changing picture of life. The scientific advances represented by modern technology have affected industry to such an extent that vocational opportunities vary significantly within the space of the four-year span of a high-school or college education. Only a person who specializes in guidance can keep abreast of these changes. James Conant, noted educator and former president of Harvard University, in his book *The American High School Today*, says:

In a satisfactory school system the counseling should start in the elementary school, and there should be good articulation between the counseling in the junior and senior high schools, if the pattern is 6-3-3, or between the counseling in the elementary school and the high school, if the system is organized on an 8-4 basis. There should be one full-time counselor (or guidance officer) for every two hundred fifty to three hundred pupils in the high school. The counselors should have had experience as teachers but should be devoting virtually full time to the counseling work; they should be familiar with the use of tests and measurements of the aptitudes and achievements of pupils. The function of the counselor is not to supplant the parents but to supplement parental advice to a youngster.[5]

The guidance of the gifted is discussed under the following headings: Personal Guidance, Educational Guidance and Vocational Guidance. In actual practice guidance is an integrated process which includes all three areas with the em-

---

[5] James B. Conant, *The American High School Today* (New York: McGraw-Hill Book Co., 1959), pp. 44-45.

phasis on each changing in accordance with life needs. Guidance is a continuous process which covers the entire life span because problems are always present from life's beginning to its end.

Personal Guidance

The basis of all guidance is the understanding of the individual. If the gifted child is to fully realize his potential he must know at some time what his potential is in terms of his abilities, interests, and opportunities. A knowledge of self will point out handicaps and limitations as well as abilities and opportunities. Even the most gifted are subject to limitations. Sometimes limitations are imposed by poor health, defective vision, hearing loss, or other physical defects. Sometimes deep-seated emotional conflicts or maladjustments may prove severe handicaps. Personality traits which have been developed over a number of years may harm an individual's chances for success in some fields of endeavor which otherwise might have been fruitful. Superior intelligence tends to intensify some personal problems while at the same time it provides the insights which can contribute to their solutions. These insights which are essential to accurate self-diagnosis are most effective when aided by the advice and counsel of an understanding adult. However, such advice and counsel must be founded upon a fairly comprehensive knowledge of the gifted individual. Effective personal guidance involves (1) getting the facts about the individual (*observing and testing*), (2) compiling and maintaining a record of these facts (*cumulative records*), and (3) using these facts as a basis, exploring problems and working out solutions (*counseling*).

OBSERVATION AND TESTS. The earliest knowledge of the developing child is gained by observation. Despite the fact that observation yields conclusions which are quite subjective in nature, these conclusions are valuable to the guidance counselor. Many insights into the childhood personality may be obtained by the trained observer or even the interested parent, if he or she observes accurately and records these observations over a period of time. In the case of gifted children signs of superior ability are discernible at an early age. The child who walks and talks early in comparison with other children is revealing things about himself which have meaning to the intelligent observer. The three-year-old who enjoys thumping the piano keys and hammers out rhythms on his toys conveys information to the careful observer. When he grows a little older he may be given tests which will reveal a great deal about him, his abilities, and his interests.

Perhaps the basic test in establishing the personality picture is the intelligence test. There are many intelligence tests available for use in determining intellectual ability. In general they are divided into two types, the group and the individual test. Two of the most widely-used group intelligence tests are the Otis Self-Administering Test of Mental Ability and the Otis Quick-Scoring Mental Ability Test. The Kuhlman-Anderson Tests, which consist of a series of tests extending from the kindergarten to the adult level, are in some ways preferable to the Otis Tests for use with gifted children since they present a good balance among verbal, numerical, and spatial items. Such tests are helpful in identifying the gifted while at the same time give the teacher some idea of the pupil's academic potential.

However, as a basis for counseling, the individual intelligence test is preferred. First, it is usually more accurate, and second, the tester is in a better position to evaluate the attitude of the subject with respect to the test. The Terman-Merrill revision of the Stanford-Binet scale is probably the most popular and best single measure of intelligence available at the present time. The Stanford-Binet scale has undergone a number of revisions since the appearance of the original early in the century. The Terman-Merrill revisions permit the expression of its results in mental age, intelligence quotient, and standard score. The Wechsler Intelligence Test also has wide use, especially with preschool children.

A second type of test which sheds valuable light upon the nature and interests of the individual is the special aptitude test. Such tests are uniformly diagnostic in nature and therefore useful in analyzing the abilities and interests of the gifted as a basis for guidance. Aptitude tests have been developed in science, art, mechanics, and many other areas. They are in common use largely at the secondary-school level.

Personality tests, or ratings which are designed to yield a quantitative statement of personality in terms of a score or a point on a scale, can be quite helpful in studying the gifted child. Attitude and interest tests, as well as adjustment instruments, may also be used to advantage in getting a better description of the personality of the gifted child. The Bernreuter Personality Inventory is one of the oldest and most popular measurement instruments in this field. At the present time dozens of helpful testing instruments dealing with social attitudes, personal and social adjustment, emotionality, vocational interest, moral judgment, introversion, extroversion, character traits, family relationships, and neurotic tendencies are available to the guidance worker.[6]

Early observation combined with the later use of a wide variety of tests and rating scales makes it possible to secure a comprehensive picture of the gifted child as a person. This picture should form the basis for guidance in the broad field of personal and social adjustment. Certainly every gifted child needs to have such a picture taken both as an aid to self-diagnosis and as a basis for counseling by parents, teachers, and guidance workers.

CUMULATIVE RECORDS. The cumulative record is a very useful instrument in the guidance of the gifted. It preserves in black and white the story of the child's growth and development over the years. Often it begins with the child's entrance into the school program. Unfortunately in many schools such a record is meager or nonexistent. In some school systems it consists merely of a record of grades and the name and address of the parents. A comprehensive cumulative record of maximum value in the guidance of gifted children will include:

[6] See Lee Cronbach, *Essentials of Psychological Testing*, rev. ed. (New York: Harper & Brothers, 1959).

1. Family background of the child
2. Physical measurements
3. A mental measurement record
4. A record of personality, aptitude, and similar type tests
5. Scholastic achievement and progress record, including courses, grades, and standardized achievement test scores
6. A record of interests, extracurricular activities, leadership roles, and educational and vocational plans
7. Anecdotal records revealing behavior characteristics, social adjustments, unusual experiences, special abilities, talents, and character and personality traits
8. Work samples showing growth and development of abilities

If a preschool record compiled by the parents is available to supplement or be incorporated in the school cumulative record file it will be more comprehensive and as a result more valuable. In such a case the counselor and teacher will have a record covering the entire life span of the child up to the current time. The development of personality traits and special abilities can be traced from earliest childhood. The permanency of interests, changes in behavior, and growth of social characteristics can be traced almost from infancy through the school years. Such a complete record is particularly important for the gifted child since his interests and abilities often develop quite early in life.

The parental record of the preschool child should include:

1. Dates of the child's earliest accomplishments, such as crawling, walking, and talking
2. Health history, including serious illnesses and physical defects
3. A record of any tests taken in the preschool period
4. Special interests and abilities exhibited by the child and typical behavior patterns
5. Social awareness and adjustment including his attitudes toward playmates, parents, and other adults

Often the very act of compiling the record over the preschool years encourages the parents to deal more objectively with the child. They can see the effects, in many cases, of their own attitudes and behavior reflected in the child. If they study the record carefully they may find explanations for what might seem inexplicable conduct on the part of their child. They may discover hitherto hidden reasons for childish frustrations. If the preschool record is to be of maximum value the parents must be completely impartial, objective, and accurate. This, of course, is very difficult for a parent dealing with his son or daughter. However, once he realizes that the value of the record both for himself and school personnel is directly related to its impartiality, objectivity, and accuracy, he will tend to achieve them to a greater degree.

Some parents feel that teachers do not welcome such records. Unfortunately in some cases this is true. However, the good teacher is aware of their value and appreciates the parent's interest and thoughtfulness in maintaining such a record and making it available to the school. It is the thoughtless teacher who says he doesn't want to know anything about the pupil because it may be prejudicial in dealing with him. Such a teacher, in effect, admits his inability to interpret and use information wisely. If all teachers held to such a position they would have no use for cumulative records at all except, perhaps, as a place to record grades.

The cumulative record should follow the child through elementary and secondary school and be available as a source of information for the college in which he may enroll. Pertinent data from the record may be supplied to the prospective employer. The record should be kept by the school and made available only to responsible persons directly concerned with the welfare of the child. It is a valuable source of information for the parent-teacher, parent-counselor, and teacher-principal conferences on personal problems of the pupil. Without it all who deal with the gifted child are handicapped in diagnosing and developing satisfactory solutions to his adjustment problems.

COUNSELING. Lewis Terman said, ". . . more and better counselors are imperative for the encouragement of talent of *all* levels."[7] The importance of counseling in the school pro-

---

[7] National Society for the Study of Education, *Education for the Gifted* (Chicago: University of Chicago Press, 1958), p. 19.

gram is slowly but surely gaining the recognition it deserves. Counseling may be defined as the process of helping the subject to identify and clarify problems which face him, improve his understanding of himself and his environment, develop, examine, and test alternative solutions and select the best one. For the most part counseling is an individual matter with two people sharing experiences in seeking a solution to a problem. However, the shortage of trained counselors has encouraged experimentation in group counseling. While group counseling has obvious limitations, it has the advantage of being economical of the counselor's time. The general objectives of individual and group counseling are the same but the situation in which the counselor works is quite different. He must develop rapport not only with his subjects but among them also. The counselor must convey a sense of group warmth and understanding and common purpose to each individual so that each feels free to pose his problem for discussion and his proposed solution, if any, for group reactions. In this way members of the group obtain assistance while helping others. Group counseling is probably most effective in the vocational and educational fields and least effective in solving personal problems.

Counseling usually begins with the parent when the child is quite young. In fact, informal counseling begins when the mother cautions the child about the danger of the hot stove or the sharp knife. When he is old enough to play by himself he is cautioned against running into the street. He is advised by his parents to share his toys with playmates, refrain from venting his wrath by striking others, and return borrowed things to their rightful owners. Often older brothers and sisters, uncles and aunts, and grandfathers and grandmothers join parents in counseling the child.

When the gifted child enrolls in school he adds another counselor in the form of the teacher. Although the primary guidance interest of the teacher is educational, he realizes that the attitudes, interests, abilities, and behavior patterns of the child are vital factors in his success in school. Particularly is this true with respect to the gifted child who, in pursuing the regular school program, will have much of his time unoccupied by study and many of his interests untouched in the curriculum. The teacher who is aware of this and has a comprehensive cumulative record as a source of information can be of much help in counseling the gifted child. Most schools do not offer expert counseling service in the elementary grades, so the classroom teacher is usually the representative of the school in the counseling program in the early years of the child's school career. When the teacher has the full cooperation of the parents his job of counseling is easier and more effective. Several parent-teacher conferences on the gifted child each year are essential. More may be necessary if his personal or social adjustments are unsatisfactory. Since the superior child as a rule can do a superior job of self-diagnosis, the teacher should be frank in giving him the facts. He will appreciate such frankness and profit by it.

The good teacher must also be a guidance worker. Teaching and guidance are inseparable. Often it is more important that he know the child than that the child knows the subject matter. In the case of the gifted child knowledge of the subject matter will usually come easily, but personal and social adjustments and emotional stability may be difficult to achieve. By careful observation and use of tests and a comprehensive cumulative record, the teacher can do much to help the gifted child solve his personal and social problems, both within and outside the school. Needless to say parental cooperation is essential to his success.

When the gifted pupil reaches the secondary school level, he will in many school systems have the advantage of guidance personnel specially trained in counseling. It has been suggested by guidance experts that there be one full-time counselor for each two hundred fifty to three hundred pupils. When this is the case adequate counseling may be given each student.

The gifted youth when faced with a personal or social problem will usually attempt to meet it with his strongest asset, his intelligence. In some cases, particularly if it is an emotional problem, it may fail him. The experience may be so frustrating, particularly if repeated, as to actually cause him to discard intellectual analysis as a tool of investigation and substitute popular generalizations or mysticism. For example, the problem of his own origin and destiny may develop just such a type of frustration. It is at this point that skillful counseling can save the day. However, the counselor, parent, teacher, or guidance worker, whichever he may be, must be able to recognize the problem situation in the youth and get him to share his problem with the counselor. Sometimes this is not an easy task, since the typical gifted person is inclined to be independent and self-reliant. It means that the counselor must have rapport or he may not know that a problem exists until it is too late. The importance of there being at least one interested adult who shares the youth's confidence can hardly be overestimated. Many successful gifted individuals give much of the credit for their achievement to some teacher or guidance worker who served as a confidant. Often such a person served in the dual role of both confidant and hero or idol—an inspiration as well as a counselor.

The cumulative record of the secondary student, if it has been properly kept, provides the counselor with the needed background information for effective counseling. It is at this age that the gifted student encounters many of the personal and social problems of adolescence. Often he is a year or so younger than his classmates and sometimes not as socially mature. Dating presents its usual problems for the gifted as well as the average youth. Skillful counseling may free many of the anxieties and tensions of growing up so that the gifted student may be better able to pursue formal learning. Skillful counseling consists, however, of more than simply giving advice. It includes the sharing of experience. It includes helping the gifted youth to see himself as he is and as others see him. It includes getting him to set personal goals which are consistent with his abilities. It includes helping him to face problems courageously and accept both success and failure philosophically. In short, the counselor should use every skill and every fact at his command to aid the gifted boy or girl to establish and maintain good mental health. Such health is essential if the gifted youth is to make his maximum contribution to society.

Educational Guidance

The gifted pupil presents a challenge for educational guidance since in most cases he will secure his education in a school system which is geared to the average child. Even when enriched programs are offered or acceleration made possible, wise guidance is important if maximum benefits are to be secured from these educational adaptations.

The primary problem in the educational guidance of the gifted is underachievement. Underachievement, as the name indicates, is achievement which is below the level expected. The underachiever is the pupil whose scholastic achievement is less than that which is consistent with his mental ability. His performance is below that which might reasonably be expected from him. His opposite, the overachiever whose performance level is higher than might reasonably be expected, presents no problem academically, although he may develop emotional difficulties or mental health problems.

Underachievement among gifted children is often due to habits of idleness, lack of study, and general laziness growing out of their ability to meet school standards without serious effort. Content to "pass," they develop poor study habits which persist over their school careers. In some cases immaturity, emotional instability, and social maladjustment may be factors in causing underachievement. Not infrequently gifted pupils actually become disgusted with routine drills and teaching which stifles initiative, and react by turning their attention elsewhere. In such cases underachievement may be said to be due to underteaching. Occasionally the gifted underachiever is a boy or girl who prefers to be like the crowd and avoid the reputation of being an "intellectual highbrow" or a "brain." Other and infrequent causes of underachievement include broken homes, ill health, and language and reading difficulties. It should be noted, however, that in some cases these conditions spur the pupil to great achievement.

Overachievement, desirable in itself, may arise out of circumstances which are undesirable. For example, the gifted student who fails to achieve the social satisfactions and recognition that he desires may turn to academic endeavor to compensate for his social failures. In such cases, scholastic achievement becomes an escape and may lead to greater maladjustments which may preclude any major contribution to social progress. A case in point is the Phi Beta Kappa student who whiles away the time between trips reading Greek literature in the original as he operates a hotel elevator. His case history includes a series of incidents which led to his seeking escape in academic pursuits. Being a bright pupil, his success in school encouraged him to the extent that he avoided contact with others to devote all his time to classical languages. His concentration on academic work isolated him from his fellows, since he had no time for social activities. No doubt other personality traits were involved, but the early lack of adjustment clearly was the cause of the boy's adoption of scholastic work as an escape. Had his interest run along scientific lines significant social gains might have been realized, since work in an industrial or medical laboratory might have afforded a quite satisfactory adjustment. However, his antisocial attitude prevented him from securing a satisfactory job which would utilize his ability to read a dozen languages, and he settled for a job which permitted his reading Greek while earning a meager living.

Some students in the field of educating gifted children express fears lest gifted children, because of their verbal skills, become too bookish; they believe that guidance is required to help the gifted develop in other ways, socially, emotionally, and physically as well. Heck, a noted authority in the field of exceptional children, has written of the gifted:

School studies should not be allowed to absorb the child's entire attention or even the major part of it. The physical, the social, and the moral aspects of the lives of these children are of the greatest importance.

This does not mean that they are originally less well developed physically and socially than other children; they are likely to be even better developed. It means that some of them become so absorbed in academic interests that they tend to neglect other phases of life. It means that, because they are so capable, they owe it to themselves and to society to prepare themselves in such a way that the maximum good can come from their academic achievement. This does not mean equal development in all fields; it urges that other important areas shall not be ignored in the program of instruction.[8]

This can be interpreted as a caution for teachers; it is quite a temptation to give a gifted youngster all he can take of an academic diet at any one time; most teachers are pleased and proud to work with highly intelligent youngsters and may urge them into a program which overfeeds them with one kind of academic achievement at the expense of neglecting other important parts of the child's necessary development. A balanced program seems to be more satisfactory in helping a gifted child to become what he is capable of being: a citizen who can contribute to the progress of his society as he himself benefits from full usage of his personal abilities.

Educational guidance as well as personal guidance should be based on observation and testing, records, and counseling.

OBSERVATION AND TESTS. Educational guidance in the best sense begins even before the child enters school. Tests which are helpful in educational guidance are available for preschool children. The reading readiness test is a good example of such an instrument. The results of this test are most helpful in adjusting the gifted child as he enters school. As the child grows older less and less dependence is placed on observation and more and more on testing in providing educational guidance. This in no sense minimizes the value of careful observation on the part of teachers and other school personnel. Observation may reveal attitudes and conditions affecting educational progress which test results fail to uncover. For example, there are many cases recorded of pupils who can express themselves well in writing but are handi-

---

[8] Arch O. Heck, *The Education of Exceptional Children*, rev. ed. (New York: McGraw-Hill Book Co., 1953), p. 376.

capped in oral expression. As a result they fail to participate fully in classwork; they show up poorly in recitation, sometimes preferring to remain silent rather than reveal a lack of facility in speech. Nearsightedness may cause a gifted child to guess what is on the blackboard and leave the impression that he is unable to read well. Some gifted children who are sensitive to this handicap actually memorize the eye chart and are able to make a perfect score in vision. In such cases testing without accurate observation results in errors. Both testing and observation are invaluable in educational guidance and both have their place in a forward-looking guidance program.

The intelligence tests discussed in the section on Personal Guidance provide a basis for estimating the pupil's achievement potential. On the basis of these tests the teacher and counselor can make a fairly accurate estimate of the pupil's ability to do school work.

There are many tests designed to measure achievement, most of which are standardized in terms of grade or age norms. The tests are available for every grade in the elementary school and every subject in the secondary-school curriculum. The standardized test is a valuable supplement to the informal essay-type test which the teacher uses, as he seeks to determine pupil progress. However, the primary value of these tests in guidance of the gifted is diagnostic. Ofttimes the pupil's grasp of the subject matter as indicated by standardized test results is at great variance with teacher estimates. When such cases are studied by teacher and counselor some hidden factors affecting school progress may be brought to light.

The standardized tests are quite helpful in determining whether a bright pupil should skip a grade. They are useful in deciding whether he should be assigned to an enrichment class or be given individual enrichment. They point out strengths and weaknesses in subject mastery which prove helpful in course selection in the high school. In the elementary school in particular, standardized reading tests may reveal the cause of poor performance in geography, history, and similar subjects. Not infrequently a pupil with a high intelligence quotient makes unsatisfactory progress in school simply because his reading ability is poor or his reading time slow, or both.

In the elementary school the Modern School Achievement Tests, the Stanford Achievement Tests, the Metropolitan Achievement Tests, and the California Achievement Tests are popular general achievement tests. The Gates Basic Reading Test and the Iowa Silent Reading Test are widely used as diagnostic tests in reading. In the secondary-school programs many schools make use of the series of Cooperative Tests, in English, German, chemistry, economics, plane geometry, and many other subjects. The Iowa Tests of Educational Development are also widely used in secondary schools.

CUMULATIVE RECORDS. Practically all cumulative files contain a complete record of school marks and the progress of the pupil from grade to grade. This information is essential to proper educational guidance but the additional information contained in the complete file described earlier in this chapter is valuable in supplementing the bare academic record if a fairly complete battery of tests has been given and the results recorded. The family background, health history, and anecdotal records have a direct bearing on educational guidance. It should always be kept in mind that educational achievement can be affected by many factors, and that proper guidance requires a fairly complete knowledge of the pupil as well as the school program. Decisions regarding acceleration, enrichment, and choice of academic subjects will often depend as much on these nonscholastic factors as on the pupil's marks.

COUNSELING. Adequate and effective counseling of gifted pupils is essential if maximum academic achievement is to be realized. In the early years of his school career the pupil usually must depend on the teacher for advice on his schoolwork. If the teacher has full information about the gifted pupil he is in a position to counsel with parents on the child's learning problems. In deciding whether or not it would be best for him to skip a grade or what type of enrichment would be most desirable, a parent-teacher conference is in most cases clearly indicated. Nor should the pupil's wishes be disregarded. He should have a voice in the decisions and greater weight should be given to his opinions as he grows older.

Effective counseling does much to insure that the gifted student not only pursues an academic program consistent with his abilities and interests but that he completes that program. Although the drop-out rate for superior pupils is quite low in the first twelve years of their schooling it becomes quite high between the twelfth and thirteenth year. Studies indicate that less than 70 per cent of high-school pupils who rank in the upper quartile of the senior class go on to college. Boys go to college in greater number than girls. The loss of female talent of high caliber is great at this level.

The reason for failure to go on to college in some cases is financial but there are other significant factors at work. Parents who don't value a college education are powerful deterrents. Many high-school graduates prefer a car to a college education. When parents consent and help provide the car they aid and abet the loss of talent. Family background is an important factor. In some families college attendance is traditional; in others going to work after high-school graduation is the accepted thing to do. In homes where the father is a professional man the graduating son or daughter is much more likely to go to college than is the case in homes where the father is a semiskilled worker.

One of the real problems of school counselors is to route superior secondary graduates into college. In order to do this they must be cognizant of the family background and able to deal with the parents as well as the gifted student.

Vocational Guidance

It has been shown that educational guidance is inextricably bound up with personal guidance. In this section, it will be shown that vocational guidance is inextricably bound up with both. Whatever vocation may be chosen, interests, abilities, and educational achievement are all major factors in selection. Effective vocational guidance in common with personal and educational guidance is based on observation and tests, comprehensive records, and adequate counseling.

OBSERVATION AND TESTS. Parental observation will often discover that early in life the gifted child is likely to show marked preferences for certain types of activities as opposed to others. One child may be intensely interested in birds and insects, another in airplanes and mechanical toys, and a third in drawing or painting with water colors. Such interests often persist through elementary and secondary school. In some cases, these interests may be superseded by others as the child grows up. Regardless of the fate of his early interests they furnish clues for perceptive guidance. This is not to say that the child who collects rocks should become a geologist or that the boy who enjoys making various concoctions by mixing water and assorted chemicals should choose industrial chemistry as a career. It does mean that such interests have significance and should be recorded.

Vocational aptitude tests are many, covering almost every phase of the occupational world.[9] Such tests, when properly administered and accurately interpreted, can be quite helpful in the hands of the counselor. Intelligence tests, achievement tests, and personality ratings as well as interest inventories have value for the counselor as he seeks to guide the student toward the vocation or vocations which will be most satisfying to him and in which he will contribute most to society. School marks, particularly in high-school subjects, contribute to the fund of information needed in selecting a life work.

THE CUMULATIVE RECORD. The comprehensive cumulative record is just as valuable for vocational guidance as for any other type of guidance. It presents in chronological sequence the changing interests and the developing abilities of the

[9] See Lee J. Cronbach, *Essentials of Psychological Testing* (New York: Harper & Brothers, 1959).

gifted youth. It records test results and the teacher's interpretations of them. Family background and health history have considerable significance in vocational choice. Anecdotal records may reveal social attitudes and behavior patterns which might enhance the chance for success in one vocation and act as an obstacle to success in another. Vocational choices, with the possible exception of music and science, are not usually made before the junior or senior year in high school. By this time, the cumulative record, if conscientiously kept, will be replete with information and consequently of maximum value.

COUNSELING. In some respects, vocational counseling is more important and certainly more difficult than educational counseling, although the two go hand-in-hand at the upper levels of the student's school career. In the modern highly specialized vocational field, it is quite difficult to shift from one profession to another. Shifts in the student's educational program are much easier. In the case of the gifted, vocational counseling assumes great importance because so much potential is at stake. Misdirected vocational efforts may mean great loss to society as well as to the individual.

Vocational counseling of the gifted does not differ greatly from counseling of other students. However, the range of vocational opportunities, theoretically, is much greater for the gifted than for the average person. All the professions and high-level positions in industry and business are within their grasp when interests and personality factors are favorable. It has been estimated that 99 per cent of the major contributions to human progress have been made by less than 1 per cent of the total population. This emphasizes the importance of proper vocational adjustment of the gifted. If the gifted student is to have the opportunity to make the maximum contribution which his ability permits, he must choose a lifework for which he is eminently fitted.

The old concept of the "round peg and the square hole," reflecting the idea of inflexibility both of the person and the job, has yielded to the multi-potentiality concept of both job and worker. However, this does not make vocational choices easier; in fact, it adds to the complexity of the problem. If the very best choice is sought, which should certainly be the rule in the case of the gifted, rather than simply a satisfactory choice, the selection presents a multiplicity of factors to be considered. This is true because the gifted student even more than the average student possesses a multitude of potentials, and because the upper-level positions to be filled are many-faceted with respect to abilities required and are ever changing in nature as society changes. In the modern technological world, rapid changes in training requirements, as well as in professional duties, are not unusual.

In actual practice, gifted students almost universally select vocations from the upper level of occupations, thus narrowing the range of selection. Furthermore, the fact that they are better able to analyze and appraise their own interests and abilities than are the average students is a favorable factor in vocational selection. The counselor can place considerable reliance on their ability to diagnose and evaluate their own handicaps and limitations.

It is not unusual for the gifted student to encounter rather severe pressures in selecting a life career. In some cases, his parents may insist that he follow in the vocational footsteps of his father. Not infrequently, a favorite teacher strongly urges that he follow teaching as a career. A classmate of whom he is especially fond may attempt to sway his judgment. Then, again, the gifted student may himself feel that in view of society's needs, he should become a scientist or medical research worker. Such altruism should not be discouraged but neither should it be allowed to determine the final choice. The counselor should seek to isolate the student as far as possible from external pressures. He should be made to realize that such pressures tend to dissipate once his choice is made, and he should therefore regard them as temporary factors. More nearly permanent factors, such as his abilities, interests, personality traits, behavior patterns, attitudes, and academic record, should receive primary consideration.

Some gifted youths have a particular person in mind whom they would like to emulate. He may be the student's father, uncle, teacher, or some political figure whom he admires. In such cases, the profession must be separated from the person. It is the duty of the counselor to help the student determine whether it is the person who gives the vocation its attraction or whether it is the characteristics of the job itself which appeal to him.

Often, for the bright student, high-school vocational and educational guidance are synonymous. When he chooses his college he also chooses the lifework for which he will seek training. For example, if he chooses medicine he will choose the school which offers the best premedical course from among those available to him. If law is his selection, his college and his college program will be chosen with a law career in mind.

In view of the fact that most gifted students have multiple potentials, counseling them becomes a difficult and complicated task. One case is reported by Rothney,[10] an authority in the field of pupil guidance, of a youth in the Wisconsin Counseling Study who, on the basis of his academic record, test scores, and other achievements, was eligible to enter any program in any college in the United States. Success might be confidently predicted for him in engineering, commerce, law, medicine, or teaching. In his case, as in many others, the problem is not in which career will he be successful, but in which will he be most successful. Then, again, how should success be defined? Certainly not in terms of the individual solely, but rather in terms of both his individual satisfaction and the social contribution he makes. Another question which naturally arises is the extent to which current shortages in certain professions should influence choices. In other words, to what extent should social welfare affect the selection of a career by the bright boy or girl whose potential is great?

[10] J. W. M. Rothney. *The High School Student: A Book of Cases* (New York: Dryden Press, 1954), p. 271.

With our greatest human resources involved and with our national existence as well as our way of life in the balance, the stakes are indeed high. Those who counsel the gifted assume great responsibility. If the young man, who as a scientist would have discovered the perfect defense for atomic attack, becomes a lawyer, our nation is the loser. Such a loss could be fatal. If the girl, who, as a medical researcher would have discovered a cure for cancer, becomes a teacher, society itself is the loser. Regardless of how proficient each might become in his work, one could hardly conceive of their making social contributions of comparable value. The importance of adequate and thoughtful guidance of the gifted in the choice of their life careers can hardly be overestimated.

SELECTED READINGS

CRONBACH, LEE J. *Essentials of Psychological Testing,* revised ed. New York: Harper & Brothers, 1959.
> This book is a comprehensive treatment of the field of psychological testing, with a particularly valuable treatment of uses and interpretation of the various types of tests.

FRENCH, JOSEPH L. *Educating the Gifted: A Book of Readings.* New York: Henry Holt & Co., Inc., 1959. 555 pp. Pp. 103-15, 377-89, 395-426.
> Wilson and Jenkins discuss the results of specific tests given to various populations; Bonsall and Stefflre propose some interesting questions regarding the effect of socioeconomic status upon the temperaments of gifted children; Strang presents data concerning gifted adolescents' concepts of self. The remaining four articles deal with underachievement on the part of gifted students.

NATIONAL SOCIETY FOR THE STUDY OF EDUCATION. *Education for the Gifted.* Chicago: University of Chicago Press, 1958. 420 pp. Chapters 4 and 5.
> Chapter 4 covers Strang's discussion of concepts of giftedness. Group characteristics as well as individual differences are indicated, and the kinds of conditions conducive to the development and the stifling of talent and giftedness are explored. Chapter 5 deals with some of the societal factors influencing the development of talent, and the individual factors related to achievement.

NUNALLY, JUM C., JR. *Tests and Measurements: Assessment and Prediction.* New York: McGraw-Hill Book Co., 1959. 464 pp. Chapters 5, 6, 7, 9, 11, and 12.
> The chapters cited give the reader a clear picture of the values and limitations of tests in connection with guidance of the student.

TERMAN, LEWIS M., *et al. Genetic Studies of Genius.* Stanford, Calif.: Stanford University Press, 1926-1959 incl.

The volumes dealing with the mental and personality traits of the gifted group studied give much information that has implications for the guidance of the gifted. The records of grades earned in college, for example, indicate that more successful pursuit of this part of their careers might have been achieved, had the gifted students been better understood and guided.

TRAXLER, A. E. *Techniques of Guidance.* New York: Harper & Brothers, 1945. 394 pp.

This book presents in a well-organized form the best of modern techniques and procedures available for the complex job of counseling and guidance. An annotated listing of the principal psychological tests of various types used in guidance is a valuable feature of the book.

WITTY, PAUL A. (ed.). *The Gifted Child.* Boston: D. C. Heath & Company, 1951. 338 pp. Chapter 7.

This chapter, a discussion of the mental hygiene of gifted children, was written by Ruth Strang and is replete with illustrations drawn from real life.

6

Administration of Education
for the Gifted

Administration of education for the gifted, like all administration, involves the organization of persons, ideas, and facilities into effective working units for the accomplishment of specific goals. Once these units are established, the task of administration is that of continuous evaluation. On the basis of such evaluation, the effectiveness of the operation may be maintained and improved. Chapter 6 deals with the common types of organization of education for the gifted from the administrative or superintendent's viewpoint, and includes a list of criteria which may be used for evaluation. Chapter 7 deals with present organization and practice from the instructional or teacher's point of view, and includes a discussion of classroom practices and procedures.

The problem of administering educational programs for gifted children has centered around two major factors; namely, the small number of such children in comparison to the total pupil population, and the reluctance of many administrators as well as lay people to support homogeneous grouping of pupils in the school.

Even with a liberal interpretation of intellectual giftedness most schools will have no more than one or two out of twenty pupils who can be so classified. This means that the typical elementary classroom will have possibly one and no more than two gifted pupils. In high school the percentage of gifted pupils will be slightly higher but still comparatively small. The typical elementary school of three hundred pupils might have fifteen or at most twenty gifted pupils of varying ages, representative of every grade level. A secondary school of the same size might have as many as twenty-five.

Some authorities maintain that on a nationwide basis a ratio of one gifted out of each twenty-five elementary pupils and one out of every twenty high-school students is probably a more realistic picture. In either case the problem of administration of a program of special education at the elementary and secondary levels for those of superior intellectual potential is a formidable one.

When education for the superior student is organized on the basis of the upper 10 or 15 per cent of the total pupil population, sometimes referred to as the academically talented, the problem of sparsity is not as great. Many elementary classrooms have four or five such pupils and a high school of five hundred in some communities will have as many as a hundred students falling in this classification. Of course, there are many communities in which the number is less than 10 per cent.

However, it should be noted that in this classification are included bright children who by virtue of industry, persistence, and strong motivation are quite successful academically but not intellectually gifted as the term is defined in this text. Many children with I.Q.'s of between 110 and 120 qualify for the 10 or 15 per cent referred to as academically talented.

On the other hand, the child with great creative imagination whose primary interest is in music, poetry, or graphic arts might not be included in a selection of academic talent.

At the college level the nature and organization of the program, the maturity of the students, and the size and selective nature of the student body considerably lessen administrative problems. A comparatively large percentage of students at the college level are in the gifted classification, and the nature and variety of courses offered challenge the ability of the superior student. The maturity of college students permits unlimited individual study and research. Probably the greatest administrative problem is the provision of an adequate guidance and counseling program. Early admission and admission with advanced standing are administrative practices quite feasible at the college level. In short, the problem of administration is most serious at the elementary and secondary levels and becomes less acute once the student reaches the college level. This is not to say that the college may disregard superior students in administrative planning but rather that it should utilize the opportunity for capitalizing on superior ability once the gifted student enrolls in an institution of higher learning.

ADMINISTRATION IN THE SCHOOL SYSTEM

The administrative head of the local district, usually the superintendent of schools, is the key person in the administration of education for the gifted just as he is for other phases of the educational program. However, it is the local board of education which by law is the policy-making body which will enact the policies under which education of the gifted will be organized and administered. Back of the board is the community, which in the final analysis will determine policies by its control over its representatives.

Policies with respect to the education of the gifted are in reality to a large extent determined by the people of the community, enacted by their representatives, the board members, and administered by the superintendent of schools with the aid of the principals and teachers. In large systems a program supervisor is an added staff member with administrative responsibilities. All have a significant part in bringing effective education to the mentally superior child.

The administrative role of each group is different but there is also much in common. The superintendent is the key person since he forms the bridge between the lay groups which determine policies and the professional groups which execute them. In his role of executive officer for the board he not only sees that policies are carried out, but he also advises the board on policies from the professional point of view. The good superintendent will in time seek the advice of his staff with regard to policy in the education of the gifted. Once a set of policies is adopted, he and his staff proceed to carry them out in the most effective manner until such time as changes are made. Suggestions for change may and should be initiated by both the professional and lay groups in the interest of progress.

In planning the inauguration of a program for the education of the gifted in any system, each of these groups should be involved to a greater or lesser degree. No program is likely to succeed unless it has community support. Such support will normally be reflected in the board. If the superintendent is not able or willing to counsel with and advise the board, then the program will be seriously handicapped if not a complete failure. In turn, if the staff does not understand or is unsympathetic to the program, it is probably doomed to failure.

ADMINISTRATION IN THE INDIVIDUAL SCHOOL

Assuming a system-wide set of policies, the individual school still must have an administrative plan in its own operation. This plan must, of course, be consistent with and subject to the over-all policies enacted by the board for the entire system.

In each school unit the principal is the key person in interpreting general policy to the teachers and exerting leadership among them in developing internal policies for carrying on the program in his school. For example, if the system-wide policy of enrichment on an individual basis has been adopted, then it is the responsibility of the principal and his staff to formulate internal policies for the most effective education possible within the framework of individual enrichment. This will involve arrangement of instructional schedules, teaching responsibilities, and pupil assignments. When these decisions are made on the basis of common discussion among teachers and principal and plans are developed cooperatively, the program is likely to be more successful than when arbitrary decisions are made and handed down. The principal, as an administrator, will make every effort to provide facilities, equipment, and materials of instruction as they are needed. In cases where a program supervisor or consultant is employed, it is the responsibility of the principal to arrange for her visits so that she may work cooperatively with the teachers to the maximum benefit of the program.

The best type of program supervisor or consultant is one who really does not supervise in the traditional sense of the word but rather stimulates and guides the teachers in developing and carrying out the program for the gifted. One of the most valuable services the supervisor or consultant can render is that of making best and most successful practices common throughout the school system. In systems where no such person circulates, an outstandingly successful practice may be limited to one school simply because teachers in other schools know nothing about it.

In the absence of a general program supervisor or consultant a program coordinator in each school may serve many of the functions of the system-wide worker. This person may be a teacher in the school who has a special interest in the gifted or who has had broad experience in dealing with exceptional children. In some cases the principal may wish to assume the task of the coordinator. In practically every case the job of coordinator of necessity must be a part-time one. A teacher may be relieved of part of his teaching load or given an overload for which he receives additional pay. The former practice is recommended since it frees the coordinator during some part of the school day. The major task of the program coordinator, as the title indicates, is to tie the program together in the school. She assumes responsibility not only for coordinating the program but also for bringing new ideas and new enthusiasm to the teachers. She is an advisor on problems of instruction, a counselor who helps the staff to do a better job in dealing with the gifted. The coordinator is usually appointed by the principal with the advice of the faculty.

In order to have a systematic way of getting advice from the faculty on this and other matters a staff advisory committee may be called upon. This committee may be selected specifically to advise on the program for the gifted or it may be a general advisory group which deals with this program along with the other aspects of the school. In either case the committee should be selected by the staff itself rather than appointed by the principal. In small elementary schools this committee may well embrace the entire staff. In the larger elementary schools one or two teachers from each grade level or each division—primary, intermediate, and upper—may be selected in order to get a broad representation. In secondary schools representation from each department or area of study is advisable. Although the principal sometimes serves as the chairman of this group, in most cases the committee will function better if chaired by the program coordinator or a member of the group itself. There is usually freer discussion and greater frankness when the administrator is not identified with the committee.

The function of the committee is to act in advisory capacity in the planning, establishment, execution, and coordination of the program. Its membership can present the views and opinions as well as the points of friction which may develop among staff members. The committee can and should be a source of many ideas and suggestions with respect to the program. Through such a group the staff may contribute to the administration of the program and inject into it a vitality which will go far to insure its success.

ADMINISTRATIVE PRACTICES

Administrative practice in the education of the gifted may be divided into two general categories. One is acceleration which, as the name implies, involves "speeding up" the educational program and accomplishing more in less time or at an earlier pupil age. Acceleration is based on the theory that it is desirable for a pupil to move ahead as rapidly as possible in educational achievement. Content mastery is the primary consideration while physical, social, and emotional maturity are generally regarded as secondary in importance. It is further assumed that the program of the typical child is also suitable for the gifted child. Acceleration does not differentiate between the typical and the gifted as far as course content is concerned.

Acceleration may be accomplished by early admission to school, skipping of grade levels, or rapid progress. The first two practices are ordinarily on an individual pupil basis while the last-named usually involves the grouping of children of similar intellectual or academic ability.

The second category is that of enrichment which, as the name implies, involves making the program for gifted children "richer" than that for the typical student. It provides additional kinds of learning experiences. The "enriched program" aims at greater breadth, depth, and height. Here the emphasis is on widening the scope of learning at each grade level, increasing its depth, and raising its aims and expectations.

The enrichment program may be organized on an individual pupil basis with regular or special teachers given responsibility for enrichment or on a group basis with the special school, special class, or seminar plan in operation.

Acceleration and Its Forms

Perhaps the best-known and most commonly used administrative practice in connection with gifted children is acceleration. In this connection an acceleration program is defined as *one which makes possible pupil attainment of given educational level in a shorter time or at an earlier age than is normally expected.* For example, a pupil may complete the elementary eight-year program in six years. Thus a child may complete the eighth grade at the age of twelve while the customary age is fourteen. The same pupil may complete the normal four-year high-school course in three years and be ready for college at fifteen. If he is able to duplicate his high-school acceleration rate he would graduate from college at eighteen years of age instead of the usual age of twenty-two.

Acceleration takes various forms, differing a great deal according to the nature of administrative provisions required. Each form has its advantages and disadvantages. Combinations of the various forms of acceleration are not uncommon. Each form will be discussed in detail with regard to administrative implications.

EARLY ADMISSION. The practice of early admission, as the name implies, means *admitting the pupil earlier than is normally the case.* The customary time of admission to the elementary school is, in the case of the kindergarten, when the pupil is approximately five years of age; and in the case of the first grade, six years. These standard admission ages are, of course, chronological in nature. No consideration is given to the mental age, intelligence quotient, or social and emotional maturity of the child. The chronological age is convenient and objective. It is much easier to administer an admission policy based upon such age than one based on less objective criteria.

Admission to the secondary school is ordinarily not a matter of age but rather of satisfactory completion of the elementary program, which usually terminates at the end of the sixth or the eighth grade. Early admission to the secondary school in terms of grade level is unusual but occurs occasionally when a pupil skips the last grade of the elementary school. In terms of chronological age early admission is somewhat more common since a pupil admitted early to the elementary program will, if he makes only normal progress, enter the secondary school earlier than at the normal age.

Early admission to the college program is not unusual. Although normally graduation from high school is prerequisite to college entrance, there are numerous exceptions. Many colleges allow students to qualify for entrance by examination without regard to high-school courses. Others allow the high-school student to enter college if he has satisfactorily completed specified courses even though he does not have a high-school diploma. The University of Chicago, later joined by Columbia, Wisconsin, and Yale, has provided notable programs for special students qualifying for early admission by extra-achievement tests. Students in these programs average sixteen and one-half years of age at entrance, and most leave the high school at the completion of the tenth or eleventh grade.

The most difficult problem in connection with the practice of early admission is found at the elementary level. In many states the chronological age standard for entrance into school is set by the state either by legislation or ruling of the state department of education. Even the use of chronological age as the single criterion for admission to the elementary school poses administrative problems. When such criteria as mental age, intelligence quotient, reading readiness, and social maturity are introduced, the situation is further complicated. However, if we are to permit the superior child to enter the elementary school when he is ready these factors must be taken into consideration.

The difficulty in securing accurate information concerning the intellectual ability of children under six years is of course a major obstacle to the establishment of a policy of admission based on mental age or the intelligence quotient. Reading readiness is likewise subjective and at best shows only part of the picture. Social and emotional maturity are even more difficult to measure.

An admission policy based on mental age and social and emotional maturity has been suggested by some psychologists and students of child development. However, such a policy poses problems of administration which so far have prevented any widespread adoption of the plan.

Probably, the most practical policy with regard to early admission of gifted children to the elementary school is one of providing exceptions to chronological age standards. Thus a child whose mental age exceeds his chronological age by six months or more might be eligible for early admission. Evidence of reading readiness and social and emotional maturity may be required as additional qualifications. In any case the school would have to provide psychometric testing service in order to carry out such a policy. However, this would not prove a great burden, particularly for a large system with guidance personnel, since many parents would not seek early admission for their children. In fact, it might be necessary to encourage some parents to seek early admission for children showing evidence of superior mental ability.

At the secondary level admission policies are ordinarily based on elementary-school achievement. A pupil who successfully completes the work of the highest grade in the elementary school automatically qualifies himself for high school. In many private schools and a few public schools an elementary pupil may obtain early admission by passing prescribed standardized achievement tests.

The administration of a policy of early admission to the high school is considerably easier than a comparable policy for the elementary school. In the first place a record of scholastic achievement is available, and second, the pupil has reached an age at which psychometric testing is more easily administered and more effective in measuring over-all ability.

Since most pupils enter high schools which are part of the same system which embraces their elementary schools, such entrance is not admission in the real sense but rather a continuation of the pupil's educational program.

College entrance, however, is in most cases a change from one school system to another. This is true with the exception of those systems which provide a thirteenth and fourteenth year of training in the junior or community college. Since colleges and universities are with the exception noted administratively independent, they can establish such policies of early admission as they see fit. Gifted students can and are in some institutions of higher learning encouraged to enter college early. Proficiency examinations usually provide the way for such early admission.

A sound, well-administered policy of early admission at the elementary level can accelerate the progress of the typical gifted child so that he is ready for high school a year before he otherwise would be. It is also quite possible that with proper guidance the same high-school student might find it possible and desirable to enter college via proficiency examinations after three years in high school. Thus, by early admissions our typical gifted child would have entered college two years younger than his fellows.

Early admission in the elementary school serves to place the gifted child with those near his intelligence level and, therefore, challenges him immediately before he has the opportunity to develop habits of laziness or dawdling as is often the case otherwise. Early admission to high school and college serves to broaden opportunities for challenging learning experiences.

SKIPPING. Skipping is the term commonly used to describe *the practice of pupils omitting one or more grades in ascending the educational ladder.* For example, a superior child might be promoted from the third grade to the fifth, thus "skipping" the fourth grade. This practice poses no great administrative problems, which may be one of the reasons for its popularity. Of all forms of acceleration, skipping a grade is probably the one practiced most frequently.

In skipping a grade the pupil is usually presumed to be able to pursue the advanced work successfully because he already has some knowledge of the work missed and can acquire the rest of the knowledge and skills taught in the grade skipped while pursuing the work of the next grade. When this is the case, the bright child gains a year academically without causing any administrative problem. The procedure is not only economical in terms of the pupil's time and that of the teaching staff, but also in terms of money. The monetary saving, while secondary to the economy of time for the pupil, is welcomed in the modern era of crowded schools and increasing school taxes.

RAPID PROGRESS. Rapid progress is defined as *the practice of pupils proceeding through the school program faster than is normal.* Thus a gifted pupil might complete the work of the regular six-year elementary program in five years. In rapid progress nothing is skipped. The pupil simply accomplishes the work of the program faster than the normal rate.

Rapid progress has the advantage of giving the pupil an opportunity to become acquainted with the entire content of the program while at the same time allowing him to proceed at an accelerated pace. The teaching staff can see to it that all the skills and knowledge are achieved by the pupil in the established sequence. In skipping this is seldom possible. Furthermore, rapid progress eliminates the necessity of bright students sitting back and waiting for their fellow students to catch up. When skipping is practiced this waiting period often occurs during the year immediately preceding the pupil's double promotion.

The practice of rapid progress permits the gifted child to move forward at approximately his own pace or that of his fellow students of similar intelligence. He is constantly challenged by new and more complex things to learn and thus avoids developing habits of inattention and laziness.

The administrative problem involved is not an easily solved one. Rapid progress usually involves the grouping of children of like ability and approximately the same age. Thus a group of children of superior mental ability might be placed together at the beginning of the first-grade work and pursue the program of the elementary school at their own speed. As a result this group of children might well finish the work of the elementary program in one or two years less than those making normal progress.

A modification of this procedure is the practice of grouping children of two, three, or even four grades together for instructional purposes. In this way large groups of superior pupils might be given instruction which would allow them to make rapid progress. For example, a group of such children six to eight years of age inclusive might accomplish the work of the first three grades in two years and move on as an advanced group into the work of the second three years of the elementary program. By completing the second three years in two the group might then enter the seventh grade or junior high school at the end of four years instead of the normal six.

The principal administrative problem in such grouping is that of numbers. Few elementary schools have a sufficient number of gifted pupils to form a single grade group for efficient operation. An elementary school which has four rooms for each grade is likely to have fewer than a dozen pupils in each grade who can qualify for a rapid progress group. The typical elementary school, being smaller, would have even fewer. In large school systems this difficulty may be overcome by having the gifted of three or four elementary schools come to one of the schools in which a rapid progress program is established. This may require some pupils to travel excessive distances, which is particularly undesirable in the case of very young children. On the other hand, to operate a rapid progress program with fewer than a dozen pupils per teacher is inefficient.

Out of this dilemma has come the multiple-grade group which allows even the smaller elementary schools to have an acceptable number in each unit of the rapid progress program. However, such an arrangement has the disadvantage of increasing the age range of the group and imposing a heavier burden on the teacher.

Once the pupil enters the secondary school the problem becomes less difficult. In the large secondary school there is no difficulty in securing a sufficient number of gifted students at each grade level to compose a rapid progress group. For example, a high school of sixteen hundred pupils would typically provide at least twenty clearly superior students at each grade level and possibly ten more who could be included in the rapid progress group. At the present time some high schools have three-track systems which permit rapid progress for the superior group.

The small high school, however, faces the problem of insufficient numbers, and in grouping for rapid progress must establish multiple-grade groups or include some pupils who although considerably above average cannot qualify as gifted under the usual definitions. In some cases both of these modifications are necessary to secure a large enough group for efficient operation.

At the college level there is little grouping for rapid progress inasmuch as the college program permits rapid progress comparatively effectively on an individual basis. However, such grouping is found in some first-year English, mathematics and social studies courses, particularly in the larger universities. It is not infrequently used in make-up courses designed to remedy high-school deficiencies.

Although rapid progress ordinarily involves grouping there is the possibility of an individual student making rapid progress. In fact, such is fairly common at the college level. However, at the elementary level rapid progress by an individual pupil encounters numerous obstacles. In cases where individual instruction is given, a pupil may advance to the next grade at midyear. The individual instruction provided either by the regular classroom teacher in the classroom or outside, or by someone else, must be designed to supplement the regular work to the extent that the work of the entire year is covered. Standardized tests are helpful in evaluating the coverage obtained by the combination of classroom and individual learning.

If the pupil does not cover all of the content of a given grade before moving on to the next he is in reality "skipping" rather than making rapid progress as it is here defined.

In the elementary school rapid progress by the individual imposes somewhat of a burden on the teacher and limits to some extent the opportunity for group discussion and learning with others on the part of the gifted pupil. This is true because a considerable part of the work covered by him must be on the basis of individual effort. In cases where two or three pupils are given the opportunity for individual rapid progress some opportunity for exchange of ideas and discussion may be provided if time and facilities permit.

In the secondary school rapid progress by the individual pupil may be achieved as in the elementary school, but it is much more commonly achieved by the gifted student assuming more than the normal load. Thus while four units or subjects (in addition to physical education and similar-type courses) is considered the usual load, a gifted student might take five or even six units. In this way he would be able to complete a four-year high-school program in three years. Likewise summer school provides an opportunity for speeding up the high-school program of the gifted student.

Rapid progress in college is almost solely a matter of above-normal course loads, although it may be achieved in many schools by the student taking the normal load for twelve months a year instead of the customary nine or ten. Thus a student attending four summer sessions, each equivalent to one-half a semester of work, would be graduated at the time the typical student would enroll for his fourth year of college.

As can be seen from the discussion above, the administrative difficulties of individual rapid progress tend to decrease as the pupil ascends the educational ladder. At the college level there is little if any problem in providing the opportunity for a willing and able student to proceed at his own pace.

Enrichment

Enrichment is usually defined as *the practice of providing additional kinds of learning experiences beyond those offered in the regular program.* This definition rules out simply providing more of the same kind of work, which duplicates and gives no additional learning experiences. For example, enrichment in mathematics may be achieved by exploring the origin of geometrical theorems but not by assigning more problems of the same type. The latter device is sometimes used to keep superior pupils busy and may be falsely labeled "enrichment." True enrichment widens, deepens, and enhances learning. Repetition and extra drill do not enrich and are boring and tiresome to gifted students.

Enrichment is most effective when it is coordinated with the regular program. Particularly is this true in the case of individual enrichment programs as opposed to group enrichment. The additional learning experiences of enrichment, if properly coordinated with the regular program at each level, can establish meaningful relationships which are beyond the scope of the regular program.

While enrichment is essentially an individual process adapted to the interests, needs, and abilities of the pupil, it may, like acceleration, be organized and administered both on a group and an individual basis. Each will be discussed briefly.

GROUP ENRICHMENT IN SPECIAL SCHOOLS. The special school for gifted children represents the ultimate in group enrichment. Needless to say, such a school requires a large pupil group from which to draw its enrollment. Only comparatively large cities are able to populate such a school on a nonresidence basis. Perhaps the outstanding example of this type of school is the Hunter College Elementary School in New York City. As a rule only children who are able to make a very high score on an individual intelligence test are admitted.

Such a special school can carry on an enrichment program which is limited only by physical facilities and the ingenuity of teachers and pupils. The whole administration and instructional program can be geared to the gifted pupil. An elementary school of this type might include equipment such as typewriters, printing presses, specialized science equipment, and extensive library facilities including maps, globes, and various visual aids.

When such schools at the secondary level provide living accommodations they may be even further specialized by providing emphasis in various areas of learning. For example, one special school might be equipped for, and devoted to, the instruction of gifted children with a special interest in science; another, for pupils specializing in the humanities. According to some students of Russian education this specialized type of special school is a logical development in the Soviet scheme of education which at present embraces the idea in an embryonic form.

The special school for the gifted has a number of advantages. The major one is the opportunity it offers for providing a rich, meaningful and challenging program for the gifted without the limitations imposed by the regular school. Furthermore, it represents an efficient and economical use of facilities, services, and instruction personnel. The most obvious disadvantage is the difficulty in populating the school without extending attendance area boundaries unreasonably, or providing living quarters. In the case of the special school which includes elementary pupils, living away from home is generally undesirable, and even at the secondary level poses difficult problems. Many educators feel that this obstacle alone rules out the special school for gifted children except in the largest cities. Other objections cited include the complete isolation of gifted students from other pupils during a considerable period of their school life and the possibility of creating an intellectual aristocracy.

Although the primary purpose of the special school is enrichment, it lends itself quite well administratively to acceleration, particularly in the form of rapid progress.

IN SPECIAL CLASSES. Special classes for enrichment are more common than the special school. Special classes may represent a section for each grade in the elementary school and for each subject at each year level in the secondary school. Thus an elementary school of eight grades might provide eight sections of an enrichment program for the gifted paralleling the regular program. Two or more sections may be combined in order to secure groups of adequate size. The gifted child upon entering such a school is assigned to the enrichment program with children of like intelligence. The entire group of gifted pupils moves along at the same pace as other pupils in the school, but receives a broader program. The gifted pupils in this situation are able to participate in extracurricular activities of the school and otherwise freely associate with pupils in the regular program.

In order to secure special classes of adequate size it is common practice to operate such a program in a school designated as a center which serves several attendance areas. In Cleveland, which is recognized as a pioneer in this type of program, these centers are called Major Work centers.

The size of many secondary schools permits the maintenance of special sections for the gifted without resorting to drawing from other schools. Woodruff High School of Peoria,

Illinois, has for a number of years provided entering freshmen with the opportunity to enroll in enrichment sections taught by instructors carefully chosen for their ability to provide challenging learning opportunities in their subject fields.

Special classes for enrichment may be provided on a full-time or a part-time basis. In some elementary schools the enrichment classes are on a half-time basis with gifted pupils attending regular classes the other half of the day. Likewise in the secondary school the program may include, for example, only science, mathematics, and social studies, while home economics, industrial arts, commercial work, and other subjects are offered only in regular classes.

The special class program of enrichment provides gifted children with the opportunity to associate with other pupils and thus overcomes to a large extent one of the chief objections to the special school program. In practice gifted students in these special classes often assume positions of leadership on athletic teams, win leading roles in dramatic productions, and become valuable members of school bands and orchestras.

A further modification of the special class program includes such procedures as having a library period once a week attended by gifted pupils who leave regular classes for this period. During the period the librarian introduces pupils to the world of books and stimulates and guides their reading in biography, travel, and similar areas which enrich their school experience. Discussion of books read can occupy many interesting special class periods. The absence from regular classes proves no hardship for the superior pupil. The special class meeting one or two periods each week can give opportunity for exploration and enrichment in such areas as current events, creative writing, practical arts, science, and in other areas as well. Teachers for these classes may be drawn from the faculty of the school, from a system-wide staff of special teachers, or from people in the community who have the knowledge, ability, and interest needed.

In Seminars. Seminar programs for the gifted have been developed in some high schools. Such seminars are usually organized around areas of interest such as science, mathematics, or the humanities. Seminar sessions are held in the late afternoon, in the evening, or on Saturday. Leaders may be high-school teachers, college professors, or professional and business people of the community. Attendance is usually on the basis of invitation and is completely voluntary.

In general, these seminars seek to develop not only content information, but also skills in communication, in the use of mature resource materials, and in the formation of advanced concepts. They are designed to challenge the abilities of students who are capable of handling a full program of regular secondary courses and yet have considerable free time on their hands.

The content of the seminars is ordinarily close to if not on the college level. Experience at a mature level is provided in individual and group projects, in group discussion, and in critical analysis.

Large high schools such as Niles Township High School in Skokie, Illinois, offer complete seminar programs by themselves, providing the staff leadership from their own communities. Some smaller high schools such as those in the Catskill area in New York join in forming a cooperative group to sponsor such a program. By pooling resources and transporting gifted students, a high-quality program may be achieved.

INDIVIDUAL ENRICHMENT IN GENERAL. Individual enrichment programs require no adjustments in grade organization but do require planned adaptations in the regular school. Much of the success of any program of individual enrichment depends on the instructional staff available. The attitude and ability of the teacher is of primary importance. He must be skilled in creative teaching, in individualizing instruction and in pupil-teacher planning. A second requirement is a wealth of equipment and instructional material appropriate to a wide variety of interests. Without such physical properties a teacher will be handicapped in planning and developing enrichment programs for gifted pupils.

Two general plans of individual enrichment in terms of staff assignments are presented here. The first is the program carried on by the regular classroom staff, and the second that carried on by a special teacher of the gifted who specializes in planning for and working with gifted pupils. A combination of these two plans probably offers the greatest promise for a successful program.

Regardless of whether the enrichment program is staffed by regular teachers or special teachers or both, it is at the elementary level that most such planned programs are found. This is not a result of chance but undoubtedly at least in part due to the realization that it is during early school life that most of the habits of study and attitudes toward learning are developed. The gifted child is likely to develop interests at an early age, and these can be capitalized on in the elementary school. Furthermore, the younger child is in greater need of help in exploring his interests and abilities than is his older brother in the secondary school. At the elementary level the enrichment of a pupil's program is the responsibility of a single teacher sometimes aided by a special teacher, or the reverse. In the departmentalized secondary school where a student may have four or five classroom teachers, the task is more complicated. On the other hand, much individual enrichment is available in elective courses which may be taken in the high school. The special teacher can be most helpful at the secondary level in guidance and counseling and assisting subject area teachers in planning enrichment activities. He can also arrange for college correspondence courses for gifted high-school juniors and seniors. At the college level, the gifted student has a broad opportunity to enrich his program not only by elective course work, but also by independent study and research. He is usually mature enough to develop his own program of enrichment with a minimum of guidance from his instructors.

THROUGH THE REGULAR CLASSROOM TEACHER PLAN. In this plan each teacher is asked to provide enriching experiences for his gifted pupils both inside and outside the classroom.

It requires that the classroom teacher know the special interests and abilities of his gifted pupils and plan a program for each with these in mind. Such a program should involve reading and exploration outside the classroom and opportunity to contribute knowledge thus acquired in the regular classroom work. The effective teacher is able to correlate the enrichment experiences of the gifted with the regular program so that the regular work becomes more meaningful not only to the gifted but to all pupils. In all probability it can be demonstrated that an enrichment program skillfully administered will raise the level of learning for the entire class.

The most successful enrichment in the regular teacher plan is usually characterized by the following:

1. A thorough knowledge of the pupil, including his interests, aptitudes, abilities, and general personality characteristics
2. Imagination, understanding, desire, and creative ability on the part of the teacher
3. Good pupil-parent-teacher relationships
4. Adequate variety of instructional facilities and materials
5. Classes of small or medium size
6. Adequate teacher time for planning, and individual counseling
7. Flexibility in classroom procedures
8. Ample classroom space for enrichment materials and activity

THROUGH THE SPECIAL TEACHER PLAN. In this plan there are one or more special teachers who devote part or full time to working with gifted pupils. They work with the regular teacher and develop plans for individual enrichment cooperatively with him and his gifted pupils. Pupils are usually allowed to leave regular classes at intervals to work with the special teacher. He provides guidance and counsel in out-of-class work, helps the pupil evaluate his enrichment activities, and in general nurtures his interest and curiosity in learning beyond the requirements of the regular schoolwork.

Such a teacher may work at all grade levels in a small school system. However, because of the departmentalized work at the secondary level few such special teachers feel themselves capable of their best work over such a wide range. By far the greatest number of special teachers work in the elementary school and many of them specialize in either the lower or upper grades of the elementary program.

The special teacher plan offers a number of advantages over the regular teacher plan. First of all, it adds a specialist to the staff who by devoting his undivided attention to the gifted pupil is able to give him more effective help. His freedom from regular classroom activities allows him to do more planning and counseling. His experience with the gifted will be much broader than that of the regular teacher. He can bring best practices from all schools to every school. Usually such a teacher has special training in his work and is abreast of current thought in the psychology and education of the gifted. Furthermore, while some regular classroom teachers are unsympathetic to the problem of the gifted, the special teacher by virtue of his interest and training is sympathetic and understanding and many times has a favorable influence on the attitude of the teachers with whom he works.

The most successful enrichment by the special teacher plan embodies the following characteristics in addition to those listed under the regular classroom teacher plan.

1. Special teachers with imagination and ingenuity who through training and experience have a clear understanding of the problem and methods of educating the gifted
2. Complete and willing cooperation between the special and regular teacher
3. Considerable opportunity for pupils to leave the regular classroom to engage in enrichment activities under the direction or supervision of the special teacher

CRITERIA FOR ADMINISTRATION

1. *Is the program system-wide?*

A system-wide program can be much better coordinated and integrated than one which is carried on only in one or two schools in the system.

2. *Is there an effective screening program for the discovery of gifted children?*

An effective screening program is the best insurance against overlooking gifted children and including the non-gifted. Gifted children who are unmotivated are likely to be underachievers and as such are easily overlooked. On the other hand, the industrious, aggressive child with a pleasing personality may well be included even though he possesses only average mental ability. An inclusive and systematic plan for testing and observing is essential in the administration of a program for gifted pupils.

3. *Are the responsibilities of all personnel working in the program specifically defined and their relationship to the regular professional staff and to each other clearly set forth?*

Much confusion, omission, and duplication can be avoided if this is done.

4. *Is there a carefully designed plan for selecting teachers for the program?*

The program is much more likely to succeed if teachers are chosen with due regard to interests, adaptability, tolerance, broadmindedness, mental flexibility, imagination, ingenuity, and tactfulness. Such characteristics are not likely to be given proper consideration unless carefully designed selection procedures are in use.

5. *Are provisions made for orienting teachers to the program?*

Even an experienced teacher should be given some orientation before he is expected to assume responsibilities for a part of the program. The goals of the program should be so defined and the philosophy so clearly stated that the teacher will be able to direct his efforts effectively from the beginning. It is in the early stages of development that the success or failure of the program is usually determined.

6. *Is provision made for all staff personnel to contribute to the development and success of the program?*

The program should be a school program rather than an independent operation. Every teacher should be encouraged to make suggestions and otherwise assist in planning new procedures and methods.

7. *Are lines of communication established between the school and the parents of children in the program?*

Such lines should be two-way channels of communication, carrying information to parents and bringing back parental reactions and suggestions.

8. *Is there an adequate pupil guidance program?*

Proper guidance is just as important for the gifted as for the typical child. It might be argued that it is even more important since the potential of the gifted is so much greater. Adequate pupil guidance will help insure that the special program is effective in meeting the needs of the gifted.

9. *Are there adequate and suitable physical facilities and equipment?*

The chance for success in any program for the gifted will be greatly enhanced by modern science laboratories, adequate libraries, and a variety of equipment which will encourage the gifted student to exercise his abilities.

10. *Are provisions made for periodic evaluation of the program?*

Evaluation may be made internally in terms of comparisons of the relative effectiveness of teaching procedures, administrative provisions, and organization. External evaluations may be made by comparing results with those of the regular program. Reactions of pupils themselves, of parents, and of teachers may be quite helpful in this regard. Few school systems will be able to achieve the rigid control of variables necessary to completely scientific evaluation. However, this fact should not deter them from securing such evidence as is available.

FINANCING

Every genuine program for the education of the gifted costs. The costs are assessed in the form of extra planning, extra effort, extra time, extra materials, and extra money. Even when a full-sized class of bright pupils is instructed by a regular teacher there is usually an added expense just in bringing such a group together. Such expense is real whether borne by the school or the parent. The problem of financing is one which the administration is constantly called upon to face whether it be for the regular program or a special one. Many school systems include the costs of special programs in the regular budget without identifying any extra costs. Some, however, budget the cost of the program as a separate item. Extra costs in a program for the gifted are usually occasioned by one or more of the following: smaller classes, more expensive materials and equipment, more testing, more guidance, more supervision, more field experiences, extra transportation of pupils, more teachers, and additional administrative time.

Of all special programs for exceptional children commonly in operation, those for the gifted incur the least additional expense. While it is not uncommon for programs for the crippled and the deaf to cost several times as much as the regular program on a per-pupil basis, it is seldom that a program for gifted children exceeds the regular program cost by more than 50 per cent. The extra cost, of course, will be determined to a large extent by the nature of and the scope of the program. The major portion of the extra cost is in personnel—teachers, supervisors, guidance workers, psychologists, and administrators.

In a school system where the program for the education of the gifted consists of individual acceleration or enrichment, the additional costs will be slight. They will be occasioned principally by extra testing, counseling, and materials. Programs involving homogeneous grouping in most cases include additional personnel to a greater extent and therefore cost more.

Estimating costs of a program for the gifted on an over-all basis involves quite a number of arbitrary decisions with regard to the proper proportion of general expenses to be assigned to the special program. However, the general rule is to ascribe to the program as excess costs any expenses which would not have been incurred had the pupils in the special program been provided with the same program as the typical pupil. This assumes, for example, that the principal of a school in which a special program is carried on is receiving the same salary as he would have if no program were in operation unless he is given extra pay for this specific reason.

The direct cost of special programs for the gifted may be borne by the local district, the intermediate district, the state, or a combination of these. In reality the state shares in the cost to the extent that it supplements local funds in the general school budget, when the program is financed by the local district from that budget. In some states the intermediate district, which often is the county, provides special services in the form of supervision. While these services are most often supplied for handicapped children, the same administrative framework will serve for a program for the education of the gifted. The cost of such programs, while coming from the intermediate budget, is in effect a state expenditure in most cases, since the intermediate district usually draws its operating funds from state sources.

Most states provide financial aid to local districts with special programs for handicapped children. A number of states also extend this aid to districts with programs for the gifted. The amount of such aid is usually based upon the excess cost of the special program. Such aid may cover all or part of the excess costs. To be eligible for state aid the local district usually must meet specific requirements regarding class size and teacher qualifications.

SELECTED READINGS

BENTLEY, JOHN EDWARD. *Superior Children.* New York: W. W. Norton & Company, Inc., 1937. 331 pp. Chapter 9.
      Five methods of working with gifted children are discussed: acceleration, enrichment, individualized instruction, homogeneous grouping, and the special class. Specific enrichment programs are presented in outline form, showing what portion of the work is basic to all students, and what additional enrichment can be provided for the gifted in the classroom.
DEHAAN, ROBERT F., and HAVIGHURST, ROBERT J. *Educating Gifted Children.* Chicago: University of Chicago Press, 1957. 276 pp. Chapters 5 through 8.

Chapter 5 presents an analysis of a method by which school systems may inaugurate a program for the education of the gifted; it shows the division of responsibilities advisable among the staff members.

Chapter 6 presents case studies of two programs: the first is in the initial stages, the second well-established and accepted in the community of Portland, Oregon.

Chapter 7 discusses possibilities for successful enrichment of education for the gifted in elementary and secondary schools.

Chapter 8 analyzes the questions involved with organizing special classes for the gifted, and with accelerating them. Special classes as a means of enrichment are related to the community values.

GARRISON, KARL C., and FORCE, DEWEY G., JR. *The Psychology of Exceptional Children* (3d ed.). New York: The Ronald Press Co., 1959. 586 pp. Chapter 8.

Chapter 8 discusses various methods of educating the gifted and special educational provisions for the talented.

HAVIGHURST, ROBERT J., STIVERS, EUGENE, and DeHAAN, ROBERT F. *A Survey of the Education of Gifted Children.* Chicago: University of Chicago Press, 1955. 114 pp. Chapters 1 and 6.

Chapter 1 develops some criteria for a good program of enrichment; Chapter 6 discusses briefly methods of educating gifted children found in the public schools.

KLAUSMEIER, HERBERT J. *Teaching in the Secondary School.* New York: Harper & Brothers, 1958. 499 pp. Chapter 13.

The variety of administrative and over-all curriculum provisions for educating the gifted is pointed out, and the author stresses the need for continuous and systematic programs of identification as well as the necessity of enriched learning activities at all levels.

NATIONAL SOCIETY FOR THE STUDY OF EDUCATION. *Education for the Gifted.* Chicago: University of Chicago Press, 1958. 420 pp. Chapter 18.

Williams discusses some of the problems to be met in organizing and administering a program for the gifted. He includes plans for making a beginning, for staff responsibilities, for financing the program, for evaluation of it, and for developing community acceptance and support. He draws upon specific instances of programs in operation as examples of the procedures discussed.

TRUMP, J. LLOYD. *Images of the Future: A New Approach to the Secondary School.* Commission on the Experimental Study of the Utilization of the Staff in the Secondary School, 1959. 48 pp.

This publication looks at the secondary school of the future and projects a flexible program which will provide opportunity for every student to achieve to the limit of his ability. A brief section on the implications for the education of the gifted is included.

WITTY, PAUL A. (ed.). *The Gifted Child.* Boston: D. C. Heath & Company, 1951. 338 pp. Chapter 13.

The typical administrative devices used in the education of the gifted are set forth in a brief and concise manner in this chapter. Teaching procedures are treated from the administrative viewpoint.

7

Present Organization
and Practice

Historically there are two basic ways of handling the education of gifted students; these are acceleration and enrichment, with various interpretations and combinations of these for individuals or groups of students. Each plan has its group of faithful adherents; each has a group of people who argue against it. Each arrangement has been shown to be successful; probably, in certain cases, each could be shown to be unsuccessful, depending upon the criteria set up as bases for judging, and the way in which each criterion is interpreted.

Were public-school people concerned only with the intellectual development of pupils (and there are those who say this should be the school's only purpose for existence) acceleration would surely be the favored choice. Gifted students would be promoted and advanced as rapidly as they showed by performance and achievement that they were capable of moving to a higher level. It would not be unusual then to find a six- or seven-year-old taking his academic work beside eleven- or twelve-year-olds. To push possible outcomes even further, gifted students might well be found entering college at the age of twelve or thirteen. This kind of procedure would be based on the assumption that students should be placed at a grade level or in a course in which they could be academically successful; the students' social, emotional, and physical maturation levels would not be considered in such a procedure. It should be noted that in the examples mentioned, extremes of the possibilities have been given; those people who speak against acceleration often draw upon just such extreme variants of the scheme as examples for their points of attack.

Individual enrichment as a proposal for working with gifted students seems at first glance to be completely possible in any classroom. It would create the least disturbance of administrative procedures already in operation, and would have great benefits to the students involved as they developed intellectually, socially, emotionally, and physically. Any good teacher should be able to handle enrichment procedures, and probably does anyway in his quest to meet the individual needs of his pupils in the day-by-day program. Enrichment would give greater depth and breadth to the studies of all the children and thus would not single out any one or any group as different from any other. Actually enrichment can be explained as merely greater breadth and depth in teaching, aimed at dealing with the individual differences present in every classroom.

Let us consider this proposal critically. Consider for a moment the numbers of youngsters in elementary classrooms, and in secondary-school classes. Review the kinds of instructional materials that are typically available to teachers as they pursue their task of educating each child to his optimum development and capacity. Think of the demands made upon the school program in terms of time, time to be taken away from regular study and given to other community causes such as fund drives. Take into consideration the time the teacher must give to planning lessons for the class, evaluating their work, preparing tests and analyzing their results, and checking plans with individuals and small groups, in addition to the time he spends actually working with the pupils in the classroom. In consideration of these items and others which will occur to the reader, is individual enrichment feasible as a way of educating the gifted? And not only is it feasible; is it possible of accomplishment, in the regular classrooms of the typical public school today?

Grouping of gifted pupils offers much greater opportunity for enrichment. However, while individualized instruction with attention to the individual differences of students seems acceptable to most people, the concept of grouping students for such instruction is much more likely to stir up unfavorable and loud reaction. Actually, students have always been "grouped" in some way. If the age for entrance to school is accepted as six years, then six-year-olds are grouped as first graders. If twenty-seven students sign for third-year French, then they are grouped into that class. In a large high school that requires two or three shifts for the lunch period, the students are grouped accordingly. Grouping is not new in working with boys and girls in school.

If there are ninety students and three teachers for seventh grade, there may very well be three seventh-grade groups. In this case, there may also very well be questions as to the basis for the grouping, the selection of certain students for one group instead of another. It is not the mere grouping of students that raises questions; it is the basis for such grouping which is questioned, though few question the grouping of athletic teams, or the selection of casts for musical productions. It is usually assumed that the students so chosen have exhibited high-level ability in the area of the choice. When that area of choice becomes intellectual ability rather than athletic prowess or musical achievement, there are many more questions raised, even among the teachers themselves. Few teachers choose to be charged with the task of educating the below-average groups, which they see as a possibility once the intellectually gifted have been grouped into one section. Few parents choose to have their children placed in a group labeled average or below-average. There is somehow a feeling of stigma attached to such groups, a feeling that if all people are really created equal, such grouping goes against that precept and should not be tolerated. This stigma is not ordinarily attached to the athletic groupings. A boy may be hurt because he does not make the first team, but he can realize that his capabilities simply did not justify his being named to that team. He and perhaps his parents and teachers are not quite so ready to accept the fact that he does not have the intellectual ability to be chosen on the academic first team. The reader may recall George Orwell's classic statement from *The Animal Farm:* All animals are created equal, but some are more equal than others.

There is no basic agreement among educators as to the one best way of educating gifted students. Perhaps there should not be. Each of the proposals for their education will be examined in the remaining sections of this chapter. Some of the advantages and disadvantages of each will be presented, from the viewpoint of their relationship to the instructional program, the teaching-learning process, which includes the best interests of the students involved. These best interests should surely be of primary concern to teachers of boys and girls at any level of the educational program. Before any of these proposals, or any combination of them, can be chosen as the one best way of working with gifted boys and girls in a certain school, the objectives of the educational program of that school should be considered. It is only in terms of such aims as are held for the instructional program and in terms of the students themselves that the "best" method may be adopted, and even this may need to be adjusted from time to time, as goals may change and differing individuals are to be educated. This chosen best method will not be and probably should not be the same for every school situation.

ACCELERATION

Acceleration was one of the first methods tried in adjusting or bringing closer together the abilities of gifted students and the programs of the schools. William T. Harris, as superintendent of the St. Louis Public Schools, began a plan of flexible promotion in 1867 whereby students were allowed to advance more rapidly than the pace that was considered normal at the time. This program involved promotion as often as every five weeks during the school year, when such promotion was merited by the child's performance in his academic work. The net effect was to graduate him from public school at an age younger than that accepted as normal. This program, initiated nearly a century ago, contained the elements of what is today accepted as a definition of acceleration:

moving through an educational program in less time or at a younger age than is considered normal.

These two factors of speed and youth are both significant and necessary to understanding acceleration. Obviously, a student who moves through a program more rapidly than is considered regular will complete it at an age younger than the expected age. However, the youngster who begins his educational program at an age younger than the customary one is also accelerated, though he may not have any extra promotions or make more rapid progress throughout his school career.

Forms of Acceleration

EARLY ENTRANCE. One type of acceleration is that of early entrance to school. This has been practiced with and without scientific knowledge of the abilities of the youngsters involved. One such program was begun because there had been a lower birth rate for a time, and there were not sufficient pupils in the district to fill the classrooms unless the four-and-one-half-year-olds were accepted into the kindergarten program. Today's birth rate does not seem destined to provide the schools with that particular problem in the very near future.

Early entrance to kindergarten and first grade based upon accurate knowledge of a child's capabilities and potentialities does seem to have some merit. When a youngster is "ready" to begin his schooling insofar as appropriate testing and observational methods can determine, there would seem to be very little reason for forcing him to wait another six months or a year so that his chronological age will be more nearly like that of his classmates. Chronological age is not a factor that is related to academic progress and success nearly as positively as are mental age, social and physical development, and emotional stability. Studies have indicated that early entrance upon an educational program is not detrimental to a child's progress, his health, his social and emotional growth. No scientific studies have yet shown the harm that may be done a youngster by having him held back, actually retarded, because he happens to be four instead of five, or five instead of six years of age when he is ready to begin his school career.

Early entrance has advantages in helping a youngster reach his productive adult status at least one year earlier than the accepted normal age of entrance would. It removes the fears of missing some significant educational attainment that are associated with grade skipping. It supports the concept of readiness, and it assures that the youngster will be placed with others more nearly like him in aspects other than chronological age.

SKIPPING. Probably the type of acceleration most familiar to the profession is that which involves extra promotions, double promotions, or skipping of grades. This is much more likely to be found at the elementary-school level, though it is possible at the college level, particularly in graduate study, to take a proficiency examination and thus acquire credit for a course that has not actually been taken. This process might also be called skipping. In this instance the student is given credit for his demonstrated knowledge and not forced into what would merely be a repetitious course for him to have on his schedule, and thus a waste of his time. More recent practice on a somewhat smaller scale allows high-school graduates to obtain advanced standing in college through similar procedures.

For the most part, skipping of grades is limited to elementary-school pupils. A danger and possible disadvantage to the youngster may result from grade skipping unless his teachers work closely with him to insure that he has not skipped any fundamental process or any basic knowledge in skill areas, the lack of which might well hamper his later progress. This checking should involve the teacher's working with each individual accelerant to ascertain his actual understanding of the content he is expected to have mastered for the grade in which he is placed. A superficial knowledge may not be sufficient for the child. Use of diagnostic tests can be helpful to the teacher as he attempts to discover the status of the pupil's understanding of basic processes.

Within the past several years there has been a tendency on the part of some educators to advocate what are called "social promotion" policies. By this they usually mean that a group enters school together and graduates together, moving along at regular intervals, regardless of the scholastic achievement rate of each individual within the group. The purpose has been to emphasize the social development of the students involved, and to help them to become socially adjusted to their groups, to develop their ability to get along with others. Surely this is a worthwhile purpose, and one which ought to have some consideration, though not at the expense of other aspects of each pupil's growth and development. This kind of a policy tends to be unfair to both the gifted and the slower learners in the group in that they may soon feel that there is no use in putting forth effort, as they will be promoted regardless of what they may accomplish in the classroom. This policy may seldom have been practiced to the extreme described; yet it is a subject quite likely to be mentioned by parents at conferences. The phrase "social promotion" has become widely known.

RAPID PROGRESS CLASSES. The skipping of grades or awarding of double promotions in elementary school can be done in at least two ways: individuals may be promoted alone into the next highest grade, or groups of pupils may be accelerated together. The latter practice may have developed in an effort to help achieve group feeling and social awareness. It is obviously not possible unless there happens to be a large enough group of gifted youngsters available to accelerate in this fashion. Such groups may well complete eight years of study in six or seven, or six years in four or five, accelerating at whatever speed seems appropriate to the teachers and attainable by the pupils. The gifted youngsters are not held back to the pace of the average as in most regular classrooms, but are allowed and encouraged to progress at their own speeds, both in individual projects and in group study.

Rapid progress classes have been organized in large school systems such as that of New York City, particularly on the junior-high-school level. A gifted child can easily do the work of three years in two, covering what would ordinarily be grades seven, eight, and nine, as he is quite capable of completing his school tasks for each day in a half-day session of applying himself to his studies.

To enter such a rapid progress class in junior high school, a pupil is usually expected to have grade-equivalent scores of at least 8.5 in reading achievement and 8.0 in arithmetic achievement, including both the ability to reason and knowledge of the fundamentals. In many schools he is required to have an I.Q. of 130, or more. He is expected to be at least eleven years old, but to have the social maturity associated with the average twelve-year-old. He must be healthy both physically and emotionally and must indicate his willingness to work and show some evidence of enthusiasm and initiative. The intellectual ability of each youngster is not the only factor considered in allowing him to enter a rapid progress class.

Though these classes are often discussed as accelerated programs they usually involve enriched activities as well in order to provide the best educational opportunities to the gifted who are enrolled in them. The youngsters do not skip any of the content of the courses ordinarily included in these specific grades, but they do have opportunity to delve more deeply into the meanings of their tasks even though they are advancing at greater speed than ordinary classes can manage. Studies indicate that they attain greater achievement than do youngsters equally gifted who for one reason or another remain in normal progress classes; the personal and social adjustments of the rapid progress pupils remain at a high level. When the youngsters who have had the advantages of rapid progress classes enter the high school, they continue to maintain their academic superiority and their emotional stability, though they are younger by at least a year than the other pupils in the classes to which they are assigned.

Secondary-School and College Practices

Once a gifted youngster reaches the secondary school, he is very seldom skipped as an acceleration practice, though this may happen in isolated and special instances. For example, a student who has experienced quite a thorough training in a foreign language by reason of living in a home or a country in which he had learned to speak and understand it creditably would surely be allowed to take examinations that would help his teachers to place him in the appropriate year of that language according to the school curriculum, and would not be forced to begin with the first year of study regardless of his accomplishment. Similarly, a child who had studied harmony and composition with a private music teacher should be allowed to demonstrate his proficiency in these areas to determine proper placement for the pursuit of his musical studies in school.

In both secondary schools and colleges there are other methods that have been used in acceleration procedures. One of these involves the lengthened school year. In such a situation the high-school student might attend summer school for the purpose of studying certain courses and accumulating needed credits so that he might graduate earlier than "his class." The college student might also attend classes for eleven or twelve months each year instead of the regulation nine or ten and thus move toward earlier graduation. Each could, if the circumstances of courses offered were favorable, complete his course of study in three years rather than four.

A second way of accelerating at the high-school and college level is carrying a heavier load of courses during the regular academic year. Though increasing one's program beyond the recommended load for students often involves much arrangement through seeking permission of guidance counselors, advisers, deans, parents, and other concerned authorities, it can be accomplished if the student is sincere and potentially able. Some high schools and colleges that have available a great amount of relevant information about their students will encourage the capable ones to carry a heavier load of subjects. Sometimes the student finds it difficult to meet graduation requirements because courses may not be offered during the semester in which he is able to carry them, in addition to his regular load. A combination of summer school study plus heavier course loads during the academic year may help solve this problem. Also, sometimes he is encouraged to take more subjects as a form of enrichment of his program, rather than as an acceleration measure.

Within the past several years other methods of acceleration at the secondary-school level have evolved. One of these is early admission to college, which incidentally was not generally favored by the secondary schools when it was proposed. Although meeting with greater favor today, opposition still remains, despite the success of students who have gone through such programs and entered upon successful careers as young adults. The distinct parts of the American educational ladder have a tendency to remain exactly that—separate units—though there is much discussion of articulation and cooperative effort. Notwithstanding the excellent results of allowing gifted students to move into college, take courses that stimulate and challenge their thinking, and become productive and contributing adults at an earlier age than is customary, there remain many high-school faculties which regard the practice with disfavor.

Another recent development, the giving of college-level courses to gifted seniors in high school, has not met nearly so much opposition from the secondary school, as it is allowed to keep the students the regulation four years, and it is the college that loses a year or a course or two of the student's education. Perhaps in the last two examples of methods of acceleration, the difficulty lies in the unqualified acceptance of four years as the right and proper amount of time for both high-school and college attendance. The mere fact that such a pattern has developed in American education does not attest to its being the only possible or acceptable system of operation. The underlying question ought to be directed to what is best for the student, not what has always been the practice in the past.

A third recent application of the principle of acceleration involves admission to college with advanced standing. This possibility was touched upon previously in connection with the student's taking proficiency examinations and being allowed credit for knowledge and skills already possessed, rather than being put into a first-year course simply because he is labeled a freshman.

Some of these practices in acceleration may have seemed something like enrichment as they were explained. This is entirely possible and not a bit out of the ordinary; someone has said that any course a gifted student may follow becomes enrichment for him by the very nature of the rich experiential background which he brings to it. The division of this chapter has been made merely to clarify and simplify the presentation; the separate sections are not meant to imply that each aspect of working with gifted students is necessarily separated from other possible means. Combinations of varying amounts of acceleration and enrichment both for individuals and for groups have been practiced with results most worthwhile for the progress and development of the students enrolled in the programs. This should surely be fundamental to any instructional program designed: that the students involved derive the best in educational benefits possible at the time and under the circumstances. Mere acceleration, without any attempts at enriching the advanced classes thus entered, would not, in most cases, meet such specifications.

Advantages and Disadvantages of Acceleration

With the welfare of the students concerned uppermost in the consideration of a choice of ways of working with the gifted, it is advisable to be aware of the possible dangers as well as the probable advantages that may be expected in such programs. Neither the benefits nor the dangers occur automatically, merely because a program is called by a name such as acceleration. They will depend rather upon the ways in which the program is implemented in actual practice with the pupils involved in it.

ADVANTAGES. The weight of the evidence from research favors acceleration as not only a possible but a successful method of accommodating gifted students in the educational program. Research studies indicate that most of the fears related to accelerated progress are groundless; the students involved not only survive but appear to be better prepared and more ready for their future lives and careers. Some of the quotations given in Chapter 4 show evidence of the greater amount of success achieved by young gifted students in the very areas objectors stress as being harmed by acceleration.

There are significant values attached to a well-planned and well-executed program of acceleration. They can be stated as follows:

1. A gifted student who obviously learns more rapidly than average students is allowed to make the rapid progress of which he is capable. His development is helped rather than hindered by placing him in a grade level or a course which more nearly corresponds to his maturity level.

2. Keeping a gifted student in the same class with his age-mates and requiring him to progress only at the speed of the average may well result in the development of poor study habits. If a pupil does not have to put forth any effort to remain at the top of his class, he will be totally unprepared to meet the increased competition of high-school and college classes. He may become an underachiever and his potential be lost to him and to society. Boredom with school tasks that require no effort and seem to have no purpose to the gifted student is another possibility. Either of these could lead to emotional difficulties. Acceleration tends to prevent such eventualities.

3. Differences in ability are much less obvious when a gifted student is accelerated to a level that offers him greater stimulation rather than held back in a class of his age-mates. In the latter case both the gifted student and his average classmates can easily see who always knows the answers to questions, who need not study but still does above-average work.

4. The factor of time necessitates rapid advancement of gifted students if they are to be helped to achieve their complete professional preparation at an age young enough to enable them to use the early adult years as creative, productive ones. Without acceleration these years would be filled with school studies and preparation for careers.

5. The typical gifted youngster is quite likely to be somewhat advanced physically, socially, and emotionally as well, though not in all these respects as far beyond his chronological age as in the case of intellectual ability. He is thus able to work with older students without necessarily losing opportunities for leadership or social contacts, and to share the similar advanced interests of the older groups.

6. Since little correlation has been found to exist between the length of time spent in study of a given subject area and knowledge of it, it does not seem necessary to hold a gifted youngster to the pattern of elementary and secondary education developed in the community, whether it be eight-four or six-three-three. Keeping a gifted student with his age peers amounts to actual retardation for him; accelerating him allows him to study further with greater benefit and increased learning.

7. Acceleration, when properly conceived and carried out, provides opportunities for various studies, at any grade level or in any course. It could very well be considered enrichment for a gifted student in that it enables him to progress further, delve more deeply, and possibly to investigate areas of interest unfamiliar to him.

To conclude this discussion of the relative values of acceleration for gifted students versus regular progress through school, it seems appropriate to return to the studies of Terman.[1] He and Oden wrote:

No universal rule can be laid down governing the amount of acceleration that is desirable. Some gifted children are less injured by acceleration of three or four years than are others by one or two years. Important factors are the child's social experience and his natural aptitude for social adjustment. So far as physique is concerned, perfect health is probably less crucial than physical maturity or even mere size. The oversized, physically mature, and socially experienced child of twelve may be at less disadvantage in high school than the under-sized, immature, and socially inexperienced child of fourteen.

It is our opinion that children of 135 IQ or higher should be promoted sufficiently to permit college entrance by the age of seventeen at latest, and that a majority of this group would be better off to enter at sixteen. Acceleration to this extent is especially desirable for those who plan to complete two or more years of graduate study in preparation for a professional career.

Pressey,[2] who is a leader in research on the effects of acceleration of the gifted, goes even further in his conclusions about the values of acceleration for gifted students. He writes, "Superior students apparently have such great potentialities that even unsatisfactory methods of acceleration are better than continued holding back with the average."

He advocates that superior children should begin school earlier than the average, should be selected for advancement in elementary and secondary schools with sufficient guidance to help them make the most of their educational programs, and that they be encouraged to complete college work in three years. In view of the evidence from controlled scientific studies, this should lead to greater productivity from the superior people of the nation; with accelerated school programs, it has been shown that superior students continue to produce superior work, follow their planned programs

[1] Lewis M. Terman and Melita H. Oden, *The Gifted Child Grows Up. Twenty-five Years Follow-up of a Superior Group* (Stanford, Calif.: Stanford University Press, 1947), p. 281.

[2] Sidney L. Pressey, *Educational Acceleration, Appraisals and Basic Problems* (Columbus, Ohio: Bureau of Educational Research. Ohio State University, 1949), p. 143.

through to completion, and attain successful adulthood status earlier.

DISADVANTAGES. The main arguments advanced against the use of acceleration in educating the gifted can be summarized as follows:

1. Valuable learning experiences are not necessarily a part of a certain sequential approach to a subject. The assumption here is that a student who is accelerated will study the more advanced subject in the same way it is offered to regular students, that no changes will be made in subject content or methods of teaching in order to educate the gifted as fully as possible.

2. Skipping grades or courses may allow students to omit a needed area of understanding or the desirable development of a skill process.

3. Though gifted students may be bored by regular progress which may lead to their sitting in nonstimulating, nonchallenging classes, there are better ways of combating that boredom than by mere reduction of the time spent in class. It is contended that the teacher should provide learning experiences calculated to interest the gifted pupil and challenge his abilities. Certainly the program of the gifted child will be furthered by such activity, but this is in reality more of an argument for enrichment than against acceleration.

4. Younger students who are moved into classes with older ones may not be socially and emotionally as mature as their new classmates and may lose opportunities for leadership because of this immaturity. Many of the studies cited in Chapter 4 dealt specifically with gifted children who were underage for their academic placement at the time of the studies; it will be recalled that honors and leadership positions did not seem to be jeopardized by the comparative youth of the gifted individuals involved.

5. Younger students who are accelerated may develop personality difficulties because of being thus singled out as different from their chronological age peers. Children, like adolescents and adults, can recognize differences among

their peers without their being specifically pointed out. Ask a group of youngsters who are the best spellers, the best readers, the fastest in arithmetic, the best at playing basketball, and they will know. They do not have to be told who are the best ones in their classes as far as reliability and responsibility for work are concerned. The whole idea back of sociometric devices takes into account the fact that children in school or play groups come to know each other's qualities quite well. Intellectual ability, skill in athletics, ability to lead a group successfully—none of these is a dark secret hidden from the members of a group. The old methods of classifying children as Robins, Sparrows, and Blackbirds hid none of the differences involved from the children; they knew which was the fast, the average, the slow group. It is common to call groups X, Y, and Z—the children will understand the designations if they indicate fast- or slow-learning students. Only the teacher is fooled by such ruses, if he believes that they hide the facts from the youngsters. Thus, difference in intellectual ability is known to the individual and to the group whether he stays with his age-mates or moves to a group which is expected to be more nearly on a par with him according to mental age.

The way in which acceleration is handled may lead to some personality problems; but that way or method is in the hands of the administrative and teaching staff, and the possible dangers do not arise solely from the fact that a child is moved into another grade or another section of a class.

6. Acceleration may cause social and emotional maladjustments due to the fact that the gifted are closely associated with classmates who are older, larger, and more mature socially and emotionally. This argument is cited particularly in connection with problems of adolescence, especially dating and other boy-girl relationships. That there is validity in this argument cannot be denied. However, the fact that as a group the gifted are physically better developed and more socially mature and emotionally stable than the average pupil reduces somewhat the force of the arguments. Nevertheless, there are individual cases in which it can be shown

that acceleration, particularly when excessive, has caused social and emotional problems among the gifted.

7. Gifted children require, as do all children, sufficient time to absorb the experiences of learning and living richly and creatively. They need time to reflect upon their experiences, to absorb their learnings, to explore new areas of interest, to appreciate what they see and feel. Accelerating a gifted child takes away the time needed for these activities. This argument gives little weight to the fact that the gifted youngsters absorb so much more than average youngsters from each experience, and that one of the reasons they are designated as gifted is this very speed of intellectual processes. They do not need as much time as other youngsters do for learning skills or for creative work. They are so much more sensitive to the values of their experiences, and to the implications of their studies. One wonders if perhaps this argument might be for keeping them "children" as long as is possible; yet an inquisitive mind should surely be helped to explore and to learn rather than be engaged in some childish activity mistakenly believed to involve rich and full learning. It is no more possible to keep a youngster a child mentally than it is to stop his physical growth. It is somewhat doubtful that the construction of a model of the Colosseum will help a gifted student in his study of Latin; might it not take time that he could be applying to further and more beneficial pursuits in his actual study? Does the gifted student actually require such concreteness of study? One of his attributes is his ability to handle abstractions readily.

8. Since a child's progress in subject areas as well as in personal development may be uneven, he might not be ready for acceleration in all areas; yet in a more advanced class he would be under pressure to achieve at a higher level and standard in all of his subjects. Granted he may be at a higher level of achievement in one area than in another; this is typical of most youngsters, gifted or not. Until the specific instance is studied and causes found and remedied if possible, it should not be assumed that no acceleration is the best policy. This statement also carries a bit of the idea of want-

ing all-round development for every child; it seems quite possible that in insisting upon well-roundedness, teachers and parents may be filing off the very sharp edges that might lead to originality of thought and creative production.

9. Finally, the mere provision of more advanced or more difficult work may not give the youngster the best educational experiences for his optimum growth and development. This objection can be overcome to a large extent by the practice of individualized instruction to which most teachers are or should be committed, and which they attempt to carry out insofar as they are able under the circumstances in which they work. The fact that a gifted child is quite likely to be highly advanced in his grasp of subject matter anyway—further even than the grade level into which he may be placed when he is accelerated beyond his chronological age-mates—detracts further from this argument.

These nine statements are traditionally the ones heard from those people who argue against acceleration in any form. What does research say about the progress and development of gifted students who are accelerated? In general, there have been few serious maladjustments either socially or emotionally that can be attributed to the accelerated progress of students within reasonable limits. On the contrary, the acceleration of gifted students by a year or two has helped their personal adjustments as they worked with people who were more nearly their equals in achievement and outlook. Academically, of course, they have experienced little difficulty. They have found opportunities for leadership in extracurricular activities despite their comparative youth. They are not socially handicapped to any extent and they are enabled by wise acceleration to enter productive adult status at an earlier age.

The 1957 report of the Fund for the Advancement of Education includes this provocative statement, which is apparently not often considered by those who speak against moderate acceleration for gifted students:

It is much too early yet to predict the future of the early admission idea, but the evidence in this report clearly indicates that under the proper circumstances it represents a promising approach to the problem of enabling the very best students to realize their full potential. The risks of entering college early have been the subject of much popular concern, and properly so. But too little thought has been given to the risks run by an able student in an unchallenging environment in *not* entering college early.[3] [Italics in original]

This study as well as several of those cited in Chapter 4 seem to stress a concern for graduating the gifted students at a younger age than normal, for getting them into the productive adult status earlier than usual, and the emphasis may be somewhat puzzling to the reader. Why should it be considered necessary to show concern for getting gifted students started in their adult careers sooner than other persons?

There has been some research within the past decade which seems to indicate that by and large the most productive years are those of young adulthood. Creation, discovery, invention—all seem to occur more often early in life than later. To hold an obviously gifted person to the normal rate of progress through elementary and secondary school, through college and graduate study, would tend to use these creative years in completing an educational program rather than in freeing them for productive achievement. Pressey[4] refers to this as "the concept of prime as the period of peak total biological potentialities." As programs of graduate study consume more of the gifted student's years they also subtract from the number of years in which he might well be engaged in creative work to the benefit of society as well as himself. Historically there seems to have been a trend toward lengthening the time required for professional careers; if the concept of early productivity has any valid basis, surely educational programs should not be lengthened, particularly for gifted individuals. The studies made by Pressey[5] on accelerated progress tend to support this viewpoint. He suggests that:

---

[3] Fund for the Advancement of Education. *They Went to College Early* (Evaluation Report No. 2 [New York: The Fund, 1957]), p. 90.

[4] Pressey, *op. cit.*, p. 37.

[5] *Ibid.*, p. 134.

The need for much greater flexibility of programs, and especially for greater opportunities for superior students, seems patent. Since, in general, the abler young persons tend in all respects to mature somewhat more rapidly than the average, to be in fact far ahead in educational attainment, and to continue into advanced training, ways by which they might more readily accelerate their educational pace seem needed.

ENRICHMENT

Enrichment, by the very nature of the word structure itself, must involve something that is valuable and desirable. The act of enriching should supply worthwhile elements or ingredients to produce finer quality in that which is being enriched. Familiar applications of enrichment include bread and Vitamin D enriched milk. In the classroom, enrichment ought also to supply some wealth or richness to the learning of the students.

Enrichment develops and enhances the learning experiences of gifted students in such a way as to add both breadth and depth of meaning beyond what is normally acquired by the typical student. Enrichment involves more than merely good teaching; the greater ability of gifted students to grasp more fully, see abstract relationships, and understand quickly, interacts with the teaching to develop a richer, more meaningful, and more valuable learning situation for the participants. The same good teaching when presented to and developed with students of average ability would not produce comparable results, as the average students do not bring as much to contribute to the teaching-learning process as do the gifted.

Enrichment can also include learning experiences beyond those expected of average students. It may consist of additional and different subjects or topics of use and interest to the gifted. It need not be limited to greater depth and breadth of study but can involve differences in kind as well as degree.

Enrichment really ought not to be considered as a certain program to be followed by gifted students. Such a designation belies the concept that good instruction ought to be based on knowledge of the needs, interests, problems, and abilities of the persons involved; it tends to allow the program to take precedence, rather than consideration of what beneficial effects the pupils may derive from it. The students themselves must remain central to the learning; what is enrichment for one may be totally unnecessary, boring, or even frustrating to another. Good enrichment does not consist of a series of planned exercises through which each student progresses in a certain sequence; that is merely another educational lock step and should not be dignified by the name of enrichment.

It might be well to mention several other things enrichment is not, before getting to specific examples of the ways in which enrichment can be used properly in public-school classes. Enriching is not requiring the gifted student to produce eight compositions in the same time that average students write five; it is not assigning him several more pages of problems of the same type; it is not requiring reading in "spare" time after regular classwork is satisfactorily completed; it is not having him work puzzles or play spelling games with another student; it is not asking him to carry messages for the teacher, or act as a monitor, or clean the chalk board and the erasers. Enrichment is not merely extra work provided for the explicit purpose of keeping a gifted youngster occupied during school hours.

Enrichment must be carefully planned. Both the teacher and the individual student must understand the purposes, the plans to be followed, the goals to be reached, and the devices and techniques to be used for evaluating the completed job as well as the steps in progress. For an experience to be enriching for the gifted pupil, there must be much more involved than merely a haphazard "go find yourself something to do" approach.

Enrichment cannot be valuable if it is a casual, unplanned, or one-shot effort. It should be so organized as to help a given youngster develop his known abilities, explore further his professed interests, delve into areas that may provide new and profitable interests, and increase his knowledge and understanding of himself, his society, his world, and his personal ability to contribute to a good life. Enrichment as a title cannot be given to plans which upon analysis involve nothing more than busy work for the youngsters. Enrichment must consist of valuable activities unless it is to be completely misused, and degenerate into a contradiction of terms.

Individual Enrichment

ENRICHMENT IN REGULAR CLASSES. The enrichment of instruction for youngsters in their regular classrooms with their own age-group and their regular teacher is favored as a method of working with gifted students by those who fear accelerated programs and any special kind of grouping beyond that which occurs inside the classroom as the teacher attempts to develop efficient ways of handling large classes of children. Grouping children for instruction within their regular classes seems somehow more acceptable. It may be because such groups change: some are task-centered; some are interest groups; some are ability groups; some are friendship groups. The basis for these groups depends upon the activity being pursued at a particular time. Grouping whole classes on the other hand seems more objectionable to some because it assumes a rigidity of structure which may not be conducive to teaching and learning in the most effective manner. The idea of ability grouping in particular has the tendency to cause some persons to raise strenuous objections based on somewhat nebulous conceptions of equality and democracy.

There are also those who insist, however, that if there is to be special work for any of the children, it should be offered to all of them. This feeling also seems to stem from a faulty conception of equality of opportunity.

Enrichment within the class certainly causes the least disturbance to administration, as the burden for developing and carrying out plans for enrichment falls upon each individual teacher. He must first be sufficiently concerned about the progress of his gifted students to desire to help them develop as best they can; he must also be prepared to devote the necessary time and energy to organizing special activities designed to help each student grow intellectually, socially, and emotionally. One should not be so naïve as to believe that such efforts just happen as a good teacher works with good students; behind the scenes and after school hours much hard work must be given to planning activities, gathering materials, and learning about each student, so that the most helpful activities can be devised with and for him. Good teaching does not just happen, though observations of good teachers at work may lead uninformed persons to that opinion; good teachers do appear to teach easily, but they have undoubtedly put in many hours of preparation for the particular activities that may be seen under way in their classrooms. It is not purely luck that they just happen to have appropriate materials at hand, or know which suggestions seem most fruitful, or are able to name people and places which can be used as resources to gather needed information. These things happen too consistently in the classroom work of good teachers to be accounted for by mere chance.

Enrichment for gifted pupils in the regular classroom then involves much hard and extra effort on the part of the teacher. What else does it entail? First and perhaps most obvious of all the requirements of an enrichment policy is the absolute necessity of having a wide variety of useful materials available at all times. Gone are the days when teachers can confidently assume that for each subject taught one set of textbooks geared to a certain level of reading comprehension is sufficient for the needs of the students in any class —elementary, secondary, or collegiate. Beginning with first grade and continuing throughout college and adult life there is evidence of wide individual differences in reading ability alone, not to mention the many other differences in abilities and interests evident among groups of people of like chronological age. The assumption that the same textbook will prove satisfactory for every student enrolled in a class is false. It may perhaps be used as a starting point but it should not be the only source available to the students as they attempt to develop their understanding of the subject.

Let us assume for purposes of discussion that all six-year-olds do enter school at the same level of understanding, even though this is contrary to fact. If all beginners are exactly alike in their readiness to read, for example, good teaching plus the varying abilities of the pupils to learn will tend to develop differences among the youngsters very soon. It can even be said that the better the teaching, the wider the spread will be as each youngster is helped to progress at the speed of which he is capable. Enrichment, like good teaching, will tend to increase differences, to increase the spread between the most and least able of the classroom group. It is not uncommon to find classes in secondary schools wherein there may be a spread or range of as many as nine years in reading ability alone. The idea of providing one and the same textbook for each of these students becomes farcical when looked at in terms of the realities of the situation. Since it is a comic and yet tragic occurrence in regular classrooms, how much more serious an offense to the children such procedure becomes when among those of varying individual differences can be found a student or two of very high I.Q.

There must be reading materials at many levels of comprehension dealing with the various topics the class is expected to study, and these must have equal status and acceptance value as "the text" for the course. There must also be many sources of reference available for the students' use within the classroom and for their borrowing for use in their homes. A resourceful teacher will have begun collections of many sorts of otherwise fugitive materials in addition to pamphlets and booklets that can be used by the students in their work. If there is money available for him to use for the purchase of instructional materials he will choose carefully to make the best use of the amount he has to spend so that the classroom collection will have maximum value.

Beyond these there ought also to be a well-supplied library with a librarian who understands her function as a resource person for the ongoing learning of the students. This may be a school library, used by all pupils in the school building. If there is not that facility, use may be made of the public library or the traveling bookmobile whose staff will be eager to help locate and distribute the kinds of books the youngsters must have for an enriched school program. A trained and interested librarian is a most valuable asset to the gifted students and their teacher. She can help with their free reading choices as well as their choices of books applicable to their studies.

Though the need for books has been discussed first and stressed heavily this must not be misunderstood as implying that books are the only materials of instruction which can add enrichment. Books of all sorts *are* required: dictionaries, atlases, biographies, encyclopedias, and books on the many subjects to be studied. These should be at many reading levels with emphasis on the higher levels of interpretation and viewpoint to carry the gifted student further into his studies and understanding. But there should also be audio-visual materials—slides, films, filmstrips, pictures, models, maps, charts, phonograph records, tapes, and the equipment for using these—to show specifically the important points and phases of a topic or a field of study.

In a self-contained elementary classroom one would expect to find live materials as well as inanimate ones. There will be need to have living plants and animals for the children to observe, learn from and about, and experiment with during the year. In a primary classroom there will be things to experiment with as well—things to build with, to manipulate, to control and to structure. The less structured these materials are in their original forms, the more creative uses the children can make of them. In nearly any classroom there should also be supplies to carry out artistic expression of ideas.

Rather than continuing to list the specifics needed for the education of gifted children in a regular classroom, it would be wise to look at the implications of this brief presentation. One stands out: the mere having of such items in a classroom implies a need for space in which they can be stored and space in which they can be used. This, in turn, implies also some flexible type of classroom furniture which can be so arranged as to make room for the many items essential to the pupils' learning. It also implies classes of a size which can be handled in small teachable groups and in which methods involving a greater degree of individual instruction than is typical can be used. The third implication increases the difficulty for the teacher as the enrichment proves profitable, and the students require continually increasing amounts of individual instruction if they are to progress to their optimum levels of development.

Another question may have occurred to the student: why are such items and the myriad others that have not been specified required? What are the goals of a policy of enrichment in the regular classroom? The existence of goals is certainly implicit in the insistence upon a variety of useful aids to learning. Explicitly these goals include:

1. Stress upon independent work
2. Development of initiative and creativity
3. Emphasis upon skills of learning and habits of research
4. Insistence upon high standards of achievement
5. Individual attention to the pupils by the teacher
6. Increasing the students' ability to use knowledge as well as to secure it
7. Wide reading plus plenty of valuable direct experience
8. Learning to plan carefully and to share the outcomes of research projects
9. Development of increased inner motivation to continue to learn
10. Development of feelings of social responsibility
11. Development of leadership abilities

A further question involves whether or not these should be and in fact are the expressed goals applicable to the best educational program for all students, assuming that each would develop in each area to the best of his ability. With this, the writers would not argue; surely there should be as effective an instructional program as can be devised for all students, given the materials, the abilities of the teachers and the students, and the support by the administration that prevails in any particular set of circumstances. The goals for the education of the gifted do not differ significantly from general educational goals. The difference lies in the emphasis which is placed on those goals which promise greatest rewards in connection with the education of superior students.

Many specific suggestions as to how these goals may be achieved or approached by the gifted child in the regular classroom have been made in the growing literature of the field. Examples of such publications include: 97 *Ideas for Classroom Teachers to Use with Gifted Children (Primary Grades, and Intermediate and Upper Grades)*, from the Portland, Oregon, Public Schools; *The Gifted Child in the Regular Classroom*, by Marian Scheifele; *Curriculum Enrichment for Gifted Elementary School Children in Regular Classes*, edited by Henry J. Otto and used as a curriculum bulletin in the Austin, Texas, Public Schools; and Birch and McWilliams' *Challenging Gifted Children*. Each of these contains a wealth of suggestions that can be valuable to the teacher searching for ideas for ways in which he can improve and enrich the program for the gifted in his classroom. The ideas must, of course, be evaluated in terms of the goals to be achieved and the specific youngsters involved; they ought not to be applied as recipes supposed to produce excellent results regardless of the differences of these ingredients in each classroom program.

Actually there is no limit to the activities which may be planned and worked out as enrichment except those limitations which are due to the teacher's lack of imagination, lack of facilities or equipment, or the lack of time to pursue and develop such activities. A gifted student can usually do the work of his regular grade in half the time ordinarily devoted to it, so enrichment will not use time required for regular studies. He may then have supplementary or additional work to pursue involving reading, creative projects, experimentation in science and other fields, independent study in areas of interest, interviews and consultations with experts in the fields he is studying, further work to develop knowledge of and skills in research—the possibilities are limitless insofar as the child's program is concerned.

Enrichment within the regular classroom seems to possess many advantages:

1. It eliminates fears resulting from beliefs about harmful acceleration and harmful special grouping, so it is the least controversial of the methods for educating gifted children.
2. It is a part of each teacher's normal work as he tries to provide for the individual differences of all the youngsters enrolled in his class.
3. It helps gifted youngsters to learn to work with others of all levels and thus develops their understanding of others of varying level of intelligence.
4. It develops leadership as the gifted take the roles of which they are naturally capable in the class group; it thus develops democratic values.
5. It allows the average to profit from the stimulation offered by the gifted.
6. It helps the child develop intellectually, socially, and emotionally at his own rate, with whatever unevenness of abilities and growth he may display.
7. It requires a minimum of administrative effort or change except perhaps in an in-service program to help teachers learn to utilize opportunities for enrichment for the gifted.
8. In small school systems it is possibly the only feasible way of working with the few gifted boys and girls who are enrolled.
9. As teachers become more aware of enrichment possibilities for the gifted, the instructional program for all children is improved.

Each of these items seems plausible considered alone as a simple statement. However, not all of these so-called advantages can be accepted as truth, since they do not take into account all the facts which impinge upon them. The main purpose of any program should be to offer the best possible education to all the youngsters involved; these statements of advantages do not take into account what actually and unfortunately happens in most classrooms where all children are expected to learn together regardless of intelligence or any other individual differences.

The main disadvantage of relying exclusively upon enrichment in the classroom program to provide for the education of gifted children was stated most succinctly by Carroll,[6] a leading psychologist, in 1940 when he wrote:

> The principal objection to enrichment for gifted children in the heterogeneous class is that in most cases it fails to work. Teachers are human beings with all the failings of human beings. Consequently most of them prefer teaching procedures which require the least amount of time. They find it much easier to treat the class as a unit than as a loosely organized group of subgroups and individuals.

Obviously such a program as that outlined to explain enrichment in the regular classroom is not the easiest for teachers or students to follow. It takes much work and much time on the part of both. Good results can and do occur from enrichment in regular classes; they do not occur purely automatically but only with concentrated effort expended by those involved.

ENRICHMENT BY SPECIAL TEACHERS. Another way of developing enrichment for gifted individuals involves the use of a special teacher. In this plan a gifted student may do his regular grade work in the classroom with his age-mates and his grade teacher, and then engage in enrichment activities with a special teacher for the remainder of the day. By using extra teachers such competencies as they possess can be utilized in working individually with the gifted. These competencies may be in many subject fields, but the instruction involved is individualized to suit the project, study, or investigation being made by the student under the special teacher's guidance and direction.

The special teacher must possess many skills; it would be futile for him to attempt to teach French as an enrichment class, for example, were he not able to use that language himself, and to teach it effectively. He ought to know not

---

[6] Herbert A. Carroll, *Genius in the Making* (New York: McGraw-Hill Book Co., 1940), pp. 246-47.

only the subject but the best of methods in helping young-sters to learn it, such as the aural-oral approach to the study of modern languages.

In addition to being fully prepared with subjects and methods of teaching, the special teacher should certainly understand the youngsters with whom he is working—their motivations, skills, personal attributes, and feelings. He must be alert to the variations of method and curriculum which are most appropriate for gifted children; teaching French to elementary youngsters involves a great deal more than a mere watering down of the regular high-school French class methods and content. In fact, there should be no feeling of watering down any subject in which gifted students are con-cerned; their interests and abilities tend to make necessary a far more solid approach. Less drill will be required, though this definitely is not to say that no drill will be needed. For another thing, gifted children can respond rapidly to a mini-mum of suggestion and direction; they grasp almost im-mediately what is said, and they can usually work profitably for long periods of time without constant checking or over-seeing of their progress. The teacher must be there for needed help; he must not halt the learning process of the gifted by unnecessary interference.

The plan offers help to the regular teacher as well, in that he is released to a degree from the requirement of providing individual instruction in all areas for all of his pupils. He still must, of course, provide for the differences the children show in their regular classroom work, and he must also in some way develop his program so that the gifted student who is out of the classroom for as much as half a day does not skip or miss any vital instruction in a new skill or process which he introduces.

This plan involves a high degree of staff cooperation and planning if it is to operate effectively. Ideally there should be sufficient time for the teachers to plan together so that the work each does is known to the other, and each can supple-ment and reinforce so that the youngster receives the great-est possible benefits from the instruction of both. The special teacher will require time to study the students and to learn about them from their present behavior as well as their past records. He must be as fully aware of the student's needs, problems, interests, and abilities as the regular teacher is, if the special work is to be a real contribution to the child's total development. He ought not to see him only as an art pupil, or a science pupil, or a student of French. He needs the whole picture in order to develop an effective program of supplementary enrichment.

The regular teacher must accept and support the program wholeheartedly. He must realize his own inadequacies and accept the fact that his gifted students can learn some things from him and other things from other teachers. He must back the program. His attitudes will be quickly sensed by his pupils; if faulty, they may sabotage the possible worth of such a divided program. This support of the program is also necessary for the special teacher; he, too, must realize that the whole purpose is for the child to receive benefits from each of his teachers.

Administrative backing and arrangement are, of course, fundamental to the success of the special teacher plan. Without this, few programs have a chance to succeed. There will be the special teacher himself, whose hiring and position may increase the pupil loads of each regular teacher; there must be some rooms and equipment available for the special teacher to work in and to use; he will need some time in which to examine the records of his students, and some space in which he may work with them as individuals. He will probably be working with much smaller groups than those of the regular teachers and often with only one or two children. All these factors require explanation and understanding support by the faculty and the administration.

Effective operation of the special teacher plan for enrichment requires much staff cooperation; petty jealousies must be set aside. The development of the skills and abilities of the gifted pupil is paramount, and the teachers must work together to that end. The special teacher plan and the regular class plan for enrichment may be combined to produce a better program than can be achieved by either plan in itself. This combination is a logical one since the special teacher can be most helpful in planning regular classroom work with the regular teachers and supplementing their efforts in his own program.

Group Enrichment

Unfortunately, it is rare to find regular classrooms where enrichment of the curriculum actually operates to educate gifted students to their optimum capacities. With few exceptions, the only places in which enrichment functions as it should are those in which groups of children are especially organized for that purpose.

SPECIAL SCHOOLS. At the present stage of development in programs designed to offer the best possible education to gifted students, the special schools devoted wholly to the gifted represent the most complete programs. In such schools, of which Hunter College Elementary School in New York City is a well-known example, the entire pupil population is composed of gifted students. Every class in the building is an enrichment class and the teachers are selected for their ability to profitably carry out enriched learning experiences with the youngsters.

At the secondary level, New York City offers several special high schools designed to further the growth of students gifted in many areas, such as science, the arts, journalism, the theater arts, music, and the like. Other cities have developed somewhat similar programs, though their high schools are not as many in number nor as varied in specializations offered.

In a special school of this nature the gifted student is segregated from those of average and below-average intelligence. However, the schools are not the only agency in which youngsters have contact with other people; there are the churches, scout groups, and other community organizations in which youngsters meet and deal with all kinds of people. Students of special schools are not completely cut off from others, though one objection to special schools is based on that assumption. Further, it may be that associating with people at all levels of intelligence is not quite as necessary as is sometimes assumed in preparing a gifted youngster for life.

Choices are made in adult associations as well as in childhood; the argument that the gifted should stay with average and below-average pupils in schools because they will then be prepared to work with them later may not hold as much truth as is sometimes credited to it.

It is difficult to discover what school grade a youngster is in when he attends one of these special schools. He cannot fairly be compared with youngsters of a specific grade level in another school because his schoolwork differs from theirs. He has greater opportunity for enrichment and for rapid progress; he studies the basic skills, of course, but he is not held to the specific work considered as right and proper for a certain grade level according to the course of study. In the special school a teacher must actually be prepared to accept each child where he is in any area of learning and development, and carry him to the farthest points of which he is capable during the time they work together. Though this is often expressed verbally as a goal for all youngsters and all teachers, few regular classes demonstrate it in actual practice. One school which believed in and tried to practice enrichment in depth and breadth also had a hands-off policy insofar as the established and accepted work of the next grade was concerned. After all, if a child had already learned the eighth-grade work in the seventh grade, what could his eighth-grade teacher do with him? This is a real problem for many schools, and one which must be faced by administration, faculty, students, and parents. Again, if a student can profitably study and absorb and apply in his writing the principles governing the punctuation of divided quotations in sixth grade, who shall say that he ought not be taught these until the eighth? Is this not retardation? And does it not militate against the best interests of the gifted student?

Articulation between grade levels has been touched upon, and another problem to be considered is the articulation between elementary and secondary schools. A student who has pursued an enriched curriculum plan throughout elementary school will obviously have had many more experiences and gathered a greater store of useful knowledge about many more things than a youngster who has followed the ordinary curriculum of the greater number of public schools. To put them together in classes in secondary schools and expect them to perform in the same way and proceed at the same pace is thoughtless and lacks consideration for the best progress of each group. It does not represent very good educational practice, either. To solve the problem involved here, some high schools have developed sections for each subject offered and have divided their students on the basis of knowledge of their abilities, both intellectual and scholastic, derived from previous performance and test scores. As high schools may draw pupils from a number of elementary schools, and they have a larger population to subdivide, this is one possibility, though if the groups are rigidly selected and a student cannot shift from one to another according to his ability in various subjects, there are obvious objections to such a plan.

The actual class work of the youngsters in special schools for the gifted is very like that in special classes. They learn basic skills, pursue individual interests, use research methods, evaluate their work, read widely, and investigate many subjects and topics as a group as well as individually. They require talented teachers and many material resources to carry out their school program. The schoolwork is geared to the specific youngsters involved in the program, with the final goal being that of helping the gifted to develop to their optimum capacity.

The children know they are gifted; they are certainly not so unaware or insensitive as to fail to recognize that they are somewhat different from others in their ability to learn. They usually possess a sensitivity to social problems and can be helped to realize their obligations in helping to solve those problems. This does not imply that six-year-olds will be made aware of substandard housing conditions in their school and expected to do something about them; there is little value in pushing sensitive youngsters into problems over which they know they can have little influence. However, this feeling of awareness and desire to improve unsatisfactory situations can be effectively developed in the special school at the child's continually increasing level of understanding, and the responsibility for the welfare of his school can be translated into social responsibility which may be formed and fostered in the special school.

SPECIAL CLASSES. Special classes for the entire program of the education of gifted youngsters have been established and maintained by cities recognized as leaders in their work with the gifted. Cleveland's plan of Major Work classes is probably the best known among them; having been organized in 1921, it is one of the earliest recorded. New York City operates both rapid progress classes and intellectually gifted classes, each of which involves some enrichment of the gifted students' school studies.

When gifted children are selected for special classes, there is usually much more involved as basis for selection than an I.Q. measurement, though this is of course one of the factors to be considered. Others are social maturity, emotional stability, physical health and size, and, of course, the scholastic achievement. The judgments of parents and teachers are considered also, on the question of whether or not working in a special class would be the most effective way of educating each gifted individual. Docility and tractability of the child, two traits that may make teaching him an easier job, may not be indicative of a need for a special class; problem behavior related to lack of satisfying programs may also be a factor in deciding whether or not a certain child may profit from a special class. Not all of the factors noted in this paragraph may be positive characteristics; it may be that a child's social maturity or emotional growth have been hampered by his experiences in a regular classroom, and the decision for placing him in a special group made as an attempt to promote better growth in these areas, as well as in the academic field.

Special classes for gifted children do not represent complete homogeneous grouping. Despite the fact that the youngsters in a gifted class will be superior intellectually, they are still individuals and will have many differences. They are not merely to be taught as a group for whom sights are raised, more achievement is expected, and greater creative productivity is anticipated. They are individual persons requiring a great amount of individual instruction suited to their individual needs, problems, interests, and abilities. About the only way to get a really homogeneous group is to consider each child as an individual. Even though I.Q. test scores, reading achievement scores, personality traits, and the like may be similar, differences within the group of youngsters remain, and must be taken into account as the teaching-learning process is developed.

The purpose of segregating gifted students into special classes is to provide opportunities for enrichment, to help bright youngsters to develop their abilities, and to provide them with the intellectual stimulation offered by other gifted students. They should gain a rich background of information and develop creativity and originality of working and thinking. The mere organization of special classes does not guarantee these results, but it does set a situation in which pupils can be guided in their achievement much more adequately than they are in regular classrooms. The special class for the gifted also stimulates continued growth in every area of the child's school studies; it removes the distinction between regular work and enrichment classes, when each of these is operated on a part-time schedule.

Segregating gifted children in special classes also encourages hiring teachers who are sympathetic to the needs of the gifted, who have shown ability and interest in developing their capabilities, and who can teach them effectively, making use of the many resources needed in such a program, and capitalizing upon the resources offered by the gifted students themselves. These teachers should be able to develop a curriculum as they work with the youngsters in the classroom; they ought not to be bound to the course of study or the curriculum guide planned for regular classes. They must be flexible in their work and receptive to the ideas and suggestions the gifted can offer to help develop their own programs and augment their progress.

When these special classes are located in classrooms of regular schools, the gifted youngsters have opportunities to participate in the all-school activities such as the assemblies, the student government program, the safety patrol, and the clubs and hobby activities, and in some cases regular classes in such subjects as home economics and physical education. They are not cut off from contact with average and below-average students; they work with them in the various organizations that are offered to all the pupils of the school. They do make much greater progress in their studies than the other pupils do, and they benefit from these special classes enormously. They learn to make worthwhile contributions to the all-school programs, and the average students can learn to appreciate such help. Some school systems try to avoid "brain" or "egghead" classifications and distinctions by having at least two gifted classes in a school building designated as an attendance center for children who are gifted. Research indicates that even in regular classrooms gifted students produce better work and are emotionally more stable when there are two or more such children in the class group; they seem to derive emotional satisfaction and moral support from their intellectual peers.

Obviously the materials and equipment suggested as necessary for general enrichment are required in these special enrichment classrooms. The youngsters cannot work profitably without these extra facilities, and they can be quite helpful in collecting materials, and competent in organizing them to best advantage for their classroom use.

SEMINARS. Seminar programs are carried on for the most part in junior and senior high schools although there is no reason they cannot be conducted in the elementary school on a modified basis. In such case they would assume the nature of a part-time special class with a special teacher, meeting either during or after class hours and in addition to the regular class program. When the gifted child is taken from his regular elementary classroom for such work he ordinarily has no difficulty in keeping up with his regular classmates, so such absence is not likely to create any problem. It is usually better for these special groups or classes to meet during regular school hours; both pupils and special teachers would be inconvenienced by excessive after-school hours.

Once again it is possible to use a special teacher, but here he works with groups of students rather than almost entirely with individuals. These special part-time enrichment classes can be made up of pupils from more than one grade level in order to develop a group of workable size.

In some cities the enrichment classes are organized as workshop groups. The Colfax plan in Pittsburgh segregates the gifted for intensive study of skill subjects and allows the youngsters to work with their regular classes for special subjects such as art, music, and physical education. The classrooms in which the workshop groups meet have little equipment beyond that found in an ordinary classroom except for typewriters and microscopes. The experimental or laboratory methods of learning used involve the problem approach in group study and individual projects. The actual work pursued by the youngsters includes the topics and skills expected of all children and delineated in the study guides for the public schools. The children have the opportunity to expand these topics and explore related issues as well as to pursue individual and small group interests in addition to the regular work of the grade level.

The actual subjects that these elementary groups investigate with their special teachers depend to a large extent upon the interests and problems of the gifted pupils themselves. The topics may have vocational or avocational value; they will be socially significant, as this kind of interest is usually a characteristic of gifted children. They are concerned deeply with social issues, and of course can pursue their studies far more beneficially and understandingly than can average students.

The gifted students flourish much more noticeably with helpful guidance and direction than they do with a dominant teacher who holds the reins of the classroom procedures tightly in his own hands. It is not necessary that he know everything about every topic that may be studied; this is obviously an impossibility. He must be willing to work with and to learn with the students; teaching is not merely the imparting of knowledge. He is trying to help these students develop their own understanding of society and of themselves. This can be achieved much more effectively as they grow in ability to help with the planning and evaluation of each project and activity. This does not imply a laissez-faire approach; that is just about as faulty as a heavily autocratic one. Development of self-direction requires some opportunities for practicing self-direction, not merely reliance upon what someone else offers as direction. This implies a teacher who can guide and direct valuable learning experiences with youngsters as they learn to be more and more responsible for their progress and for themselves. It is admittedly more difficult to teach in such a manner; it is so easy to "tell the answer" in reponse to a question. Yet the student's learning is not helped nearly so much by telling as by helping him to discover for himself. The special teacher ought not be considered an oracle or a fountain of knowledge to be consulted at each turn; he is a guide to seeking knowledge rather than a dispenser of ultimate authority on every question.

French or other modern languages have been mentioned as examples of subject matter for the part-time enrichment class to be taught by a special teacher. All kinds of art activities, music, science, reading and discussion of books, creative writing—almost any activity that is ordinarily classified as a subject—may also be used as the basis for such a class as well as the interests of the youngsters referred to previously. In fact, though gifted students will gain a great deal from the subject of the enrichment, that in itself may not be the primary gain; developing the skills and abilities listed previously as goals for enrichment may have greater and more far-reaching significance to the student.

Advantages of the seminar or part-time special class plan in educating gifted children in the elementary school seem somewhat similar to those sought when the special teacher deals with the gifted individually. It lightens the tasks of the regular teacher by helping him meet the individual differences with which he must deal, and it strengthens the program offered to the gifted. The gifted benefit by learning of their capabilities and how to use these to greater advantage. They work with others who are intellectual peers, and they find they must work hard; they cannot get by in a seminar with minimum study as they may be able to do in a regular class. Time and effort are devoted specifically to the gifted; they are not so likely to be neglected as in a regular classroom situation where the teacher must deal with the lower levels of ability represented in the class. They can investigate thoughtfully areas in which they can profit by the competencies of the special teacher, competencies which their regular teacher may not possess or may not be able to bring to bear upon their learning, burdened as he is with children at so many levels of development. The gifted are not held back to the average pace, and they are much less likely to get an overestimated idea of their own worth because they face their intellectual peers. As they do not require a full school day to complete their regular work, the special teacher plan for part-time enrichment classes urges them to work rapidly and fully in both areas, and they are less likely to become underachievers.

Since these advantages can be shown to be valid by studies of youngsters learning in such a plan, there seems no question of its value. The question is rather whether the seminar or part-time special class plan offers sufficient stimulation to the gifted student, or whether he should be with his intellectual peers throughout all of his school program. Those who believe the latter plan more valuable have established full-time special classes and special schools for gifted children.

At the secondary-school level the special teacher may be supplemented from time to time in the seminar by professional and business men such as chemists, physicists, doctors, medical researchers, accountants, public relations men, and others who are interested in meeting with bright young men and women to discuss problems and issues and provide new insights and information for the group. In some cases, the special teacher may spend most of his time arranging for materials and seminar leadership and a minimum of time actually conducting the seminar. The utilization of such valuable resources as those represented by an insurance executive who might lead a series of seminars on the theory and practice of insurance is possible under this plan.

In one reported case, an industrial chemist not only provided seminar leadership but demonstrated by the use of chemicals the actual process of paper-making and followed up the seminar with an arrangement for the group to tour the paper-making plant.

The skillful special teacher can organize these seminars around the interests of the students, and by utilizing human and material resources of the community, provide rich and challenging learning experiences for the gifted group. While such seminars may be held during daylight hours, evenings have proven more satisfactory in many communities because of the greater availability of nonschool leadership. Saturday mornings also prove satisfactory since school classrooms and laboratories can be made completely available without conflict with other school classes.

GROUPING THE GIFTED FOR INSTRUCTION

Advantages

There are many obvious advantages to placing gifted children in groups made up only of the gifted. They can be listed as follows:

1. The gifted can work at their own speed and within their own abilities. The program can be planned to achieve these ends without their being obliged to wait for the slower students. The individual needs of each gifted student can be more easily met when the teacher is not held responsible for slower students at the same time he is expected to teach gifted ones.

2. The gifted student can obtain a better perspective of his own worth, his actual potential, when he is with other students of superior ability; in a regular class he might feel

superior to the others without having to put forth definite effort. Here, his abilities and potential can be challenged to a greater degree.

3. An enrichment policy for the special classes (or special schools) makes possible full learning experiences without pushing a gifted youngster beyond his depth socially or emotionally. Since children may be uneven in areas of development, special classes can offer them a greater degree of support and intellectual stimulation, while at the same time avoiding harmful effects of overacceleration, and habits of careless preparation for their studies.

4. In a special group gifted students can explore their ideas and activities and may experiment with various media of expression without sacrificing group acceptance as may be the case in the regular class. Studies have indicated that gifted children support one another as they work together.

5. The rich knowledge and experiential background of each gifted student spurs the individuals and the group to increased learning. The gifted act as an added stimulus upon each other, as does the much richer curriculum which can be provided for them in special groups.

6. The special class makes feasible the hiring of a teacher who is specially qualified to teach gifted students, and can guide them in valuable learning experiences. He can develop a good intellectual environment for them and give much attention to helping them learn how to study as well as to learn many things they would not acquire in a regular class.

7. Special classes can provide for rapid progress as well as an enriched learning environment; more challenging activities can be developed by a flexible program.

8. Grouping the gifted provides better opportunities for developing leadership and the ability to follow as the students work both together and individually.

9. Grouping gifted students into one section is beneficial to the other students of a school too; average students are thus allowed greater opportunities to exercise the leadership of which they are capable. They have been known to develop better attitudes toward their schoolwork and to show greater

achievement when they are not so consistently thrown up against the superior achievements of the gifted students, as occurs in the regular classroom.

10. Grouping by special classes is a tried and tested method of organizing students for the best instructional program, to develop each student to his fullest potential.

Disadvantages

The traditional objection to grouping students on the basis of intellectual ability, even when as in any worthwhile program other factors are considered, has been that such grouping is undemocratic in that it extends special privileges to some students. These special privileges, if that is what grouping offers, have been extended to crippled children, to youngsters who need sight-saving classes, to those hard-of-hearing or deaf, to delicate children, and to those who cannot learn very much—not everyone immediately wishes to take advantage of those special privileges. Perhaps the reason is related to the fact that such children have fewer advantages, have less of the natural endowments than most. "Equality" of treatment, that is, educational programs planned for average children, can be seen to be totally ineffective for those atypical youngsters who by reason of heredity or accident are patently unable to benefit from such programs. When the differences appear at the positive end of the scale, cries of concern about democracy, equality, and fair play, come forth.

Someone said long ago that there is nothing quite so unequal as the equal treatment of unequals. Unequal treatment appears acceptable when the inequality is observable as a deficiency; when it is a proficiency somewhat beyond what most humans possess, there are objections to providing special education for its development. A gifted child typically is not a pathetic-looking individual who immediately arouses sympathy among those who see him. People are unfortunately less prone to accept the fact that he too requires help and additional educational opportunities to develop to his fullest, for the good of the society as well as for his own benefit. Is not providing only one scheme of education, geared to the average, and forcing its acceptance upon all, unpalatable in this day when teachers are supposed to be caring for individual differences of the youngsters whom they teach? Might it not also be conferring special privileges upon the average, to the detriment of the gifted child and his talents?

In addition to this traditional objection, other disadvantages of special groupings are cited by those who speak against that method of helping gifted students to achieve to their fullest. These further objections include:

1. Special groups for the gifted promote snobbery and conceit among the gifted. In other words, in a group in which gifted students are challenged constantly both by the program and by the performances of other gifted children, they would develop feelings of self-importance beyond any reasonable cause. It seems more likely that this result would occur from their staying in regular classes where their superiority to the others would be continually evident.

2. Grouping, especially in entire schools devoted to the education of the gifted, prevents the students from having rich school life, participating in many activities with many other people. This may become a problem, but it seems to be an administrative one rather than a natural result of grouping for the gifted. Provisions can be made for their association with other students at varying levels of ability through extraclass activities.

3. Leadership opportunities are limited in a special group in which all may have leadership potential, but fewer opportunities to practice and develop skills in this area. Not all gifted children are so constituted as to become leaders; one of the purposes of the special group is to develop greater opportunities for followership as well as leadership. A further assumption seems to be that in a regular class there exists relatively greater opportunity to develop leadership. Such an assumption would be difficult to prove; in fact, most evidence is to the contrary.

4. Average children suffer from the lack of stimulation afforded them by the gifted when the gifted are removed

from regular classrooms. Average children are as likely to be discouraged by the presence of gifted students in the class because of the unfavorable comparison. When the teacher has a narrower range of differences to cope with, he can devote more time to each individual child and thus effect greater stimulation be the child gifted, average, slow, or dull.

5. Since the instruments and procedures used for identifying gifted children are not adequate, they do not assure that every gifted child will be located; there is the possibility that some will be omitted and neglected in the selection. The assumption here seems to be that if all cannot profit, none should. So long as the search for the gifted is begun early and continues throughout a student's school years, and the opportunity is provided for him to enter a special group at any time, this is an invalid objection. Likewise, if a youngster is placed in a special group and later is found unable to manage the work adequately, there should be provision for removing him to a class in which his needs can be more nearly met. Underlying this objection seems to be a somewhat unwilling feeling that grouping is really all right, but that it should not be employed unless there is assurance that all who might profit from it are singled out and included in the special classes.

6. Students may actually be overworked in such classes. Higher standards of achievement, greater pressures for success, and more requirements may lead to excessive work for the students, or worse, to lowering the aspirations of some gifted students, and to their becoming underachievers. These are possible outcomes of a program geared to students' requirements, but are more directly related to the manner in which the class is conducted, and the personal motivations of each student, than to grouping. One of the authors has had the experience of being requested by parents to stop assigning so much homework when in reality none at all was being assigned; the students in question were so interested and involved in the problem being investigated that they continued their study each evening when they were at home.

7. One objection which cannot be overridden in a general

fashion is that special classes cost money. They do. However, it also is not known how much money is being lost by not providing special classes and developing the potentials of the gifted students to their fullest. It seems that the loss is certainly greater in the long run when special classes are not provided.

Those school systems which have long operated special classes or special schools for the gifted have found over a period of years that most of these objections based on beliefs about the probable poor outcomes of such programs simply are not valid. The gifted do not necessarily become conceited or snobbish, they are not cut off from all other contact with boys and girls, as a group they do not overwork seriously, nor is there a proportionately large number of underachievers. In the experience of such systems as Cleveland, the advantages of the special classes far outweigh the disadvantages, especially since most of the latter fail to materialize in actual practice in special classes for the gifted students.

CONCLUSIONS

There ought to be no disagreement in school systems over whether enrichment or acceleration should guide their thinking in dealing with gifted students. Each is significant in the education of the gifted, and each occurs with or without the help of the school, as is shown by the typical test scores made by most gifted students on tests of general knowledge and tests of achievement in school subjects. This is not to say that the gifted will get along all right without help; it is to point out once again their capacity for learning rapidly and extensively. Acceleration is unlikely without enrichment in depth, breadth, and further study that naturally accompanies it, regardless of whether a child is considered to be in grade three or grade ten. Acceleration should not be a purely mechanical moving of a student ahead of his grade without attention to curricular adjustments. There is no argument between the two; they reinforce each other, and each will be appropriate at various times in planning the best possible progress of individual students in terms of the goals of education which are accepted in any system. The important points seem to be rather that schools become aware of their obligations toward their gifted students, and that they plan some kind of program which will benefit them.

Much research is available on each method of teaching gifted children that has been discussed in this chapter; especially has much study been conducted on homogeneous versus heterogeneous grouping. The results are not conclusive to the degree that they can be used as definitive guides to establishing programs in other areas. Studies of acceleration and enrichment both indicate that gifted students have profited from following these programs. One is led to the feeling that nearly any reasonable plan set up earnestly to try to help the gifted can be of value to them. The merits of any one suggestion over another will need to be debated and decided upon by each school as it becomes aware of the need to do something for its gifted students. Each community has an obligation to work toward that end if the wealth of human resources is to be used wisely and not allowed to be lost.

The problems of grouping or of holding the gifted in regular classes will also have to be decided upon the basis of the beliefs held by those vitally concerned in each school: the administration, faculty, parents, other lay citizens in the community, and students who would be within the special groups and those who would not be so scheduled. If there are such strong prejudices against grouping as to jeopardize its probable success, it would not be a wise choice until such time as the opinions can be altered. Heck[7] has written:

> When teachers, parents, and school patrons understand that the organization of the special class is just a part of the professionalized program of providing a more suitable classification or "grading" of school children, this problem of avoiding prejudice will be eliminated. For years the public has accepted the grouping of school children in grades from the first through the twelfth; just so will special classes for the gifted be accepted as soon as the public understands what is being done.

[7] Arch O. Heck, *The Education of Exceptional Children* (revised ed.; New York: McGraw-Hill Book Co., 1953), p. 392.

SELECTED READINGS

BIRCH, JACK W., and McWILLIAMS, EARL M. *Challenging Gifted Children.* Bloomington, Ill.: Public School Publishing Company, 1955. 49 pp.

The pamphlet contains suggestions both practical and useful for teachers working with gifted school children in regular classrooms. There are enrichment ideas for primary and intermediate grade levels as well as for basic subjects at the secondary-school level. General suggestions for identifying gifted children and working profitably with their parents are included.

CUTTS, NORMA E., and MOSELEY, NICHOLAS. *Teaching the Bright and Gifted.* Englewood Cliffs, N.J.: Prentice-Hall, Inc., 1957. 268 pp. Chapters 3, 4, 6, and 7.

Chapters 3 and 4 deal with enrichment, its objectives and necessary planning, and some content and methods suggested for use.

Chapter 6 discusses the advantages and disadvantages of special grouping, drawing upon established elementary- and secondary-school programs as examples.

Chapter 7 presents arguments in favor of accelerated progress for gifted students, and examples of possible acceleration methods from kindergarten through college.

DeHAAN, ROBERT F., and HAVIGHURST, ROBERT J. *Educating Gifted Children.* Chicago: University of Chicago Press, 1957. 276 pp. Chapters 6, 7, 8, 10, and 12.

Chapters 6 and 12 describe programs and classes for gifted children, stressing the aspect of enriched learning.

Chapter 7 discusses possibilities for enrichment in the elementary and secondary schools, developing some criteria for judging the quality of enrichment.

Chapter 8 presents the ideas of special grouping and accelerated progress for gifted children as the two methods of dealing with their education currently favored, and points out that each method has been used with favorable results for the children concerned.

Chapter 10 presents suggestions for the kinds of things that teachers in regular classrooms can do for the gifted enrolled there. Problems of physical facilities, grouping within the class, guidance, and the use of community resources are explored as well.

HALL, THEODORE. *Gifted Children: The Cleveland Story.* Cleveland: The World Publishing Company, 1956. 90 pp.

Mr. Hall tells in an informal, easy style the story of the Major Work program in Cleveland, Ohio. He takes the reader into the classroom and gives him a clear picture of education of the gifted in action.

HECK, ARCH O. *The Education of Exceptional Children*, revised ed. New York: McGraw-Hill Book Co., 1953. 513 pp. Chapters 26, 27, and 28.

The three chapters cited present what the author believes should be the guiding principles of educating the gifted, the advantages and common objections, the major problems to be solved, and his conception of the challenge of such education to professional and lay people.

HILDRETH, GERTRUDE H., *et al. Educating Gifted Children at Hunter College Elementary School.* New York: Harper & Brothers, 1952. 272 pp. Chapters 3, 4, and 5.

In these three chapters the author describes and discusses the curriculum, organization, teaching methods, and instructional resources of Hunter College Elementary School.

MARTENS, ELISE H. *Curriculum Adjustments for Gifted Children.* (U.S. Office of Education Bulletin 1946, No. 1.) Washington, D.C.: U.S. Government Printing Office, 1946. 82 pp.

Part 1 deals with the basic theory behind the education of the gifted, and some analysis of the various ways in which this is carried out; part 2 describes some programs in operation at different grade levels of the public schools.

NATIONAL SOCIETY FOR THE STUDY OF EDUCATION. *The Education of Exceptional Children.* Chicago: University of Chicago Press, 1950. 350 pp. Chapter 14.

This chapter on "Special Education for the Gifted Child" draws upon basic philosophy and research studies to support the viewpoint that acceleration and enrichment complement each other to provide adequate education for the gifted child.

NATIONAL SOCIETY FOR THE STUDY OF EDUCATION. *Education for the Gifted.* Chicago: University of Chicago Press, 1958. 420 pp. Chapter 10.

Passow analyzes and discusses the arguments for and against the several ways in which enrichment can be provided for the improved education of the gifted. He draws upon many research materials to support the statements he makes, and emphasizes the need for continuing research and evaluation of programs for the gifted.

OTTO, HENRY J. *Curriculum Enrichment for Gifted Elementary School Children in Regular Classes.* (Bureau of Laboratory Schools Publication No. 6.) Austin: University of Texas Press, 1957. 136 pp.

This bulletin was prepared by a workshop group in order to supply philosophy, ideas, methods, and content designed to be useful to teachers who have gifted children in their regular elementary classrooms. Enrichment suggestions are made for communications, science, social studies, arithmetic, physical education, art, and music activities.

SCHEIFELE, MARIAN. *The Gifted Child in the Regular Classroom.* (Practical Suggestions for Teaching, No. 12.) New York: Bureau of Publications, Teachers College, Columbia University, 1953. 84 pp.

Since most gifted children are to be found in regular classrooms, the author describes several kinds of activities which can be carried on easily by the teacher and the gifted child. The suggestions are based on practical possibilities for almost any class, showing how the gifted child's special work can be correlated with that of his classmates.

WORCESTER, D. A. *The Education of Children of Above-Average Mentality.* Lincoln, Neb.: University of Nebraska Press, 1956. 68 pp.

Acceleration and enrichment are discussed with special emphasis upon the values of early admission shown by studies made by the author.

8

Teachers for
the Gifted

To state that the teacher in any given situation determines the quality of the learning that will take place has become a truism. A good teacher helps boys and girls to have
worthwhile learning experiences, often despite the handicaps
of poor or inadequate physical resources and equipment.
What qualities does a good teacher possess that are related to
his success in the classroom? More specifically, what qualifications should be expected in teachers of gifted children and
youth? Can these be developed through programs of teacher
education? Who should teach the gifted?

QUALIFICATIONS

Superior Intelligence

Most lists of the qualities administrators or supervisors
wish to find in selecting teachers for the gifted include a
reference to intelligence decidedly above the average. In
fact, this might well be a qualification for the teachers of all
children, regardless of *their* intellectual potential. A teacher
should be a person of high intelligence if he is to carry out
the kind of program that includes the many applications of
what he has learned to the greatest degree for each of his
students. Gifted students especially require teachers of superior intelligence to direct their work and allow them the free
choice needed for experimentation along the lines of their

interests, at the same time that they are learning the true fundamentals of communicating their findings to others, and developing some idea of the social obligations they have because of their giftedness.

Interest in Students

The teacher must possess deep and sincere interest in his students as people. He must be interested in their interests; he listens as they talk and is genuinely concerned with their thoughts and expressions. This is not meant to imply a somewhat saccharine "love for all children" but rather a real desire to know as much as he can about these boys and girls, and to make use of this knowledge as he plans the program of studies with them. He is sympathetic and helpful as they explore among their many avenues of learning; he is truly interested in teaching them as well as he possibly can.

The teacher of gifted children is truly interested in helping them to achieve the best of which they are capable. He does not subscribe to the unfortunately too prevalent theory that the gifted can direct themselves and that the teacher should devote most of his time and effort to helping those who learn more slowly. He realizes that many times a simple suggestion to the gifted will give them sufficient direction for hours of work; he does not misinterpret this as indicating that they need only a little help. He knows that the many ramifications of their investigations will certainly keep him busy helping to secure materials, interpreting findings, and making judgments, as he works right along with his gifted students. Granted they do not require nearly as much drill in fundamental processes as do their slower classmates; but they do require a sufficient amount so that they can progress to the next step, that of using their skill in some profitable and beneficial manner.

Creativity

The teacher of the gifted should be a creative person. He is not hemmed in by ordinary methods or the usual ways of doing things; he can develop original approaches to his own work, and he can appreciate those original approaches made by his students. He is not a stifler of creativity or ingenuity; students in his classroom are not coerced into well-beaten paths of organization, but they are rather released and encouraged to find new ways, to develop original methods of procedure. He realizes also that creativity is not necessarily confined to those aspects of living and learning that are called "the arts," but that it exists and can be developed in many fields of human endeavor. He can see new ideas, new implications or novel uses of an otherwise prosaic item. He is not restricted in his own thinking and approaches to problems, nor does he restrict his students only to "tried and true" methods of working.

Having opened the pathway to creative development among the students, he must also be prepared to accept unusual responses from them, reactions that may be out of the ordinary. He should not be an inflexible person, thinking or acting only in stereotypes. As the teacher stimulates youngsters toward creative expression, so must he be ready to work with their creativity. A different reply must not be rejected merely because of its difference; it may have resulted from a genuinely creative approach to the problem at hand.

Resourcefulness in Method

This quality of creativity, or at least of sensitivity to creativity in others, implies ingenuity or resourcefulness as another quality the teacher of the gifted should have. He cannot rely on printed courses of study or curriculum guides alone for knowledge of what to teach and how to work with these gifted boys and girls. He must be able to develop many of the methods and problem areas as he works with the youngsters in the classroom. Surely he can find suggestions from other programs designed for the gifted; he will need to interpret these—judge, qualify, revise, and possibly reject them—on the basis of their fitness or suitability for his particular class. He does not attempt to impose a pattern of progress developed for other students upon those with whom he works.

As he and his class develop their program together, he needs to be aware of and alert to many possibilities for activities, many ways in which the study can be carried on. The gifted youngsters will have many ideas of their own to suggest and these are usually useful and worthwhile. The teacher needs in addition a knowledge of resources in the forms of people, books, pamphlets, films, filmstrips, sites for field excursions, and the like, so that he can supplement the learning with references to these, and make them available to the students. He should also be resourceful, able to procure needed supplies and materials, create them from nothing when money is not available for their purchase, and encourage his students to do likewise.

Broad Knowledge

Certainly the teacher of the gifted must have a broad general background of knowledge upon which he may draw as he attempts to help his students increase their understandings of the problems which confront them. He is an educated person. He probably possesses greater knowledge and interest in certain specialized areas of learning, but he guards against his personal interests hampering his students' exploration into many fields of learning.

At the same time, he is not afraid to admit that he may be uninformed about some specific point which arises in the class. He learns with his students; it is entirely possible that they investigate a problem or question together. He does not try to feign knowledge where he does not possess it. Most youngsters in an average classroom can see through such a bluff, and gifted students would recognize false pretense even more rapidly; worse still, such action could destroy whatever respect they may have had for him as their teacher.

Diversified Personal Interests

The teacher of gifted youngsters should be a person of diversified interests himself. He is not mired in a set pattern of activity, but he has, and continues to develop, many interests of his own. He needs to be abreast of current social and political trends and developments, read widely in many fields, see plays and hear concerts and lectures, travel, and study. He must be a dynamic person, not a static one. He realizes that education or learning does not stop when one steps out of a classroom, and is continuing on his own, as he works with the gifted to try to help them realize that drive for further knowledge which should characterize their lives. He is a part of the community in which he lives and works; he participates actively in its affairs. He studies not only to increase his own personal understandings of the world in which he lives, but also to gain further insight into ways in which he may help the gifted students with whom he works.

Good Physical and Emotional Health

Excellent physical and emotional health seem requisite to the task of teaching the gifted. The need of good physical condition for teachers of all youngsters regardless of their standing on the scale of intelligence seems obvious. As the teaching of the gifted seems to involve more and more individualized instruction in the classroom and the necessary preparation of materials and evaluation of students' work and progress as well, it will strain the energies of the most vigorous. As the classroom teacher becomes more widely recognized as the key person in the guidance function with those youngsters whom he knows best, the necessity for stability, for good emotional health, can be realized. It seems obvious that a well-balanced personality can do a more effective guidance job than one with quirks or bents that shift it off balance.

The teacher of the gifted must be a mature person, not necessarily in age, but in acceptance of himself. He must be secure as he works with young people as they are, and as they strive toward ever-increasing maturity themselves. Being a mature person, he can accept independent thought and action from his students. He is not a person to stifle interest, to stultify reaction, to hamper experimentation; he is much more apt to respond to a novel suggestion with, "Maybe it would work that way. Let's try it and find out." It is assumed, of course, that the process involves no physical danger or extreme risk to the participants.

This maturity frees the teacher from jealousy, either overt or unrecognized, of these gifted students and their abilities.

A teacher who harbors some jealous reactions to his students is not the best person to work with them. He may be unable to free them to work with their problems in ways in which he feels incapable of proceeding. Worse, he may vocalize his reactions to the degree that he stops learning and growth in understanding. Jealousy has no place in the classroom, on the part of the teacher or the students.

Understanding of Democracy

This teacher possesses knowledge of and faith in the principles of the democratic way of life. He is convinced of the dignity and worth of each individual, and respects him for what he is and can do. He believes in the values of a cooperative attack on common problems as he works with his class. He has faith in the method of intelligence for the solution of man's problems. And he helps his students to learn, understand, and practice these democratic values as they work together.

The teacher of the gifted has usually had some experiences in teaching average groups of youngsters in regular classroom situations. He has recognized the need for individualized instruction with normal children; he knows that as children progress through school, the span of achievement increases noticeably. In secondary classrooms, for example, it is not unusual to find a span of as many as nine or ten years between the achievement of the highest and the lowest pupil in one class. He recognizes that even when gifted children are grouped together for instructional purposes, there will still be a range of achievement and potential evident; they cannot be treated as one group in every part of their work. He has surely moved from lock-step instruction or the use of one text exclusively as he has worked with varying groups of boys and girls.

Personal Qualifications

About his person the teacher for the gifted is neat and clean. He dresses attractively, suitably to his job, and is well-groomed. In every way he is a good example for the students in his classroom. Of course, he speaks and writes excellent English, exhibits good manners, and knows how to get along well with the people with whom he deals.

PREPARATION

Preservice Education

The teacher education program designed for prospective teachers of gifted children, and this includes every teacher of youngsters, should certainly be of the highest quality available. A basically good program of teacher preparation in this country can be divided for purposes of discussion into three areas: there are (1) the general education segment which is required of all students, (2) the special education part which could include courses required for some specialization as well as those elected in the pursuit of some specific interest, and (3) the professional education segment, designed to lead to a particular professional career.

GENERAL EDUCATION. The general education courses are those required of all students in the belief that they lead to the development and improvement of the basic skills, the fundamental processes needed by educated citizens of a democracy. These include English courses to develop skill in communicating one's own thoughts and understanding those of others; mathematics courses to improve one's numerical concepts and quantitative reasoning; and social science courses to increase one's knowledge of the people of the world in which we live, the factors which influence their actions, and the growth of democracy with its rights and responsibilities for its citizens. In today's world, general education ought also to include some specific study of science, as a part of a prospective teacher's own knowledge and understanding, regardless of his determination to specialize in that or some other areas. Arts, music, and physical education have also a contribution to make to each teacher's general education.

SPECIALIZED EDUCATION. The specialized section of the program cuts two ways. It may include courses required to earn certification in some area of instruction, or it may involve courses elected on the basis that the prospective teacher chooses them for broadening his knowledge of some field or to begin exploration in some other. Some courses that are required for students following a certain pattern to obtain a teaching license may also be elected by others who wish to enrich their own background or develop an interest in the field. Granting the superior intelligence expected of a teacher of the gifted, he will, in his preparation for teaching, avail himself of the many opportunities offered by elective courses to develop a wide range of general knowledge, and to specialize in his fields of interest.

PROFESSIONAL EDUCATION. The professional education courses are those required specifically in the belief that the teacher will need to have the knowledge that they offer in order to do an effective job of teaching. Child study can be used as an illustration of one significant area in the professional experiences of preservice teachers. They need to know what to expect from youngsters at various ages and stages of growth and development—physically, socially, intellectually, and emotionally. Though they may never meet that hypothetical average child, knowledge of the norms of growth and behavior will help them to see deviations from the expected pattern. They will need to see children as they study from a textbook or other reference materials, and as they listen to explanations made by their instructor. Reading and studying certainly comprise one method of learning; for students of above-average intelligence it can be a fruitful one. It is further enhanced and made meaningful by watching real children and comparing their apparent growth and behavior with what has been studied. The teacher of gifted children will need knowledge of these possibilities of growth, so that he may be better able to understand children in his classes and the problems they may present as he works with them.

The professional side of teacher education generally includes such courses as those dealing with general psychology, child growth and development, principles and techniques of teaching, philosophy of education, educational psychology, and some student teaching experiences. A student preparing to teach gifted youngsters will need the understandings developed in such courses as these, and more. He ought to study the psychology of the gifted, with their special needs in addition to those common needs of all youngsters. Involved are the acceptance of their own mental ability plus accepting that of others without developing impatience, intolerance, or lack of sympathy with those who may be slower in learning than the gifted are. The prospective teacher's understanding of individual differences will help him to realize that even in homogeneous groupings, the differences may quite likely outweigh the likeness which reflects only the one factor on which the selection was based. If the likeness is intelligence, a study of the tests used might indicate differences within the various components of those tests; if it is reading ability, again examination of the tests will indicate that the youngsters missed different questions and require help on different reading skills, and so the only likeness is the final score, which is again based on a large number of items.

As he will be expected to develop a program of learning experiences with his class group, and probably to work with faculty groups striving to improve the over-all offerings of the school, a knowledge of curriculum design and the bases for its construction will certainly be helpful. The curriculum is the content of experiences in the classroom as the teacher and the students plan and work together; it can be achieved without knowledge of the basic design but it will not be nearly so effective as when it is built on common beliefs and understandings, and is well articulated with the program of the entire school.

From the study of educational psychology, the teacher should become well aware of the accepted theories of learning and their implications for the ways in which he will teach his gifted students. They can learn quite rapidly, particularly from their wide reading; they may be inclined to sidestep less tasteful activities in which their skills are not so well developed. Yet these skills, especially in expressing ideas in written form, are essential to their continuing learning.

The uses and interpretations of tests take on a significant aspect when the teacher is dealing with gifted students. There are many kinds of tests—aptitude, intelligence, interest, achievement, and the like—and he will need knowledge of how to interpret the results and make use of them in his contacts with his students and their parents.

As the guidance function of the classroom teacher becomes better understood, the teacher of the gifted must study in this area. He will be an important part of the life of the youngsters for at least one year; he knows them better than other adults do, as he learns to watch behavior and search for its causes, to talk *with* students instead of *to* them, and to keep informative records. The accepted purposes of guidance are to help youngsters make wise choices, to become capably self-directive, and this certainly is a part of the work involved in teaching gifted youngsters. A further point which should be stated is that a good teacher must be able to realize at what point his guidance ability ends, and be able to seek help from trained guidance personnel or other sources.

Another course which should be part of the preparation of teachers for the gifted is one that deals with methods and teaching techniques suitably adapted to varying needs and speeds of learning. This is not to imply that there is available a bag of tricks from which any teacher may pluck the exact method to use in any situation with insured results, because such a thing does not exist. There are some skills of teaching, however, that have been found to be very successful in work with gifted children, and a teacher should know them and have the ability to make them properly useful in appropriate situations with his class.

Discussion instead of straight recitation or question-and-answer lessons is such a method. Because these are gifted youngsters, each of them undoubtedly has much to contribute to the discussion, and skill is needed to help them realize the importance of speaking understandably, waiting their turns, avoiding unnecessary interruptions, listening as the others speak, and staying on the chosen subject rather than introducing extraneous material. They need help in setting goals for discussions, understanding procedures, taking part helpfully, and learning to disagree in an agreeable manner. To develop good discussion technique is not easy; the explanation, practice, and evaluation of results are worth the time they require to help the youngsters learn the skills involved, share enthusiastically in effective class discussion, and learn from the subject matter content that is explored through discussion.

Problem-centered teaching seems ideally suited to gifted youngsters, as it allows them to develop and practice the skills involved in critical thinking, group work, and independent study. They have a high potential for seeing relationships among various phases of a problem, and they are well able to deal with abstractions and ideas. They can reason on a high level and they are equally able to generalize, to draw principles from their findings. Skills in research will be necessary to their progress, and as they understand the relationship to their goals of locating reliable sources of information, note-taking, outlining, and organizing their materials logically, they can see the necessity for learning and applying these skills. Their teacher then must be prepared to help them learn and use the skills required by the problems approach to learning.

The teacher of the gifted will also need to become skilled in individualizing instruction. Mass instruction is out of place as a regular way of working with the gifted, as it is with most other youngsters. It tends to squelch any initiative a child may possess, and it has the disadvantage of being a broadside approach aimed usually at the center of the group in the hope that each child will learn something. For the few youngsters who may be at the point upon which the mass instruction centers, it may be helpful; for the many more who extend to either side of that point, it is of little value. It may even be destructive, as it wastes time for those already aware of the content as well as for those who may not have reached the point at which the lesson could be meaningful to them. Individualized instruction is a must for the classroom teacher if he is trying in any degree to put to use what he has learned about youngsters, how they grow and how they learn, each at his own rate. Thus he will need help in learning how to work with one or two students at a time, and what to expect from the remainder of the class as he concentrates his attention upon a few students or a single individual.

A wide variety of materials for instruction is needed in any classroom in which the teacher professes to be dealing with youngsters according to their levels of achievement and intelligence. As gifted youngsters can learn quite early to use resources effectively, the need for such materials as unabridged dictionaries, sets of encyclopedias, biographical books, and single reference books such as almanacs and atlases, can be seen. The gifted progress beyond children's reference books very soon; not only do they enjoy using adult resources, but they profit from them. Those written and simplified for children do not contain the kind of information for which they are searching. A teacher of the gifted will need many resources available and will need to know and make use of the school library and community facilities as well.

Resources of information are not merely books. The teacher needs to be aware of the many possibilities of other audiovisual materials and to help his gifted students make effective use of these as well. Some authorities stress that the teacher must see to it that the gifted do not concentrate their time upon reading exclusively, though this can be a rewarding method of learning for them. The teacher will need to be skilled in introducing sound films, strips, recordings, pictures, three-dimensional exhibits, and the like, into the classroom as he attempts to provide a lush environment for enriched learning. He will need to learn about these resources, and how he may obtain them.

PRACTICE TEACHING. Perhaps most significant of all, the prospective teacher of the gifted must be exposed to the most vital of teachers in his own career as a student. Teaching is quite a personal activity; teachers cannot copy exactly what another teacher does in his classroom and expect it to have the same beneficial results in a different one. Each teacher needs to develop his own ways of working with boys and girls, based on sound principles of learning and teaching. Exposure to stimulating members of the teaching profession may help the student to realize the need for being a real and interesting person, and for developing his own talents to challenge students as best he can.

Observation of and participation in instruction with an experienced teacher who is skilled in meeting the needs of youngsters, providing for individual differences, and enriching the program for gifted youngsters are two ways at least in which a student teacher can see how the principles he has learned can be put into effective practice. Again, he must not be merely an imitation, but must develop his own best methods of working with the boys and girls in his own classroom.

In-Service Education

After a teacher has had some years of successful experience in an average classroom, he may express his desire and interest in working with gifted youngsters particularly. If so, he can be helped effectively in a number of ways.

ADMINISTRATIVE AID. Supervisors and administrators can bring ideas for increased enrichment of the classroom program and procedures. These may involve certain activities associated with fundamental processes, as well as material resources. Supervisors ordinarily have greater opportunity for attending national conferences, seeing exhibits of new materials, and exchanging ideas with people from all over the country than do classroom teachers. They can also encourage the classroom teacher to try new ideas and activities, and stand squarely back of such intelligently planned experimentation. This assumes that they conceive of their job in terms of democratic leadership, and that there are positive relations between the administrative and the teaching staff.

WORKSHOPS. Workshops have been held to help interested teachers explore the possibilities involved in the teaching of the gifted. Again with effective leadership such workshops invite teachers to participate in planning, studying, and developing workable programs in their own location. They provide opportunities for hearing authorities in the field present their viewpoints, for exploring the research available about gifted, and for reading and discussing what is being done in other localities. Perhaps one of the most valuable aspects of the workshop is the coffee hour or the break between sessions when teachers can talk together, mulling over the points they have heard and read, listen to others' reactions, and thus sharpen their own thoughts on the subject. A stimulating leader for a group session is a vital part of the workshop; with such leadership teachers often continue to discuss the topics even during time set aside as breaks from the study hours.

CLASSES AND STUDY GROUPS. Near many schools are colleges and universities which as part of their extension or field services will organize classes on the expressed interest and need of a number of teachers. Classes to study the gifted have been formed as a result of these groups asking to have such a course presented in their area. While this is a more formal approach than a workshop, it can be quite helpful in acquainting teachers with the knowledge and understandings required in teaching the gifted. Along the same line it should be mentioned that courses on educating gifted children are offered at the graduate level by many colleges and universities; teachers can make arrangements individually to attend these during the summer or in evening sessions as they prefer.

Study groups can be formed if there is a sufficient number of teachers who express a desire to investigate improved ways of working with the gifted. Some of the most successful have included both parents and teachers, surely the two groups deeply interested in and involved with the welfare of gifted children.

TEACHER INSTITUTES. County institutes and state meetings of teacher groups ordinarily offer sessions in which they present speakers, panels, and symposia dealing with topics of interest to their teachers. This is admittedly just a one-shot approach but it can kindle a flame from a spark already in existence, or perhaps strike the spark. Certain teachers may be inspired to improve their programs and continue their study as a result of hearing a well-presented talk on the subject of the gifted, and an alert supervisor can continue stimulation as he becomes aware of the interest.

READING. Individual reading and study by a teacher who desires to improve his teaching of the gifted can be very significant. He can learn satisfactorily from a program of study which he has blocked out for himself. He can crystallize some of his beliefs and perhaps find that others do not stand up in the light of applicable research findings. He can clarify his understanding, increase his knowledge, and locate some things that will be effective in making him a more successful teacher of the gifted. Probably he has not had the program of preparation discussed previously, so the suggestion does not necessarily imply a fruitless repetition of what he has already learned. Books, articles, and pamphlets dealing with the gifted exist in plenty; he may seek help in choosing from the available supply, and his supervisor will probably welcome the opportunity to work with him and incidentally watch his progress so that he may be assigned to teaching the gifted when the time is deemed opportune.

INFORMAL METHODS. Good teachers never stop seeking ways of working more effectively with their classes. Less formal methods than those named above can sometimes be just as valuable and helpful. Not the least significant is that of informal conversation among teachers, the exchange of ideas as they search for ways of helping a student who presents problems, or one with whom they all have contact. Caution against attempting a wholesale transplantation of these ideas must be exercised. What has admirable results in one classroom with a certain group of boys and girls and one teacher may be disastrous or fall flat in other circumstances. Good sense is needed in applying the parts that may be workable in particular situations.

Perhaps a few days of observing an already successful teacher of the gifted in the classroom may be another helpful activity for an individual teacher. Such visitation can be arranged, with the help of interested administrators.

SELECTION

In many of the existing programs for the education of gifted children and youth are found teachers who have had some years of professional experience with classes of average youngsters. This is often cited as a qualification for choosing a teacher to work in such a program. A second outstanding characteristic mentioned as expected by administrators and supervisors of programs for gifted children is that of interest in working with superior students. A teacher who feels and expresses a sincere interest in the welfare of the gifted is much more likely to be successful in building a program suitable to their needs and the development of their potential than is one who has no such concern.

These experienced teachers, in many cases, have developed concern for the plight of the gifted, as they have worked with youngsters of varying intelligence levels. They are not the teachers who are constantly concerned with the students at the lower levels of achievement, though in their teaching they have not neglected the slower learners in the classroom. They have had success in individualizing instruction, in working with small groups, and in creating a rich environment for the learning of all their students. Having had these experiences they are thus better able to judge their desires for teaching children who represent the higher portion of the intellectual scale.

That gifted students themselves realize and express their need for better teachers has been shown in studies. They must not be subjected to teachers who show very little interest in or adaptability to the program in operation if worthwhile results are to be expected.

Merely checking off a list of qualifications, scanning a transcript of credits showing college preparation, and determining previous success in teaching in some fashion will not, in and of themselves, guarantee the selection of a teacher who will be consistently successful in working with gifted students. There is something beyond what can be put onto a paper and analyzed; there is the quality of the person himself which must be judged by the administrator or supervisor in charge of employing teachers. It is that indefinable spark that makes the difference between people of similar preparation and experiences; it is that nameless attribute that makes one person a stimulating, inspiring teacher, and another individual a droning bore.

Sometimes these challenging personalities can be discovered in some in-service program, such as a workshop. They are interested in the problems being studied; they care deeply about the progress made; they are in attendance to seek improvement in their teaching, not merely to earn another credit which will advance them upon the salary schedule. They contribute more than just their share to the work, and they accept responsibilities and carry them out promptly and effectively.

They are quick to make use of timely events; they capitalize upon opportunities for growth that may arise beyond what was planned. They are not opportunistic in that they flit from one question to another without purpose or plan, but they can see the possibilities of being flexible and making good use of current happenings.

They would not be interested in teaching the gifted because of whatever status this might carry in the eyes of other teachers or of the community. They are sincerely interested in doing as good a job as they are capable of doing with these often neglected youngsters.

Perhaps it would be possible to select a teacher for the gifted before he completes his undergraduate work and becomes a full-fledged teacher in his own classroom. This earlier selection would have at least one advantage in that the program of studies the candidate planned might be geared more directly to the teaching of the gifted, and the teacher would thus be somewhat better prepared as he began his work.

Here again, expression of interest would seem important. This could be discovered during advisory or counseling sessions, as the student's program was being planned. Instructors might note students of high intelligence coupled with high achievement and make this information available to the advisor. The college testing program could surely provide some indication of the expected potential of the student. It can be seen that in looking for prospective teachers of the gifted one should not depend upon any one criterion, but rather attempt to gather as much evidence as is available about the ability, interest, and performance of the student as he progresses through his program of teacher education. A consistent advisory system is necessary here, one person at least who knows this student well, can collect and keep the information concerning him, and help to plan a program that provides the greatest possible opportunity for helping the student develop and realize his teaching potential.

Whether it would be wise to choose inexperienced teachers to begin their careers with gifted youngsters is another point to be considered. Some might say that the first year of teaching presents sufficient difficulties without adding another stress point; perhaps that consideration in itself might indicate that beginners are not the best selection for teachers of the gifted.

RELATIONSHIPS WITH OTHER TEACHERS

Having been chosen as a teacher of the gifted, and assigned to a certain task, the teacher will find that many problems of adjustment and human relationships can arise. A teacher works ordinarily in a building which houses many other people, adults as well as children. His task becomes easier to accomplish if he can establish positive relationships with his co-workers.

If he meets the qualifications previously discussed, he is free of the mistaken feeling that he is somehow better than the other teachers. He views the faculty members as people who are striving together toward the same objective: to do their best in helping the boys and girls of the school grow into dependable, socially responsible citizens who can make their ways in the world and contribute to its improvement.

There may be, however, other teachers within the building who feel inferior in some way because they teach only normal children. Perhaps they feel threatened by the newcomer who may bring new methods or become better liked by the students. Here he must work to establish that he certainly does not share this feeling. A willingness to pitch into the everyday routine work of school people, to serve on committees, to count books, and so forth, may help in setting other teachers more at ease.

In working with the students in the classroom, the teacher of the gifted will need help which may be available from other staff members. With the amount of knowledge man now possesses, and its continuing growth as further discoveries are made, it is impossible for one person ever to be able to encompass the whole that is available. It is, indeed, impossible for one person to know all that there is to know in just one field of knowledge, and the special knowledge areas of other teachers on the staff can be used to supplement his own. For example, as his youngsters explore various areas of science they may ask questions which he cannot answer; nor can he help locate reference material for the children to use in finding information. The teacher whose specialty is science can be interviewed by the youngster who posed the question; the two teachers can pool their resources to locate helpful informational sources; the science teacher may be invited into the classroom to discuss the point with the youngsters as a resource person. Another time, as a group of children are illustrating some of their findings on charts and posters, they may seek the advice of the teacher whose specialty is art. Still another instance might involve a mathematics teacher, when the classroom teacher wishes to be sure of the youngsters' knowledge of percentages, or their skills in the preparation of bar or other sorts of graphs, as these are needed in presenting their information or exploring source materials. He does not wish to break down the other teacher's work by presenting the topic in an entirely different manner. It is certainly wiser to consult with these special teachers in advance of the need if it can be foreseen in time to plan such a conference.

Other teachers in the school building may be helpful to the teacher of the gifted in sharing their knowledge of the youngsters with him. Some may have been the students' previous teachers, and he can draw upon their experiences as necessary in planning the best program possible with the students. The records kept by previous teachers are an invaluable source of information about each child, assuming that the school has developed a good system of cumulative records, and each teacher feels his responsibility to contribute useful information. In a situation where youngsters spend half a day in class with other gifted students and explore various special subject areas during the remainder of the day, the teachers of these classes may sit down together for an hour or so each week to pool their knowledge of each student and work toward improving their programs, as they increase their understanding of the youngsters.

At times teaching methods may develop a raw spot of friction among teachers. The teacher of the gifted, in trying to help his students develop increasing self-direction and self-discipline, works quite differently in the classroom from the teacher who believes that his main task is to cover the content of a textbook within a certain period of time. The latter may well take upon himself the responsibility for all planning and decision-making, and expect the students merely to follow his directions. He may look upon questions in regard to procedures or additional and possibly contradictory information as expressions of impertinence or impudence. Youngsters who are penalized in one class for the same kind of behavior that is welcomed and praised in another class may have a difficult time. Gifted students can learn to make the necessary adjustment to the differing expectations of teachers quite rapidly, but they may be confused as to the value of what is happening to them in school.

The teachers involved would do well to iron out such problems with each other, in order to provide a good program of education for the boys and girls in their classes. Administrators and supervisors may help also by trying to aid each teacher to understand the point of view of the other, and striving for a clearer conception of what they are all trying to achieve with their students, and how these objectives may best be reached.

Professionally, as part of his job, the teacher of the gifted will work with the other staff members as is expected in the school system. He will not criticize them or their teaching and will not allow children to indulge in unwise comments. He does not have to like every one of his colleagues; the mere fact that they work in the same building should not be interpreted to mean that they must therefore become his fast friends. He is a human being and has his preferences in choosing for himself those people with whom he wishes to be friendly. He will, however, keep his professional relationships on an adult level, and will not become involved with any cliques if he is so unfortunate as to teach in a school where these exist.

On a personal basis he should surely feel free to make friends with certain of the faculty whose interests are similar to his. These personal relationships ought not interfere with the performance of his tasks in the school. Free choice of personal associates ought to be a privilege granted to adults in any profession.

TEACHER LOAD

This is an area in which most teachers have quite definite feelings, but in which there is little definitive research upon which to base conclusions. Teachers are sure that they can do a more effective job with a smaller class, in which they can give individualized attention to each student, than they can in a larger class, which requires that much of their time be spent merely in routine business and keeping order. Yet they are unable to say with exactness just what an ideal class number may be. Recommendations exist in plenty, but they seem to be based on feelings rather than upon objective evidence.

It has been said that elementary classes should be no larger than thirty students and secondary classes no larger than twenty-five. The differential appears to be based upon the fact that a secondary teacher may meet as many as six classes each day, and so have a total of 150 students whom he is expected to instruct effectively. The National Education Association suggests that elementary classes be limited, as well, to twenty-five students.

From personal experience the authors offer a belief that twenty-five youngsters are not too large a number to work with individually, and that this number can be divided into workable small groups for the exploration of various facets of a problem which is being studied. They have managed to operate in somewhat the same manner with groups of forty or more but this requires a great deal of extra effort and energy. Furthermore large classes do not permit the frequent contact with parents that is considered essential to a good educational program.

Of those school systems that have established programs of some sort designed to educate the gifted, only a very few report any differences in the size of gifted classes as compared to others in the same system. The pattern of development up to the present has been rather to keep the classes somewhat equalized whether they be at elementary or secondary level.

Some secondary schools offer honors courses or seminars to certain of their more advanced students. These may be smaller in size than the usual classes; not every secondary school contains exactly the same number of gifted children. Quite often these seminars are held after school hours, and are staffed by interested and talented adults of the community.

Regardless of personal feelings and beliefs about the numbers of youngsters who can be taught well at one time, teachers are at present confronted with more and more students in the elementary and secondary schools. It is not possible to send these children back; they are here, and they deserve the best educational program that can be provided. In some school systems classes have had to be put on shifts; in others, classes have increased to forty, fifty, and more youngsters; in still others, there has been sufficient foresight on the part of the school people and the community to provide additional building and classroom space and qualified teachers so that the children have a reasonably good opportunity to attend school in a good learning situation.

EXTRACURRICULAR SERVICES

Extracurricular activities can be found by the score in secondary schools though they are not quite so numerous in most elementary-school programs. There are club activities to interest almost every student, though not every student in a given school will be participating in the program. It is much more common to find that a small proportion of the students may be sharing in many of the activities offered.

For a time there was a trend toward naming these after-school clubs and sessions "co-curricular" to indicate that they should be considered on the same basis as the curricular offerings, those found within the time limits of the regular school day. There is at least one excellent reason behind such a belief: the values to be derived from active participation in a well-planned activity are often more closely related to the written philosophy of a school than are those evident in its classroom procedures. Students can have real experience with self-government as they direct an activity with the guidance of a faculty sponsor. They learn to plan, to carry out their plans, to judge results in terms of consequences, and to revise plans as mistakes are noted and procedures improved. In a live activity program students accept direct responsibility for what occurs. They learn ways of working in groups and ways of getting along with their fellow students. As they have a share in the planning, so are they directly involved with the outcomes, and they work hard to insure the success of their projects.

Some schools have moved to a program which includes the extracurricular activities in the class schedule. If these activities are to be sponsored by the school, they should have educative value; there should be nothing in the program that does not meet this criterion.

Teachers of the gifted will very probably have their part to play in sponsoring extracurricular activities. That a competent adult leader is required for the success of the program seems obvious if the participating youngsters are to have vital learning experience. The teachers of the gifted must pull their share of the load of work in the school, and as long as extra-class activities are sponsored by the school they have an obligation to that part of the program as well as to classroom teaching.

Each teacher has his own talents and likes and dislikes, and in assigning faculty sponsors to activities an administrator would do well to consider these. A teacher who has little patience with the sometimes rambling discussion of youngsters or who prefers to direct all of an activity himself probably would not be the best choice to sponsor a student council. Many administrators today offer a first, second, and third choice to their teachers in an attempt to fit the right person to each activity.

Teachers of the gifted are members of a faculty whether they teach in a school with only one class of gifted children or with many. These teachers will be expected to contribute to every part of the educational program of the school to the best of their skills and abilities.

SELECTED READINGS

BRANDWEIN, PAUL F. *The Gifted Student as Future Scientist.* New York: Harcourt, Brace & Co., 1955. 107 pp. Chapter 5.

> The role of the influential teacher is explored as Brandwein describes a study of those science teachers at Forest Hills High School most often cited as having encouraged their gifted students by the students themselves. He proposes that it is not so much the teaching, though that is important, as it is the teacher as a person who can have the best effect upon the students' learning and development.

CRONBACH, LEE J. *Educational Psychology.* New York: Harcourt, Brace & Co., 1954. 628 pp. Chapter 15.

The role of the teacher as group leader in the classroom is explored in relation to methods of planning activities, and methods of control developed with the group. An interesting discussion is presented on the idea that disciplinary problems can reflect failure in the leadership role.

FRENCH, JOSEPH L. (ed.). *Educating the Gifted: A Book of Readings.* New York: Henry Holt & Co., Inc., 1959. 555 pp. Section 9.

Four articles discuss the qualifications of teachers for the gifted, their preparation and in-service training programs, and a study dealing with the attitudes of certain teachers toward special groups of mentally superior children.

GODDARD, HENRY HERBERT. *School Training of Gifted Children.* Yonkers, N.Y.: World Book Co., 1928. 226 pp. Chapter 7.

In this chapter, the author discusses the qualifications sought in selecting teachers for gifted children in the Major Work program of the Cleveland, Ohio, public school system.

HILDRETH, GERTRUDE H., et al. *Educating Gifted Children at Hunter College Elementary School.* New York: Harper & Brothers, 1952. 272 pp. Chapter 10.

In this chapter, the author enumerates and briefly describes the personal and professional qualifications which, based on her experience at Hunter College Elementary School, she has found desirable in a teacher of the gifted.

NATIONAL SOCIETY FOR THE STUDY OF EDUCATION. *Education for the Gifted.* Chicago: University of Chicago Press, 1958. 420 pp. Chapter 15.

Wilson proposes that every teacher should be able to work with gifted children, describes some on-going programs of teacher education institutions and public school systems, and makes practical suggestions for undergraduate programs designed to prepare teachers for the gifted.

TRUMP, J. LLOYD. *Images of the Future: A New Approach to the Secondary School.* Urbana, Illinois: Commission on the Experimental Study of the Utilization of the Staff in the Secondary School, 1959. 48 pp.

This publication looks at the secondary school of the future and projects a flexible program which will provide opportunity for every student to achieve to the limit of his ability. A brief section on the implications for the education of the gifted is included.

WITTY, PAUL A. (ed.). *The Gifted Child.* Boston: D. C. Heath & Company, 1951. 338 pp. Chapter 6.

This chapter discusses the kind of teachers gifted children want as revealed in the remarks and testimony of gifted children themselves. A brief discussion of the preparation of teachers of the gifted is also included in this chapter.

9

The Role of
the Community

Society has, in the past, shown but little concern for seeking out and developing unusual mental ability. With notable exceptions the predominant philosophy is expressed in the sentiment, "Genius will out." Or in other words, the gifted will get along all right so there is no reason to be concerned about them. Attention has, for the most part, been directed toward the mentally and physically handicapped. Their need is evident and the enlistment of aid for them has been less difficult.

However, a more intelligent philosophy is superseding the "laissez-faire" attitude toward the gifted. It is based on the principle that every individual should have the opportunity to develop his abilities to the utmost. This does not mean the same opportunity but rather opportunity commensurate with ability.

Hughes and Lancelot[1] in their book, *Education—America's Magic,* have put the proposition well:

We have long held a confused idea of "democracy." It does not mean that all men are equal in ability. It does not mean that identical schooling might be open to all. It does mean that opportunity to reach the highest posts should be provided for all, regardless of wealth or poverty, or of high or humble birth. It means that every promise

[1] Raymond M. Hughes and William H. Lancelot, *Education: America's Magic* (Ames, Iowa: Iowa State College Press, 1946), p. 133.

258

of ability is entitled to recognition and encouragement. It means that each youth should have the education that is best fitted to his needs and capacity.

This is true democracy in education. Such a philosophy makes special education for the gifted just as necessary and justifiable as special education for the mentally retarded. Each is an adaptation of the regular program to meet the needs of divergent mental abilities. While it may be true that the gifted individual is able to develop his abilities more successfully than his counterpart at the other end of the intelligence scale, this in no way obviates the principle of equal opportunity. If the institutions of society are to be fair to all, they must adapt educational practice to meet the needs of all.

Eugene Ayres,[2] writing in the *American Scientist*, said, "If it is possible to teach genius, instead of merely hoping it will come along, the future will belong to the society that first discovers how." This statement reflects a point of view which recognizes the responsibility of society to cultivate, as it were, the best of its human resources. People recognize now more closely than ever before the overwhelming importance of human talent in a world whose complexity is constantly increasing. Furthermore, in a world as fiercely competitive as the one in which we live the nation can ill afford to neglect those who offer greatest promise in the intellectual field.

If our society is to meet successfully the challenge of rapidly changing times, it seems almost elementary that we must search out the superior mind and do all possible to stimulate and guide its development. Almost every day the frontiers of human knowledge are pushed a little farther into the unknown. Every week marks an advance in technological development. Each year records the unlocking of one or more of the secrets of nature which have lain hidden for centuries. Yet men are faced with greater problems as a result.

[2] Eugene Ayres, "Social Attitude Toward Invention," *American Scientist*, XLIII, 4 (October, 1955), 521-40.

The situation is aptly expressed in the old Oriental proverb, "The larger the circle of light, the greater is the periphery of darkness."

The very discoveries which make man's physical life easier and more comfortable increase his mental burdens. Advances in communication and methods of travel have placed a greater strain on intergroup and international relations. Inventions in the field of weapons and armament have forced the world to recognize the interdependence of nations. Whether we like it or not we no longer can think and plan exclusively at the national level. We must think and act in global terms because we live in a world which science and technology have made interdependent. The vast populations of Asia and Africa are stirring like sleeping giants. Once these populations become industrialized they may well become decisive powers in a world which heretofore has been little concerned with them.

The development of human resources goes on at an accelerated pace throughout the modern world. It is in effect an international movement in which each nation competes within itself and with the other nations of the world. The objective may be a higher standard of living, territorial expansion, industrial supremacy, military superiority, self-rule, or even self-preservation. Regardless of the objective, its attainment depends on effective development and utilization of the men, women, and children who make up the available human resources.

Such a world places a high premium on intelligence. Our society demands that its leaders be able to think on highly complex conceptual levels. Scientific advances require a tremendous background of knowledge as well as creative imagination and ingenuity. Domestic affairs and foreign relations present problems which to the average person appear insoluble. In such an atmosphere few will argue against the full utilization of the most able of our human resources.

The existing social and political structure of American democracy places the primary responsibility for identifying and developing these resources upon the community. The thousands of communities spreading from coast to coast form the solid foundation upon which the social structure rests. Communities vary widely in geographical size, wealth, population, and the many other characteristics of sociological units. However, they have much in common also. They are all integral parts of sovereign states and exist and function within the framework of state governments. The states in turn are bound together in national unity with common customs, traditions, laws, and government.

In such a social context, it is obvious that whatever is done for the gifted in the community will be directly reflected in the welfare of the nation and of society as a whole.

THE AMERICAN COMMUNITY

Historically, the American community has possessed a large measure of local autonomy. Within limits set by the state and national governments, the American community has functioned as a sociological unit. It has had great freedom in determining its form of government, educational policies, cultural provisions, public health program, provisions for safety and public welfare, and the nature and extent of its recreational facilities.

The public educational system is a good example of community self-determination. The public school in America is essentially a community institution. Although the legal structure in the United States places the responsibility for education on the state, this responsibility to a great extent has been delegated to the local community. The state can and does impose certain minimum standards, but the nature and quality of education in a community is largely determined by the community itself. Local control allows each community to adapt its educational program to its peculiar needs. Local control also permits the type of experimentation in the schools which can lead to better and more comprehensive education.

Local control of education is quite consistent with the democratic way of life. It permits a freedom of action which encourages the individual to participate to the fullest extent in the development of educational policy. It opens the way to close and mutually beneficial cooperation between school and community. In this cooperative venture of providing education, it is the responsibility of the people of the community through their representatives to establish, within limitations, the purposes and the local policies of the school, and it is the responsibility of the professional educators to translate those purposes and policies into an educational program calculated to serve the best interests of the people of the community. These "best interests" are not interpreted in terms of the community alone, but in terms of the state, the nation, and the world.

This close and continuous relationship between school and community lends itself admirably to the development of an adequate and effective program for the education of the gifted. The "school-community" is the logical combination for developing this type of program. To encourage such developments, a number of states have appropriated funds to cover the excess cost of special provisions for the education of the gifted. On a national basis, scholarship funds have been established by the federal government as well as by a number of foundations and public-spirited corporations. While state provisions tend to encourage the community to act and national scholarships offer an inducement to the gifted to seek higher levels of training, the essential responsibility for the education of the gifted rests upon the "school-community."

Unfortunately, the concern for the gifted shown by the vast majority of communities is considerably less than that shown for soil conservation, wild life preservation, industrial expansion, and even the education of the physically and mentally handicapped. This apparent lack of concern about the full development of the abilities of gifted children and youth is probably based on a widely prevalent philosophy expressed in the quotation, "Why worry about the gifted? They'll get along all right." In addition, many people still hold to the notion that special educational opportunities for the gifted constitute special privilege, favoritism, and undemocratic practice. Furthermore, such programs necessitate some increase in financial outlay for teaching personnel, supervisors, and extra equipment and materials. Also, the difficulty in securing teachers who have the knowledge and skill required to make curricular adjustments for the gifted, guide their independent study, or conduct special classes for them has no doubt been a factor. Last but not least, the administrative problems which are encountered in providing special classes, making curricular adjustments, and providing opportunity for independent study and experimentation are not small obstacles.

Community Provisions for the Gifted

No matter what the skills or the experiences may be that are provided by community agencies or by private individuals and groups of the locality, the factors of awareness of the need for offering the gifted these varieties of stimulating and rewarding experiences, and sufficient interest to provide the time, space, facilities, and personnel needed to carry out the program are required.

Realization of the need for these added experiences is undoubtedly basic to setting up such facilities or programs. It must be acknowledged that although the school can and should expose all its students to the cultural and educational values to be obtained from acquaintance with many fields of knowledge, it cannot do the entire job of producing completely trained specialists and artists in any field. The school is only one of the agencies or institutions the community establishes to enable its people to learn; unless some of the other institutions act to supplement the school's work, the job is but partially done.

Once the need for added valuable services beyond those provided by the school is realized and accepted as a community responsibilty, there will be interest in developing programs on the part of those who have attained understanding of the situation. A wide base of thoughtful support will enhance the possibilities of enlisting the help of variously skilled and talented adults to provide leadership for the services offered. Adults who have had the experience of working with eager and enthusiastic youngsters will probably realize that the leaders derive much benefit from the association with gifted youth; others may need some persuasion to give their time to the projects that are planned. Sometimes the teachers of the community work in summer programs, thereby adding their professional knowledge of how best to work with boys and girls in developmental activities. Communities, however, ought not expect their teachers automatically to be available for such extra programs, particularly during the school year when their time and energy are required to handle their regularly assigned teaching load properly. Skilled adult leadership from outside the school system remains an important factor in developing effective programs.

A community that has already developed offerings for creative adults such as ceramics classes, great books seminars, art appreciation courses, and drama groups, is more likely to realize the values of such services for gifted youth. A community barren of interests for one age level may show more reluctance in establishing services to benefit others.

Cost is another factor to be considered. That programs designed to help locate, develop, and release talent cost money cannot be denied. Money is needed to build or rent suitable space, to purchase appropriate equipment and supplies, and to engage skilled leadership. A community may be more willing to establish and support the kinds of agencies that benefit large numbers of its residents than to organize services that seemingly benefit only a small proportion. In the case of libraries, art galleries, concert halls, museums, civic auditoriums, and sports arenas, this qualification does not seem to be prohibitive. These kinds of places are accepted as community buildings. If there are known services already established for other small groups, such as the provision of "talking books" for the use of the blind, or the provision of special recreation facilities for the crippled, there are precedents to provide for the gifted groups in the community.

Often groups of private citizens assume responsibility for some improvement project in the community as a public service. Some of the Braille book purchases, and the supplying of materials for use in retarded children's groups, come from such sources. It would be possible for a few adults who recognize the need for helping gifted children as a worthy project to interest their clubs in such work. Though this would not be a comprehensive community action, it might well start more people thinking along these lines. Particularly would this be true as the club's activities were publicized in local newspapers. Often such ventures develop into a community project from such a small beginning.

Four factors that influence the nature of school provisions for the gifted are: "(1) Size, complexity, and wealth of the community. (2) Social structure and social values of the community. (3) Leadership in the community. (4) Getting community understanding and support."[3]

These same factors would seem to be influential in community-sponsored action for the gifted to provide effective programs beyond that which the schools are able to offer.

The size of a community as well as its geographical proximity to a metropolitan area may determine whether or not it will or should provide the museums, galleries, and concert halls previously mentioned. The wealth upon which the community draws for its support usually determines the adequacy of such general facilities as are provided. Public-spirited individuals, in some cases, give libraries and art museums to their home communities and often make substantial endowments for their maintenance. However, most communities do not have this good fortune to augment the services their tax money can provide. Small communities at a prohibitive distance from population centers that do offer such services may band together to develop programs accessible to each, and thus benefit the gifted youth and adults from several areas with one cooperative enterprise.

The social structure of the community may dictate the provision of general services and facilities for all residents, as opposed to those which would benefit a small selected group. The gifted can select from these services all those that are most helpful to them. Programs specifically for the

[3] Havighurst, NSSE, *Education for the Gifted, op. cit.,* pp. 393-94.

gifted are not characteristic of this social climate. Even in these cases, however, the Saturday morning classes at the museum, while theoretically established for all, will tend to be composed of selected youngsters who continue to attend because of interest or ability or even parental pressure, after those less interested and less able have dropped out of the group.

The social values of the community will influence community action for any group. If the prevalent beliefs hold that equal opportunity should be interpreted as identical opportunity, any community-sponsored program will reflect that belief. If the emphasis is placed on opportunities for all residents to fully develop their abilities, a different sort of a program may evolve. The accepted and trusted leadership in the community could influence it to develop and offer programs different from those expected in the light of the other factors involved. If the leadership viewed as responsible and informed decided that there was value to be gained for the community in operating a program to help discover and develop its gifted citizens, this would probably form the pattern of the community program. If the relied-upon leadership elements felt otherwise, community acceptance of responsibility toward the gifted would likely be less.

None of these factors operates separately from the others; all are interwoven into the fabric that makes the community what it is. Awareness of the need for providing services for the gifted, plus acceptance of this responsibility as a proper function of the community, seem paramount; the other enabling and limiting factors follow logically once this base is established.

Community Agencies Serving the Gifted

The community through its agencies can and in some cases does play an important role in the education of gifted boys and girls. The school, as a community agency whose responsibility and support goes beyond community boundaries, is the primary agency for the education of the gifted as well as all other members of the community. However, there are many other community agencies which are uniquely qualified to share in the educative process and specifically to aid in the education of the gifted. The attitudes of the community and the institutions it supports obviously can affect the development of its gifted citizens favorably or unfavorably. The community can be a laboratory in which the gifted are encouraged to explore, develop, and learn, or it can be a place of meager opportunity from which people wish to escape.

A basic attitude necessary to community support of opportunities for the gifted to enrich their lives involves community awareness of its responsibility to all of its residents, gifted included. A community that accepts responsibilities in the area of worthwhile leisure time activities may offer recreational programs outdoors when weather permits and in community buildings during cold seasons. The presence of a system of parks, and recreation facilities such as swimming pools, playgrounds, tennis courts, and ice skating rinks, gives some evidence of the community's acceptance of its obligation to provide space and facilities for the worthy use of its residents' leisure time. A further step will include planned programs of a recreational nature staffed by people who are willing to use their skills to help others to learn profitable uses for leisure time. Such programs can include sports and games for all ages, crafts, music activities, dancing of various types, swimming lessons—all kinds of supervised recreational activities planned not only for the spending of leisure time, but for its wise use in recreation.

Another worthy use of leisure time as well as an opportunity to enhance the educational and cultural lives of the citizens involves the library supported by the community. For gifted people, a more than merely adequate library is an essential feature of any community. The printed materials, fiction and nonfiction, offer much that is of value in entertainment and in extending one's horizons beyond the scope of one's own circumscribed life. Gifted boys and girls especially can make use of a well-selected library, as they are able to gain much valuable information through their reading. The community has a duty to provide library facilities for all its citizens, even though these may seem to be benefitting only a small proportion of the residents. A further or concomitant responsibility might be to encourage greater or wider use of the library by more people. The annual bookweek observation may be supplemented by other campaigns to help the citizens realize the values they can receive from increased use of the library.

Reading, enjoying, and learning from the books available is just one aspect of the contributions a library can make to the citizens of the community. Adequate research materials can be useful to almost anyone who is working on a research project, designing stage setting for a play and verifying costume details, or writing a history of the area. A well-chosen selection of worthwhile periodicals, including those magazines and newspapers less likely to be available in the homes, will be welcomed by the gifted students and the gifted adults of the community as well.

Of fully as much significance as the varied collections of reading matter is the valuable assistance which is offered to the community by a well-trained librarian who is interested in helping people to choose materials that will be useful and pleasurable to them. The enthusiastic librarian can aid school and home in developing the desire for continued reading throughout life. Some librarians organize books clubs to encourage children's reading during the summer months when school is not in session. Many librarians offer weekly story hours for different age groups. Some have even developed creative writing groups to which children may bring their stories and poems for helpful criticism and recognition of merit. Tasteful exhibits embodying notices of newly published books and established classics can encourage wider reading; such bulletins or posters can be shown in city buildings, department stores, and banks, as well as in the library itself. Librarians can offer valuable guidance to all the community, and the gifted can benefit materially from this help, even though the library is not established for them exclusively.

Museums, zoos, and botanical gardens supported by community funds form another source of learning and pleasure open to all members of the community. Quite often the establishment of such facilities may be at least partially supported by private endowments, but they are managed by the community.

Museums of art, history, natural science, and industry, will be familiar to the reader. Each with its authentic exhibits and trained curators offers expanded learning opportunities for the members of the community who wish to take advantage of the opportunities thus available. Each variety of museum may develop Saturday study groups in which interested youngsters may participate during the year. Many art museums offer classes for children interested in art expression; such classes can be helpful to all children, but as time progresses, it is usually the talented ones who continue to attend the sessions and profit most from them. In essence then, these become classes for gifted children in the field of art and art appreciation.

Lectures are often planned as part of a museum's program; a gifted child may read notices of such opportunities in the local newspaper and ask to be taken to one on a subject of interest to him. His parents may initiate this attendance too. As the youngster becomes familiar with the museums and their exhibits, he may become acquainted with the guards or curators. Many a gifted child has profited from such an acquaintanceship with a specialist in a field in which the two are able to study and learn, the child working with the sympathetic guidance of the older person.

Museums of science, while admittedly not common to many communities, can offer much advanced knowledge as well as entertainment for their visitors. Particularly those museums that are so organized that the visitors may manipulate the exhibits and thus participate in the action, offer valuable learning experiences for gifted students. They can analyze the processes they initiate, and learn from the intricacies of the operations involved. The possibility of seeing scale models of the universe, of creatures of the past, of mines, railroads, submarines, and the like, are exciting to most children, though gifted ones will undoubtedly profit more from them, because of their ability to make more from their experiences.

Zoos at first thought appear in childhood memories to contain entirely entertainment values—the performing animals, the picnic areas, the fun of seeing the elephants, the hippopotamuses, and the ancient Galapagos tortoises. More reflective analysis will show the learning values of the examples of many species of birds, reptiles, and mammals that are displayed. A gifted youngster whose interests lie in the direction of learning about living things has a wealth of information available in such animal exhibits. He can study the explanatory cards attached to the cages or houses, and learn a great deal of value from them. He can also become acquainted with the men who care for the animals, and may be permitted to work with them, and thus extend even further his learning about the habits of the animals.

Community institutions often include YMCA, YWCA, YMHA, and YWHA organizations dedicated to helping people achieve better living within the framework of a particular religious pattern. They schedule classes in indoor and outdoor sports for the learning of the skills, and for the recreational values offered. As these institutions operate with groups of people, the program has social as well as educational significance. They offer crafts, games, conversation groups, language study, and guidance and counsel. Such classes are usually organized by age groups within the boys' and men's and the girls' and women's divisions. The gifted of any age level can participate in the activities offered, and profit by increased skill and social contacts as their interests are challenged and stimulated. The life-saving courses sponsored by the Red Cross are often part of the swimming program; this allows the acquisition of greater useful skill than can be achieved by swimming for recreational purposes only.

The directors, instructors, and other staff members of such institutions can help to discover and foster talents in the areas with which they are most familiar as they work with and learn to know the members and their specific skills.

So far the discussion has dealt with agencies supported by the community for the betterment of its citizens. Admission is open to all; the uses of libraries, recreational facilities, museums, zoos, and Y organizations are available to every citizen of the community. They are not restricted to certain groups. There are some other kinds of agencies, approved by the community in the sense that they are allowed to function within the area, that are more nearly pointed to people of a certain talent or interest. Children's theaters and choirs or other musical organizations are examples of such selected opportunities.

Summer theater for adults is growing rapidly in many towns and cities over the country. Interest in such activities for grown people may sometimes lead to the establishment of similar opportunities for youngsters.

Many communities offer children's theaters which under the direction of a talented adult give children experiences in acting, designing, choreography, costuming, and performing as members of a dramatic group. Children can thus learn the business of dramatics as they participate actively with such groups. The actual performances, open to the public, offer other youngsters opportunities to see plays they might otherwise miss, and to profit from the children's theater as spectators.

Depending somewhat upon the kinds of talents available from the adults who are willing to give time to such activities for talented children, children's theaters can branch into puppetry and marionettes. This activity can involve crafts experiences as well as those related to dramatics, as the youngsters would be helped to design, make, and clothe their puppets as well as to construct the stage settings needed for different plays to be performed.

Musical activities unrelated to school are found in many cities. A number have developed boys' choirs open to youths with good voices, no matter where they may live in the city. Some churches offer musical training to youngsters who then sing at the various church services. Good choirs are in demand to perform for service clubs and other organizations. Some cities stress community music activities as much as others stress athletic teams. Interest runs high as the community band marches in parades and competes in contests. Community orchestras also flourish in an atmosphere of support for musical activities. These are not amateurish groups though they may be composed of musicians of amateur status. Ordinarily, the director or someone in charge will have had some professional experience from which the others benefit as they work to produce creditable performances. Such organizations offer talented youth excellent opportunities for learning and performance beyond that which the school can supply.

Communities located within short distances of colleges and universities often take advantage of the educational and cultural opportunities offered by them. Interested townspeople, including both gifted youngsters and gifted adults, can take part in the activities sponsored by the colleges. These may include performances by gifted actors, talented musicians, athletes, and able speakers on many topics, which offer spectator opportunities, as well as lessons in the many fields of knowledge represented in the college program. Music departments give lessons which can be used for discovering and fostering talent; art departments often schedule classes for children talented in art, with the college professors giving their time to helping these youngsters advance in their use of various art media; the foreign language departments arrange lessons for interested and able students and adults. It may be possible for a youngster sincerely interested in science to work in the laboratories as a supplement to the opportunities his own school can offer him. Gifted students may be accepted as special registrants in courses they are qualified to study and able to profitably pursue.

Some communities support theaters that schedule foreign films or art films which present informational material well-filmed and well-acted, for the residents to enjoy. These films are usually of somewhat better quality in conception, acting, photography, and direction than the customary movie production available in commercial movie houses. These more worthwhile films can help gifted people to see plays and operas they would otherwise have little opportunity to enjoy and to learn about. Gifted youngsters may profit from the acting, the language, the music, and the evidences of well-handled technical production.

Each institution or agency which has been described depends upon community support in terms of money contributed to its continuance, and time and energy given by interested adults, both based upon a feeling that such opportunities are part of the community's responsibilities to its citizens. The schools of the community are obviously unable to supply all the kinds of experiences that can be helpful to the development of the potential of gifted children. The community must recognize its responsibility to supplement the school's work with additional opportunities for worthwhile experience, even though these may seemingly benefit only a small proportion of the residents. From a somewhat selfish point of view a community may wish to hold its gifted youngsters, to keep them aware of the contributions they can make to society right in their own community, and thus provide incentives to influence them to remain in that area. A rich environment is required so that giftedness can be nurtured, developed, and usefully applied; communities can add a great deal to the lives of all their people when they become aware of, and plan for, meeting the variety of needs of the gifted. Just as enriched school experiences for the gifted ordinarily increase the effectiveness of the total school program, so can communities enrich the lives of all their people with the attention given to the values sought for the gifted segment of their population.

Such provisions as are offered for the stimulation and development of giftedness by community agencies should consider all ages, from the early preschool years to creative adulthood. It would be shortsighted as well as unfair to establish offerings for one age group and ignore another. Gifted people profit from a continued challenge to their development throughout their lives; their potential can be stimulated and released for their own benefit and that of society, over many years.

Whether or not there are organized community attempts to offer worthwhile programs for the gifted, there may be private individuals and groups who realize the need for such stimulation and do what they can to supply it from their own skills and knowledge.

The skill and knowledge of business and professional men and women can be utilized for the benefit of gifted youngsters in a variety of ways. Many of the seminar programs operated by the schools call upon these people for the specialized help they can give to the youngster's development. They can serve as counselors, bringing intimate knowledge of various professions and occupations to young people and helping them to see the responsibilities entailed in the performances of many kinds of jobs. Individually they may talk with gifted students concerning their specialties, offering personal information that is difficult to obtain in any other way. These personal contacts with competent adults who exhibit sincere interest in their growth will tend to inspire the gifted youths to strive for the maximum development of their potential.

A local industry can arrange to have students gifted in science spend time in the research laboratories working with the technicians, not only to learn the skills involved, but to see the contributions research can make to modern living. Supervised experiences can be provided in the executive offices of the companies so that the gifted may secure an over-all picture of the industry involved.

Service clubs such as Rotary, Kiwanis, and Optimists have sponsored programs in which boys are encouraged to develop their public speaking ability. Interested boys are helped by qualified college students specializing in speech. Reputable judges evaluate the boys' progress in improving the organization and presentation of their material. There may or may not be a contest situation involved, but it is the time and effort given to help the boys improve their speaking ability that offers the greatest values for the gifted students in such programs.

National organizations such as scouting, 4-H, and others active in similar ways, offer programs designed for all youngsters, but the gifted can use these programs for the pursuit of certain knowledges and the development of particular skills they wish to possess but are unable to attain in other ways. Although not strictly community activities, they must depend upon local leadership and support for their existence in each locality.

Junior Achievement is the name given to a plan whereby interested industrialists and civic leaders sponsor and furnish working capital for small business enterprises operated by talented juniors and seniors in high school. These enterprises provide real experiences for youth in producing valuable goods and services for consumption by the citizens of the community. Since its beginning in 1919, Junior Achievement has grown to include more than 80,000 youngsters in over 300 cities in the country. The boys and girls develop a workable product, incorporate as a company, keep complete and accurate records of their transactions, report periodically to their sponsors or stockholders, and in general operate their businesses along lines comparable to any established business or industry. The businessmen who back these operations provide rewards for outstanding achievement in manufacturing the products and giving the services; these rewards have included trips to conferences of industries related to the high-school students' production. At such conferences, students participate in analysis and discussions of problems with the men established in such businesses. Rewards in the form of scholarships for the study of economics, commerce, and industrial relations at colleges and universities have also been made. For gifted students the opportunity to continue their education is essential to the full use of their potential; Junior Achievement offers them both valuable experience in the business world, and a chance to advance their formal education.

Junior Achievement in the cities has been compared to 4-H in rural areas; each organization helps youngsters to learn the basic facts of the enterprise in which they may earn their living. They are encouraged and helped to test their abilities and improve their skills by doing, by engaging in a purposeful activity that is meaningful to them at the time they engage in it. They can learn about economics and agriculture in the schools; they can put their knowledge to the test in Junior Achievement and 4-H.

There are boys' state and girls' state operations in which gifted students may participate. Though these are state-wide activities, each local community has the opportunity to choose boys and girls to attend these meetings. The youngsters form model legislatures, elect candidates for government offices, and operate a model state government, sometimes for a week at a time. Variations of this plan include such programs as those in which interested students work with the elected governmental officers of a community for a day. The participants see democratic government in action, and have the opportunity to put the principles to work themselves. Another form of a similar program involves model United Nations Assemblies which are usually a cooperative endeavor of several communities.

In each of these cases, boys and girls interested in government and politics have opportunity to participate actively in programs modeled on the adult ones. The youngsters learn the structure of government and secure the information necessary to discuss current issues intelligently. They derive not only educational values but also social ones as they test their skills in government and politics as well as increase their acquaintanceship with others of similar interests.

The descriptions of the kinds of community agencies and the varied opportunities they can afford for providing extended educational and cultural values for the gifted are not intended to be exhaustive. Sufficient numbers of examples have been given to indicate the many kinds of things that communities can do if they accept the responsibility for helping to discover and develop giftedness among their people of all age groups. Not many communities will provide every opportunity discussed here; but each is in successful operation in many communities throughout the nation.

It is not suggested that all gifted children should be involved in all of these community opportunities. It is suggested that all activities such as those described can be helpful in nurturing, developing, and releasing giftedness, and that they represent part of the community's responsibility in providing facilities to the end that people may live richly and satisfyingly in the community.

Community Motivation of the Gifted

The provisions made by community agencies, institutions, and private citizens or groups for helping the gifted to discover and develop their interests and abilities usually involve effective use of various kinds of motivation. The child is usually conscious of the superior level at which he performs in chosen activities or he would not continue to participate in them. Guidance and counseling are given by the talented adults who give of their skills and energy to lead or sponsor the activities. The successful business and civic leaders who work with the youngsters may also provide examples for them to aspire to, as well as extend the personal, sincere interest that can develop and enhance the desire to achieve in the youngsters. Rewards exist in community programs such as those that have been described; there is the honor of being selected to participate in model government activities; there are exhibits of art creations; there are public performances connected with the speech, music, and dramatic productions. Rewards may take the form of trips to conferences related to the activity; the Junior Achievement program uses such rewards, and so do business and industry as they select youths as delegates to such activities as the National Youth Conference on the Atom, the first meeting of which was held in Atlantic City, New Jersey, on April 30 and May 1, 1959. Three hundred and fifty high-school students and two hundred and fifty of their teachers attended this meeting. The friendly and personal contacts made with adult figures have

been shown to be very influential in helping gifted youngsters make progress in their schooling; the same factors may
be at work in community programs. For that reason if for
no other, the quality of leadership in this connection must be
of the highest.

In the case of the gifted, perhaps the greatest motivation
is the opportunity to learn by doing, to explore new horizons,
to try and fail and try again, and to pursue their interests beyond the bounds of formal education.

Community Action

Effective community action in the education of the gifted,
as in most endeavors, must be based upon wholehearted and
unselfish cooperation among the individuals and agencies involved. Although the school is recognized as the major agency
for the task, it is by no means the sole one. Business, industry,
labor unions, and professional organizations have a responsibility in the discovery and development of superior ability.

The community by active support of its school program can
encourage the school to provide the personnel, equipment,
and type of learning opportunities which will be most beneficial to the gifted student. In some cases it is some interested
and dedicated individual or civic group in the community
that supplies the motivation and sometimes the resources for
special programs for the gifted. The Major Work program of
the Cleveland, Ohio schools, one of the oldest and largest
special programs for the gifted, is a case in point. It was
established in 1921 through the efforts of the Women's City
Club of Cleveland, which assumed financial responsibility
for the extra expense of the program. Much of the credit for
the success of the program is due to the vision of a dedicated
member of the club, the late Mrs. Benjamin Patterson Bole,
and the indefatigable efforts of Mrs. Dorothy Norris, the
person chosen to guide the program from its inception.

Too often the assumption is made that the school can and
does do an adequate job of identifying and meeting the
developmental needs of talented youth. A nationwide survey
of educators in high schools, colleges, universities, and state

departments of education in 1949 revealed that these people thought of the education of the gifted largely in terms of the school program. Although they acknowledged the need for community involvement, few examples of cooperative action along these lines were cited. Today such a survey would likely show a somewhat broader concept of the function of the community in developing the potential of its most able youth. Certainly instances of community involvement could be cited in a number of states. A few examples appear in a later section of the chapter. However, the situation is far from ideal and certainly encourages no sense of complacency among educators and other public-spirited citizens.

Community action programs may be classified under five headings for purposes of discussion. They are:

1. Identification programs
2. Opportunity center programs
3. Supplemental programs
4. General community programs
5. Special community programs

PROGRAMS FOR IDENTIFYING THE GIFTED. The early identification of gifted youth is not only highly desirable but often necessary for their full development. Granted that the parents and the school are the primary sources of identification, it should be recognized that the community as such has a distinct responsibility in this regard. It may discharge this responsibility in part, but only in part, by seeing that the school is provided with every resource necessary to discover talent among its pupils. There are many preschool children, youths who have dropped out of school for one reason or another, and adults who do not come within the purview of the school. If giftedness is to be identified in these groups, parents or some agency of the community must do the job.

The problem of identification outside the school is admittedly a difficult one. Probably it is best approached through the provision for a wide variety of opportunities to exercise ability and then systematically observe people in action. The informal observation corps might consist of persons who possess competencies which would aid in identification. Such people as psychologists, teachers, personnel workers, lawyers, and social workers possess skills and knowledge which would be helpful in the enterprise. Librarians, playground supervisors, YMCA and YWCA directors, and museum curators are often in a position to observe performance and also to note intense interests which may be the harbingers of superior ability.

A second technique which has promise is the community self-survey. Although it has hitherto been largely used in connection with civil rights and employment opportunities and the development of school building programs, there appears to be no reason why it could not be used as a device for locating the gifted. Such a survey might take a number of forms, each of which would provide valuable information in the identification of superior ability. One form might seek to discover all those with a specific talent such as painting, musical composition, or scientific ability. A second form might have as its objective the discovery of talent in whatever guise it might appear. In its broadest form such a survey might seek to compile a list of all the human resources available in the community. An intensive examination might reveal valuable leads in discovering talent.

A second type of self-survey is that designed to locate all types of exceptional children in the community. A particularly effective instrument for such a project is the one developed by T. Ernest Newland[4] and associates called *How to Conduct a Self-Survey of Special Education Needs*. The information secured by such a survey if it is carefully and accurately done can be extremely valuable.

A third approach to community identification is actual testing. Intelligence and aptitude as well as achievement tests may be administered by a psychologist or guidance worker employed by the community on a part-time basis. Or persons who show indications of superior ability may be referred to a commercial testing service and the bill paid by

[4] T. Ernest Newland, Herbert F. Boyd, Donald L. Edwards, Nancy J. Maroney, and Lloyd L. Wolf, *How to Conduct a Self-Survey of Special Education Needs* (Washington, D.C.: International Council for Exceptional Children, 1958), 48 pp.

the community. In cases where the school has adequate testing services incorporated in its program, arrangements may be made to refer preschool children and adults there. Any such plan of course has as its prerequisite an alert group of people throughout the community who are on the lookout for talent, and suggest people for referral to the testing service.

Regardless of the approach used, effective work in the discovery of superior ability is dependent on the social consciousness and keen awareness of a group of public-spirited people in the community.

OPPORTUNITY CENTERS. Opportunity centers is the name given by the authors to a miscellaneous group of agencies which seek to provide opportunities for human self-development. In one community, such a center may be a guidance clinic which provides guidance and counseling free or at a small charge. In another, it may be a little-theater project in which people with dramatic talent may participate. In still another, it may be an art center which provides the materials necessary for the young artist to test and develop his creative ability. Often such centers offer some free instruction as well as lectures in art appreciation. Still another type of opportunity center is the observatory which provides the young student of astronomy an opportunity to view the heavens through a high-powered telescope. Such a center is usually established in cooperation with a college or university which possesses the necessary facilities.

A somewhat different type of center is represented by a scholarship and student loan service set up by a group of businessmen in one community. Although the service is housed in the local high school, it is largely staffed by the businessmen who established it. They search out and secure scholarships and fellowships from large corporations and small businesses for the ablest youth of the community. In case a superior youth lacks the finances to pursue his education, they are supplied from a revolving loan fund. This service represents a real opportunity for many poor but gifted young people.

A third type of opportunity center which could well become the most productive of all is the community research center. A good example of this type of center is the Upjohn Institute for Community Research in Kalamazoo, Michigan. While this particular research center is chiefly concerned with research into the causes and effects of unemployment, its format would lend itself just as readily to research in the identification, nature, and development of superior ability.

Opportunity centers may be supported fully or in part by public funds. They may be established as the result of endowments by wealthy individuals or by foundations. They may be financed by a group of public-spirited citizens. But regardless of their sponsorship, they make valuable contributions to their respective communities in aiding in the development of human talent.

SUPPLEMENTING THE SCHOOL. Often the community is in a favorable position to supplement the program of the school in such a way as to permit the superior student to go far beyond the offerings of the school in the pursuit of his interest and the development of his abilities. The community can open its doors to the high-school student who wants to learn more than his school teaches about the science of government, the process of justice, the art of community planning, and the operation of social service agencies.

Under community sponsorship, the internal workings of industry may be made available for the student's observation. He may spend hours in the laboratories of a manufacturing chemist or the research headquarters of a corporation producing electronic devices. A day's visit to an oil refinery makes a profitable addition to the education of any boy who dreams of becoming a petroleum engineer. With proper cooperation between school and community, the latter may become a vast and interesting laboratory of supplemental learning experiences for talented boys and girls.

Many school systems provide a program of music education for students who desire it. However, in most schools the program is somewhat limited in nature for the talented musi-

cal student. If the community supports a community choir or
a concert band under the leadership of a highly trained con-
ductor, this type of student may have the opportunity to enrich and develop his ability far beyond the limits of the
school program.

In developing supplementary programs, it will probably
be found helpful to form an informal advisory committee
made up of representatives of the school board, the recreation commission, the library board, and perhaps representatives of industry and labor. Such a board could develop plans
and make facilities available and serve as a facilitating
agency for supplementary programs. Such an arrangement
offers many advantages, not the least of which is the development of closer cooperation among the various agencies
which serve the community.

GENERAL COMMUNITY PROGRAMS. There are in most communities a number of general activity programs which are
open to all but from which the gifted may profit. In fact,
such programs are much more numerous than the other
types mentioned in this chapter. Many of these activities
are sponsored by national organizations with chapters or
branches in the local community. The local group operates
with considerable autonomy with certain common goals and
within a broad framework established by the national organization. Examples of such organizations are the YMCA,
YWCA, Boy Scouts, Girl Scouts, Jewish Youth League,
Junior Achievement, and Junior Red Cross.

Local programs of this nature, of course, vary from community to community. In one community it may be a library
program in which the librarian serves as a leader in the study
and practice of creative writing, discussions of great books, or
the analysis of current events. Often authors, travelers, and
lecturers serve as guest leaders at meetings. Meetings may
be held monthly or sometimes biweekly. In another community an art program may be sponsored; in another, a
dramatic club.

All such programs offer opportunities for gifted people to pursue their interests and develop their abilities. Most, if not all such activities, are available after work or school hours, so no one is excluded because of work or school attendance.

While these programs are open to all they do not preclude individual performance at any level of achievement. The lock-step procedure which exists to some extent in all schools is not present. Since activities are largely on an individual basis, the gifted have unlimited freedom to excel and achieve.

SPECIAL COMMUNITY PROGRAMS. In some places community programs have been organized especially for the gifted. Although such communities are at present few in number, their numbers are increasing. Interested citizens and civic groups are becoming increasingly aware of the need for locating and developing the most able human resources of the community. Programs involving opportunity for the gifted to study and practice painting, ceramic art, drama, architectural design, sculpture, and aeronautics are in existence at the present time. More are being proposed. Large corporations are acutely conscious of the need for the development of able business leadership and in many cases are willing to sponsor and financially support youth programs aimed at developing leadership qualities. Often the only obstacle to the establishment of such programs is the lack of qualified personnel.

In Illinois, the Quincy Youth Development Commission project described briefly later in this chapter is one of the most comprehensive and ambitious community programs in behalf of the gifted so far inaugurated. The project is a joint effort of the community and the Committee on Human Development of the University of Chicago. It is to be hoped that this project will be the forerunner of many such cooperative efforts involving the community and institutions or agencies devoted to the development of our most valuable resources.

Although many problems are faced in establishing such special programs, they can and will be solved if the people of the community believe strongly in the necessity of providing for the gifted as well as for the handicapped. Problems of identification, sponsorship, financing, housing, and securing qualified personnel to work in the program have all been solved in one way or another in various communities throughout the country. It is not too much to expect that they will be solved in many more.

Community Programs in Action

A few current programs are identified and briefly described in this section. Many similar ones are in operation in various communities throughout the nation.

DALLAS. A creative writing club for able and interested children is sponsored by the children's department of the Dallas Public Library. Each year the board of education sends notices concerning the program of the club to all schools; the librarian in charge of the children's department herself publicizes the classes through informal talks and speeches to various groups.

There are usually two classes, each enrolling about twenty children, one for elementary- and one for secondary-school students. The librarian helps the youngsters criticize their own writings; she also encourages reading and observation as well as writing in various forms, both prose and poetry.

There are exhibits of the children's writing, some contest activity, and occasionally publication in magazines and newspapers. Some of the participants have earned college scholarships in recognition of their creative writing ability.

DAYTON. The Rotary Club of Dayton, Ohio, sponsors the Dayton Boys' Choir which is composed of about ninety boys aged nine to eighteen. As additional voices are needed, voice and music-reading tests are given to applicants who are recommended by parents and teachers, or volunteer to join. The director of the group is the music supervisor in the public schools. Student officers are elected; social and leadership qualities as well as musical ability are developed. The more talented boys are asked to sing solos as a part of the programs which are presented before both private and public audiences.

LAWRENCE. In Lawrence, Kansas, the Children's Summer
Studio sponsored by the recreation council of the city serves
about two hundred children who work with half a dozen
teachers in four-week sessions each summer. They study
crafts, drawing, and painting. Any child who is enrolled in
the public schools during the year may attend. Originally the
program was financed by private individuals and interested
groups, but currently costs are assumed by the board of education and the community chest.

Creative work is emphasized and a wide variety of art
materials is available for the youngsters' use. Young children
explore and experiment widely with many materials; older
ones register in classes using media such as clay, wood, water
colors, and the like.

Art majors from the University of Kansas get student
teaching experience at the workshops; the children enrolled
can develop talents and learn skills contributing to the worthy
and profitable use of leisure time.

QUINCY. The Youth Development Commission of Quincy,
Illinois, began a ten-year program in 1951 to try to locate
and help children with special needs—gifted and talented
children, children who are educationally, emotionally, or
socially maladjusted, and children who are physically handicapped in any way. The Commission believed that early discovery of such children, and programs designed to help them,
would lead to lessening of delinquency, fostering of ability,
and development of constructive people. The University of
Chicago supplied resident consultants for the project; the
community supplied the usual services for boys and girls,
including schools, Y's, scouting, church organizations, and
others. The project involved the Commission, the community
and the consultants. Four handbooks for teachers have been
written, giving suggestions to help teachers identify these
children, and ideas for helping them in the classroom, at
both the elementary- and secondary-school levels.

The public schools have done a great deal of the work
connected with the project, but some of it has been accomplished by community groups. Specifically for the gifted the

adult drama group located children talented in dramatics and developed theater groups for young children and adolescents. Drama teachers were hired, paid from the ten-dollar fee collected from the youngsters. Scholarships were available for those talented children who were unable to pay. Plays were presented by the groups after several weeks of study. It was intended that such an initial program would lead to a permanently established community activity.

WORCESTER. The Worcester Art Museum in Worcester, Massachusetts, offers classes in block printing, drawing, modeling, and painting for all youngsters in the city, aged four through eighteen. Talent is not a criterion for entrance into the classes, but those who do exhibit ability are asked to attend the after-school classes two days a week, as more individual attention can be given them than in the crowded Saturday morning classes. About 1,250 youngsters are registered for these classes each year.

The program is supported by the museum's endowment fund. For the children enrolled the purposes include experience, understanding, and enjoyment of art. Student teachers from Clark University also participate in the program.

The Worcester Girls' Club, supported partially by a small endowment but mostly by community chest funds, aims to promote responsible citizenship among school-age girls. Several thousand girls participate in the program each year. The music activities particularly attract girls talented in vocal and instrumental music.

Related State and National Programs

STATE PROGRAMS. A number of states stimulate and encourage the education of the gifted by appropriating funds for use in research on the gifted at the state level. Most state departments include personnel whose duties are to aid the local schools in improving their programs for exceptional children. Although major attention has been given to the handicapped, some states include a specialist in the education of the gifted on their staffs. Furthermore, a number of states provide funds for paying the excess cost of programs for the education of the gifted, over the regular program.

A new and encouraging trend appearing among the states is the offering of college and university scholarships by the state department of education. Recipients are usually high-school seniors who qualify by examination. Although such scholarships are available to all on an equal basis, they provide a genuine opportunity for the gifted to continue their education at the college level.

NATIONAL PROGRAMS. At the present time the federal government offers scholarships to superior students who are able to qualify in various fields of learning. Indications are that this program will be expanded to a considerable degree in the years ahead.

Many large corporations have established scholarship funds for youth who have interest and ability in science, industry, business, labor unionism, government, law, and international relations. These scholarships are in many cases quite generous and entitle the recipient to attend some of the outstanding institutions in the country.

Finally, there are a number of national organizations whose purpose is to promote the identification and development of superior mental ability in the community and as a consequence in the state and the nation. Such organizations include the American Association for Gifted Children, New York, New York, the Metropolitan Association for the Study of the Gifted, New York, New York, and the National Association for Gifted Children, Cincinnati, Ohio.

These and similar organizations sponsor research and hold conferences on the gifted as well as publish books and journals dealing with the gifted. They provide help to communities which desire to establish programs for the gifted and are sources of information for on-going programs.

SELECTED READINGS

MELBY, ERNEST O. *Administering Community Education.* Englewood Cliffs, N.J.: Prentice-Hall, Inc., 1955. 325 pp. Chapter 2.

    In this chapter, the author points out the far-reaching changes in community organization and structure which have taken place over recent years, and their implications for education.

MERCER, BLAINE E. *The American Community.* New York: Random House, 1956. 304 pp. Chapter 3.

A sociological interpretation of the American community as it functions in our national life is presented in this chapter.

NATIONAL SOCIETY FOR THE STUDY OF EDUCATION. *Education for the Gifted.* Chicago: University of Chicago Press, 1958. 420 pp. Chapters 16 and 17.

Chapter 16 provides criteria for developing a sound program for the enrichment of the lives of the gifted of a community, and gives some examples of community programs developed to serve all the young people of the area, as well as some that are designed specifically for gifted youth.

Chapter 17 indicates the ways in which the social, economic, and cultural factors operative in a community tend to influence the kind of program that may be developed for the gifted youth of the community.

OLSEN, EDWARD G. *School and Community.* Englewood Cliffs, N.J.: Prentice-Hall, Inc., 1945. 422 pp. Chapters 3 and 19.

Chapter 3 presents the major techniques of community analysis together with a brief discussion of the uses and value of each technique. Chapter 19 emphasizes the importance of school-community coordination since "the child is a whole being who is educated by a total environment."

SUMPTION, MERLE R. *How to Conduct a Citizens School Survey.* Englewood Cliffs, N.J.: Prentice-Hall, Inc., 1952. 209 pp. Chapters 1, 2, 4, and 5.

This book, in the chapters cited, describes a procedure by which lay citizens may conduct a school survey which will provide the basis for intelligent planning for the improvement of education in the community. How to select a survey committee, organize it for the job, and the procedures involved in fact-finding, are treated in detail.

WITTY, PAUL A. (ed.). *The Gifted Child.* Boston: D. C. Heath & Company, 1951, 338 pp. Chapter 8.

This chapter, written by Nicholas Hobbs, is devoted to the important factors to be taken into consideration in organizing community programs for the gifted. Descriptions of a number of programs of different types are included in the chapter.

WORMSER, MARGOT HAAS, and SELLTIZ, CLAIRE. *How to Conduct a Community Self-Survey of Civil Rights.* New York: Association Press, 1951. 271 pp. (Copyright, National Board of Young Men's Christian Association.) Pages 1-16, 68-89.

This reference explains why the self-survey is so valuable in securing the necessary facts about a community preliminary to intelligent action. It discusses the resources needed and ways in which community support for the self-survey may be developed. While the authors are mainly concerned with the problem of civil rights, the techniques and procedures have wide application.

10

The Preschool Program

Because the gifted child progresses rapidly in language and concept development in his early childhood, the kinds of developmental experiences he should have are important in these years. Because he is first of all a child, he needs for his best growth and development satisfactions like those of any child, and it is necessary to understand how he grows and why he behaves as he does in order that these common needs may be met. Since he is laying the foundation for his future growth and development, the first stages must be well cared for to the best of his parents' (and teachers') knowledge and ability.

This chapter consequently will point out some of the basic needs of early childhood, and the patterns of growth that are followed by all young children. It will show some possible deviations that may be expected in the gifted child. Suggestions will be given to help adults understand the kinds of experiences helpful to young gifted children, and the values they can derive from such experiences. To insure a good transition from home to school environment and activities, the need for keeping records of the child's early life is stressed. The responsibilities of both home and school are discussed in detail; there is need for both to be concerned with the gifted child in his early years if he is to have the maximum opportunity for growth and development over the years.

CHILD GROWTH AND DEVELOPMENT

During the first five or six years of a child's life he does more growing and developing than he will ever again in a comparable period; the only later period in his life when he even remotely approaches such rapid growth is that of adolescence.

Not only does he grow physically, though the evidence of height and weight and abilities that depend upon physical growth are prominent parts of his development. He grows intellectually, socially, and emotionally as well as physically; he begins to show some of the facets of his developing personality almost as soon as he is born. Some children seem more placid than others by nature; some are actively moving and reaching out insofar as their limited physical development will allow. For example, babies react differently to the withholding of a feeding, or the removal of the bottle midway in their feedings; some protest vigorously while others wait quietly for the bottle's return. They seem to show evidence of the personality which will develop throughout their lives, even at this very early age.

This is not to say that their personality pattern is already formed, and adults may merely sit back and watch as each further manifestation appears; environment plays a significant part in the development of each person as he grows. Parents have it within their power to supply a favorable environment in which a healthy personality can be fostered; they can also hinder or snuff out healthy development. The same statement can be made for physical growth; although growth of a sort will occur, what adults do for a child in feeding, clothing, supplying vitamins, establishing a proper schedule of rest, exercise, and fresh air, as well as developing a supportive aura of affection and discipline, can influence the child's physical growth also.

Obviously, most parents want the best that is possible for their children, and they want this best in terms of physical health as well as emotional stability, intellectual development, and social responses. Not all would state it so concretely; yet most will strive to help their children grow in the best ways in which they can. This best is not always the same as the best that other parents might be striving for with their particular children, but the feelings are basically alike. There are some exceptions; there are unwanted and unloved children; there are parents who pursue their own ends more zealously than they act in helping their children; there are children who are practically forced to fend for themselves. These are unfortunate exceptions; the gifted children to whom this book is devoted may be found in such families and as a result the problems of the schools and teachers will be increased. However, the vast majority of parents in America fall into that group which wants its children to be successful, to live fully and richly, and to develop to the optimum.

Every child passes through a recognizable pattern of development as he progresses from infancy into childhood and indeed into mature adulthood. These growth stages can be expected by parents and teachers; it is not unusual for a two-year-old, for example, to exhibit some negativism in his actions. He may say "no" to mean various things, not the least of which is that he has learned "no" as a word and likes to experiment with its sound as well as to watch the reactions he gets from its use. Somewhere between the ages of eighteen months and three years some experimentation with "no" can be expected, and it becomes easier to deal with as adults realize that it is merely a developmental stage in the child's exploration and growth. It ought not be accepted as evidence that the child is developing an antagonistic personality; it also ought not be ignored as merely something he will outgrow. It requires definite attention, yet that attention need not be of a tense anxious sort if recognition of the normality of "no" is acquired.

Though each youngster does follow a recognizable pattern in his growth physically, intellectually, socially, and emotionally, it is important to realize that the *rate* of growth will be the child's own. He will reach childhood, adolescence, and adult status, but at his own speed. He may surpass the accepted norms at one stage and fall short of them at another; he will continue to grow and he will need to pass through each step on his way. Norms are derived from facts concerning many children, and they represent merely an average; parents need to realize that deviation from the norms is not an automatic cause for alarm. Gifted children should be expected to deviate in some degree from the norms for the growth and development of average children; they may not deviate quite as far in every respect, but some positive deviation should be expected as the child grows. This is one evidence of his giftedness.

A third point about growth which needs to be considered by adults who are concerned with young children is that there may be plateaus along the way. Children grow by leaps and bounds, and they also seem to pass through periods when they make little noticeable advance. The organism may be readying itself for the next step it is to make; growth continues though it may not be noticeable externally to an observer seeking for outward evidence in one aspect of growth. A youngster may concentrate on language development while he persists in coming downstairs by bringing one foot carefully to the other before moving to the next step.

An understanding of growth patterns is basic to understanding how best to help children develop and how to prepare them to manage the next stage successfully. Havighurst believes that it is essential that each developmental task be achieved at its proper time in order for the growing child to be successful in his later achievements. He defines a developmental task as one "which arises at or about a certain period in the life of the individual, successful achievement of which leads to his happiness and to success with later tasks, while failure leads to unhappiness in the individual, disapproval by the society, and difficulty with later tasks."[1] These tasks are forced by the maturation of the individual, the expectations of the society in which he lives, and the desires of the growing personality, or some combination of these factors. They fall somewhere between a purely individual need and a definite demand by society. They are psychologically, biologically, and socially necessary to a person's successful growth. For the infancy and early childhood stages of life with which this chapter is concerned, Havighurst lists these developmental tasks:

[1] Robert J. Havighurst, *Developmental Tasks and Education* (New York: Longmans, Green & Co., Inc., 1952), p. 2.

1. Learning to walk
2. Learning to take solid foods
3. Learning to talk
4. Learning to control the elimination of body wastes
5. Learning sex differences and sexual modesty
6. Achieving physiological stability
7. Forming simple concepts of social and physical reality
8. Learning to relate oneself emotionally to parents, siblings, and other people
9. Learning to distinguish right and wrong and developing a conscience[2]

These developmental tasks and the principles of growth enumerated above can provide practical guides to what parents and other adults ought to be doing to help youngsters develop successfully during their preschool years. Since the gifted youngster must abide by the rules of growth and maturation, and since he must achieve each of these developmental tasks successfully, it seems only logical that adults need to work with these needs, not against them.

There is a certain time in the life of each youngster when he is ready to take a certain step, and no amount of teaching can help him to take that step properly before the organism is ready. For example, there is a great amount of growth and control of muscle and bone structure which is necessary before a child can walk; walking is such a common means of moving about for older people that they sometimes fail to take into account all the parts of the involved process, when they move away from a standing baby and implore or perhaps command him to walk to them. He will walk only when his maturational pattern allows him to, and when his emotional and social growth is sufficient that he can turn loose of supports and move away on his own feet. This certain time, when all the aspects of each individual reach a point at which the organism can make the next step will, of course, be at a different time for different children. The implications for parents and teachers of such a statement are vitally impor-

[2] *Ibid.*, pp. 6-14, *passim.*

tant. They point quite definitely to individualized treatment and instruction, to the necessity of noting carefully the significance of the individual differences of each child.

There are societal expectations for youngsters also to be noted and taken into account, thus compounding the difficulties of dealing with young children. A five-year-old is not expected to use baby talk; but some of them do. A four-year-old is expected to manage his own coat and hat; but some of them cannot. Nursery, kindergarten, and Sunday-school teachers meet these problems as they work with children of varying abilities and differing stages of maturation. Knowledge of expected growth patterns and developmental tasks appropriate to a given age level helps them to understand the youngsters' present stage of development and to assist in further successful achievement. Knowledge of the expectations of the succeeding stages also gives direction to the activities that these teachers plan with their groups of pupils, and to the guidance they provide for each individual child.

EDUCATIONAL GOALS

The goals and objectives for educating a youngster during his preschool years obviously must take the fundamental facts of child growth and development into account. It is futile to set the learning of the skill of handwriting as a goal for a child who is still working at large muscle control and development; yet one task of parents might be to supply materials of appropriate size and weight so that a youngster may be helped in this area of gaining control over large muscle activities to the end that he may be able to use his smaller muscles with adequate and satisfying control when the time comes for him to do so.

In general, the basic goal of education for all stages of development is the same; it is fully developing the child's interests and abilities in such ways that he will grow into a happy and contributing member of his society. This involves self-fulfillment, and surely during the preschool years self-interests seem uppermost. Each society has certain ways of behaving that are considered acceptable; in each, the child's particular self-interests may need to be redirected so that he may grow into these societally accepted and supported ways of acting. Conflicts may occur in which he will need to learn to suppress individual likes to those appropriate to the situation; this is learning and progress in assuming the ways, the customs, the mores of his groups. This does not negate the possibility that some of society's ways may not be the best, and as the individual grows, he may find ways of helping to change and improve them.

The fundamental goal for educating gifted children is like that for educating all children; the differences lie in the stress placed on wider knowledge resulting from broader offerings with more advanced work for the gifted, and the emphasis upon the necessity for more individualized work in the teaching-learning process. The young child requires both security and ever-growing independence; he needs to know that he is wanted and loved and cared for, and yet he strives to achieve those measures of independence of which he is capable in feeding and dressing himself, and in his play, which is a very significant part of his learning and development. In fact, play is the work of childhood.

Hildreth[3] states three goals in the education of gifted children from ages three to eleven as self-exploration, self-direction, and self-management. Self-exploration can be related to the discovering and developing of worthwhile interests; self-direction implies independence with responsibility for one's own actions; self-management can be actively stated as accepting responsibility for oneself behaviorally and in other ways. Each of these is patently related to the idea of independence stated above; adequate assumption of such responsibilities must be based on a fundamental feeling of security as well.

Hollingworth[4] has written that "the education of the best thinkers should be an education for initiative and originality."

---

[3] Gertrude H. Hildreth, *Educating Gifted Children* (New York: Harper & Brothers, 1952), p. 43.

[4] Leta S. Hollingworth. *Children Above 180 IQ* (Yonkers, N.Y.: World Book Co., 1942), p. 290.

Young children are actively curious about everything they experience. They are constantly asking "Why?" and exploring to find "why" for themselves. Sometimes these explorations lead them into difficulties. For example, this need for discovery may yield the fact that a quart container holds more liquid than can be poured into a juice glass. The child learns from his experimentation with many quantities and many things; it is natural for him to pick up an empty locust shell, touch it all over, look at it from every angle, sniff it carefully, and then taste it. He has learned much from tasting when he was quite young; this remains one of his avenues of learning until he realizes that he does not always have to use his sense of taste to complete his analysis of an object. Dirt, mud, sticks, leaves, blocks, dolls—many things may be tasted as the youngster explores and seeks to learn about the things of his world. Adults sometimes scream "No!" when they might better be channeling the youngster's eager curiosity into safe and acceptable patterns of analysis. Yet how many adults dip a finger into some spilled white substance and taste it to find whether it is sugar or salt? A bug is not necessarily a dirty creature to be thrown down to the ground and stepped on; it may be the object from which a child begins to build his concepts of many kinds of animals. Initiative in learning can easily be curbed by emphasis on cleanliness, or not touching, or not exploring; yet initiative in learning is most important to a gifted child who should be helped to form methods and attitudes which will help him to continue his learning and exploring as long as he lives.

Originality and creativity are likewise easily obstructed. All that is necessary is to insist that a child operate according to accepted adult standards and to force these standards upon him regardless of the fact that he is a child with a child's view of and feelings about situations he meets. It is much more helpful to the child's development if he is encouraged to be curious about what he sees, and aided in his attempts at forming concepts according to his own levels of experience. He should be praised for originality of approach whether the exact situation involves block building or the setting up of his train tracks when he is a bit older. Rachel Carson[5] expressed this idea when she wrote "Help Your Child to Wonder." Keep his imagination operative; if he is to develop creative ways of living and learning he needs his curiosity to help him.

Parents, as the first adults with whom children have contact, have definite responsibilities in the children's first learnings. Parents are teachers, and children learn not only much subject matter from them, but they also pick up their parents' feelings and attitudes about the subjects. These first informal teaching-learning situations in which parents and child participate can be haphazard or they can be planned with accurate knowledge of the people involved. Sometimes opportunities arise which have not been planned and advantage must be taken of them at the time when they are available. The appearance of a crew of workers to cut down and haul away a dead tree is an opportunity for learning which may occur right outside one's front door. In other words, while these beginning learning experiences may surely be somewhat informal, they ought to be recognized as bases for learning, and they should be built upon a plan which takes account of the knowledge of how children grow, and yet is flexible enough to allow for some unplanned activities as opportunities present themselves. For these reasons, parents have been mentioned in their teaching guise during this discussion of goals and objectives in learning. Parents do not lose this role when their youngsters start more formal schooling; they continue to teach their children many things though not so formally and not in such large units as schools commonly do.

PARENTAL RESPONSIBILITIES

Parents have some specific duties in the rearing of a gifted preschool child, in addition to their functions as the child's first teachers, and in addition to those commonly accepted responsibilities in the rearing of any child as expressed in

[5] Rachel Carson, "Help Your Child to Wonder," *Woman's Home Companion*, 83: 24-7, July, 1956.

the developmental tasks concept referred to above. For a gifted child to make his best progress in school from the very beginning of his first experience with a school, it is necessary that his teacher have as much relevant information about him as can be obtained. Parents can help by keeping records of the child's growth and development during his pre-school years. As the study of the individual child should be the basis for sound educational procedures, so it is the basis for being a good parent; these records are thus helpful to the parents as well as to the teachers. They are also of interest to the child in his later years.

Keeping Records

BABY BOOKS. Many parents keep baby books as records of their child's growth during his first years of life. The commercial booklets ordinarily provide space for entering information as to when the youngster accomplished many firsts: first smile, first laugh, first tooth, first sitting unaided, first words, first steps alone, and so forth. They may have pages for listing important events such as Christmas and birthday celebrations, playmates and friends, and baptismal records. There are usually blanks for keeping age, height, and weight records, and some provide space to write about the travels the child takes. Oftentimes there are pages on which records of immunizations can be made.

These notes should be kept up-to-date as the events occur; their contents are more likely to be accurate when each item is entered as it happens than when memory is relied upon exclusively. Memories become mixed with other events; while retrospection can be of some help, it is not usually as accurate as the daily or weekly or monthly systematic approach to writing down the significant events in the child's life.

Some parents prefer to make their own records, to have them more personalized than the commercial books allow. These can follow somewhat the same pattern, but offer greater space for recording the child's development more thoroughly and over a longer period of time. They can be of loose-leaf construction to allow additions as the child has more experiences. One set of parents report they have kept and are continuing to keep records of their three children who are now in their teens. These records are known as "Davy's Diary," "Marilyn's Memoirs," and "Bobby's Boyhood." Such carefully-kept written records as these will surely be of interest to the youngsters themselves as they grow older; they also provide much needed pertinent information which the parents can share with the teachers as they work to help each child have the most appropriate and meaningful educational experiences.

PICTURES. In addition to the written records, many parents also keep a file of snapshots of their youngsters. This may well be done systematically too, taking pictures of the youngster each month or quarterly. These offer a pictorial supplement to a mere listing of height and weight measurements; they can also help show the child's personality growth and his interests as he smiles or frowns, as his favorite toys and playmates begin to appear in the pictures as he grows older, and as his parents prepare explanatory paragraphs for each snapshot at the time it is put into the file or mounted in an album.

HOME MOVIES. Another means of keeping pictorial records of children is the home movie. To be used to the greatest advantage there should be a systematic or regular pattern or sequence followed in these movies. Some parents take movies of each birthday, or each Christmas, and supplement them with vacation movies. The movies have an advantage over still pictures in that they can show action, and the child's ability to move; one disadvantage is the relatively greater cost and the need of extra equipment for taking the movies, viewing them, and sharing their contents with other interested adults.

Color slides can be made by some still picture cameras. and a three-dimensional viewer can be almost as effective in showing the pictures as a projector and screen. Such slides would also be easier to share and to use than movies, but they fail to show a youngster's dexterity and agility as he moves about.

TAPE RECORDINGS. A somewhat newer method of record-keeping involves the use of the tape recorder to preserve sounds, language attempts, stories, and events deemed significant to the child's development. The youngster's own voice can be recorded and the tapes preserved to indicate his growth in language, understanding of concepts, conversational ability and word usage, and knowledge of various subjects. The only limits to what might be helpfully recorded would be the limits of the parents' and children's ideas on the subject. Here again there are expenses to be considered in purchasing the necessary equipment to record and to play back the sounds.

RECORD COMBINATIONS. The most complete record combines aspects of all that have been mentioned. If expense is a limiting factor in this task of record-keeping, the personalized baby book combined with a snapshot file can be quite satisfactory. The others offer excellent supplementary information to the basic records, but descriptions of such events can be written into the record when the costs of action movies and tape recordings make their use prohibitive.

SUGGESTED RECORD CONTENT. What should this record consist of? There should be the important firsts mentioned above, the listings in chronological order of height and weight gains, the trips taken by the youngster and his reactions to them, his childhood illnesses and immunizations against possible illness, his visits for check-ups to the doctor, dentist, oculist, or other special care that he might require, his playmates, and his interests in various toys and games. Each item should be dated, and comments should be attached by the parents concerning the child's apparent reactions to his experiences. As these ought to be individualized records, each will contain many different items as well as the basic ones. Each parent will need to judge what has been of significance in his own child's development; to that extent the choice of items and incidents to record by written comment or by snapshot will be somewhat subjective. The pictures will be objective, and the comments should be written as objectively as a parent can make them when he is writing about his own youngster. An example of a full record of a child's first ten years may be found in Gilmer's *How to Help Your Child Develop Successfully*.[6]

Providing a Favorable Environment

LOVE AND SECURITY. The human infant is more completely dependent upon adults for the necessities of life than is the young of any other species, and he remains dependent for a much longer time than do other young animals, who are able to forage for themselves soon after they are born. The human baby requires complete care at the time he is born, and continues to need the almost constant attention of one or the other of his parents for many months. He is learning all through this phase of his existence, however; he learns that this world is a good place in which to live and that it is peopled with friendly adults as he is handled lovingly while his needs are attended to—or he learns that this is an uncomfortable world in which he is left wet, soiled, or hungry despite his cries which are his only means of signifying his needs. It is the adults who care for the infant who give him his first feelings of security, or lack of security. A child's parents thus have a basic responsibility in building his emotional stability, his feeling of security. Infants and children require tender, loving care if they are to build good foundations for future emotional stability.

As the child grows, he moves from complete dependence to an ever-increasing need for independence. There comes a time when he insists on feeding himself, on buttoning his own buttons, on putting on his own socks and shoes. Since his parents know that he must move from the egocenteredness of babyhood to the social responsibility of adulthood, they allow him to try to feed and dress himself even though they are quite aware that they could manage these tasks much more efficiently. Their refusal to allow him to experiment would hamper his growth and his learning.

At the same time that the child is cared for with sincere affection to help build his emotional health, his needs for

[6] B. Von Haller Gilmer, *How to Help Your Child Develop Successfully* (Englewood Cliffs, N.J.: Prentice-Hall, Inc., 1951).

physical health must also be satisfied. He requires certain nourishment to insure good physical health and his parents supply this for him. He must be fed and dressed for good physical growth as certainly as he must be cherished to promote his best emotional and mental health.

As a youngster becomes more mobile through his learning to creep and then to walk, his parents must set limits for his activities. He must not be allowed to become destructive; overpermissiveness on the part of the parents can be just as frustrating to a youngster as can overprotectiveness or prohibitiveness. In order to begin the development of his sense of right and wrong, his realization that some things may be played with while others may not, a child must be taught that there are boundaries beyond which he must not go. This very setting of reasonable limits often assures a youngster that his parents do care about him, about what he does and what happens to him. He requires adult help in learning how to behave in ways acceptable to the society of which he is a part, and in ways which insure his own safety. There is, however, a certain time at which such safety measures make sense to a youngster within the limits of his own experience; spanking a two-year-old who runs into alleys or streets does not teach him to stay away from those places, because he has not had sufficient experience to understand the dangers which are obvious to his parents.

Adults must also exercise some judgment in protecting their prized possessions from the curiosity of the youngster, even if this involves putting them away beyond the reach of the child for a time. And some objects will be broken as the child explores to learn about his environment. Common sense dictates that while absolute freedom of exploration is not best, there ought not be too many tempting objects for the child to be cautioned against touching, either. It is not wise to have an excessive number of "no-no's" that keep both parents and child anxious.

RICH VITAL EXPERIENCES. A young child approaches nearly everything he meets as a brand-new experience. Adults have become so accustomed to green grass, blue sky, varicolored flowers, brick, stone, wood, and steel structures, dirt, gravel, concrete and macadamized roads, and the like, that they sometimes forget that all these things are new to a child when he meets them for the first time. He needs time to savor his experiences with each new object, and to absorb and assimilate them into his growing knowledge. Parents can provide many experiences to make their child's environment a lush one from which he can learn and build his concepts of living effectively.

The child must have experiences upon which he may draw for his interpretive and creative play. The simplest things to him are bright and new. Each object that meets his curious glance is to be fully explored so that he may grow in understanding. He touches and handles, using his sense of feeling to establish understandings of fuzziness or smoothness, or sharp edges. He squeezes, developing concepts of firmness or plasticity, or rigidity or softness. He tastes; he learns sour or tart, sweet or palatable, chewy or creamy. He shakes objects and throws them. In all these ways he develops understanding of his immediate environment. He learns.

He watches motion; he sees branches of trees sway as the wind strikes them; he sees birds fly, settle to a perch, drink sips of water, and stretch their heads back as they swallow. He watches processions of automobiles, trucks, and buses on the streets near his home. He sees trains on tracks, boats in water, planes in the sky. He sees all kinds of people engaging in many different activities.

He watches animals; he may possibly see a horse pulling a wagon, a squirrel jumping among the branches of a tree, cats stalking a grasshopper, dogs playing and running in his neighborhood. He may catch sight of a hummingbird poised over a flower in his garden; he may hear bees humming as they go about their work; brightly colored butterflies fly around his yard; he sees fireflies in the twilight. As he sees these things, he also hears the noises that accompany them: the chattering of the squirrels, the barking of the dogs, the whirring of the wings of birds and butterflies. He is building understanding of the things about him as they impinge upon his senses. For the gifted this understanding comes more rapidly and is broader in scope than is the case with the average child.

He sees; he sniffs; he listens; he touches and feels; he manipulates; he tastes; and he asks questions. Not only have his parents seen to it that he has had all these experiences, but they are with him to help his interpretations of what he has experienced. Parents are responsible for the child's growing understanding of his environment. Through answers to his questions, he learns; questions must be honored, and answered truthfully and sincerely. The wise parent can distinguish between the questions asked so that the child may enjoy the sound of his voice and establish contact with the adult, and those that are asked in all sincerity because the child truly wishes to know. If a child is mature enough to ask an honest question, he deserves a correct answer suited to that maturity. Perhaps the parent can find pictures that show attractive explanations for some of the queries; perhaps models can be constructed from the child's own collection of toys to help his understanding. The gifted child should be encouraged to develop concepts out of his new experiences.

Mere watching of what others do does not satisfy an active child for a very long period of time; he wishes to become involved in the activities, to play them out creatively with his toys, and parents need to supply materials that encourage the child's doing for himself. This desire should be cultivated so that the superior abilities may gain expression in whatever desirable lines interest leads.

Toys. Playthings properly used are the stuff of a preschool child's growth in learning. They can help him to exercise his creativity and to explore with originality, or they can be presented to him as completed objects that offer him no opportunity for further exploration and growth.

Very young children can grasp rattles, soft stuffed toys, and rubber or wooden or plastic blocks and large beads. They can squeeze them, turn them over and over, make noises with them, and suck on them. They are forming con-

cepts of size, hardness and softness, fuzziness and smoothness, and the like, from these simple toys. Each item should
be large enough to preclude its being swallowed, and yet
small enough to be grasped by the child's whole hand. At
the age of about three months, when a baby can distinguish
some movement, light, and sound, he may be fascinated by
a mobile hung over his crib, or a Japanese wind harp in a
nearby window or doorway where he can see it move in the
breeze and hear its tinkling sounds.

The less structured his early toys are of themselves, the
more the child can exercise his creativity and originality in
his play. Blocks of various sizes which the child can handle
successfully may be built into any sort of structure the child
desires. A visit to a nearby farm may lead to the construction
of barns and barnyards. Small blocks can become chickens
and ducks; round blocks become troughs for drinking water;
a combination of blocks may become a horse and wagon.
Beyond the construction aspect of using blocks, and the development of dexterity in the use of the hand and arm
muscles, is the actual dramatic play in which a child can
create scenes and characters and play them out as he
chooses.

If space is available, blocks large enough to build structures that a child may get into are an excellent source of
pleasure and learning for him. Barring such huge blocks, a
large crate may serve. If he can build a house and walk in
through its door, or build a counter and use cans and boxes
for a grocery store, or construct a locomotive and sit inside
it as the engineer, in each of these ways he is building his
concepts of living today. Each activity described presupposes that the child has had direct experience with the sort
of activity portrayed; if he had never seen a barnyard, he
could not be expected to build one in creative play with his
boxes, blocks, and boards.

Plain ordinary kitchen utensils provide a source of learning and exploration also. A couple of lids from saucepans
make excellent cymbals; an egg beater serves to stir concoctions in the sandbox; a large wooden spoon or paddle can be
used for digging or dipping; these are all common utensils

which the child may use in his creative play as he learns. Using his imagination plus a few real-life objects may lead to very original and dramatic play. At the same time, the child is building understanding of his world, concepts that help him to increase his basic knowledge.

Later on the youngster will need dolls and cars and other such toys to add the ideas of people and their activities to his blocks and his buildings. As he grows larger he will want a tricycle and a wagon, roller skates and a scooter—each of these common toys, as he develops skill in operating them, helps in building the strength and control of his muscles.

Some helpful catalogs from which parents may get ideas for selecting well-designed playthings and unstructured materials for creative play for their youngsters are those from the Judy Company and Creative Playthings, Incorporated.

Crafts supplies of many kinds help the child in his creative exploration and interpretation of his environment. Colored construction paper plus blunt scissors and some paste provide an unstructured situation from which he may create. Blank paper and a box of crayons large enough so that he may grasp them comfortably with his little-developed small muscle control can help him to attempt representations of things he has seen. Perhaps he will create purely imaginative pictures of lines and colors, experimental scribbles. A wise parent does not name the child's pictures scribbles even though that may be exactly what they look like to him. He does not impose adult standards of line, form, and color combinations; he respects the child's efforts and commends him for them, offering suggestions only when they are requested. Commercial coloring books are to be avoided when one's aim is to help keep the imaginative and creative approach of the preschool child; they offer merely outlines which constrict the child's activity to simple filling in. He is too young to exercise that much control anyway, and may easily become discouraged when he is unable to color a picture as neatly as some older person in the household.

Paints of clear true colors and large brushes offer yet another way in which a child may try to express what he is feeling and thinking and experiencing. He may express desires, or show needs for further experiences, or indicate some misunderstandings of past experiences. He may satisfy his own aesthetic leanings toward the use of colors, as well.

Finger paints help to satisfy his desire for messing. Many children enjoy the purely manipulative act of squeezing the soft, starch-like, part-liquid part-solid gobs of finger paint between their fingers. As they move their hands across a paper, designs appear. A stroke in one direction may wipe out one design and produce another which in turn may be obliterated by a single movement. Freedom of movement and individuality of design are significant to the child; so also is the fact that here he can destroy if he does not like what he produces. Naturally, to enjoy fully the creative as well as the manipulative aspect of finger painting, the child must be dressed in clothes that will not be spoiled should the starchy mixture splash around a bit. Trying to keep himself, the table, and the floor clean will be enough to stifle a most creative child, and to stunt that desire for the good feeling as the mixture is pressed and handled and moved about on the paper. To save the parent's nerves and help the child retain and develop and experiment with his own creativity, a situation in which keeping clean is not a necessity should be provided.

The use of clay is another manipulative experience beneficial to young children. Whether or not the result is a recognizable object, to be used as a paperweight, perhaps, is of no consequence in the early exploration of this material; if the child chooses to model an animal he has seen, all well and good. If he delights in rolling long worms or in punching the clay into various shapes, he is not wasting his time. He is learning about this new plastic material, and bending it to his will, creating and destroying as he chooses. With clay, or with any of the other inexpensive materials mentioned thus far, it really does not matter if his final products are unrecognizable to adults. The child has gained further understanding of his environment, has expressed his ideas with solid materials, and has had a good deal of fun. Children enjoy messing, whether it be in mud puddles, with clay, or with paints on an oilcloth-covered table. They learn from the very manipulation of materials; they develop their small muscles of control; they make themselves ready to handle chalk and crayon and pencil and pen; they have satisfying experiences; and they grow.

Pictures with bright clear colors, pictures of things the child knows, and things or activities strange to him stimulate his interest in learning still more about his world. These pictures may be hung at his eye-level in his room or play area. They should be pleasingly arranged as to color combinations and grouping of the pictures themselves. Perhaps the child can be encouraged to show interest in clipping pictures he has seen in family magazines. This may also help him to understand expected care of magazines. He may not be able to manipulate his scissors as satisfactorily as he wishes nor mount his pictures straight, but he can be helped to do this, and he will increase control of his muscles as he tries.

These pictures may develop interest in seeing new sights, talking about trips that may be taken in the future, or learning about jobs of people with whom he is unfamiliar. Changed periodically with the child's help and his selection of new ones for replacements, such pictures can lead to developing concepts of pleasing color, interests in the various activities depicted, attractive arrangement and design, and the like.

LITERATURE FOR YOUNG CHILDREN. Books are an important aspect of the growth of a youngster, particularly a gifted one. They provide another avenue through which he may interpret experiences he has had and share new and unfamiliar experiences vicariously with the adventures of the people and animals in his story books. Books to buy for youngsters are available at low cost almost everywhere, in drug stores and supermarkets in addition to bookstores where they might logically be expected to be found. The problem is not so much in procuring the books or realizing their values, but rather in making wise choices from the wide selection at hand.

Parents of gifted children are most likely lovers of reading and of books themselves; there is probably a large and useful collection of books in the home which are being read and discussed and referred to quite regularly. Magazines and newspapers are another source of reading materials and information that are to be expected in the homes where most gifted youngsters live. Reading has been so much a natural part of living for the family that the gifted child often accepts it as an interesting activity in which he participates with his family. He has to be taught to take care of books, magazines, and newspapers; fragile things tear quite easily and he may make a few missteps before he grows enough to realize that such objects have value and he is expected to care for them properly. He needs quite a bit of growth before he can distinguish those magazines that are supplied to him as raw materials from which he selects for his picture collections or his scrapbooks, from those that are to be read and enjoyed quietly but not cut or torn.

A family that loves books will also supply some for the child to have as his own. Simple pages of a linen-like paper with pictures on them plus a few words may be among the first chosen for him. The child who sees reading as a vital part of the family life learns to "read" and enjoy his own books too, as he is helped to learn about their care and as the simple stories are read to him at various times of the day when he is quiet. A child who has been talked to and read to often as a normal part of his daily program may be reciting from his books as early as the age of two or two-and-one-half; he has heard his stories so often that he is able to "read" them from his personal book collections.

Since children enjoy hearing books read repeatedly, it is wise to select stories that can be read over and over without the parents' growing too weary of them. Another significant point is that these early stories actually help develop a child's taste for literature; if he is surrounded with stories that have well-written sentences and interesting plots and actions, he can more easily choose better stories and reject poorly developed ones as he grows. A book ought not be chosen for its pictorial values alone; though locating a book that combines good pictures with a worthwhile story requires more time and judgment, wise selection holds values for both parents and child.

Fortunate is the youngster whose parents know and share with him the traditional Mother Goose rhymes and the folk tales and legends of the past. Here are worlds of rich imagery which can also supply beauty and understanding of good language for the child. He can come to appreciate poetry through such simple beginnings, and he can enjoy many poems that are thought to be more adult as well. Sound and variations of sound are fascinating to youngsters; rhythmic structure of language likewise holds their interest. It is not necessary to stay with simple rhyming verses or couplets merely because the child is young; in fact he can enjoy some of the language of Shakespeare when it is well-spoken to him. The attraction of "eye of newt" or "While greasy Joan doth keel the pot" can be made very real to the youngster whose family takes time to share literature with him.

It is difficult to discuss literature, particularly poetry, without mentioning music as well. The traditional lullabies combine the two, and a mother or father can sing or hum "Bye, Baby Bunting," "Hush-a-Bye," and the lullabies of Brahms and Handel to a very young child as he settles for his nap. These poems and their music set an emotional tone to which a youngster may respond as much as he does to the poetry and the rhythm and the melodies he hears.

Several good anthologies are suggested by Nancy Larrick in her *Parents' Guide to Children's Reading*. Those parents who need to add to their own sources, such as previous collections and their memories, will find that this book offers quite helpful ideas for selecting stories and poems for children up to the age of thirteen, as well as the anthologies which the parents themselves may use when the children are quite young. Larrick also interprets some reading interests of youngsters in ways that may help parents work with their children for the purpose of having them continue to enjoy reading as they grow older.

Other sources of literature for youngsters are the children's book sections from the *Saturday Review,* the *Chicago Sunday Tribune,* and the *New York Times* Sunday book supplement. The *Bulletin* from the Center for Children's Books of the Graduate Library School of the University of Chicago is another rich source.

Not all books need to be purchased and owned by the family. There are good collections of children's books in most libraries from which books may be borrowed and used for certain periods of time. One of the best habits a parent can help his gifted child to develop is that of wise use of the library resources which are available for him. The library offers story hours as well, and these may be valuable to individual three-, four-, and five-year-olds. Whether a child has the maturity to join a story group is to be decided by the parents and the librarians as they observe the particular youngster in question. These story hours give the children another opportunity to hear excellent stories well told, to see the books available, and to grow in their ability to make some choices of books to borrow and use at home. Story hours at the library are not merely a free public baby-sitting service; the parents of gifted children can use them as one more kind of experience to help the children grow in understanding and appreciating the area of literature. A parent who shies away from storytelling himself may find the children's librarian a good source for this sort of experience, which he wishes his child to have though he cannot supply it easily or skillfully himself.

Sometimes there are story hours, presented by local radio stations, to which youngsters and parents may listen to make use of yet another medium for having experiences with the field of literature. Some television programs also offer good stories for youngsters; these of course give visual stimulation as well as experiences with words. There are children who reject the visual presentation, because it is somewhat different from the pictures they have made in their own minds as they have listened to the stories previously. Both radio and television programs should be subject to judicious selection by the parents in order to help the development of taste and discrimination in the youngsters, in addition to offering them further growth in experiences with literature.

It has been stated previously that about half of all gifted youngsters learn to read before they begin their regular attendance at school. Such experiences as have been discussed here have undoubtedly acted as readiness programs for the youngsters involved, and have helped to develop in them the desire as well as the ability to read. Since reading offers so fruitful a way of learning for gifted children, it is wise to offer them many pleasurable experiences with literature while they are small, and before they begin to go to school. There is a further responsibility involved too; it is up to the parents to tell the child's teacher of his ability and progress in reading so that he will not be forced into another readiness program merely because the teacher himself does not have time in the first weeks of school to learn all the background information about every individual child. Such sharing of vital information will help the youngster to continue to progress rather than having him held where he is for a time, and possibly run the risk of developing faulty attitudes toward learning because he is not challenged to show what he can do in his early schooling.

Music. As young children respond to sound and rhythmic structure of language, so do they react to the same elements in music. Even very primitive societies develop dances and songs as part of their expression and communication. Youngsters who strike blocks together or bang spoons are experimenting with sound; as they are able to stand and walk, they respond with their whole bodies to the sounds and rhythms of the music they hear, whether its source be radio, television, tapes, phonograph records, or a musical instrument played by some member of the family. This response is natural to the stimulation they receive from what they hear.

Natural expression is the important aspect here. It is totally unnecessary and in fact wrong to insist that a baby who can barely maneuver himself adequately respond with marching to a piece of military music or gliding to a waltz. The natural expression of his own bodily responses is much more significant in leading to creative development. Forcing a child to conform to adult standards or expectations in reacting to music can stultify his creativity in this area, just as it does in other expressive acts. The child's personal inventions are more helpful to his developing originality.

Songs sung to youngsters need not be confined to nursery rhymes or lullabies. Obviously, if his mother does her work to the accompaniment of radio programs, he will hear the popular music of his day, too. He needs the experience of music that has more depth to it as well, music that has lasted and has been designated as classical because of its permanence and value to many generations. Just as there should be no rule for his hearing only poetry written for children, he should not be confined to music or songs written especially for children. When given the opportunity, children can appreciate and understand much of the program music that is available; and they do not need to be aware of the stories which have been supplied by the composers or their interpreters. They respond to the music itself. Though the Irving Caesar safety songs may teach the child lessons when he is old enough to grasp their meaning and apply it to his own experiences, they are not the only or the best examples of music with which gifted youngsters should have opportunities to become familiar.

Musical toys are often given to children, and the supply of them is varied. There are jack-in-the-boxes that operate to the tune of "Pop Goes the Weasel," and there are toy pianos, bells, and xylophones as well as pull-and-push toys and tops that create sounds as they are manipulated. A youngster who is experimenting with the pleasurable aspects of various sounds seems to possess a much greater tolerance to loudness than his parents have. Sometimes this is explained as one way in which the child can expend some of his almost endless supply of energy. This tendency to loudness extends through adolescence; it cannot well be tackled on the basis of courtesy alone because the child sees no discourtesy in playing his phonograph or radio at full volume. This is the way it sounds best to him, and the tot who hammers his xylophone with all his force is not in his own mind being unduly loud. Parents need to help the children grasp the realization that instruments or toys need not always be used at full volume; at the same time, they need to see the reasons back of such behavior.

To play with musical toys can be fun for youngsters. Their use will involve repetition of what to the parents may seem like purely monotonous noise; to the child it is pleasurable sound or music. One cannot realistically expect adult performance from a child working with a toy instrument; children grow from experimenting with the stuff of their environment, and they may use harmonicas, drums, and pianos enthusiastically in their trials.

Youngsters who are responsive to the melodies they hear may reproduce them by singing or humming as they go about their play. This is not the easiest process for a child to achieve; many youngsters will require help at six, seven, or even eight years of age, to find their singing voices. To a youngster who grows in a family where singing, whistling, humming, or hearing good music is just an ordinary part of living, these activities may arise naturally as a part of his expression of his feelings, too. They offer another way of exploring his ideas and expressing himself.

Lessons in the various musical arts, singing, dancing, playing an instrument, are usually decided upon by judging the response of the individual youngster—his evident maturity, his physical growth, and any other factors which might be significant to the particular activity and child. It is wise to remember that creativity of expression is of greater importance to the child's growth than is conformity to rigid standards, as a general rule for the great bulk of children. A child who indicates a talent for one of these arts may prosper in the hands of a good teacher. Each case should be decided individually, with the weight of the judgment being given to the best possible choice for the youngster's own development. It is hoped that adult understanding of children's needs and children's growth has progressed beyond the point of having rhythm bands or lines of three- and four-year-olds trying to follow a routine dance pattern.

Preschool children can often create their own tunes and rhythms. They enjoy experimenting with sound, and they are fortunate when parents pick up their tunes and words and copy them for later singing, too. A child responds to hearing his own music and poetry as he does to hearing his own stories told to him.

EXPERIENCE WITH LIVING THINGS. Observing and working with living plants and animals provides another experience in important areas of living for preschool youngsters. They cannot be expected to assume full responsibility for the care of a pet in the home when they cannot yet accept responsibility for their own care; their senses of time and consequences of failing to feed or water an animal, for example, are not well enough matured for that. They can gain much valuable experience, however; they can watch patterns of seasonal growth and learn how living animals feel and respond.

Unless parents are willing to be completely responsible for pet animals, they are not a good source of learning for preschool children. When the jobs involved are shared, with the parents bearing the greater burden, pets can offer both pleasure and knowledge for a youngster. A dog can be a good lively companion for an outdoor romp, under the supervision of an adult. A dog can be the recipient of shared confidences in quiet play. Again the adult must be assured that the animal in question is gentle and responsive to the youngster. Helping to feed, groom, and clean the dog offers situations in which parents and child can work together, and in which the parents can by comments help the youngster to understand the animal and its needs. Having a pet in his own home may help a youngster to become friendly with and develop his understanding of animals at large.

Working with the grass and flowers, vegetables, bushes, and trees in the yard can also help the child to increase his store of knowledge. He can trundle his wheelbarrow right behind his father as they work to build a lawn. He can rake and collect grass cuttings. He can help his mother in harvesting lettuce and pulling radishes for salad. The learning about the plants is important to the youngster's knowledge; perhaps more important to the preschooler is his working with his parents, participating with them in real-life activities, learning from them as they attempt to answer his questions, and realizing their value to him as people interested in his welfare.

Experiences with living things can also involve trips to woods and lakes in various seasons to explore them for growing plants and animals. Here is another pleasurable outing that can be shared by parents and child as each learns to know the other, appreciate the beauties of the outdoors, and learn about the specific plants and animals that may be seen.

Pots of herbs growing on the kitchen window sill, bowls of guppies in the den, a parakeet or canary in its cage, fruit trees in the yard, cats and dogs to play with—all offer pleasure and satisfaction to the youngster as he learns about the habits and needs of growing things.

RELATIONSHIPS WITH OTHER PEOPLE. Another important aspect in providing a favorable environment for the preschool child's optimum growth is that of guiding his relationships with other people. He will know his immediate family quite well from his closeness in living with them. Wise parents realize that there are other people who can contribute to their child's growth and learning in the area of social living, and they plan for expanding his relationships.

The child meets strangers with his parents from the first time that he is old enough to be taken outdoors in his carriage or stroller. A baby in a stroller or a toddler held by the hand offers sufficient stimulus to serve as the object of introductory conversation among adult neighbors, and the child is included in these social overtures. Salespeople in stores usually make comments about and to the young child. His parents' friends who come to visit before he is tucked into bed for the night will probably play with him and talk with him. All these are adult contacts in which the child is likely to be the center of attraction and the recipient of all attention; before too long children must have experiences which involve other children about their own age. If a preschooler is the oldest child, an only child, or the youngest of the family, these needed child contacts may best be found among playmates outside the home.

PLAYMATES. Playmates for children are usually available in the immediate neighborhood. It is necessary for the parents to meet and to make arrangements for their young children to play together under adult supervision, usually that of the mother in whose home or yard the youngsters play. Very young children need continuous and undivided attention as they have their first experiences with other children. They do not play together at all in the beginning; they play beside each other, or in the same room with each other, with varying amounts of friction depending somewhat upon which child wants to play with which toy, and how quietly the other child gives it up, or how vociferously he fights to retain possession of it. Sharing is a totally new experience, especially as it involves objects the child has learned are his own. Sharing bits of cookie with his mother he may have done; sharing his prized toys with a strange child is another thing altogether. He cannot accept this as a natural way of behaving without much experience, much learning, and enough growth so that sharing becomes an accepted way of behavior. He cannot give up one of his own toys for very long at a time even when he accepts sharing without obvious protest; he expects and needs a turn to use the toy so that he realizes it is still his, and was only being borrowed for a short time.

It is not until sometime in the year following the fifth birthday that most youngsters can actually play together. Until that time, they are playing separately, even in the nursery school and kindergarten program; they require time to grow in understanding of the concepts involved in working with someone as opposed to working beside him.

PLAY GROUPS. With somewhat older children, neighborhood play groups still under enlightened adult supervision can be established. It is less expensive for a group of parents to purchase large outdoor play equipment like jungle gyms on which children may climb, swings and slides on which they may play, and sandboxes or patches of dirt in which they may dig. These are play groups, not nursery schools, and the two should not be confused as to their purposes. The well set-up play group does offer mothers free time to do their work without the interruptions that caring for preschool children bring; at the same time the youngster himself is being allowed to widen his world of experiences. Mothers and fathers usually arrange to give certain amounts of time to supervising the neighborhood play group each week, with some flexibility of these times to allow for trading hours or days with other parents on a reciprocal basis.

In the control of adults untrained professionally in the handling of groups of small children, these neighborhood play centers offer merely custodial care for the children. The adults in charge are not usually equipped to help the youngsters develop as well as trained teachers can. The centers do offer the youngster opportunities to use large pieces of equipment which he does not have access to otherwise, and to learn some skills in getting along with other people. These will not be taught in the skillful manner of a nursery school teacher, however; the problems that arise in the youngsters' activities will be handled in the fashion that the supervising adult deems best from his or her own personal experience with small children. These neighborhood play centers help to widen the youngster's acquaintance with others, and they give him more time outdoors than he might otherwise be able to enjoy, as his mother has her daily tasks to occupy a great portion of her time, thus curtailing the amount of time she can spend with him outdoors.

Supervised play groups are sometimes established by churches as morning or afternoon activities provided for the youngsters of the neighborhood. Also, YWCA's often have programs in which both mother and child may participate, sometimes together, sometimes separately as the adults follow a planned program while someone baby-sits with the children in an area where there are toys they may use. These groups offer some experience in playing with other children but they do not offer the kinds of growth experiences a professionally prepared nursery school teacher can give in a well-organized nursery school program.

Many play group projects are called nursery schools, as this phrase has come into popular usage. Parents need to investigate these schools to learn the qualifications of the adults who operate them, and to see the equipment and experiences offered, so that they may judge whether the group actually has something educational to offer to their child, and whether it is a real nursery school, or a play group that offers only custodial care to the youngsters for a certain period of time each day.

PLAY AREAS. Some communities have developed parks in which recreational programs are offered for many ages of youngsters. Usually the play areas have some equipment that can be used by preschool children, but always with close supervision by the parents. These are not the sort of places to which children may be sent for growth experiences, but to which they may be taken for an hour or so of outdoor play. The preschool child requires much supervision as he swings, slides, plays on the merry-go-round or the seesaw, climbs on the jungle gym, or digs in the sand pile. He has not yet the knowledge necessary to care completely for himself as he plays; he learns from such play and becomes more familiar with the needed safety precautions as he experiments with exercising and controlling his body on such large equipment. Most of his play will and should take place in the playroom, on the lawn, or in the back yard at home.

SCHOOL RESPONSIBILITIES

The responsibilities involved in the early years of a child's existence rest almost entirely upon the parents and other adults who care for him. When he reaches the age of four, the public school system has some responsibilities which it should assume. A child who has been heretofore merely a figure in the census of the preschool children of a community becomes a person for whom the school can offer some definite programs, designed to help him to grow and learn satisfactorily. The public schools ought to provide some preschool experiences for young children.

Liaison with Home

One important aspect of providing preschool experiences for youngsters three, four, and five years of age lies in the area of communications. Parents and other lay citizens of a community have sources from which they learn about the schools to which they will be sending their children for what they hope will be a good, sound educational program. The knowledge comes from local newspapers, the radio and television stations of the vicinity, and perhaps most significantly it comes from other people of the community. Parents learn about the program offered by the school, its physical facilities, the qualifications of the teaching staff, the policies of the administration—but all too frequently this information comes not directly from the school itself but as hearsay from other people who speak in terms of the feelings they have developed as their children have progressed through the schools. This information is strained through attitudes toward the school built quite largely upon individual reactions rather than upon essentially factual information. The schools themselves should seek time and space in the mass media of communications afforded by each community to be sure that facts are presented to the citizens who in the final analysis furnish the support upon which the schools depend. Too few schools have an adequate program of disseminating information to their communities and their patrons; they accept the publicity received for the sports or music programs but make few further attempts to acquaint the community with the bulk of the school's program: its fundamental beliefs, specific aims, needs and problems, and successes or failures. There is a real need for such information to be placed before the community, and it should stem from those who know the schools best, the school people themselves.

Some school systems publish periodical newsletters to inform the community of what is happening in the schools. The contents of such letters should include information about what the students are learning as well as the special activities that take place. These papers should go into every home, to help all the citizens keep informed of the school's progress; they should not be sent merely to those citizens who have youngsters attending school at the present time.

Open house or parents' nights for visitation are common practices in many school systems. Here again too often the invitation to attend goes only to the parents of the youngsters in each class. It should be extended in a genuine fashion to all interested citizens of the community, and particularly to the parents of the preschool children. Such visitation will provide them with the opportunity to see for themselves the kind of facilities available to their youngsters as they begin their schoolwork, and to meet and speak with the teachers who will be their children's guides for so large a part of the day. Such occasions ought not to be "shows"; their purpose is to acquaint the citizens with the school's business, and the school's business is not involved with the presentation of entertainment for adults. It is teaching children. When the children have in the natural course of their studies developed and collected information they wish to share, then they might well "show" what they have accomplished to their parents, perhaps as a culminating activity for a specific unit of work. Developing a program purely for entertainment is not basically the business of any department or grade of a school.

Radio and television programs often are based on the show idea too. They would be much more valuable if the work of the school was presented as it actually is in the day-to-day program of the youngsters involved.

The parents of preschool youngsters need to know as much as they can learn about the schools of their community. They need to be included in the lists for distributing the informational newsletters, and to be invited to the occasional open houses and parents' nights. They need also to be invited to participate in whatever parents' organization there is to work with the school. The parents' organization might well be one of the first steps in acquainting parents of preschool children with the school's programs and policies, and helping parents new to the school district become familiar with its worthwhile activities. Too many parents' organizations degenerate into mere money-making activities to provide uniforms for the school band, or into tea parties at which the third grade sings a series of songs and the fifth grade presents a tortuously memorized play. Though the school band may desire uniforms and the community may wish to help provide them, the parents' organizations can contribute much more to the growth of schools and the welfare of the children by forming cooperative study groups with the faculty and other citizens, and by working to make worthwhile contributions to, and gain valuable understandings of, the school's real tasks.

In addition to sending factual information into the homes of preschool children, the schools should be ready and willing to receive questions and hear comments from the parents of preschoolers. The line of communication established should accommodate a two-way flow; the school should not be merely a disseminator of information but should be receptive to the many queries and suggestions which parents have. Parents who are about to entrust their most precious possessions to an institution require specific information about it, and reassurance as to its values. Face-to-face conferences with the teacher of young children and the building principal, both individually and in small groups, offer opportunities for parents to learn about this step their children are taking into the public school world. A brief office call to present the birth certificate and records of immunizations, and to receive a printed card indicating where and when a child should report for his first day of school, are not sufficient to establish good feeling.

The schools then are obliged to work with all citizens of the community, the parents of preschool children as well as those who have youngsters already attending the school; they must produce and distribute unbiased information about the school's programs; they must plan satisfactory ways of working with parents to improve the programs offered for each youngster; they must honor sincere questions and help citizens to build depth of understanding about the public schools they support. Teachers and parents alike must give time to talking together about the best ways of working with children and about the school's task in educating them properly.

Testing Service

A more specific need than the general one for establishing and using concrete channels of communication through which accurate and pertinent information may be dispersed to the community and sincere and relevant questions may be funneled to those school people who are best qualified to respond to them, concerns the provision of testing services by the public schools for the preschool children of the community. If the early identification of gifted children has significance for their optimum progress, then the means by which they may be identified must be available. Since early entrance to school has proven its value and since teachers can do a more adequate job of teaching youngsters with whose abilities and potential they are familiar, it seems reasonable that public schools should establish testing services for the preschool children. This is as important a part of the whole testing program as are the periodic diagnostic, achievement, aptitude, and intelligence tests that are administered to those youngsters already in attendance at school.

Nursery school and kindergarten teachers should be able to administer tests to their own classes; the intrusion of a stranger even though he be the guidance counselor for the school or the qualified psychometrist of the school system does not always create a favorable testing situation for these young children who are still somewhat dependent upon mother or a mother-figure. It may be possible to arrange times when qualified teachers of young children can give tests to the preschool youngsters, as they are now given to those attending school. If the preschool youngsters know these teachers, at least as the people with whom they will be spending a good deal of their time in the near future, they will accept them as friends and cooperate during the actual administration of the tests.

Group tests can be given to young children though the groups are quite small, consisting of no more than three or four children at a time. In this way the teacher may note the children's responses as they take the test. These tests should probably include an intelligence test and a test to discover the general readiness level of each youngster for the school program.

A child who scores well on a group test may be further tested by the psychometrist at either the parents' or the teacher's request and recommendation. A youngster whose scores for some reason do not agree with what is known about his performances may be retested by the psychometrist. A gifted child who can accept testing situations and whose social maturity in relationships with adults is well advanced should have little difficulty in working with a person who is a stranger to him. Part of the psychometrist's job is to gain the child's confidence before launching into the more formal parts of the test itself. The objects used, the questions asked, and the discussions held will be of interest to the gifted preschool child who is by nature intellectually curious about everything around him.

On the basis of information derived from group and individual tests, nursery and kindergarten teachers can provide a much more effective program to help the gifted child's development than they can without such definite knowledge. They, of course, are observing the youngster and noting his behavior, his interests, and his problems, to add to their store of information, and help them provide an individually designed program. The test scores are never to be considered the final answer for any child; they furnish information which should be used in conjunction with what is learned about the youngster from many sources.

It is the responsibility of the public school system to provide such testing service as is found to be most helpful in carrying out the school's basic task, that of providing the best educational program for the optimum development of each individual child.

Nursery and Kindergarten

A third responsibility which the public schools must accept if gifted children are to be educated as effectively as possible is that of providing preschool experience for all children. At the present time no more than 30 per cent of all the preschool age children in the entire country have access to either kindergarten or nursery school education supplied as an integral part of the school program of the community. Apparently the essential values of nursery and kindergarten education have not been clearly explained or appreciated by school people and the lay public; unfortunately this aspect of a good educational program is too often considered an unnecessary frill that can be easily cut out in this day of eliminating frills and concentrating upon what is sometimes referred to as basic education.

Kindergartens have been considered a must in some sections of the country since the 1860's when Susan Blow worked to establish them in the St. Louis public schools, where they remain a fixture to this day. Some parts of the country have never seen the need for or realized the value of education for youngsters prior to the age of six, when they are placed in the first grade and expected to learn to read without spending too much time in preparation for building the necessary skills involved in that highly complex process. There is at least as much validity in having kindergartens in which youngsters have opportunity to perfect known skills, build new skills, and prepare themselves to attain future ones, as there is for having a twelfth-grade program. Each has its significant values to contribute to the progress of the students in the instructional program; each is essential to optimum development.

Few parents have the time, energy, and money to expend in an experiential program for their youngsters such as has been described in a previous portion of this chapter. Fathers are away from home daily to pursue their occupations; mothers are occupied with the care of the home and the family. Though many of the experiences pointed out as necessary can be provided by thoughtful parents who take time for them, the programs of nursery schools and kindergartens can provide these experiences without the distractions that are everyday occurrences in the home. Nursery school and kindergarten teachers can give their complete attention to the youngsters with whom they work; except for specially planned occasions, mothers and fathers have to be alert to other happenings in the home even when they are reading a story to the youngster, supervising his block play, or tucking him into bed for his nap. This spirit of undivided attention focused directly upon the child is perhaps the one most significant value which he gains from nursery school experience. He knows that some one person is with him constantly, ready to help him solve problems that may arise, willing to give him direct attention when he requires it.

Nursery schools and kindergartens can supply the firsthand experiences that youngsters need in order to expand their understanding of their environments. The more direct experiences a child can have, the better it is for his growth. He can learn from vicarious experiences such as watching a film, but they must relate directly to what he knows at this age so that he can put meaning in them and derive meaning from them. The gifted child requires wide first-hand experiences so that he may build later knowledge onto them, and so that he has some frame of reference in which he can put his later more abstract learnings.

Nursery schools for four-year-olds and kindergartens for the five-year-olds can supplement the experiences and consequent learnings a child is offered in his home and by his parents. They do not take over the responsibilities of the home; they do not solve problems the youngster may have developed as a consequence of his home situation; they cannot change an undisciplined young egoist miraculously into a well-behaved, socially acceptable youngster. They can supplement the home teaching, provide for experiences beyond the scope of the home resources, help a child understand that everyone needs to wash his hands before juice or lunch time and that this is not just a personal task his mother has thought up to bedevil him. They can give mothers time away from their youngsters so that they may regain some energy, complete their household tasks without having to keep an eye on the child, pursue some of their own interests, and be better mothers, more rested and more loving when the youngster returns home. Nursery school and kindergarten experiences can help a youngster move from his self-centeredness along the road to more socially centered interests; they help him to learn how to get along with other youngsters of his own age group; they can help him to develop good habits of eating, resting, and control of elimination processes. They can provide the large equipment necessary for his exploration activities and the growth of his body; they can give opportunity for messy play that may not be offered or tolerated in the home. They help the child to grow in ways that are proper for him at his present age and will lead him to good habits of planning and working in the future.

Entrance to either nursery school or kindergarten involves quite a change in routine for a child. Instead of being the only one to dominate his mother's attention, or to share it with other members of the family, he is put into a situation without his mother, his familiar toys and games, the environment he knows so well, and the specific routine of activities to which he has become accustomed. Though he is striving to become more and more independent, he has heretofore had his mother within sight or sound when he needed to be reassured by her. Now he is in a strange room or yard with ten or a dozen other children and a teacher, new toys, and perhaps new rules to be learned and obeyed. Some gifted youngsters take such a change in their stride; if they have anticipated going to school, they have looked toward it as an extension of their lives and their learnings, and have become familiar with the concept of school as a good place to be, as they have heard brothers and sisters, parents, and friends talk about school. School can be a welcome experience. If, on the other hand, they have grown up clinging to a parent, or if they have been warned that the teacher will correct their bad habits and that they will have to do as they are told in school or be punished, school may be a fearsome experience. Children react differently to this first move away from home and mother. Each case must be handled as the mother and teacher think best for the child's present adjustment and future development. The factors influencing the youngster's reactions must be analyzed carefully. There is no disgrace attached to either the child or the parents if the decision is that the youngster requires a bit more preparation before he enters school. The parents and teachers can plan some ways of making this a comfortable step for each child to take.

This entrance into nursery school or into kindergarten is important to the child's future because it is his first experience with a more formal learning situation. His reactions to it can easily influence his feelings about school in general; as his parents and teachers want him to develop favorable attitudes toward learning, they must help make the transition between home and school as pleasing to the child as possible.

The kinds of activities available to children in nursery schools and kindergartens have been spelled out fairly completely in the section having to do with the kinds of valuable experiences preschool children should have. These have been listed under the responsibilities of parents specifically because so few children in America are within reach of well-organized nursery schools and kindergartens directed by qualified professional people, and thus so few children have the opportunity for such experiences as are deemed helpful to their growth under the auspices of the schools. Since these activities are valuable learning experiences, parents must supply them wherever possible, and particularly where there are no established programs of nursery and kindergarten education available within a reasonable distance of the home. The authors firmly believe that such programs are, however, a direct responsibility of the public school systems of the country; until they are available as an accepted and expected part of the instructional program, parents will need to be aware of the need of their children for these experiences, and provide for them as best they can.

It will be noted that two- and three-year-olds have not been included in the discussion of the nursery program; two-year-olds do not possess sufficient maturity to derive valuable experiences from nursery schools as such. Three-year-olds alone are not a good risk for nursery school; when grouped with four-year-olds they can usually derive some values from nursery schools. It should be noted that occasionally day-care institutions which watch and feed youngsters while their mothers work are mistakenly referred to as nursery schools.

The size of the classes for preschool children should be determined by what is best for the children involved. Present thinking about nursery schools indicates that one teacher to every ten or twelve youngsters makes a manageable and workable group; when there are more than twelve children, another professionally qualified staff member should be employed. In kindergartens there should be no more than twenty children per teacher. These children are just learning some social skills, just moving away from their ego-centered babyhood. They require frequent turns with whatever toys are available, and they need the constant undivided attention of their teacher. They are not accustomed to working in groups, and they can grow toward this necessary skill more easily when they are allowed to relate to smaller numbers of people, than they can when thrust into a less manageable, larger group of youngsters.

Play is the business of childhood; through his play the youngster learns. He is not merely passing time in recreational activities; his absorbed manner as he works out problems with his toys is surely proof that play is to him a serious occupation. From play a bright child readily incorporates the meanings of his experiences into the vast fund of general knowledge he is building, and he also prepares himself for future understandings.

Hymes has written:

Play gives children language: words and meanings and sounds. Reading is based on these.

Play gives children experiences: knowing objects and people and materials first-hand. Reading is based on these.

Play gives children attention-span: sticking to a task and not hopping around. Reading requires this.

And play leads children into wanting to know more. Here is the real urge for getting the reading skill.

Play is the foundation.[7]

SELECTED READINGS

FRANK, MARY and LAWRENCE K. *How to Help Your Child in School.* New York: The Viking Press, Inc., 1950. 368 pp. Chapters 1 through 4.

Slanted toward the parents' role in helping children to develop healthy personalities, these chapters deal with the principles of growth and development in childhood, the values of nursery school attendance, the values of kindergartens, and the kinds of experiences parents should provide when nursery schools and kindergartens are not available for their youngsters.

GILMER, B. VON HALLER. *How to Help Your Child Develop Successfully.* Englewood Cliffs, N.J.: Prentice-Hall, Inc., 1951. 368 pp. Part 3.

A schedule for keeping a simplified record of the young child's development is given. It includes sections on general development and special problems, as well as the expected spaces for recording age-weight-height data, physical and dental examinations, family facts, and the like.

[7] James L. Hymes, Jr., *Three to Six (Your Child Starts to School)* (Public Affairs Pamphlet No. 163 [New York: Public Affairs Committee, Inc., 1950]), p. 20.

HAVIGHURST, ROBERT J. *Developmental Tasks and Education.* New York: Longmans, Green & Co., Inc., 1952. 100 pp. Chapters 1 and 2.

Chapter 1 discusses the learning process of human beings as dependent upon physical maturation, cultural pressures of society, and the personal values and motives of the individual. Chapter 2 summarizes and explains the principal developmental tasks of infancy and early childhood, giving the nature of each task and its bases, biological, psychological, and cultural.

HILDRETH, GERTRUDE H., *et al. Educating Gifted Children at Hunter College Elementary School.* New York: Harper & Brothers, 1952. 272 pp. Chapters 1, 3, 6, and 8.

These chapters are devoted to the need for educational opportunities for gifted children, the goals and curriculum of Hunter College Elementary School, life in the school, and the role of the parents as co-workers in educating the gifted.

HYMES, JAMES L., JR. *Understanding Your Child.* Englewood Cliffs, N.J.: Prentice-Hall, Inc., 1952. 188 pp.

The principles of child growth are explained, and their influences upon children's behavior are discussed so that parents and teachers may work with these principles and understand why a child behaves as he does.

ILG, FRANCES L., and AMES, LOUIS B. *Child Behavior.* New York: Dell Publishing Co., Inc., 1956. 384 pp.

The research of the Gesell Institute as well as the experience of the writers is formed into this practical and realistic guide to knowledge and understanding of child development and behavior. The kinds of behavior that can be expected at each age from birth to ten years of age are carefully explained, with specific suggestions made as to how parents can help each youngster.

KENT STATE UNIVERSITY. *The Role of the Parent in the Education and Training of the Mentally Superior Child.* Kent, Ohio: Department of Special Education, Kent State University, June, 1957. 47 pp.

Prepared by committees of parents and school people, this bulletin offers suggestions in outline form to help parents understand the emotional and social growth of gifted children, and to participate more understandingly in their education. The areas dealt with include: emotional adjustment and human relations; health, physical education, art, music, language, and science; library, travel, hobbies, and guidance.

LARRICK, NANCY. *A Parent's Guide to Children's Reading.* Garden City, New York: Doubleday & Company, 1958. 283 pp.

This volume contains a wealth of suggestions and information about children's reading interests, habits, attitudes, and skills. Although primarily directed to parents, teachers and those preparing to teach will find the book quite helpful.

11

The Elementary-School
Program

The elementary school represents for the majority of children their first experience with formal education, since nursery schools and kindergartens are available to only a minority of children today. For the gifted child who can make rapid progress in the ordinary curriculum offered to all children, it is important that his elementary-school experiences be made rich and satisfying, if he is to be motivated to achieve as well as he is capable of doing, and to profit from his school experiences. This chapter spells out the goals of elementary education for the gifted, discusses the influences of the school environment upon the child, and shows how programs of instruction and methods of teaching may be adapted to the particular needs of the gifted youngster, in order to reach the goals suggested.

Since children continue to grow physically, intellectually, socially, and emotionally, it is necessary to take these aspects of growth into account in planning and carrying out a good elementary-school program. Gifted children display the common problems of growing youngsters in addition to those problems peculiar to the superior child, and elementary-school teachers should be aware of their needs.

PUPIL GROWTH AND DEVELOPMENT

The principles of growth and development enumerated in the chapter dealing with preschool children continue to be operative throughout life. Elementary-school children strive to grow, to grow up, to become adult. They grow through a fairly predictable pattern of development, passing through recognizable stages along the way. And each child continues to progress toward the goal of maturity at his own particular rate.

Still required are the two basic needs of security and ever-increasing independence. The foundation of security is required so that a youngster may feel sure of his ability to grow up, which to him implies becoming an independent person in his own right.

Continuity of Growth

Growth is a continuous process; there are no definite cut-off points from one stage to another. Instead, a human being merges from one to another and continues to grow and develop in one way or another throughout his life. The guideposts which have been established so that parents and teachers may observe and analyze the growth of an individual youngster and compare it with the growth of others of his age are merely indications of what average youngsters may be like at a given time in their lives. At no time does a child suddenly stop developing. Development is a gradual process in which ages and stages may very likely overlap. A five-year-old does not abruptly give up his five-year-old ways and take on those characteristic of a six-year-old merely because he has had a birthday. Any reference to certain ages when particular developments may be expected must be interpreted as approximations and is made merely for convenience in order to have some sort of a norm as a point of reference.

Preschool children thus do not suddenly develop the characteristics of first graders because they are so classified in school records. They carry with them their feelings and attitudes, their skills in play and learning, their abilities in caring for themselves; they add to their knowledge and growth in each area, but there is not a swift shift from one stage of development to the next. It is entirely possible that some youngsters may continue to require help with the earlier developmental tasks while other youngsters have mastered some of those ordinarily placed in the age group of middle childhood. Gifted youngsters as well as average children may develop somewhat unevenly; this is not an unusual situation, but a completely normal one.

Developmental Tasks

During middle childhood, defined as being somewhere between the chronological ages of six and twelve, the following developmental tasks arise, skills and attitudes that a child needs to master and to acquire to insure his best possible development at this time, and his success with later tasks:

1. Learning physical skills necessary for ordinary games
2. Building wholesome attitudes toward oneself as a growing organism
3. Learning to get along with age-mates
4. Learning an appropriate masculine or feminine social role
5. Developing fundamental skills in reading, writing, and calculating
6. Developing concepts necessary for everyday living
7. Developing conscience, morality, and a scale of values
8. Achieving personal independence
9. Developing attitudes toward social groups and institutions[1]

These tasks must be interpreted in terms of the democratic society in which the child lives. His attitudes toward social groups and institutions, for example, would develop somewhat differently if he were living in an authoritarian society. Likewise, another society might hold differing expectations about masculine and feminine social roles than does the society which has developed in America. These roles are not fixed but are in a process of change themselves. These tasks are not exclusively the responsibility of the school; the achievement of these tasks is a basic responsibility of every institution, church, family, community, or school, to which the child's life is related.

[1] Robert J. Havighurst, *Developmental Tasks and Education* (New York: Longmans, Green & Co., Inc., 1952), pp. 15-28 *passim*.

There is obviously some interrelatedness among the tasks. A child who has an unrealistic view of himself may very well be hampered in the acquisition of the basic skills of reading, writing, and calculating. A youngster who has difficulty in relating to others may also suffer in his attempts at achieving personal independence. One who is successful in one of these areas may very likely find success in the others; each achievement is intertwined with the others to some degree.

Common Needs

Gifted children are first of all children. They pass through the steps of growth; they need to acquire the attitudes and skills expected by society; they have the human needs for affection and security and growing independence as do other children. Cutts and Moseley have written, "Parents who want the best for their child should bear in mind that, no matter how high his I.Q., he is still a child, with all of a child's feelings and with the right to share all the activities which make childhood happy."[2] This seems a significant point for teachers as well to be aware of and to consider as they plan instructional programs for their classes. Though the central task of the school may seem to relate more clearly to the development of the fundamental skills of reading, writing, calculating, and the like, the child's progress in learning these skills is subject to influence by his progress in his other developmental tasks as well. He does not leave his previous learnings at home; he brings his attitudes to school with him.

To take this point a bit further, Garrison has written, "The emotional needs of mentally gifted children are certainly similar to those of inferior or average children."[3]

Growth principles, social demands, human needs—all must be taken into account in the planning of a school program if

[2] Norma E. Cutts, and Nicholas Moseley, *Bright Children* (New York: G. P. Putnam's Sons, 1953), p. 223.

[3] Karl C. Garrison and Dewey G. Force, Jr., *The Psychology of Exceptional Children*, 3d ed. (New York: The Ronald Press Company, 1959), p. 207.

gifted children are to be encouraged and assisted to achieve their maximum potential. Overemphasis upon intellectual development to the degree that the gifted child's social, emotional, and physical growth is hindered is not a wise procedure to follow. Each aspect of the child's development needs attention; he should not be forced into premature adulthood, nor on the other hand held back to childish practices in pursuit of this goal of total optimal development.

The needs of youngsters and the demands of society are continuing as are the stages of growth; they cannot be met and satisfied one time and checked off as fully accomplished. At each stage of development the needs are evident, though the means of satisfying them may change to more mature methods as the child grows older. For example, satisfaction of his need for security and belongingness changes from purely physical contact to reassuring glances from the adults who have charge of him during this period from ages six to twelve. By and large, the youngster depends upon adults for satisfaction of his needs until the latter part of this period, when he begins to achieve greater satisfaction through association with his age-mates.

EDUCATIONAL GOALS AND OBJECTIVES

The goals for the education of gifted children in elementary school and indeed throughout their educational careers are very like those for the education of all youngsters. The differences lie in the degree of emphasis upon the greater creativity, initiative, and intellectual effort expected from gifted students, as well as the greater stress put upon social adjustment and responsibility, and the qualities required for skilled, unselfish, and socially conscious leadership.

The gifted child by definition is capable of more intellectual achievement than are youngsters of average ability; teachers must not accept accomplishment that is merely better than that of others in the class, but must insist upon achievement that appears to be consonant with the gifted child's ability insofar as that can be ascertained. It is not in the best interests of the student to be satisfied and thus teach him to be satisfied with work that is merely above average; the child must be motivated to produce the best of which he is capable in each area of his studies, and to realize that full usage of his gifts will contribute to his own success and happiness as well as to that of society as a whole.

Social Responsibility

The greater emphasis upon social responsibility and social adjustment should not be interpreted to mean that gifted students have less capability and thus greater need in these areas, but rather that they need to become socially adjusted and socially responsible so that their greater intellectual ability may be used for the benefit of the society of which they are a part. In fact, the greater sensitivity of the gifted child to his own problems of adjustment works as a helping factor in whatever guidance he may require; he can usually understand his needs and may well be able to suggest workable methods of improving his social adjustment. However, not every gifted child should be encouraged to become one of the group; blind conformity to group standards is not a desirable part of the gifted youngster's development. He may be better able to make worthwhile contributions to society by reason of his individualistic tendencies, though he should be helped to develop understanding of those people with whom he is associated who do tend to conform to the prevailing standards of the group. As in most situations, this kind of decision depends upon the child himself.

The similarity of specific statements of objectives for educating all elementary-school children, gifted, average, and below average, can be noted by comparison of those stated by Stendler and Passow. Stendler sees the task of the modern elementary school as follows:

1. Teaching children concepts and skills in communication and quantification
2. Transmitting to children the knowledge that will enable them to understand their physical and social environment
3. Encouraging the creative abilities and aesthetic development of children

4. Promoting the optimal physical and mental health of all pupils[4]

Writing in somewhat more detailed fashion, Passow believes that "regardless of their specific interests or degree of talent, all gifted students need to acquire the skills, knowledge, and attitudes which will enable them to achieve the following objectives:

1. To deal competently with themselves, their fellow men, and the world about them as human beings, citizens, parents, and participants in the "good life"
2. To build a sound liberal foundation to sustain the vigorous development of specialized competencies at the higher levels which they can handle
3. To foster self-direction, independence, a love of learning, and a desire to create and experiment with ideas and things
4. To provide the self-understanding, inner consistency, and ethical standards to see their own uniqueness in terms of responsibility to society
5. To stimulate critical thinking and a scientific approach to solving their persistent problems
6. To nurture an appreciation of the cultural heritage bequeathed by societies through the ages
7. To motivate the desire to meet the special expectations society has for individuals with unique talents[5]

Passow concludes by saying, "While these same objectives are *desirable* for all students, they are *essential* for the gifted if they are to achieve maximum self-realization and to implement their potential leadership."[6]

The main difference between the two listings seems to be the emphasis Passow gives to developing within the gifted child a realization of his responsibility to his society for cultivating and using his talents in helpful ways. This is in agreement with the opinions of most students in the field of education for the gifted: that the very uniqueness of the

[4] Celia B. Stendler, *Teaching in the Elementary School* (New York: Harcourt, Brace & Co., 1958), p. 11.

[5] A. Harry Passow in National Society for the Study of Education, *Education for the Gifted* (Chicago: University of Chicago Press, 1958), p. 194.

[6] *Ibid.*, p. 194.

abilities the gifted possess should constitute a responsibility to develop those unique qualities to serve society and improve it for all. Martens makes this point when she summarizes basic objectives for educating the gifted as including these factors:

1. The individual's relation and responsibility to his fellow men
2. The importance for maximum happiness and service of realizing one's highest potentialities[7]

These can, of course, be goals for all youngsters; the social responsibility aspect is stressed more with the gifted because they are endowed with greater powers to use for the good of society.

In order to develop social responsibilities in the gifted child, it is necessary to provide experiences of a cooperative nature in which he participates with other youngsters. These experiences must be at his level of development; he is not apt to see much use in the mere playing of simple games with few and uncomplicated rules. His mental development requires more complex ways of working and playing with others in some kind of group activity which to him seems reasonable. Unless there are at least a few more gifted children in the group, these kinds of experiences are difficult for teachers to provide. The average youngsters in the class may be completely satisfied with "drop the handkerchief" or "three deep" or similar activities; the gifted youngster requires activities of a more advanced nature if he is to develop habits of cooperative action on a reasonable basis.

Individual Responsibility

At the same time that goals and objectives of education for the gifted prescribe socialized development, they also stress individual development. The two are not incompatible; in fact an integrated, well-balanced personality is probably a basic requirement for understanding cooperation with others to purposeful ends. A gifted child who succeeds in

---

[7] Elise H. Martens, *Curriculum Adjustments for Gifted Children* (U.S. Office of Education, Bulletin 1946, No. 1 [Washington]), p. 3.

achieving the developmental tasks necessary to his satisfaction at various chronological ages, and who has opportunity to work toward the stated objectives of education with the sincere help of interested teachers, is aided substantially toward maximum development in all aspects—physical, social, and emotional, as well as intellectual.

To be of greatest use in guiding instructional programs, objectives of educating the gifted should be stated behaviorally. How does a person act when he is wisely independent and self-directive? What behaviors indicate the growth of social sensitivity? How does a youngster show that he understands himself, and that he is developing acceptable ethical standards? In what ways does he behave if he has grasped the basic skills of communication and quantification? If learning or the acquisition of knowledge does result in changed behavior, this behavior must be known in order that schools and teachers and students may evaluate their progress toward accepted goals. Each school or school system will need to state its objectives in such ways that progress toward them may be measured; then ways of measuring that progress which is considered valuable for students to achieve must be developed. Only a few of the objectives stated can be measured by standardized tests at present; yet if the objectives are accepted as worthwhile aims toward which to work, there must be methods of measuring progress. Evaluation is one of the more important problems growing out of the development of worthwhile objectives in educating gifted children. It is one to which both the psychologists and the educators may well devote their attention.

THE SCHOOL ENVIRONMENT

The environment of the school plays a large part in the values derivable from the teaching-learning situations that operate within the school. Two aspects of that environment are the physical and the attitudinal, the latter being the feelings people hold about their school and its instructional program.

The Physical Plant

Physically the school should be so constructed as to further the accepted objectives of the educational program. If it is a new building, its structure should incorporate the features deemed necessary to carry out the educational objectives planned and projected by the community. If it is an older building, at least the inner features should be so modified as to lend themselves as much as possible to developing good learning situations for the pupils.

Boys and girls are sensitive to their surroundings. It is difficult for them to develop habits of respect for public property, for example, in a building whose furniture and fixtures bear the scars of previous occupants. Likewise, it is hard to develop interest in one's work in drab dirty rooms that are dark and not pleasing to the senses. These difficulties add to the job of the teacher because he must plan ways of surmounting them while he tries to teach his pupils the content prescribed by the accepted curriculum guides of the school.

Old buildings can be kept clean, well ventilated, and unscarred; they can be redecorated in pleasing fashion and oftentimes remodeled to provide the necessary features for today's learning. Movable bookshelves, tables, and chairs can be purchased to replace the fixed ones and thus allow pupils to have more usable and useful space for working in their classrooms. Storage shelves and cupboards can be provided for the many materials needed for an enriched program for gifted pupils, and for the safekeeping of work in progress. Work centers and display areas are needed. Furniture must fit the children who use it. It is hard to concentrate in study when one must sit in a chair that is uncomfortable. Ceilings can be soundproofed to eliminate or muffle the working noise that busy interested children generate. Floors can be treated so that legitimate movement inside the room does not prove disturbing to others working at more quiet tasks.

It would be expected that well-planned new buildings would contain these features and would also provide running water and electrical and gas outlets for use in the learning program. Older buildings do not always have the necessary pipes to allow such facilities as water and gas to be available in every classroom. Sometimes the physical size of the classroom itself operates to limit the kinds of activities that are deemed necessary to children's full learning. Creative and resourceful teachers can devise ways of operating with substitute facilities; less imaginative teachers allow the physical handicaps of older school buildings to provide them with excuses for limited programs of education and thus for limited learning for the boys and girls in their classes. Teachers as well as pupils can be inspired to good work in pleasant surroundings, or discouraged by unpleasant ones.

The Attitudinal Climate

Important as helpful physical facilities are to a program of good education for gifted boys and girls in elementary school, the attitudes of the school and community toward education of the gifted are equally significant, if not more so. If the faculty of the school and the other people of the community hold warm supporting attitudes toward the need for special education of the gifted and the program which has been adopted to achieve it, the limitations of poor physical facilities are not nearly so oppressive to those who are trying to educate the gifted as would otherwise be the case. Resourcefulness with methods and materials can overcome the limitations of existing physical facilities more effectively with the cooperative understanding of the community than it can when there is even slight opposition to offering special programs to educate gifted boys and girls.

A planned program of working with the people of the community can develop understanding of the school's tasks and the ways in which it is trying to fulfill them. Such a cooperative program of school and community working together forms a solid base for any school program, whether it be to educate every child in the community, or to deal specifically with the problems involved in special education for the gifted. Understanding of a program, the reasons behind it, the methods by which it operates, and the ways in which its success may be measured and reported, often leads to support of that program. Involvement of the people of the community with the very first steps of planning a program for the gifted can pay dividends in support; ignoring the contributions which the members of the community can make to the planning and to the carrying out of the program can lead to active opposition.

As the programs for educating gifted boys and girls must make full use of community resources, as should the learning experiences for all the children in the school, understanding and active cooperation are needed. When the attitudinal environment is favorable, a program can thrive and grow and produce excellent results; when this encouragement is lacking, the program has no roots from which to draw continued support, and it may wither. At the very least, poor attitudes in the community may be reflected by poor attitudes toward the gifted on the part of other children in the school. This is a situation which should not be allowed to develop. Since gifted children have the potential to become leaders in the community, their full development demands the support of the community and is actually essential to its future progress.

THE INSTRUCTIONAL PROGRAM

The actual program of education which is planned to help youngsters achieve the accepted objectives depends upon several factors, including the expectations of the community and the larger society of which the community is a part, the individual needs of the youngster himself, and a working knowledge of how children learn. Unless these factors are considered as a basic part of the planning, the instructional program may well be a paper development, unworkable, or ineffective in practice.

In the past one often heard that the main purpose of the elementary school was to have children "learn to read" so that in the secondary schools and institutions of higher education they might "read to learn." The unnecessary division of purpose is evident, as is also the fact that youngsters involved in the program were not considered important enough to have much bearing on its development. At a later date educators and psychologists gave much time and thought to developing logical sequences of facts to be learned at each age throughout the grades. Here again, the purposes and needs of the learner were ignored; at most the learner was considered a receptacle into which certain learnings might be poured at certain times with guaranteed effective results.

Today's elementary school operates somewhat differently. Knowing that what a child learns is related to what he does, it becomes necessary that he do something besides sitting and listening, if the teacher wishes him to learn anything more than how to sit and to listen. Realizing that effective adults must have the ability to solve problems as they arise, it becomes necessary that children have problem-solving experiences throughout their school careers. It is known that it is impossible to teach a child how to solve the exact problems he will face throughout life, as it is impossible to predict with any certainty what these problems may be. Yet through learning methods of tackling problems effectively and efficiently in the here and now, a child can develop the knowledges and skills required for solving problems that arise at later periods. He should also be developing a rich, full life for himself at the present time; education ought not be concerned only with preparation for future living but should stress the good living of the youngsters at each stage of their development. This ties in with the belief that accomplishment of present tasks has a bearing upon a child's ability to accomplish later tasks satisfactorily.

Obviously one must have facts with which to think. One can no more teach a child how to solve problems in the abstract than one can teach him how to swim without water. Nowhere does good elementary education today negate the importance of the learning of facts and the mastery of basic skills and fundamental processes. The skills of critical thinking and problem-solving must be taught in connection with real problems whose solution is necessary to the boys and girls involved; there is little use in parroting a list of problem-solving techniques. It is the ability to apply such techniques that shows whether or not a child is proficient in solving problems on his level of development. There is no single, all-purpose method of problem-solving, just as there is no one method of scientific experimentation which leads to the solution of all problems. There is no charm or incantation to be memorized and applied each time a problem arises; there are several methods by which problems may be attacked and reasoned judgment applied to their solution.

Learning is difficult to define simply. Most psychologists will agree that when a person has learned something he changes his behavior accordingly. When a child has learned to subtract he is able to solve subtraction examples presented to him. His ability to decide whether or not subtraction is the process to apply to certain problems will depend somewhat upon his grasp of the facts involved in stating the problems. Gifted children who read well may find themselves more able to interpret the problems as stated than to apply accurately the computation processes required in solving the problems. It has been found that some gifted children do not develop skill in mathematical processes to the same degree that they have developed their processes of reasoning. They often require some help to fully realize their need for continued study of basic processes in order that they may exploit their reasoning powers more adequately.

Learning involves several factors. Cronbach identifies seven elements of learning as follows:

1. Goal. The goal of the learner is some consequence which he wishes to attain.
2. Readiness. A person's readiness consists of the sum-total of response-patterns and abilities he possesses at any one time.
3. Situation. The situation consists of all the objects, persons, and symbols in the learner's environment.
4. Interpretation. Interpretation is a process of directing attention to parts of the situation, relating them to past experiences, and predicting what can be expected to happen if various responses are made.

5. Response. A response is an action or some internal change that prepares the person for action.
6. Consequence: confirmation or contradiction. Some events that follow the response are regarded by the learner as the consequences of the response.
7. Reaction to thwarting. Thwarting occurs when the person fails to attain his goals.[8]

Each of these elements is vital to effective learning. When a teacher understands these aspects of learning and can plan to provide for each child learning experiences that take them into account, children can learn effectively. It is wise to remember that children can and do learn from any experience that involves these elements of the learning process, regardless of whether or not a teacher has planned the situation in which the learning occurs. Learning takes place in many situations; teachers have the task of setting up learning situations so that directed learning experiences relating to the basic objectives of education will result.

Curriculum

A good elementary program capitalizes upon the interests the children bring with them to school. It does not regard those interests as exclusive determinants of curriculum content; such teaching is haphazard, wasteful, and often unproductive in developing basic skills. The preplanned curriculum can, however, be taught in a way that is related to the children's interests; children learn what has meaning and purpose to them in terms of their present problems. For example, a youngster whose father works with rockets and jets may bring knowledge as well as interest in science to his classroom. He can be a resource person in a group study planned in this area. He can also increase his own knowledge of the subject by using it as a personal interest topic which he pursues as an individual study with his teacher's guidance and help.

[8] Lee J. Cronbach, *Educational Psychology* (New York: Harcourt, Brace & Co., 1954), pp. 49-50.

PLAY. Elementary programs must recognize that play continues to be an excellent source of learning, especially for the primary children. Moving into first grade should not signify the end of opportunities for the children to explore and experiment with their environment through the use of much large equipment and props for creative dramatic play. Observing youngsters during a free-choice period gives the teacher much opportunity to learn about their interests and their difficulties; being informed of these needs, he can plan ways of satisfying them in constructive fashion. Sometimes a teacher must realize that a child's problems are beyond his ability; in such case the teacher must be willing to ask for help from the school psychologist, the nurse, the administrator, or any other person qualified to work with youngsters who have deep-seated problems that do not respond to normal treatment of which the teacher himself is capable.

Play and free-choice activities can contribute to the achievement of educational objectives throughout the elementary-school program, and indeed that of the secondary school as well. It has often been said that many of the well-planned extracurricular activities of the secondary school are more instrumental in helping adolescents practice skills of good citizenship than are the actual classes which they are required to attend.

Play is the proper business of childhood and it remains important to establishing a stable personality throughout life, though in society the proportion of work to play tends to increase as a person grows older. Children and adults can and do have good learning experiences from play activities; there is no basis for the notion that learning must be a painful process.

It is the duty of the teacher to help the children interpret their play experiences and generalize them into usable knowledge for application to similar situations. The best values to be achieved through play do not occur automatically; always there is need for the more experienced person to help the less experienced to appreciate the learnings that are possible in each situation, whether it be taking turns on the horizontal bars or finding reference materials concerning the people who live on Formosa.

GENERAL CONTENT. The curriculum of the elementary program for gifted children is ordinarily built upon that which has been established for all children of the community. There are several reasons behind such practice.

Usually there are a number of state requirements which must be met at certain grade levels, though these are not nearly so numerous as teachers sometimes believe. They may include a study of the child's own state in grade four and a beginning course in American history in grade five, for example; there may also be some specific scientific concepts that are expected to be taught and learned at certain grade levels. It would pay every teacher to read carefully the state requirements for education at the level at which he teaches; though this information might prompt a revision of one of his favorite units of work, it might also free him from false and unfounded beliefs about what he may and may not teach in his classroom, and open the way to more effective organization of learning experiences for the children he teaches.

In some areas where the school system is expected to follow state adoptions of textbooks for various subject areas, it is felt that the gifted children should have the opportunity to become acquainted with the materials presented therein. Even where such adoptions of specific texts are made, it should not be assumed by the teacher that the chosen books constitute the entire content for any grade. They can be used to build common background knowledge in the beginning of a unit of work; they can supply general information for a topic which the children are investigating; they should not, in the light of what is known about how children learn, be expected to teach every child every fact or skill he requires at any one time. They can serve as starting points; they should not be accepted as the final statements on what children should be learning.

When there are certain specific expectations held for children's accomplishments before they enter the junior high school, many elementary teachers feel that every child, the gifted included, should be prepared as well as is possible to meet those expectations. When gifted children attend junior and senior high schools with all other children, and are expected to participate in the same classes with them, some teachers believe they should see to it that the gifted children cover the materials in each of the texts in each of the suggested areas of work so that their future progress is not jeopardized by any lack of specific knowledge in any area. If the junior-high-school English teachers expect that children should have knowledge of formal grammar in terms of accepted definitions, elementary teachers may feel constrained as a matter of status to teach so that children may repeat, "A noun is the name of a person, place, or thing," and, "A verb is a word that shows action, being, or state of being." Elementary teachers realize full well that not every child in their classes will learn what is presented, but they do try to meet the expectations of the next higher step of the educational ladder in their efforts to develop better articulation between the two for the good of the children involved. It would also be worthwhile to put some time and effort into the development of a better understanding of individual differences among groups of youngsters, and the ways in which they learn. This holds true for all the teachers of the school system.

Most schools have prepared study guides, courses of study, resource units, or curriculum guides to assist teachers in planning appropriate learning experiences for boys and girls at various grade levels. None of these aids is given to the elementary-school teacher as a specific pattern that he is expected to follow without deviation; each is developed as a guide to good learning for boys and girls and it is expected that each teacher will make adaptations in terms of the specific individuals with whom he is working each year. Supervising teachers and other administrative personnel can help teachers in the classroom to understand the proper use of such guides as they assist in developing good learning experiences for boys and girls. There are unfortunately still elementary teachers (and teachers in the secondary schools as well) who persist in following the letter of the guide and the related text; there are teachers who are not secure enough in themselves to depart from the accepted printed word. Children can and do learn from such teachers; however, gifted as well as all other children can learn more, make better individual progress, and retain more of what they learn if they are in a program geared to their needs rather than to an impersonal study guide or series of textbooks. Particularly in elementary schools the curriculum should be structured on the basis of a study of the children plus knowledge of expectations; here is where most children develop their feelings about school and about learning. If school is a pleasant place in which they can see real achievement, they can develop attitudes helpful to their entire learning experience throughout school and adult life.

In the elementary school gifted children will study reading and the other language arts, social studies, science, physical education, music and art, and the myriad subject areas involved in each. They will develop greater understanding than average children as they have power to learn and to appreciate more fully than do the average. However, they are able easily to complete the basic work expected in the general curriculum in one-half and sometimes one-third of the school day, so there must be more work for them to do, more learning experiences for them to have, more valuable activities in which they can participate in order that they make the best use of their time, develop intellectually as they are able, learn good study habits, and form good attitudes toward learning and living.

Even in the regular curriculum gifted children must be expected to work harder than, and differently from, most of the children in the class. Since the instruction in reading is considered of great significance for the primary grades, and since about half of all gifted children enter school knowing how to read, the area of reading can be used as a good example of the need for differentiating instruction even when the subject is considered of importance for all children.

READING. No child who has learned to read, and who has read for himself in the interesting books that are being published for beginning readers, can be expected to be satisfied for any length of time to read about a dog and a cat, or a boy and a girl, whose conversation consists of "Oh!" "Look!" "See!" and other such absorbing comments. A child who has read and giggled over *The 500 Hats of Bartholomew Cubbins* may pick up and read *The Cat in the Hat* and *The Cat in the Hat Comes Back* within his first few days at school. That is, assuming that supplementary reading materials are available to him for his choice. He will require other materials than those preprimers and primers which are perfectly right for other youngsters in the class—but such easy books do not serve the needs of the gifted child who is already reading for himself. Placing him in the top group for reading instruction is one way of trying to help him, but it is seldom the best way; the needs of the gifted child may be beyond those of the other bright children in the class.

If there is a library corner or table in the room which the teacher keeps supplied with reading materials at various levels of difficulty, the gifted child can be directed to choose among these to increase his knowledge and his reading ability. But not all gifted children are content to sit and read alone while the teacher works with other youngsters. Especially if the primary teacher uses the well-known three-group method of reading instruction, he will be occupied with the other children in the class for a great portion of the time, and the gifted child is likely to be left to himself. If the teacher is to learn to know the needs, developmental stages, and readiness levels of all the youngsters in the class, some way of giving time to directing the learning of each must be found. It is not sufficient to direct the gifted child to more difficult materials and then go off to the others in the class, assuming that the gifted primary youngster can direct his own learning as long as he has access to a rich supply of materials. Even with grouping for instruction, there remain significant individual differences within the groups that are not cared for by this approach alone.

Some teachers concerned with the problem have developed quite effective individualized reading programs. Here children may choose their reading materials from any that are available in the room. Youngsters may be working with charts, books, pictures, puzzles, or scripts of their own dictated stories, yet all are having experiences dealing with some aspect of reading—the learning of skills, the development of readiness, the addition of vocabulary, or reading for pleasure. Such a program develops a high degree of self-direction among the children and certainly requires a great deal of skill, knowledge, and preparation on the part of the teacher who organizes it.

Since grouping for instruction has been found to have some value, and to be economical of time usage in the classroom, some teachers observe children as they work individually and then form groups on the basis of what has been seen as needed instruction at any one time. These groups are not selected early in the year and then held constant; their structure changes as the purpose of the instruction changes. The authors have observed one first-grade room in which children were seated in six rows of chairs, each row representing a fixed reading group. The row nearest the windows was pointed out by the teacher in charge as containing those children who would fail the first grade; this incident occurred in November of the first-grade year. Such reading instruction may not produce good reading, but it can be almost guaranteed to produce poor attitudes toward schoolwork.

Friendship groupings have been found to be quite effective in teaching reading in the primary grades, and the idea is workable throughout the grades in any reading program. Here the children work together in two's and three's, each reading his own chosen book or chart or words or sentences, getting help from his partner as needed. The teacher moves from one group to another as he sees that help is required, and as he observes the progress being made by each child. He learns more about the youngsters than their reading abilities; he learns something of the sociometric structure of his group—which pupils are at ease in working with others, which ones seem to prefer to work alone—and he can attempt to determine probable causes and decide courses of action to deal with the situations that arise.

Children also are learning more than whatever the subject may be that they are pursuing at any time; they are learning attitudes as well as skills, and they learn these as consequences of the total of the experiences they have with the school subjects involved.

Reading materials available in quantity at many levels of difficulty, time and opportunity to make use of them, and directed individual instruction by the teacher are some of the factors involved in a good reading program for children. For gifted children the difficulty of the materials must not be confined to any specific grade level; horizontal enrichment, that is, reading many books of the same difficulty merely to fill in the school day, does not help the gifted youngster to make the progress of which he is capable. If teachers believe that part of their job involves accepting each child where he is and helping him to make as much progress as he can during the year, the gifted youngster must be offered opportunity to extend his level of reading ability and comprehension and not be limited to a certain grade level.

Because ability in reading is fundamental to the study of any area in which the gifted child may develop interest and skill, it is necessary that his reading skills be carefully checked and that he be helped to develop the needed ones all through the elementary grades. He is not to be taught reading merely by choosing a book and reading it for himself; he requires the help of the teacher to build his knowledge of efficient ways of tackling new words, to learn to read differently for differing purposes, to analyze materials read, and to summarize the main points of informational reading. He needs help in the many complex skills which reading involves; he is expected to grasp these more quickly than average learners do, but he should not be expected to teach them to himself. No conscientious teacher can shunt the gifted child off into a corner of the room with a good supply of books and believe that the job is satisfactorily done.

OTHER LANGUAGE ARTS. Though skill in reading is basic to the gifted child's pursuit of other subjects, it is not the only subject to be studied in elementary school. The other language arts—speaking, writing, and listening—form important parts of the entire program of communication. Language is fundamentally related to all aspects of life; a child needs to use language effectively in everything he does.

Rich first-hand experiences help the gifted child to build a wide vocabulary which he can use effectively in speaking and writing, in communicating his ideas to others. When he writes he runs up against the problem of spelling the words he chooses to express his meaning; as English is not a phonetic language, many children, gifted as well as average, have difficulty with spelling. Since a gifted child can respond to verbal instructions concerning the need for accurate spelling in communicating accurately with others, he can usually put forth the effort required to learn to spell those words he needs. However, spelling is not an easy subject to handle in the elementary school. Too much emphasis upon correct spelling before the child has realized the need for it can hamper a sensitive child's expression; he may, if pushed too hard, resort to producing ordinary work rather than the creative work of which he is capable, merely to avoid the problem of spelling other words. This is a situation to be approached individually for each child; there can be no specific rules about spelling emphasis for all children if the objective of developing creativity is to be achieved.

A related problem concerns the skill of handwriting which is necessary for effective written communication. A gifted child develops ideas of things to write at a much greater pace than he can possibly set them down on the paper before him. Skill in legible handwriting is important to his total progress; the teacher should work with each youngster to see that such skill becomes pleasurable instead of constituting a block to his expression. A certain maturational stage must be reached before the child is capable of handling a pencil and forming his letters accurately.

Speaking can be a social experience as well as a language one. In communicating with a group of his peers, a gifted child can use his speaking vocabulary to good advantage. He can increase his skill in word selection to convey exact meanings as he explains, reports, evaluates, and plans with other children. He may find that in order to retain or acquire status with his classmates he must choose words they can understand; even a limited use of the more involved words he has learned may lead to his being called uncomplimentary names related to his intelligence and his display of it. It is not suggested that the gifted child lower himself to ordinary word usage merely to be "one of the boys" in the classroom group; it is suggested that problem situations may arise if the youngster is not helped by an alert teacher to realize differences in levels of understanding that may require substitute choices of words on his part when he is dealing with average youngsters. The very learning and use of synonyms can be a way of helping the child to increase his own vocabulary at the same time he is being helped to work comfortably with his classmates.

The development of listening as a specific skill in the language arts has been largely neglected until the past few years. Though teaching-learning situations of the past were so organized that a child was expected to learn largely by listening, he was given little help in developing that skill except as he was admonished by the teacher to "pay attention" to what was being said in the classroom. At present, studies are being conducted to try to determine good ways of teaching youngsters the skills required in effective listening; merely sitting quietly is not all that is involved in this skill. Listening requires active participation on the part of the listener; he must hear and interpret what is being said, and react to it in an intelligent manner, if he is to profit by what he hears.

The use of all aspects of language is fundamental to satisfactory achievement in all parts of the school program and in other social experiences as well. Gifted children are ordinarily very able in verbal skills. The teacher must work with each individually to help him develop basic understandings and to guard against glib generalizations that may serve to cover a lack of fundamental information.

GUIDES TO LANGUAGE ART ACTIVITIES. Suggestions for specific activities that teachers may use to help gifted children develop and extend needed skills in all the language arts areas are available in many school systems through curriculum bulletins that have been produced as part of the professional in-service experiences of the teachers. Examples of such curriculum bulletins include: *Challenging the Able Learner, Primary Grades* (Curr. Bull. 301, 114 pp.) and *Intermediate Grades* (Curr. Bull. 401, 84 pp.) from the Cincinnati, Ohio, public schools; and *Suggestions for Working with the Gifted, Grades 1-12,* from the public schools of Arlington County, Virginia. The latter guide offers many suggestions for stimulating gifted elementary-school children in reading and the other language arts. These suggestions are related to specific objectives developed for the subject areas involved, as follows:

Reading
Purpose: 1. To develop skills to a high level including comprehending, critical reading, skimming, interpreting, and pacing reading to suit the purpose.
Suggested Activities:
    a. Read widely to select material suitable for plays, tableaus, monologues, puppet shows.
    b. Determine whether material is factually accurate or opinionated, fact or fiction, probable or impossible through consideration of the date of publication, consensus with other sources, and background of author.
    c. Select and prepare material for oral reading to a younger group or to the class.

d. Evaluate reading materials, books for library, reference materials for unit study, free and inexpensive materials obtained for class work.

e. Develop skill of taking notes from material read.

f. Summarize material read in outline form.

g. Skim to select descriptive phrases, topic sentences, plot sequence. Summarize statements.

h. Read and condense study material for use of less advanced children in social studies and science.

i. Keep charts of rate of reading and work for improvement through pacing reading of selected material.

j. Read various types of materials; check comprehension to determine rate of speed required for each type.

k. Participate with a reading group for the discussion, the teaching of skills, and the developmental part of the lesson. During a part of the study time the gifted child may supplement the stories being read with stories from other books.

Purpose: 2. To become independent in the use of research skills developed by the group.

Suggested Activities:

a. Learn to use the card catalogues, graphs, charts, tables, maps, The Reader's Guide, atlases, encyclopedias, and the World Almanac as research tools.

b. Locate sources of information and extract facts.

c. Do research necessary for staging productions (scenery, costuming, stage props, make-up, appropriate choice of language).

d. Compile table of contents and glossary for class scrapbooks.

e. Locate materials for class use.

f. Organize bibliographies to accompany units of work.

Purpose: 3. To develop the ability to interpret material read in various media.

Suggested Activities:

a. Use handcrafts in presenting materials read, such as puppetry, dioramas, stage settings and costuming.

    b. Make sequence of pictures to tell the story.
    c. Tell story read through pantomime, dance, tableaus, dramatizations, choral speech.
    d. Compose original songs from material read.
    e. Follow directions to construct objects, to cook, to prepare art materials.
    f. Direct stage productions.
    g. Plan and prepare bulletin boards throughout the building.
    h. Plan and create displays related to school clubs, hobbies, and classroom projects.

Purpose: 4. To increase sensitivity to the wide variety of reading materials from which they may gain more information and a deeper understanding of the problems at hand.

Suggested Activities:
    a. Seek out additional understandings which go beyond the exact fact-finding stage to understand "why" and "how" things happen as they do.
    b. Collect library and other resource materials in setting up a learning environment in the classroom which is rich and stimulating.
    c. Study the use of own time within the framework of the class schedule to allow for the investigation of many sources of information.
    d. Organize materials gathered from various sources into composite reports, oral or written.

Purpose: 5. To develop interest in and appreciation for a variety of reading materials.

Suggested Activities:
    a. Select own reading material for individual reading from class and school libraries.
    b. Make collections which have been identified and prepared for display.
    c. Read in connection with hobbies and special interests.
    d. Plan an open house where original and unique book reports may be shared. Costumed book parades, quiz shows, puppet shows, and character sketches are examples of a few such programs.
    e. Use different materials such as supplemental books on high grade level, Landmark Books, Merrill Company Literature Series, encyclope-

      dias, newspapers, current news magazines such as Time and Newsweek, book sections of Sunday newspapers, editorials, sets of supplemental science books, and such magazines as Reader's Digest, National Geographic, Coronet, and Popular Mechanics.

  f. Study the history of books and libraries through the ages and learn how information has been recorded and transmitted through various civilizations. Make a time line to show the history of written communication.

  g. Use reading wheel to extend individual interests.

Topics for many Language Arts activities can be drawn from all subject areas, out of school experiences, and classroom living. The content for oral and written reports, discussions, and letter-writing may be obtained from a social studies unit, from a science project, or from work in arithmetic. The gifted child should be helped to develop competence in the mechanics of oral and written language through speaking and writing what is useful to him and to his class, and a high level of creativeness and originality of work should be encouraged. The functional use of reading as a tool is basic to any area of study in which the gifted may be working.

Other Language Arts
Purpose: 1. To realize satisfaction in self-expression.
Suggested Activities:

  a. Write and illustrate stories. Bind into booklets.
  b. Make collections of original stories.
  c. Dictate creative stories to teacher or older pupils (primary grades).
  d. Write stories, plays, poetry, descriptions and slogans.
  e. Create stories to tell to others.
  f. Produce and/or participate in radio and television programs.
  g. Participate in all phases of theater production (directing, stage lighting, stage craft, acting).
  h. Speak before public groups.
  i. Take part in drama and speech clubs.

j. Express own feelings about music, paintings, and other art creations.

Purpose: 2. To extend vocabulary and to develop an appreciation for our changing language.

Suggested Activities:

a. Analyze words with similar meanings to differentiate shades of meaning.
b. Use precise language.
c. Study the origin and derivation of words, names, places, persons, flowers.
d. Study the history of languages; develop collections of colloquialisms.
e. Collect folklore such as rope-jumping rhymes, counting out rhymes, legends, folk songs.
f. Develop lists of synonyms, homonyms.
g. Make crossword puzzles for other children's use.
h. Analyze stories with vivid word description of scene and action.

Purpose: 3. To refine speech skills (voice quality and control, pronunciation, enunciation, inflection, rhythm) in order to achieve clarity of expression and audience appeal.

Suggested Activities:

a. Tell stories to class or to younger children.
b. Participate in storytelling clubs.
c. Use originality and creativeness in making oral reports.
d. Develop the ability to participate in and to lead discussions (evaluating TV programs, book criticisms, group behavior, field trips, current events).
e. Give directions for playing a game, for organizing activities and for carrying out science experiments.
f. Introduce guest speaker at class program or school assembly.
g. Participate in debate or panel discussion.
h. Act as leader of group projects—planning, evaluating class and assembly programs.
i. Conduct meetings using simple parliamentary procedure.

j. Make inquiries and arrangements by telephone for material and information needed in the classroom.

k. Interview classroom visitors and community residents.

l. Direct choral speaking; assume solo roles.

m. Interpret stories from literature and student's own creative stories.

n. Make tape recordings of voices for self-evaluation and improvement.

Purpose: 4. To refine mechanics of writing (sentence structure, punctuation, word choice, word forms) in order to achieve clarity of expression and audience appeal.

Suggested Activities:

a. Write news stories and editorials for school newspaper.

b. Assemble and edit material for school or class newspapers, scrapbooks, social studies unit.

c. Write directions for playing a game, assembling articles, making things, carrying out science experiments.

d. Record scenes and characters needed to dramatize a story or event and write the sequence of action for a play or a puppet show.

e. Locate sources and illustrations for help in specific writing needs as they occur (form for writing poetry, punctuating quotations, writing business letters).

f. Write letters requesting materials for unit.

g. Write book reviews and character sketches.

h. Prepare notes or outlines for discussion and written reports.

i. Write letters to foreign correspondents.

j. Prepare folios of information and materials to exchange with children from other parts of the country and from other countries.

k. Make written reports of aesthetic experiences—concerts, plays, and art museums.

l. Write biographies and autobiographies.

m. Make anthologies of stories for different grade levels as determined by use in these grades.

       n. Keep records for class activities—committee membership, list of jobs to be done, materials to be used.

Such guides regularly offer many ideas for activities from which teachers may choose to stimulate and foster greater learning for the gifted pupils in their classes. Each teacher is expected, of course, to plan suitable activities in terms of the objectives of education and in terms of the particular child he is teaching. Suggestions in bulletins are helpful in stimulating the teacher's and pupil's own creativity and imagination in choosing appropriate learning experiences; they are not offered as lists to be followed step by step, the completion of which will insure full development of every gifted child's potential ability.

Scheifele offers the following lists of suggested activities which may be performed by gifted children in primary and intermediate grades.

The following are suggested experiences and activities that enrich the regular classroom program (note that some of the "independent activities," though developed and prepared individually, are to be shared with and/or reported to the total class; others represent the gifted child's special interests which may be beyond the understanding of the other children):

1. School- and Community-Service Activities
    A. Making rules for conduct in the school building.
    B. Planning and setting up displays in halls, offices, etc. Planning and working on a mural for the school building.
    C. Heading school drives (Red Cross, March of Dimes, etc.).
    D. Organizing and planning a school hobby show, book fair, or folk-dance festival.
    E. Serving on school committees, student council, etc.
    F. Answering the office telephone, taking and delivering messages as relief for regular employees.
    G. Writing articles and editorials for the school and community newspapers.
    H. Reading or telling stories to younger children.
    I. Scanning and classifying reading materials for the school library.

J. Setting up book displays; assisting the librarian with clerical duties.

K. Participating in a community drive, survey, or poll.

2. Activities Integrated with Group Projects

A. Making models, drawings to scale, or reproductions to show the development of an invention, to trace a series of historical events, and the like.

B. Chairing committees.

C. Leading class discussions. Summarizing class discussions orally or in written form.

D. Interviewing classroom visitors (resource persons).

E. Surveying community resources and planning class preparation for field trips.

F. Making inquiries and arrangements, by telephone or letter, for exhibits on tour to be sent to the classrooms. Locating and collecting materials in the community for classroom exhibits (pottery, shawls, tools, etc.).

G. Writing requests for, selecting, setting up and maintaining materials for class centers of interest—science center, for example.

H. Participating in a debate or panel discussion on a current issue (with children of higher grades if the topic is beyond the interest of own classmates).

I. Directing plans for a class party or other special event. Writing invitations and responses to invitations for such enterprises.

J. Devising new games; giving instructions and directing the game.

K. Singing descants (pitched high for girls, low for boys) while class sings melodies of songs. Kindergarten and first-grade children can play descants on song bells.

L. Playing instrumental accompaniments for class singing.

M. Working on creative activities related to class projects (see "Creative Activities").

N. Publishing a class newspaper.

3. Independent Activities

A. Writing letters to foreign correspondents. Learning a modern language (conversational).

B. Writing requests for materials for own use.

C. Making oral or written reports of reading, observations, excursions, and experiments (factual).

D. Making oral or written reports of aesthetic experiences—concerts, plays, art museum (interpretive).
E. Making charts, maps, graphs, drawings, dioramas, scrapbooks pertaining to experiments, observations, research reading, excursions, hobbies, etc.
F. Preparing outlines for discussions.
G. Studying and interpreting the history of classical pictures.
H. Conducting science experiments in school and at home.
I. Using magazines, periodicals, newspapers as sources of needed information. Using card catalogues, *The Reader's Guide,* and reference books such as encyclopedias, atlases, *The World Almanac,* etc.
J. Collecting and classifying materials for use in the classroom (class librarian). Scanning and classifying materials for own use.
K. Pursuing hobbies of interest. Making collections in connection with special interests.
L. Reading books on advanced levels.
M. Interviewing community residents—businessmen, city officials, etc.
N. Studying such topics as:
    Governments
    Parliamentary law
    History of own community, county, state
    Propaganda
    Own family tree
    Lives of eminent persons
    Geography and climate of own community
    Life of local pioneer
O. Studying the origin of our food supply, laws, governments, etc., as a basis for understanding the evolution of our culture (recommended for eight- and nine-year-olds).
P. Studying a problem such as the cost of building a house (involving kinds of materials, fixtures, construction, and installation labor costs).
Q. Using the typewriter, adding machine, movie projector.
R. Making a community survey of residents' recreational activities, radio- and television-listening habits, etc.
S. Participating in a community project—a drive or campaign.
T. Assisting in the organization of school clubs. Serving as an officer of a club, preparing the agenda for meetings, etc.

U. Devising functional arithmetic problems, "brain teasers," Mathematical Recreations (Magic Squares).
V. Reading stories dealing with people's behavior (with guidance for interpreting and understanding their reactions to situations).
W. Singing with choral groups of higher grades.
X. Playing instrument in school orchestra.
Y. Making independent excursions to such community facilities as:

A court in session	Industrial plants
Hospital	Library
Museum	Parks, recreation center
City government offices	Farms
Welfare organizations	Transportation centers
Large stores	Radio station
Telephone exchange	Bank

Z. Undertaking independent creative activities in art, music, writing, rhythms, dramatization.

4. Creative Activities
   A. Writing original stories and poems.
   B. Preparing oral or written book reviews and character sketches.
   C. Writing radio programs.
   D. Writing dramatizations of historical events and stories; directing their production.
   E. Writing imaginatively the life of an historical character or person living in a particular period.
   F. Expressing orally or in written form own feelings about music, paintings, etc.
   G. Listening to music—radio, concerts, records, television.
   H. Composing music (setting own or class poem to music).
   I. Writing descants for songs. Writing own instrumental descant to accompany class singing.
   J. Originating rhythms and dances related to a class study and developed from dramatization (rodeo including lariat throwing, horse breaking, etc.).
   K. Illustrating stories, plays, and poems.
   L. Sculpturing. Making models or reproductions.
   M. Making a mural for the classroom or school.
   N. Designing posters, advertisements, bulletin-board displays.
   O. Drawing illustrative sketches for programs and class books.
   P. Drawing a comic strip of some historical incident.

Q. Making slides—art, science, books.
R. Making puppets.
S. Designing costumes and props for plays.[9]

The student may find such suggestions as those quoted helpful in directing his own selection of appropriate experiences for specific gifted pupils whom he teaches; he is not expected to apply these suggestions as a recipe to each child indiscriminately but to make choices in terms of the value of the activity for the particular child in question. There may be such materials available in the professional literature owned by the school system in which the student teaches.

Though the present discussion has been confined to the language arts program in the elementary school, most general guides such as those named above include similar suggestions for making every subject of more interest and greater value to the gifted pupil. Another helpful and detailed source of ideas for working with the gifted is *Helping Children with Special Needs,* Elementary School Edition, Volume 2, by Robert F. DeHaan and Jack Kough.

The student will readily recognize many of these activities as having been among those in which he has taken part throughout his schooling. The activities pursued are important in optimum development of the gifted; the manner in which they are selected and carried out is different in method and in result depending upon whether the teacher is working with a gifted child or one of only average ability.

Each suggestion that has been made thus far is applicable to teaching gifted children in regular classrooms as well as in special classes. Special classes will usually add different learning experiences to the curriculum for gifted children, in addition to helping them achieve mastery of the basic skills expected of all elementary-school children.

Additional learning experiences for gifted children have included intensive study of biographies of eminent people of the world, modern foreign languages, personal typewriting

---

[9] Scheifele, Marian, *The Gifted Child in the Regular Classroom.* Practical Suggestions for Teaching, Number 12. Hollis L. Caswell, Editor. New York: Bureau of Publications, Teachers College, Columbia University, 1953, pp. 52-55.

as the child matures physically sufficiently to profit from use of the machine, and guided pursuit of individual interests. There is time for greater stress on projects developed to increase originality, initiative, skills of leadership, and fruitful cooperative endeavor, when gifted children are grouped in one class section, and the teacher is not continually pressed to find time to work with slower learners as he is in the regular classroom. There is time for extending the horizons of the gifted child with additional learning experiences planned specifically for him, as he does not need to spend a whole school day in the mastery of the basic skills.

There is no limit to what may be included in the gifted child's elementary-school program save those limits imposed by lack of imaginative creative teaching. Any study, any investigation, any project that will carry out the objectives of elementary education for the gifted is proper for the child to pursue.

No specific program is recommended here. Each school system must develop the one that seems best to serve the gifted boys and girls of its community.

Methods of Teaching the Gifted

The selection of methods of teaching involves the philosophy of the teacher who makes the choices. Teachers who verbalize their beliefs about varying materials to meet individual differences in need and achievement in the classroom and then assign every child the same chapter to study in the same book show that they have not actually accepted the idea of individual differences at all. Choice of method for any teaching-learning situation must be knowledgeably related to the objectives to be achieved, the individual pupils in the classroom, the subject matter to be studied, and the ways in which people learn. Anything less is not worthy of a professionally trained teacher.

Method and content are so interrelated that it is difficult to discuss one without reference to the other. The reader will have noted that method entered into the discussion of curriculum; undoubtedly content will appear in this presentation as well.

There is no one method guaranteed to be useful in teaching everything, everywhere, to all pupils. There are no tricks or techniques of teaching to be applied with assurance in any given situation. Teaching is an intensely personal activity; methods that prove valuable to one teacher with a certain group of pupils may be ineffective for another teacher with another group of pupils. In fact, the same teacher will need to change and modify his methods in terms of the needs of the youngsters with whom he works and the objectives involved in each lesson or subject or project. Oftentimes, it is the method chosen for teaching a certain skill that determines whether or not it will be successfully achieved.

INFLUENCE OF PERSONALITY. One important factor in teaching which is sometimes considered an influence upon method is the kind of person the teacher is. Elementary-school children respond favorably to a warm, friendly teacher, one who accepts and respects them as worthy individuals. The influence of the teacher's personality must not be overlooked or underrated in any consideration of method. In a classroom in which the teacher evidences real interest in the pupils as individuals rather than as enrollments to be taught so that he may earn his salary, children have greater freedom to develop profitably. A cold person has a much more difficult time generating interest among the pupils for what is taught, regardless of the specific methods he may use.

Up to the present time there are no known methods to be used exclusively in teaching the gifted. There are good methods for teaching children; from among those the teacher of the gifted must select the ones appropriate to each learning situation.

THE PROBLEM APPROACH. One method that has proved effective in teaching children so as to achieve the basic objectives of education is that which is variously called the problem approach, problem-centered teaching, and the problem-solving method. In this method children are taught through investigating and attempting to solve problem situations which they themselves have helped to plan. They define the problem for study, advance possible hypotheses for its solution, gather and evaluate pertinent data, judge the possible outcomes, report their findings, accept and reject solutions, and evaluate not only the end product but the process by which they arrived at it. They are thus learning problem-solving techniques at the same time they are adding to their usable general knowledge. Notice the plural; there is no one problem-solving technique to be applied indiscriminately to all problems any more than there is such a thing as *the* scientific method. The point is to help children develop several effective ways of approaching problem situations and solving them competently and confidently.

There must be a distinction between a problem and a question. When the problem-solving approach to learning began to be developed as a profitable classroom technique, some authorities stressed the point that problems should be stated as questions, with the result that almost any question came to be regarded as a "problem" for the children to solve. More recent thought holds that in order to be a real problem, there must be more than one answer possible. A question is not a problem if it can be answered fully by looking into a book and noting the answer given. A problem must involve real work by the students before they can consider it satisfactorily handled.

Problem-solving is effective with both group work and individual pursuits. Groups of gifted children can organize a problem, plan how to tackle it, gather many materials, weld these into a purposeful whole, report their findings before the entire class in some way, and evaluate their progress both in learning and in group processes. One gifted youngster can follow similar procedures in some study which may be of significance to him alone; he would work by himself with the guidance of his teacher in developing the resources needed. Whether or not he would report his findings before his class might depend upon several factors, including his own desires in the matter and the relationship of what he had learned to the possible benefits it held for the other children.

The problem-centered approach to learning for the gifted allows the teacher to give them much guidance and practice in needed research activities. The old idea that the teacher imparts knowledge as the foremost method of teaching is no longer effective today in producing the kind of individuals needed in a democratic society, or in helping gifted children to develop to their highest potential. Instructing gifted children by lecture en masse and expecting each to attain certain preset standards would serve merely to crush out whatever initiative they may possess. Besides that, no teacher can possibly know all the information required by a group of gifted children as they pursue their group and individual studies; practice in using research skills to locate information is much more helpful to their intellectual growth than expecting them to learn only what they are told by the teacher.

GROUP WORK. The rise of group work in the classroom has grown to be considered almost a method of teaching. A few words of caution may be in order here. Children working in groups may be a good choice when the subject at hand lends itself to a group study, but there are times when children need to work individually to perfect a skill, to follow a personal interest, to read for pleasure or for information. Group work just for the sake of having group work is not a sensible approach to teaching children. When groups are formed in terms of the task to be done, when four or five children work together to achieve some common goal, when the teacher calls together a small group to instruct them in some skill they all require at the moment, then there is reason for working in groups. There is no reason to form groups for instruction merely because one has read or heard that this is an effective or modern way of working with children. Children learn best in purposeful situations; when a group has purpose it can be useful; without purpose, it remains artificial and unnecessary.

ROUTINE DRILL. Routine assignments in specified texts which children are expected to study, to recite upon in class, and to write about on a test paper, are not designed to develop habits of self-direction in children. They tend rather to develop conformity and to snuff out thought. When a gifted child is limited to such an unimaginative method of teaching and learning, his potential cannot possibly be adequately developed.

Nothing that has been said should be interpreted to mean that gifted children require no drill in mastering the basic skills. They do. They need time to practice procedures in their skill learnings so that these may become automatic responses, skills upon which they may call as needed to solve problems. However, they do not as a rule require as much drill as learners of average ability; they prosper with functional purposeful drill, with the amount limited to their personal needs for mastering the skill. The old adage that "practice makes perfect" has long been overdone in supplying excessive amounts of materials for drill to all children in elementary schools. Someone has said that practice makes perfect only if it is perfect practice; that is, only if the skill is used correctly throughout the drill procedures. When a child has a purpose for learning, he learns; when he can drill with purpose he derives benefits from drill. The teacher must recognize that children learn at different rates; there is no educative purpose served by assigning the same number of pages or exercises in drill work for each child. The development of competent citizens obviously requires that they be able to use language and number skills effectively, but it does not require that each child be put through a routine program of drill activities.

DISCUSSION. The use of discussion as a method of teaching gifted children can be another good way of helping them attain the educational objectives. It is not easy to direct a good discussion with gifted children; each has so many ideas to put before the group that he may just speak right out without thinking of the rights of the others to express themselves or the need for the group to give serious consideration to each idea that arises. Children need practice in good discussion methods, and these go far beyond a question-answer type of activity. It is necessary to have a purpose for discussion, to plan how to reach that goal, to listen carefully to what others say, to react to the ideas put forth, to make contributions in a related manner instead of striking off at a tangent, to help keep to the point of the discussion, to develop the ability to share ideas that lead in the direction chosen. The child must learn to respect the ideas of others, to make his own comments thoughtfully and helpfully, to accept disagreement when it occurs. All of these are elements of developing a worthwhile discussion that will advance the immediate learning of the class, leading to whatever goal has been accepted as valuable, and of learning how to participate in a discussion. Gifted children also need practice in learning to lead discussions; the teacher is not the only person who acts as leader in a group of gifted youngsters.

Discussions require that youngsters have something valuable to contribute. They can seldom be based upon each child's having read the same source to gather information on the topic of the discussion. If every child has read the material, there is not much point in calling the ensuing talk period a discussion; if it is to be recitation, or question and answer, call it that.

WORK UNITS. Gifted children are more able to operate in terms of remote goals than are average children. The gifted can plan work that will carry over a longer period of time to achieve their goals; they can profit from unified or correlated teaching. In pursuing a unit of work that calls upon subject matter from many areas of knowledge, gifted children can develop their ability to perceive relationships and to draw generalizations not limited to one subject-matter field alone. They can approach problem-solving more realistically; few life problems can be solved with information taken from just one area of subject matter. Unified teaching also serves to use group work purposefully and thus to help in the socialization of gifted youngsters. At the same time, individual interests can often be correlated with the classwork, and children can learn to work together purposefully, to use research skills for a reason, and to relate individual pursuits to a group project.

When the interest of gifted children is aroused in a unit of work, they can proceed with fewer directions and much less supervision than is required for youngsters of less ability. They need help in learning how to study and this will be supplied by the teacher as required. Teachers can act more as resource people in such a situation. Gifted children must have opportunity to develop responsible self-direction and independence in study; a teacher-dominated learning situation does not supply opportunities for these skills to be taught and learned. Teachers must work directly to help children make progress in their ability to plan, to think, to do independent work. The right to learn by discovery and insight belongs to the children, but the teacher must set the stage so that such learning is made possible and encouraged.

THE COMMUNITY APPROACH. Devices have been developed to help children make better use of community resources as they learn to clarify the school's role as part of the community, to show that education belongs to the community, not to the school alone, in order to make education more real to the children than mere book-learning can be. These devices include field trips, interviewing people of the community, and asking people of the community to speak to the school or to a class of children so as to make use of the specific knowledge which they can contribute to children's learning. These are not actually methods of teaching but rather devices that implement method, and add to children's direct experiences.

Field trips can be taken in connection with any unit of work that involves learning some facts or skills that can be better learned and understood through actual experiences than through reading about the activity. Classes studying about the role of the newspaper as a communication medium in modern society may plan to watch a newspaper grow from its beginnings in the typewriters and teletypes to the place where it rolls from the press with the ink still wet. A class studying the historical development of its community may plan a trip to the places of historical interest in the area. Another group studying the occupational opportunities available in the community might travel to the various industries to watch them in operation.

In each case the trip is taken because some learning can be achieved by it; some educational purpose is served. Field trips under the auspices of the school should be planned to develop the learning of the youngsters; trips to state parks for class picnics do not ordinarily belong under the heading of educational activities.

Trips must be carefully planned and organized to insure that the pupils will derive the learnings expected from them; since it is the children who need the learning, it is they who should have the full experiences, including the planning, organizing, arranging and evaluating. The teacher does not abdicate his role as group leader; but he does exert his leadership by assisting the children to make sound plans and to evaluate the activity so that they may learn as much as possible from the experience.

It is not necessary that an entire class take every trip that is planned; perhaps a small group will plan a trip to gather information required to meet their specific responsibilities in solving the group's larger problem. In a study of communications, for example, small groups might visit the newspaper office, the radio station, the television stations, the telephone exchange, and the local Western Union office, investigating the contributions each makes to the community. Each group thus would collect information to share with the rest of the class in a planned session, and for a planned purpose.

Drawing upon the resources available from individuals in the community is another way of implementing children's learning. One woman may be able to sing the folk songs of her native country; another may be skilled at some musical instrument; still another may have been a nurse overseas and have had experiences she can share with the children. A man may have amateur radio as his hobby and be willing to share his knowledge and skill with the children; another may work at some job he can tell the youngsters about; still another may be a visitor from some foreign country about which he can inform the youngsters from his first-hand experience. In each case the knowledge brought by the visitors to the classroom is essential to the children's purposes in their units of work; the experience is planned for profitable learning.

When youngsters interview people of the community they should be prepared with a knowledge of the purposes for which they are seeking the information and with the skills of questioning to obtain it. If acquiring knowledge is the purpose of the interview, little will be accomplished unless the children know how to do what they are trying to do. The teacher must work with them through the plan, and help them to develop the needed skills. Role-playing is a helpful device in this instance, allowing the youngsters to practice a bit before they put their skills to actual test in speaking with the mayor of the community, or the president of a local industry.

Hildreth has written that:

> Gifted children need a guidance type of training rather than authoritarian methods in the opinion of Hunter teachers. A school with a narrow fixed curriculum where autocratic, regimented teaching prevails, presents a serious handicap to the gifted individual, for here he will have no scope for experimentation with his own ideas, he will not be able to forge ahead at his own pace or receive the sympathetic guidance he needs for the nurturing of his talents. . . . Teaching the gifted is largely a matter of controlling the conditions under which the children learn rather than imposing on them lessons to be learned in formal steps. The quality of the learning achieved depends upon the nature of the experiences gained, which in turn are dependent upon the environmental setting for learning both within the school and outside.[10]

Developing Creativity

One of the characteristic qualities of youngsters, their curiosity and originality in dealing with situations, unfor-

---

[10] Gertrude H. Hildreth and Others, *Educating Gifted Children* (New York: Harper & Brothers, 1952), pp. 68-69.

tunately tends to diminish as the children progress through school. Teachers of intermediate and upper grades are all too familiar with this loss of freshness, of interest in many things, of desiring to investigate and to learn. Though cause and effect relationships are difficult to establish, it may be that narrow, unimaginative teaching methods and curriculum development imposed upon youngsters have some influence in closing off the spontaneous use of their own ingenuity. Since this characteristic is a quality ordinarily present in gifted youngsters, and because it is so desperately needed in the solution of social problems, it is the responsibility of teachers to educate gifted youngsters in such ways as to keep alive the spark of curiosity, foster the development of originality and initiative, and help the gifted child to retain and increase his ability to look at situations creatively.

Recognition of the need for helping gifted children develop their creativeness is not new. In 1937 Bentley wrote, "But creativity and much of our modern educational system do not seem to be in harmony. A creative mind in a rigid system of regimented education is more or less an anomaly; it simply cannot exist. But life demands this important human and social trait."[11] As recently as 1958 Wilson stated, "The plain fact is that we know very little about the characteristics of children who are apt to become creative adults and very little about the educational or other experiences that tend to produce these characteristics."[12]

Research in the field of developing creative people is meager. For too long a time creativity has been considered only as it relates to the arts. A broader view of creativeness as it can apply to all aspects of life is the interpretation suggested here.

Independent thought and freedom of expression are two factors that most authorities agree have influence upon the development and use of creativity. When the school atmos-

[11] John Edward Bentley, *Superior Children* (New York: W. W. Norton & Company, Inc., 1937), p. 145.
[12] National Society for the Study of Education, *Education for the Gifted* (Chicago: University of Chicago Press, 1958), p. 111.

phere not only permits but encourages freedom of thought on the part of the students, it is believed that creativeness and originality are more likely to result than in situations that emphasize agreement with accepted authority. When children are allowed to question rather than being forced to conform, their originality can be brought to light and fostered. When adult standards are imposed upon children's work, an atmosphere that stultifies originality is rapidly developed.

If a youngster is afraid in some way, he is not likely to be a creative person. A child who has been trained at home to be overly conscious of the need for keeping clean will be inhibited in attempts at self-expression, particularly when they involve the use of anything that might soil his hands or his clothing. Such inhibitions seem to carry over to other fields of self-expression; a youngster who is afraid is not free to do or say anything except that which will win him the kind of approval to which children in general are accustomed.

Such children are easily recognized in the elementary classroom where all sorts of art materials are made available for children's use during a free choice of activity time. They stand back and watch the other youngsters; they may put on their smocks or other protective clothing but a great deal of time is required before they can realize that "messing" with paints or clay or sand and water or fingerpaints is approved in this particular situation. Some of them get up sufficient courage to try the materials after a time, but their efforts are hampered by their inner fears.

Youngsters who have had rich living experiences and who have had opportunities to talk about them are freer in their verbal expression, both speaking and writing. The kinds of stories and poems that have been read to them, and have been provided for them to read, have some influence upon their originality also. Stilted artificial stories and forced rhymes do not help children to develop their own creative expression.

Overemphasis upon routine drill procedures can stultify creativity too. When drill consists of supplying words for blanks left in someone else's sentences, it is difficult for youngsters to develop their own ability to speak and write in expressive ways. When reading is limited to the basal readers adopted for the classroom, creativity is hard to develop. When arithmetic processes must be done exactly as the teacher has explained, the child's ability for personal discovery and insight into the processes is stifled.

Creativity can flourish in a classroom that provides a rich environment with many materials from many fields of knowledge available for the child's use. The schedule must allow for exploration and experimentation with these materials at such times as the child needs them to express an idea. Creativity cannot be developed by allowing it to come forth only at rigidly set times. It must be encouraged by the teacher in all endeavors; one does not do creative writing, for example, every Wednesday morning between nine-thirty and ten, as if creativity were like a water tap that could be turned on and off. Creativity invades a youngster's entire life; the creative process does not operate merely on call.

Gifted children as a whole possess much drive, originality of approach to problems, and desire to achieve, along with the high level of intelligence that are believed to be operative factors in creativity. It is the duty of the elementary-school teachers to provide an environment both in material things and in permissiveness of atmosphere so that children's ideas may be forthcoming, their originality expressed and approved, their creativity encouraged and developed. While it is not the responsibility of the elementary school to train specialists in any field of living and learning, it is the responsibility of the elementary school to help the gifted child to develop whatever talents and personality characteristics he may show and need in order that his later specialization may not be hampered. Children must have opportunity to explore their known interests and to develop new interests throughout their elementary-school experiences. This is seldom accomplished through the use of a rigidly structured curriculum taught by mass methods of instruction.

The stress given to free expression and original approaches, the emphasis made upon developing a curriculum geared to children's individual needs and interests as well as upon the accepted objectives of education, may lead the uninitiated to become concerned with the possibility of discipline problems. This usually looms large in the eyes of the beginning teacher. Would not such a program lead to undisciplined children? The answer is, "No."

A school program built to handle the individual differences children exhibit actually lessens the kinds of problems of a disciplinary nature. More of such problems are found in classrooms in which every child is expected to master the same lessons in the same amount of time, and the class is treated as one identical group in the teaching-learning situation. A better curriculum for the youngsters ordinarily leads to better discipline among them.

When gifted children are interested in what they are studying, when they see the purpose of the lessons, when they see progress in valuable skills, when they are helped to learn what they need to learn, they work hard. Some gifted children have been known to develop drill exercises for themselves on skills for which they realized they needed some extra practice.

When a program is based on democratic ideals which children are living and practicing, they develop the highest order of discipline, which is, of course, responsibility for one's own actions, and self-direction with self-imposed discipline. Children need help in learning these skills as they do in mastering others. They may need reminders from the teacher or from other children, as they become so involved in their own projects that they forget to be considerate of others in the classroom. But they learn to discipline themselves much more readily in a program which deals with them as worthy individuals than they do in a program of teacher-imposed dominant authority.

Materials and Equipment

Throughout the presentation of methods of teaching the gifted and appropriate curricular experiences for them, the need for at least an adequate supply of related materials and equipment has been implicit. Children cannot learn as they should when they are limited to a meager school environment containing merely the bare essentials of furniture, chalk boards, and textbooks. A stimulating environment is necessary to offer them the opportunities for studying and exploring that they should have.

For all elementary-school children, materials supplied should be chosen for their values in encouraging learning and constructive play experiences. The arts and crafts supplies, the equipment to allow physical activity and development, the science tables with things children can do rather than things they must watch the teacher do, the books, puzzles, charts, counting materials, games, and toys, the materials for creative dramatic play—all are necessary to full growth in learning. The emphasis should remain upon unstructured materials with which the children can exercise their creativity whether they be large blocks and short ladders in the primary grades or bits and scraps of lumber and textiles for the intermediate ones.

Children learn from their experiences. Providing a setting in which guided educative experiences may be developed is part of the task of the elementary school. No child can progress toward his full potential unless he has a variety of rich experiences upon which to base his learning, and the freedom to choose among many materials those which appropriately express his ideas at any one time.

The specific kinds of materials needed to help the teacher and children plan vital learning experiences have been pointed out in the discussions relating to enrichment and to preschool programs. A creative teacher can supply those which seem best suited to the growth of the children with whom he works in his classroom.

Outcomes

The desired outcomes of the elementary program in the case of the gifted may be stated in terms of the goals and objectives presented in an earlier section of the chapter. In the consideration of outcomes, it should be recognized that the gifted share the common goals of other children in the educative process. However, because of their ability and promise it is important that some areas of learning be emphasized, that some outcomes be specifically sought. These outcomes fall under the two major headings of social responsibility and individual adjustment.

SOCIAL RESPONSIBILITY. Social responsibility includes qualities prerequisite to satisfactory social adjustment, sensitivity to social problem situations, and socially conscious skillful leadership. It is in the early years of school life that basic social concepts can and should be developed in the gifted. In many cases, the school presents the first opportunity outside the family for the child to become a member of a formal group. Most children will have had some experience in informal play groups, but upon entering school they become members of a stabilized class group which offers rich opportunity for social experiences. Here, it is to be hoped, the gifted child will learn to adjust but not necessarily to conform, to become aware of the problems of group living but not be overcome by them, to develop qualities of good leadership, and also to learn the art of constructive followership.

INDIVIDUAL ADJUSTMENT. There are certain outcomes for the gifted as individuals which should be achieved by the program. As a basis for individual adjustment, the elementary program should help the gifted child to know himself, to glimpse his potentialities and to realize his limitations. Before he moves into the secondary level, he should have developed interests which can be expanded and intensified as he climbs the educational ladder. He should have learned how he can work most effectively and where he can obtain different types of information he will need as he pursues his interests.

The general heading of individual adjustment also includes such outcomes as the mastery of the fundamental skills of learning. This is important to the future adjustment and educational progress of the gifted child as well as to that of his fellows. It is to be hoped that he will also obtain a tremendous amount of general information as well as some intensive learning experiences in areas in which he has a special interest.

It is also not too much to hope that the quality of creativeness and originality will have been sought out and nurtured and developed during these early years of the gifted child's school life. These qualities represent a rich legacy to be passed on to the secondary school and later the college or university. Every teacher of the gifted should be conscious of the necessity of preserving and fostering the growth of these traits. Together with the natural wonder and curiosity of the gifted, they form the attitudinal basis for major contributions in science, art, and human relations.

In other words, these students will have achieved the educational objectives set out for elementary education and for gifted children. They will have lived richly and satisfyingly during the elementary-school years, and they will be as well prepared for secondary and higher education as their own capabilities and their creative teachers have been able to manage.

SELECTED READINGS

Association for Supervision and Curriculum Development. *Learning and the Teacher*. Washington, D.C.: The Association, 1959. 222 pp.

This yearbook describes the teacher's role in the learning process as he plans and introduces learning tasks, helps the learners to learn through interpretation of experiences, and utilizes research sources to improve his understanding of learning, and consequently his teaching.

CRONBACH, LEE J. *Educational Psychology*. New York: Harcourt, Brace & Co., 1954. 628 pp. Chapters 1 through 3.

These chapters develop concepts basic to understanding the learning process, and indicate the aims of the socializing process. The responsibility of the teacher to organize materials of curriculum, to motivate, evaluate and provide for individual differences in the classroom, is described by an analysis of an actual classroom situation.

DeHaan, Robert F., and Kough, Jack. *Helping Children with Special Needs*. (Teacher's Guidance Handbook, Elementary School Edition, Vol. 2.) Chicago: Science Research Associates, Inc., 1956. 204 pp. Section 2.

A wealth of suggestions have been gathered in this handbook to help teachers to work with gifted and talented children in regular classes in the elementary school. The suggestions are organized in terms of various kinds of abilities, talents, and skills that children may exhibit.

Havighurst, Robert J. *Developmental Tasks and Education*. New York: Longmans, Green & Co., Inc., 1952. 100 pp. Chapter 3.

The principal developmental tasks of this age period are summarized and discussed in terms of the nature of the task and its bases in biological, psychological, and cultural factors, as well as its educational implications.

Heffernan, Helen, and Bursch, Charles. *Curriculum and the Elementary School Plant*. Washington, D.C.: The Association for Supervision and Curriculum Development, 1958.

The necessity for implementing a sound educational program with functional school buildings and facilities is presented; ways of planning buildings that will facilitate the learning of children are pointed out.

Herrick, Virgil E., and Jacobs, Leland B. (eds.). *Children and the Language Arts*. Englewood Cliffs, N.J.: Prentice-Hall, Inc., 1955. 524 pp. Chapters 1, 3, 4, and 7.

These chapters present the trends in the teaching of language arts based on acceptable theories of learning, the relationship of children's growth and development to language, the part language plays in learning, and the values of teaching listening to children.

Miel, Alice (ed.). *Individualizing Reading Practices*. (Practical Suggestions for Teaching, No. 14.) New York: Bureau of Publications, Teachers College, Columbia University, 1958. 91 pp.

In order to help teachers plan reading instruction related more adequately to the capability and maturity of each child, this booklet offers a statement of what it means to individualize reading practices, plus several reports of individualized reading instruction in specific classrooms written by the teachers who organized the programs.

National Society for the Study of Education. *Education for the Gifted*. Chicago: University of Chicago Press, 1958. 420 pp. Chapters 6 and 11.

In Chapter 6 Wilson discusses the meanings applied to creative processes, and explores some conditions that may facilitate creativity in the classroom. Ideas for stimulating creativity among gifted students are listed and explored. Chapter 11 describes several programs in operation at the elementary-school level, each of which embodies the principle of enrichment as an effective means of helping gifted youngsters develop optimally.

Stendler, Celia B. *Teaching in the Elementary School*. New York: Harcourt, Brace, & Co., 1958. 541 pp. Chapters 11, 12, and 13.

Chapter 11 presents characteristics of creativity, factors which indicate the presence of creative ability in children, and ways to identify and foster creativity. Chapter 12 discusses ways in which teachers may foster and develop creativity in children's language expression, with many examples of creative work shown. Chapter 13 presents a fully detailed exposition of ways of helping children develop and maintain creativity in the fields of music and art.

ZIRBES, LAURA. *Spurs to Creative Teaching.* New York: G. P. Putnam's Sons, 1959. 354 pp.

Teaching as a creative art is fully detailed in this effort to help teachers understand, practice, and foster creativity with their classes of youngsters, in every subject of the elementary curriculum and through every learning activity of each day.

12

The Secondary-School Program

Variations in ways of organizing public school systems exist over the country. The reader will be familiar with 8-4, 6-6, 6-3-3, 6-2-4, and K-12 as symbols used to designate what portions of the school system are considered as elementary and what portions secondary education, and perhaps the ways in which students are separated by grades, and housed in different school buildings. Less familiar are 7-5 and 6-6-2, the latter designation including a two-year community college. Regardless of the administrative organization of the school, the grades from seven through twelve, and sometimes beyond, ordinarily deal with youngsters in various stages of adolescent development.

This chapter deals with the education of gifted adolescents in the junior and senior high school. The goals of secondary education, and the additional quality of education desirable for gifted adolescents at this level, are shown. Various kinds of instructional programs are suggested, and methods of teaching and materials of instruction suited to optimum development of the gifted are discussed. Since choosing further education and exploring career possibilities become pressing problems during the period of secondary education, guidance is mentioned here, though the authors subscribe to the belief that guidance is continuous with all education and is not limited to the secondary school.

ADOLESCENT GROWTH AND DEVELOPMENT

The Adolescent Period

Adolescence is the term given to the period of development between childhood and maturity. The age or grade limits given are approximations; girls in fifth and sixth grades may give evidence of adolescent physical growth and expanded social interest; boys who are freshmen and sophomores in college may be still in a period of noticeable physical growth. Most authorities in the field agree that the ages twelve to eighteen are appropriate to assign to the adolescent stage of growth; all agree that there are individual variations from the general pattern; some believe that the upper age should be extended to twenty-four in consideration of the fact that our society prolongs at least economic dependence far beyond the age of eighteen for many people.

It is surely a fact that compulsory school attendance, child labor laws, union regulations, required ages for voting, for driving a car, for military service, and for marriage have helped to extend dependence of the young upon the adult in our society since its historical beginnings. The differences in ages at which youth are deemed able to take on the responsibilities mentioned may add confusion rather than clarification to the adolescent's quest to determine at what age he is "adult." Students of human development have come to feel that chronological age is not the best or only criterion to be applied to judging a person's maturity, but in attempting to deal with large numbers of people with one general rule, chronological age is usually the peg upon which the rule is hung.

Even though some elementary-school children do begin to exhibit the signs of physical growth and social activity generally attributed to adolescence, it is the junior and senior high schools of the secondary-school program that have been established specifically for educating adolescent boys and girls.

Characteristics of Adolescence

Adolescence is recognized as a period of increased physical growth. The child's body loses those characteristics which have kept it childish and takes on the forms and proportions associated with adulthood. Inwardly the body prepares itself to assume the function of reproduction; outwardly the differentiated secondary sex characteristics develop. The task of accepting one's physical aspects takes on greater significance for a boy or girl who remains childlike at fourteen, for a boy or girl who develops differently enough from most of the adolescents in his group to cause unsettling comparisons. With "ideal" adult figures constantly glamorized on television and in the movies, boys and girls are kept continuously aware of approved adult figures in our society, and of their own shortcomings in reaching the societal standards of handsomeness or beauty. Though they can usually understand and accept differences in rate of development intellectually, they are not always able to accept them emotionally.

Another significant point in adolescent development deals with the incomprehensibility of adults. At least, that is what it seems to be to the adolescent. Though he is on the one hand told he is "too big" for some activities that are satisfying to him, he is at the same time "too little" for others which he fully believes he is ready to adopt. This pushing and pulling is not very easy for the adolescent to understand; if he is "too old" for some activities, the adolescent may feel that he is fully "old enough" for others that remain forbidden by parents and teachers or other adult authority-figures.

In their striving to achieve personal independence from their families, adolescents seem to rely upon the standards of the peer group more than upon those of their parents, which were more or less accepted and adhered to during childhood. At the same time that adolescents push away from the apron strings of home, they bind themselves to the security of conformity to their own group. Though they insist upon individuality, upon developing as persons in their own right, they tend to stay closely to the customs of their own group in matters of dress, talk, behavior, values, study habits, attitudes, and the like. It is the rare adolescent who turns her collar down evenly all around when "all the girls" are wearing theirs turned up in back; it is the rare adolescent who keeps his shirt buttoned neatly and his belt at his natural waistline when the customs involve unbuttoned shirts and trousers belted low around the hips.

Adolescence is a time of shifting interest to activities of a heterosexual nature. The exclusive gangs and clubs of younger boys and girls dwindle from the main recreational choice as the youths naturally move toward increased interest in the opposite sex. This interest may be shown by poking and pinching or show-off behavior; the purpose is to engage the other person's attention, to establish heterosexual relationships. Youngsters may not know of approved methods, so they use the ones they have developed successfully in other situations. They learn, as they try out various ways of attracting attention, which ones are more appropriate in this new relationship. Snatching someone's billfold or notebook is seldom indicative of lack of respect for personal property; it means rather that the youngster is seeking the attention of the owner of the notebook or billfold in the only way he can at present devise to get such attention.

Economically, too, the adolescent generally tries to strike out for himself. Though society does not allow him to hold a full-time job and thus be completely independent economically, he is allowed part-time work from which he can earn some money for his needs. Money of one's own to use as one chooses represents another aspect of independence for adolescents. Baby-sitting, lawn-mowing, snow-shoveling, car-washing, house-cleaning, newspaper routes, doing errands—whatever gainful activity may be approved by the adolescent society can be used to earn money for independent use. The adolescent also looks ahead to the time when he will need to support himself and possibly a family; he is concerned not only about money for now, but about the choice of a satisfying vocation to earn money later.

Problems of Adolescence

The problems of adolescents are many and varied; they include social, emotional, physical, economic, and moral problems. It does not follow that adolescence should be a period of stress in and of itself; it is the pressures and expectations of the society in which the adolescent lives and his own developing personality that determine whether or not the period between childhood and maturity can be smoothly and naturally negotiated.

Both junior and senior high schools must be concerned with the interests and problems of adolescents. These must be known in general, and in particular as they influence each student in the school, if the school's program is to be effectively developed and carried out. Gifted youth are not immune to the problems which face adolescents in our society; they too require a school that is well informed of the needs of youth and their relationship to the instructional program and its objectives.

Havighurst[1] defines the adolescent developmental tasks, those tasks between individual needs and societal demands, as follows:

1. Achieving new and more mature relationships with age-mates of both sexes
2. Achieving a masculine or feminine social role
3. Accepting one's own physique and using the body effectively
4. Achieving emotional independence of parents and other adults
5. Achieving assurance of economic independence
6. Selecting and preparing for an occupation
7. Preparing for marriage and family life
8. Developing intellectual skills and concepts necessary for civic competence
9. Desiring and achieving socially responsible behavior
10. Acquiring a set of values and an ethical system as a guide to behavior

[1] Robert J. Havighurst, *Developmental Tasks and Education* (New York: Longmans, Green & Co., Inc., 1952), pp. 33-71 *passim*.

The Gifted Adolescent

Gifted youth, who are by nature more sensitive to problem situations, face these tasks. Gifted youngsters who have been accelerated a year or two in their educational programs and who are of average physical build may find themselves looking younger at the same time they are thinking older than their classmates. Having developed poise in social situations not only from previous experiences but from their more mature ways, they may find it difficult to understand the somewhat childish behavior of their friends, especially during early adolescence. Those who have already committed themselves to certain vocational fields and have settled into patterns of consistent study to prepare themselves for chosen professions may not be able to understand the vacillating behavior of other adolescents who are not yet guided by any specific vocational goals. There are also those gifted youth who have not made vocational choices, who are still exploring among various skills and interests to gain knowledge to help them choose wisely.

With all these problems the secondary-school program must deal in some fashion. A youngster who is working to solve personal problems and is troubled by them cannot place his entire attention profitably upon mathematics or a foreign language. His learning is influenced by the way he feels; his emotions affect his progress. In order to help youth to achieve the best education possible, the secondary schools must work with all the interrelated facets of each adolescent's being.

Hollingworth[2] believed that the main problems that face gifted youngsters exclusively include these:

1. To find enough hard and interesting work at school
2. To suffer fools gladly
3. To keep from becoming negativistic toward authority
4. To keep from becoming hermits
5. To avoid the formation of habits of extreme chicanery

[2] Leta S. Hollingworth, *Children Above 180 IQ* (Yonkers, N.Y.: World Book Co., 1942), p. 299.

Since childhood and adolescent ways of behaving merge gradually as a youngster matures, these problems cannot be ignored by those who work with secondary-school youth. A gifted child who has had the good fortune to work with creative elementary-school teachers sympathetic to his problems may have developed satisfying solutions to these problems as a child; as a youth the problems may arise again, especially if he is confined to a formal school program which offers little opportunity for self-exploration, self-realization, and self-direction. These goals remain valid and operative through the gifted child's educational experiences, whether he be in nursery, elementary, secondary school, college, or graduate studies. Though his own maturity will help him to meet these problems, his educational experiences may be of greater significance to him if he can profit from sympathetic guidance during his youth.

EDUCATIONAL GOALS AND OBJECTIVES

Goals for the education of boys and girls in public schools do not change with the grade the student has reached. Well-developed objectives apply throughout the educational system; kindergarteners and twelfth graders alike need to learn to plan and to evaluate their work, to budget their time suitably, and to get along with their age-mates. The emphasis may shift in respect to the degree of maturity attained by the students, and the amount and quality of previous experiences which they can bring to bear upon the problems which confront them, but the basic objectives remain the same. Passow[3] says, "The basic educational goal for the gifted individual—as for any student—is to develop his abilities and interests in ways consonant with his self-fulfillment and the interests of society." This statement is in agreement with previous explanations of goals developed for educating the gifted. However, as objectives ought to help teachers and

[3] A. Harry Passow, in National Society for the Study of Education, *Education for the Gifted* (Chicago: University of Chicago Press, 1958), p. 193.

students give direction to their school studies, more detailed statements are needed. Statements that are too detailed, on the other hand, tend to obscure the main purpose of the school; each school system will need to develop its statement of fundamental objectives in ways that are most helpful to the faculty as guides for directing the learning experiences of the students.

Secondary education has passed through many stages in the development of acceptable goals, from the earliest days when very few youngsters stayed in school to graduate from the twelfth grade and go on to college, to the present time when the secondary schools are charged with the responsibility of educating all the children of all the people of the country. This numerical goal has not been reached; present figures indicate that about 80 per cent of all educable youth attend secondary school, and approximately 60 per cent of those graduate from twelfth grade. Even without having all the children of all the people within its classrooms, the secondary school has had to expand its goals from the single idea of college preparation in order to deal satisfactorily with the increasing numbers of adolescents of varying abilities who do attend.

In 1952, the Educational Policies Commission released a statement which remains the most comprehensive and usable list of goals for secondary education available today. It can be applied generally in all secondary schools; each must obviously develop programs suited to its particular students, but the statement can well be used as a guide.

TEN IMPERATIVE NEEDS OF YOUTH[4]

1. All youth need to develop salable skills and those understandings and attitudes that make the worker an intelligent and productive participant in economic life. To this end, most youth need supervised work experience as well as education in the skills and knowledge of their occupations.

[4] Educational Policies Commission, *Education for All American Youth: A Further Look* (Washington, D.C.: National Education Association, 1952), p. 216.

2. All youth need to develop and maintain good health and physical fitness.
3. All youth need to understand the rights and duties of the citizens of a democratic society, and to be diligent and competent in the performance of their obligations as members of the community and citizens of the state and nation.
4. All youth need to understand the significance of the family for the individual and society and the conditions conducive to successful family life.
5. All youth need to know how to purchase and use goods and services intelligently, understanding both the values received by the consumer and the economic consequences of their acts.
6. All youth need to understand the methods of science, the influence of science on human life, and the main scientific facts concerning the nature of the world and of man.
7. All youth need opportunities to develop their capacities to appreciate beauty in literature, art, music, and nature.
8. All youth need to be able to use their leisure time well and to budget it wisely, balancing activities that yield satisfactions to the individual with those that are socially useful.
9. All youth need to develop respect for other persons, to grow in their insight into ethical values and principles, and to be able to live and work cooperatively with others.
10. All youth need to grow in their ability to think rationally, to express their thoughts clearly, and to read and listen with understanding.

"All youth" obviously includes gifted youth. The goals as stated allow for the possibility that some students may achieve at a higher standard than others, and that some may develop greater depth of understanding than others. The statement is not an attempt to establish specific standards of achievement to be reached before students are graduated from twelfth grade; it serves as a guide to the kinds of competencies needed by citizens in our democracy. The list includes objectives related to the physical, moral, social, economic, emotional, intellectual, and vocational problems of youth.

Gifted youth particularly must achieve maximum development if they are to be able to make the best use of their potential. To this end, Passow[5] suggests:

For all the gifted, the teaching-learning situation should emphasize experiences which serve the following purposes:

1. Arouse and maintain the questioning attitude, the inquisitive mind. Activities should enable the child to experience the thrill of discovery and the satisfaction of curiosity through his own efforts.
2. Develop understanding of the problem-solving process, of the tools and know-how of research, and of the resources available in problem-solving. Activities should guide students to the effective use of resources at their level for the solution of problems.
3. Motivate and develop ability to think critically, reflectively, and objectively. Activities should assist students in judging the quality of their thinking and in internalizing the importance of exercising critical judgments.
4. Foster independence of work and study. Activities should encourage students to follow their interests and to focus on tasks until self-set goals are realized.
5. Result in early mastery of foundation skills necessary for advanced specialized endeavors. Activities should provide for development of skills in communication, observation, computation, cooperation, and similar specifics which are precursors to any original creative efforts.
6. Build a consistent system of values. Activities should provide opportunities for examining values and testing their validity in practice.
7. Nurture the desire for creative expression. Activities should encourage students to formulate creative ideas, to explore areas for original expression.
8. Build skills of conceptualizing, generalizing, and synthesizing meanings. Activities should extend the building of insights and meanings through conscious attention to the processes involved.
9. Build the necessary competencies in an area of talent. Activities will not necessarily evoke the full development of a talent but should enable the student to practice the skills,

---

[5] Passow, *op. cit.*, pp. 198-99.

to explore the nature and vistas of this area, and to recognize some of his own potentialities.

Objectives of secondary education do not, as they are customarily presented, determine the content of the curriculum. They present the points of emphasis to be considered in planning and teaching any course that the secondary school offers, and in organizing and carrying out any activity that it sponsors.

Klausmeier[6] states the goals of secondary education in this manner:

The overall goal of secondary education is to develop in each youth of high-school age the understandings, skills, attitudes, and values essential to a useful life both as a member of various groups and as an individual. To this end, as community financial resources and skillful teaching procedures permit, we shall see the following developments. (1) Each student will be assisted in developing fully, according to his abilities, any talent he may possess—intellectual, social, artistic, physical. (2) Each student will learn to appreciate his common heritage, his civic rights and responsibilities, and respect for the individual. (3) Each student will learn the requirements for group living, self-discipline, and efficient independent work and study. (4) Each student will be helped, as needed, to develop and maintain good mental and physical health so that he can learn efficiently and live happily with himself and others. (5) Each student will learn the ethical values that are essential to a high level of civilized life, locally, nation-wide, and world-wide. (6) A student of high ability will learn to question our present knowledge critically and will be encouraged to propose and try out novel ideas and inventions, including those pertaining to human relationships and group living.

Relating the specific goals for educating gifted to these, he says:

. . . the teacher's goal with gifted students should be to identify and develop students who, on high-school graduation, will be rather highly specialized in at least one area concerned with their particular talents, who will find satisfaction in living with other people with varying talents and interests, and who will use their talents to improve conditions for themselves and others.[7]

6 Herbert J. Klausmeier, *Teaching in the Secondary School* (New York: Harper & Brothers, 1958), pp. 26-27.
7 *Ibid.*, p. 352.

Goals for the education of gifted students are not basically different from those for the education of all youth. The gifted require attention to their needs, their problems, their interests, and their abilities, as do all youth. In the regular classroom, it is becoming increasingly difficult for teachers to plan differentiated learning experiences for students of varying ability, as the numbers of pupils to be taught continues to grow. Individualized instruction becomes more necessary as students develop their potential and increase the span of individual differences with which conscientious teachers must deal. Goals as stated in the examples given indicate the directions toward which teachers are expected to strive, regardless of what specific course content they teach. The accepted goals of a secondary-school program serve as a unifying influence upon the learning experiences provided for the students.

The lists of goals pertaining to all students and to gifted students can serve equally well in guiding teachers and students at both the junior- and senior-high-school levels of secondary education. In the junior high school the problems involved in establishing desirable heterosexual relationships may be more pressing than those involved in selecting a vocation. Yet in the case of the gifted youngster who has committed himself to a field such as science or music which requires early commitment and continuous learning and practice of the necessary skills, this may not be true. Each gifted student is an individual with specific interests and abilities and should be so taught.

THE SCHOOL ENVIRONMENT

Secondary schools ordinarily are designed to serve a larger attendance area than elementary schools, and usually they have larger enrollments than elementary schools of the same system. Junior and senior high schools usually offer a greater number and a wider variety of subjects for students to choose from, so they need more classroom space. Specialized subjects require laboratories and other types of special facilities. As schools have taken over some responsibilities that formerly were part of the home tasks, suitable facilities have been provided for teaching homemaking, food preparation, sewing, and child care. Schools have also accepted some responsibilities that originally belonged to craftsmen, such as teaching boys and girls the elementary skills of a trade; shops and other facilities have been developed within the school building to meet these needs, as the apprentice system of learning a trade or a craft disappeared. A school building thus reflects in general the expectations the school and community held for education at the time it was built.

High schools ordinarily have classrooms designed for the teaching of certain subjects. The biology room, for example, presents a different appearance from that of an English classroom. The space for chemistry may be divided into sections designed for class lectures and for laboratory experiences. The music room may have space for instrument storage as well as a stage for chorus use. Classrooms in which students are expected to sit and absorb knowledge indicate this purpose by their construction and arrangement; classrooms in which students are allowed to move about and experiment as they learn are built accordingly.

Not all school buildings presently in use fit the needs of youth and the purposes of secondary education today. Makeshift arrangements and attempts at remodeling have come about in an attempt to make the high-school structure more nearly adequate for present expectations. Teachers and students alike must exercise ingenuity to develop satisfactory teaching-learning situations suited to the areas being studied.

Regardless of whether the building is a senior or a junior high school, it should reflect the kinds of activities considered proper for the learning of the students. To put it another way, the curriculum should determine the structure and the equipment in use. Judging from many buildings in use today, the sole objective of secondary education is the passing on of the cultural heritage.

In accordance with the goals for education of the gifted previously stated, secondary schools need to have classrooms, laboratories, and libraries. They need gymnasiums for physical activity and auditoriums for sharing large group learnings of many kinds. They should have conference rooms and rooms in which small groups may meet as needed. The students need space for quiet individual study, for active discussion, for experimenting, for exploring, for all kinds of learning activities, and for the use and storage of the supplies and equipment required for that learning.

The large well-developed school site offers opportunity for individual as well as group exploration and study. Arbors, groves, ponds, streams and similar natural features make excellent outdoor laboratories for botany, zoology, and nature study in general.

Secondary-school students, in order to do their best, require an atmosphere in the school and community which is conducive to learning. They must be supported in their experimentation and exploration if they are to profit from it as much as their abilities allow. The attitudes of the students, parents, faculty, and the entire community influence the kinds of learning experiences provided for all students. If the fundamental belief of recognizing and providing for individual differences is accepted and understood by the school and the community, good programs of education for gifted secondary-school students can be established and supported. Such programs in turn ordinarily lead to the improvement of educational experiences for all the students enrolled in the school.

THE INSTRUCTIONAL PROGRAM

The Junior High School

PURPOSES. The junior high school, comprising either grades seven and eight or grades seven, eight and nine, is a comparatively modern development in educational organization. It began as an outcome of studies of adolescents which indicated that youngsters of twelve, thirteen, fourteen, and fifteen years of age were significantly different both from younger children in elementary schools and from older adolescents, and that they therefore might profit from an educational program designed specifically to deal with them. Another stated purpose of the early junior high school was to provide for better articulation between the elementary and the high school of the time; a junior high school established for this purpose tended to take the best of the elementary practices and to offer some electives as the high-school programs did. Some junior high schools operated as upward extensions of elementary schools; others patterned themselves after the senior high schools and tended to offer less difficult courses of similar content. It is generally agreed that the school year 1909-10 saw the establishment of the first junior high schools of the country.

If it is granted that students in the early adolescent stage of development do have particular problems that differ from those of later adolescence, a junior high school can have unique functions in the American educational system. Content and method alike need revision to allow schools and teachers to plan educative experiences that help students grow physically, socially, intellectually, and emotionally.

If better articulation is accepted as a purpose for the junior-high-school program, there must be provisions to help students make the transition into senior high school. Since the establishment of a junior high school automatically makes two breaks in the educational system where before there was only one, the problem requires attention. It is not adequately solved by developing a junior high school merely as a miniature edition of a senior high school.

Integration has been offered as a basic purpose of the junior-high-school organization. A program of general education that helps students relate their learning experiences to central problems is helpful in continuing the better aspects of a good elementary-school program and for minimizing the break between elementary and secondary education. The principles affecting the ways in which people learn best apply at any section of the educational system, and the junior-high-school program must take account of them.

If the provision of a variety of exploratory experiences is accepted as a way of helping young adolescents develop satisfactorily, the junior-high-school program must offer these to each student. A broad program which allows students to develop known interests and to explore new fields is essential to carrying out this purpose adequately.

Implied in the purposes stated for the establishment of a junior high school is the need of young adolescents for effective guidance. In the early days of junior-high-school development, grades seven, eight and nine marked a period of extensive drop-outs as some of the youngsters gave up further education in favor of other pursuits. Guidance today is recognized as an integral part of the junior-high-school program; guidance is required in the personal and social development of each individual as it is for the vocational understanding and success to which he aspires.

Gruhn and Douglass summarize the basic purpose in these words: "The Junior High School is an educational program which is designed particularly to meet the needs, interests, and abilities of boys and girls during early adolescence."[8]

Pupils. Probably the most outstanding and immediately noticeable characteristic of junior-high-school pupils as a group is their differences. Physically they represent many stages of growth and development; they are of many shapes and sizes. Each, of course, is passing through a period which entails rapid growth, but each is proceeding at his own rate of speed. Since girls usually begin this adolescent growth spurt about two years before boys do, it is not at all unusual to have fully developed young ladies and small childlike boys in the same classroom. Individual physical differences immediately catch the eye of anyone who enters a junior-high-school classroom. Yet none of these youngsters may be abnormal.

The very physical differences tend to develop common problems among early adolescents. They are concerned over their growth, or the lack of it, and they need to understand what is happening to their bodies and to accept themselves as they are and as they are becoming. The adolescent girl who does not lose her childish plumpness when she thinks

[8] William T. Gruhn and Harl R. Douglass, *The Modern Junior High School* (New York: The Ronald Press Company, 1956), p. 4.

she should, may be tempted into a poor diet in order to reduce her weight. She must be helped to realize the value of balanced food intake as it relates to continued health and beauty. The adolescent boy who is striving to grow to the proper size and strength to play on a basketball team may be quite concerned over his lack of coordination as parts of his body grow at different rates. Wise counseling by teacher and parent are necessary to improve the pupil's understanding of adolescence, particularly its physical manifestations.

Behaviorally young adolescents exhibit differences also. They react to situations according to their stage of emotional maturity; they want with all their being to be grown-up but they cannot always manage their emotions as they believe grownups do. Almost anything may set off a giggling reaction among girls, and they become upset because they do not know why they behave in such a way. Once they start laughing, they often find it difficult to stop and return to their work; this inability to control emotional reactions upsets them even more. A junior-high-school teacher must be prepared to accept these emotional reactions, to help youngsters realize that they are not bad, and to help channel them into more socially acceptable ways of expressing their emotions. There is surely nothing wrong with laughing, even in a classroom. Laughter and enjoyment provide a welcome release from tension that may build up in young adolescents. A tolerant remark such as, "Phyllis, I believe you must have swallowed a feather," offers a firmer base upon which to build a good relationship than does an unwarranted scolding for some action that the youngsters positively cannot help at the moment.

Tears are not unheard of among junior-high-school youngsters. Though they are trained in this society to believe that only babies cry, young adolescents are sometimes horrified to find themselves crying, particularly before the entire class. Again they need help in realizing that emotions seem quite easily stirred during adolescence, and reassurance that they will grow more mature in control and expression of them.

Young adolescents express their concern in many kinds of behavior as they strive for maturity. They need to realize that maturity is not a specific state one reaches, but a lifelong goal toward which each person works. Not all adults behave in consistently mature fashion.

In addition to physical and emotional problems, there are also social problems that impinge upon young adolescents. As they live in a democratic society, they are expected to become aware of the privileges offered to and responsibilities required of its citizens. In their attempts at building satisfactory codes of behavior and ethical systems for themselves, they run against inconsistencies in adult standards. Particularly is this true with respect to the gifted adolescent. Many of the adolescent problems contain the idea of right: How *should* we act under different circumstances? What *should* we do in certain situations? The striving for a "white and black" right and wrong is part of the adolescent's growth, and he is sometimes unable to accept or understand the varying shades of grey which he sees in adult behavior.

Each aspect mentioned yields fruitful problems for the general education program of the junior high school. There are many more problem situations that adolescents face; for fuller discussion the reader is referred to *Guides to Curriculum Building: The Junior High School Level.*[9] In addition to a discussion of the many problems which face young adolescents, this bulletin offers suggestions as to activities the school may offer to help solve such problems.

Young adolescents have many and varied interests. If they have attended elementary schools which cherished individuality and fostered the development of children's interests, they expect to follow special areas in the junior high school, and look forward to the wider resources available to them there. If, on the other hand, their education experiences have led them to accept learning as composed purely of following directions and studying teacher-assigned materials, their interests may be way below the surface and not allowed to show during school hours. Such youngsters will wait to be

---

[9] *Guides to Curriculum Building: The Junior High School Level* (Curriculum Bulletin No. 8, Illinois Secondary-School Curriculum Program [Wisconsin State Department of Public Instruction, Madison, Wisconsin. 1950]), 181 pp.

told what to do; they will expect specific instructions for every activity, even to the number of pages they should prepare in "creative" writing. They may even be unable to work profitably in a program that demands that students as well as teachers think, and plan, and evaluate.

Gifted adolescents usually have greater knowledge and wider interests to follow than do average children. They respond to programs designed to liberate their abilities; they can be crushed by programs featured by large-group instruction, same assignments, and same standards of work expected from all. The exploratory aspect of the junior-high-school program should be so structured as to help all youngsters delve deeply enough into many fields of knowledge and living so they may strengthen their known abilities and perhaps discover and develop new ones. The purpose is not to build adult skill but rather to allow the student to become acquainted with the area sufficiently so that he may learn whether or not he would benefit from further investigation of it.

PROGRAM. In light of the preceding discussion the reader will have recognized that good junior-high-school programs are developed in accordance with the needs of the young adolescent, the expectations and needs of the society in which he lives, and the knowledge presently available about how human beings learn. The accepted objectives for educating the gifted in the secondary schools tell what kinds of people and what kinds of competencies are expected to be developed as a result of junior-high-school experiences; the programs represent the vehicles by which schools try to attain those objectives. At no time should a junior high school consider itself merely an institution established to prepare students for senior-high-school study; the unique functions of articulation, exploration, guidance, and caring for individual differences and common problems of young adolescents do not represent a program concerned only with preparation for the next educational step. A good program will serve this purpose, but not by requiring a youngster to study specifically everything he will need to know in later years; it accomplishes this end by providing for optimum growth and development during the early adolescent years.

In general, junior high schools can be divided into two categories: those that attempt to perform their functions through departmentalized classes organized according to subject matter divisions, and those that approach the problems of teaching students through specially designed general education courses, plus some special subject area offerings. The schools that offer a departmentalized program can be further divided: those that present every subject separately with a period for each, such as English, reading, spelling, writing, geography, history, science, health, nature study, physical education, art, and music; and those that have developed courses such as language arts to encompass the functions of reading, writing, speaking, and listening, and social studies to include geography and history. The division between fields of knowledge still exists in such programs, but within the field itself, all elements of which it is composed are included. The departmentalized organization is more prevalent, though recent studies indicate that general education or core classes scheduled for two or more periods of each school day are increasing in the junior high schools of the country. Some junior high schools represent compromises between these two types.

In the departmentalized approach the gifted adolescent attends different classes for five or six periods of the day. He may be helped to develop an individualized enrichment program by each of his teachers; he may be expected to conform to lessons taught, assigned, recited, and tested. Most teachers who meet different groups of youngsters each period simply do not have the time or the energy to offer personal guidance and individualized instruction for each student. When several teachers use the same classroom, the mechanics of moving supplies and sharing chalk-board and display space tend to limit the teachers' efforts. Some manage to help individual students by encouraging extra work beyond that expected of the regular class; others give up the attempt.

The guidance function of the junior high school demands that at least one teacher must know each student well and must be free to discuss problems with him, to plan ways of helping him to meet those problems, to organize present work and future possibilities. Guidance is no longer considered as another course tacked onto the student's program, in which he reads about character development or personal problems according to a system-wide syllabus. A fifteen-minute home-room period every morning or a meeting one hour each week devoted to "guidance" does not offer either the teacher or the student sufficient time and a desirable atmosphere for friendly personal relationships upon which good guidance must be built. Departmentalization limits the possibilities for adequate teacher guidance in the junior high school.

Subjects commonly offered at the junior-high-school level include English, social studies, general science, mathematics, health and physical education, fine and practical arts, typing, and foreign languages. English is designed to include all the areas of the communications arts—reading, writing, speaking, and listening. In a departmentalized program there are possibilities for developing large units of work within each subject which involve teacher-pupil planning within a pre-planned curricular structure, and opportunities for group work as well as individual study. Each student can be helped to develop initiative and resourcefulness in accordance with his abilities; each teacher can offer individual attention to the degree that the limiting circumstances of departmental-ization permit.

Most junior high schools are characterized more by re-quired subjects in which possibilities for exploratory experi-ences can be developed, than by rich elective offerings among which the youngsters can choose. This is in line with the be-lief that general education consists of those subjects required of all pupils to the end that the content leads to the develop-ment of the skills, attitudes, and knowledges required for effective citizenship in a democratic society.

In such programs, block scheduling of gifted students allows them to be assigned to rapid progress classes. They can thus complete three years of study in two years. On the surface the objective mainly served by such a practice is that of acquiring a certain body of knowledge, or covering a certain prescribed quantity of factual information. Though this method of caring for gifted students was at one time widely used, it has been retained as a useful approach in only a few places, of which New York City is probably the best known.

Cutts and Moseley[10] have said:

Strict departmentalization tends to reduce opportunities for enrichment. Even when the existence of several sections in each subject has resulted in ability grouping and the fast section covers more ground, it is still difficult to provide enrichment activities. Periods are generally short, so there is not much time left when students have finished their regular work. Many teachers use the same room during different periods of the day, and one who monopolizes the blackboards ("SAVE") and bulletin boards and clutters the window sill with models is not popular. The teachers are subject-matter specialists who think of a student's progress in terms of their own subjects.

The preparation of teachers for junior-high-school programs is a fairly recent development. Too many remain in the category of subject matter specialists with much less knowledge of human growth and development than is desirable for successful teaching of young adolescents. Since research has shown that in the past gifted students have indicated that they are influenced more by a particular teacher than by a specific program of studies, the value of well-prepared, understanding teachers seems obvious. Good teaching seems to be the predominant factor in learning, regardless of the curricular structure of the program in which the students are enrolled.

However, the need for related experiences, for application of knowledge from many subject matter fields to the solving of significant problems, and the very interrelatedness of subject matter fields themselves are not served by a wholly departmentalized program. Neither are the common needs of young adolescents. In order better to fulfill the unique func-

[10] Norma E. Cutts and Nicholas Moseley, *Teaching the Bright and Gifted* (Englewood Cliffs, N.J.: Prentice-Hall, Inc., 1957), p. 40.

tions of the junior high school, more and more schools are turning to a program that involves the use of a block of time for the solving of adolescent social, personal, civic, and economic problems. This is called by many names, but most common of these is the core curriculum.

There is a noticeably increasing trend toward establishing block-time classes, particularly at the junior-high-school level. Grace Wright[11] reports that in 1958 "the percentage for separately organized junior high schools is 31.4 and for junior-senior high schools it is 12.1." A 1949 study indicated that "for separately organized junior high schools the percentage was 15.8 and for junior-senior high schools it was 6.4."

This obvious increase in organizing core programs or block-time classes is borne out by other studies as well. The principal reason advanced for the increase is that such classes afford more opportunity for the friendly teacher-pupil relationships that develop a good basis for effective guidance in the junior high school.

Bossing[12] has stated:

In conclusion, it seems clear from the foregoing research studies covering the past eight years that block-time class programs are gaining rapidly in popularity, that this growth in popularity is most marked at the junior high school level but is steadily gaining popularity at the senior high school level, that there is a slow but marked shift away from the traditional subject centered organization of the curriculum in the direction of the problem centered organization of the curriculum around the large societal and personal-social needs of youth, that there is a growing recognition of the advantages of block-time class organization for teacher guidance activities, that block-time classes provide for greater flexibility in all aspects of the teaching function, such as, caring for individual differences, wider range of use of classroom methods, teaching materials, including greater use of library and community resources, and finally that there is every evidence that block-time programs will become the dominant pattern of class organization in the future.

11 Grace S. Wright, *Block-Time Classes and the Core Program in the Junior High School* (Washington, D.C.: U.S. Department of Health, Education, and Welfare, 1958), p. 1.

12 Nelson Bossing, Address delivered May 2, 1959, to the Indiana State Conference on Core Teaching.

This is not the place to discuss the controversial aspects of the core program. Skillful teachers have found many advantages in such organization of curriculum, and these advantages can be used effectively to further the education of the gifted, which is the subject of this book.

The core curriculum consists of the general education required of all students because it is considered essential for their best development in a democratic society. Lurry and Alberty[13] have listed the common characteristics of the core program as follows:

1. A block of time ranging from ⅓ to ½ of the total school day is allotted to the core.
2. Teacher-pupil planning as well as teacher-teacher and pupil-pupil planning is a characteristic method of the core.
3. The problem-solving approach is paramount as a process of democratic living as the core program is developed.
4. Common needs, problems and interests of adolescents in this society are the content or scope of the core program.
5. The exploration of common problems, the meeting of common needs and the widening of interests in the core program utilizes subject matter from all pertinent fields of knowledge.
6. The core is required of all pupils regardless of special needs, problems, and interests.
7. Individual and group guidance are integral parts of the core program.
8. Evaluation is a cooperative, continuous, and creative process in the core program.
9. The fundamental skills are broadly defined and taught in terms of the use made of them in the core program.
10. A wide variety of resources in men, materials and techniques are used to promote learning in the core program.
11. The democratic value system is the basis of the core program.

This list incorporates the outstanding qualities related to effective education; as such, there can be continued provision for gifted students in terms of increased assumption of re-

[13] Lucile L. Lurry and Elsie J. Alberty, *Developing a High School Core Program* (New York: The Macmillan Co., 1957), pp. 29-43.

sponsibility for self-direction, attention to individual differences, development of personal interests, growth in ability to use thoughtful and productive methods of solving problems, and acquaintance with many kinds of learning materials and experiences. The core lends itself to enabling gifted students to make as much progress as they are capable of achieving in every aspect of their development, and to helping them achieve both integration and socialization.

General education is not the entire secondary-school program. It deals with common problems; as gifted adolescents are human beings, they possess also personal interests and problems which they can pursue in special subject classes. The Educational Policies Commission[14] states:

> The educational experiences for gifted students should depend on two major considerations. First, because they are human beings, citizens, consumers, and prospective parents, they need a good general education, not unlike what is needed by all their fellow students, to equip them to deal competently with themselves, their environment, and their fellowmen. Second, in addition, because they are the potential leaders in the professions, in business, and in other fields in a contracted world at an advanced stage of technological development, they need a wide acquaintance with the record of human experience, familiarity with foreign cultures and languages, and basic training in the tools and concepts of modern science.

In addition to whatever part of the school program is required as general education, gifted students of grades seven, eight, and nine should be offered some opportunities for exploring among special fields of learning. This can be done within a core class; it can be done through the subject area classes also. Guided experiences in many aspects of arts, mathematics, music, typing, language, social studies, sciences, handicrafts, and the communications are commonly offered to junior-high-school students. For the gifted to benefit most advantageously, each teacher must continue to direct learning situations which care for individual differences in ability and interest in the special subject classes. The gifted adolescent must be stimulated and challenged in all

[14] Educational Policies Commission, *Education of the Gifted* (Washington, D.C.: National Education Association, 1950), pp. 86-87.

his classes, though he must not be expected to demonstrate equally superior competency in each.

Junior high school does not represent terminal education for most students, and least of all for the gifted. It is not the function of the junior high school to develop trained technicians in any field; it is rather for the junior-high-school program to introduce the gifted students to many challenging experiences in a variety of fields so that they may increase their understanding of their own possibilities and potentialities. All gifted students should be so taught that they develop a desire to continue learning throughout their lives, beyond their attendance at educational institutions. This is not well accomplished by programs that require memorization and recitation of factual information upon demand; it is better achieved through a program designed to help gifted students to explore deeply and broadly, to experience stimulation in learning situations, and to accomplish ever-increasing self-direction and self-realization.

Junior high schools have developed many ways to achieve these ends for gifted students. Simply knowing who the gifted are often serves to stimulate teachers to develop activities to extend their interests and expand their learnings. Gifted adolescents can study plot development and characterization when others less advanced are drilling on sentence structure. In mathematics gifted students can study number theory, advanced geometric measurement, and aspects of unknowns when less advanced pupils work at basic quantification skills. Gifted students can study the more involved relationships in international policies when others investigate simpler aspects of the social studies. In each instance given, it is the responsibility of the teacher to develop the atmosphere in which differentiated learning experiences can exist.

The use of special projects, whether they be written papers, oral reports, construction, or the use of art media, is well known as a method of advancing the understanding among gifted students. These projects, to be really effective, must have value beyond that of keeping the student occupied; he must have worthwhile reason and purpose for such activity.

Differentiated expectations in the free reading program serve to offer gifted students greater development. The differences should not be based on quantity alone; there is a distinction between doing *more* work, and doing *more advanced* work. Consideration must be given to the quality of the material read, the understandings, appreciations, and knowledges the student derives, and the skills in reading he needs to use. There is also a place in the junior-high-school program for students to read purely for the enjoyment and pleasure involved in finding out what happens to the people in the story.

The examples given have dealt with enrichment at the junior-high-school level, and its possibilities are limited only by the creative approaches of students and teachers. There are some special classes at the junior-high-school level, but they are far fewer in number than the regular heterogeneous classes with which teachers are most familiar. Special classes in foreign languages are offered to gifted children in some junior high schools. Occasionally, subject matter classes such as English, mathematics, social studies, and science are organized according to the ability of the students, but this is possible only in a school or center which enrolls sufficient numbers of students to warrant several classes at each grade level. The acknowledged purpose of these special classes is enrichment, though accelerated learning goes right along with that aim. In fact, it is possible for gifted students in mathematics classes, for example, to accelerate so that upon entrance to high school they can be immediately scheduled into the second-year course, receiving credit for the first on the basis of their performance.

There is no one program that can be rated as the one best for all junior high schools to adopt. Each school will need to develop its own approach in terms of the needs of the students and the capabilities of the faculty.

METHODS. There are certain suggested methods of teaching that have been found to be effective in meeting the objectives of education for the gifted at the junior-high-school level. Knowledge and use of these should be incorporated into whatever program is developed for gifted students.

As at the elementary level, unified teaching using a problem-solving approach provides for students to learn to exercise judgment and thought, and to apply subject matter where it is needed instead of relegating it to a certain period of the day. It offers opportunities for pupils to develop qualities of leadership and to learn to work with groups of their classmates. It promotes responsible action, as a student feels obligated to prepare his own contributions to the group's progress as well as he possibly can.

Gifted students in junior high school should also be taught as individuals. Improvement of personal methods of study should be sought as the youngster pursues individual studies. Teaching useful techniques of research is valuable for the gifted adolescent; he can apply such methods to his personal study and to the cooperative work he prepares with his classmates.

Teacher-pupil planning continues to be valuable throughout the gifted student's educational career. As he is able he should be given opportunity to assume more and more responsibility for planning, carrying out, and evaluating his work. He can improve these skills with guidance and direction given by his teacher.

Unwarranted drill or meaningless repetition has no place in the education of any students. Gifted students require less drill activity than their average classmates and they must not be forced to waste time drilling, or waiting while the others engage in drill exercises. During such time the gifted student can be released from class participation to pursue some helpful activity that he and his teacher have planned. When a gifted student needs to perfect a skill or learn a new one, he will of course be expected to participate in as much drill as he requires for mastery of that skill.

The emphasis placed on creative teaching in elementary schools earlier does not limit creativity to that level. Respect for imaginative and thoughtful approaches to learning, for creative ways of doing, should characterize the program for gifted students at all of the educational levels. It is most important that the gifted have opportunity to work creatively and with whatever originality they can muster, throughout their schooling.

MATERIALS. Developing a satisfactory teaching-learning environment for gifted students at the junior-high-school level demands a wide variety of materials and equipment for their use. The classrooms in which they work must be supplied with as many adult reference books as can be procured. They need college dictionaries, not junior editions. They need grown-up encyclopedias, not simplified ones. They must have in addition to these, many single copies of informational books written at a mature reading level. There is need for books in the classrom for immediate reference, and there is need for a well-stocked library as well, which gifted students may use as a learning laboratory. Libraries can have other learning resources, such as phonograph records, tape recordings, slides; they can be materials centers from which gifted students may select various items to extend their learning experiences. The value of a well-selected library collection and a knowledgeable librarian cannot be overemphasized in any program for the education of the gifted.

Obviously materials other than books are useful in developing good learning experiences for gifted adolescents. However, it is necessary that whatever is supplied have adult characteristics, rather than childish ones, in the eyes of the students. Most gifted children do not need the stimulus of concrete objects to help them visualize abstract concepts; even in the early grades manipulation of such concrete materials may actually slow the learning of a skill, once the youngster has grasped the concept involved. There is a fine distinction here which must be considered by the teacher in relation to the needs of each of his students, so that he may suggest such materials as will be of educative value.

Simple equipment with which gifted students may develop and construct various experiments is preferred to already finished equipment which requires only the flip of a switch to operate. Again, the creative aspect should be emphasized; allowing gifted students to originate their own experiments to illustrate some concept is more valuable for their learning than limiting them to re-performing those experiments already presented in the books they use. Stretching their thoughts beyond the proofs given offers valuable learning and thinking experiences for the gifted. They need the best materials and equipment which can be supplied, but "best" should be judged in terms of the values the students can derive as they work with the materials.

The Senior High School

PURPOSES. The overarching purposes of education for the gifted remain the same for senior-high-school students as for kindergarten and primary children. Schools continue to work toward helping boys and girls develop self-direction, self-exploration, and self-management at any grade level. The curricular structure and the teaching methods used take on more mature aspects as the students grow toward maturity.

The more specific purposes within the general framework have been given previously in this chapter. The goals of secondary education specified by Klausmeier and the Educational Policies Commission pertain to senior high school students as well as to pupils of the junior high school. Because of the differing maturity of the students, emphasis may be placed on those goals that are most applicable to their stage of development. Junior-high-school students usually plan a study of careers before they prepare their high-school schedules so that they may be intelligently guided in their choices of courses. For gifted senior-high-school students, both boys and girls, this goal becomes more immediate in terms of college preparation for a chosen profession. The increasing imminence of accepting wider civic obligations, of thinking about marriage and a home and family, of being more completely responsible for the wise use of money, of becoming independent emotionally and leaving home to attend college —all these factors should influence the specifically stated purposes and the planned curricular experiences at the senior-high-school level.

Gifted students are expected to continue their work in both general education and specialized study. The senior high school is not expected to graduate fully prepared scientists, engineers, musicians, or linguists; each gifted student who chooses to elect courses leading to such professions should have the opportunity to do so, however. In specialized courses such as languages and sciences, the gifted student will be learning new content and strengthening by now familiar ways of working. He will be expanding his knowledge and perfecting the skills required for full comprehension in each area. He should be engaging in much individualized work in special areas while he is continuing his general education experiences with his schoolmates. Each part of the program should serve to enhance, reinforce, and make use of the knowledges and skills gained in the other. There ought not be a chasm between the subject matters and methods learned and taught in general and special education classes.

The guiding purpose should be the developing of responsible citizens who understand and practice democratic ideals and who are continuing to achieve self-development in special areas of interest and ability.

PUPILS. The gifted students at the senior-high-school level will usually range in age from thirteen to seventeen. It is likely that some will have been accelerated at least one year earlier in their education in order that their teachers might more adequately meet their needs for advanced work. Regardless of their possible accelerated grade-status, gifted students exhibit more maturity both socially and emotionally than do their age peers. This advanced maturity is not so pronounced as the intellectual ability, but on the whole it is characteristic of gifted students. The well-known saying that a youngster has an old head on young shoulders represents a folk way which recognized that aspect of giftedness many years ago. Any delineation of common characteristics related to particular age levels usually must be adjusted forward to be descriptive of gifted students of that age.

The boys and girls of Gesell's studies of childhood and youth ranged from high average to superior intelligence, as determined by standardized tests.[15] The characteristics they exhibited may thus more nearly approximate those to be expected from gifted students than can developmental traits derived from a study of average children.

For fourteen-year-olds, Gesell[16] states:

> The developmental characteristics of Fourteen make him a challenging subject for education. Consider his abundant energy and outgoing friendliness, the catholicity of his interests, his insight into himself and into his teachers, a budding awareness of ideals, a growing comprehension and command of words, and an exuberant inclination to reason. These qualities, intellectual, personal, and social, pose significant questions as to the best methods and arrangements of education. The basic questions apply both to boys and girls, whether separated or combined, even granting well-recognized differences such as the rate of physical growth.
>
> . . . He may need somewhat specific rearrangements in the educational system, to bring to full realization the promising potentials which he now embodies. Perhaps he peculiarly needs an educational unit with the controls of an adapted homeroom setup. This is not a matter of soft pedagogy. It is a means of providing a more suitable congenial environment and a program which is more fully fitted to the basic maturity level of the group and the maturity patterns of the individual. Such arrangements would reduce excessive and misdirected competitions; and place Fourteen in a more favorable educational climate.
>
> The individualizing of instruction, guidance, and counseling is of peculiar importance at this stage of a youth's career . . .

Gesell characterizes fifteen-year-olds as having three noticeable maturity traits: (1) increasing self-awareness and perceptiveness, (2) a rising spirit of independence, and (3) loyalty but adjustment to groups of home, schools, and community.[17] Sixteen-year-olds display self-assurance and an achieved sense of independence.[18]

In relation to Gesell's finding that periods of stability are followed by periods of uncertainty, periods of ease followed

[15] Arnold Gesell, Frances L. Ilg, and Louise Bates Ames, *Youth: The Years from Ten to Sixteen* (New York: Harper & Brothers, 1956), p. 6.

[16] *Ibid.*, pp. 179-80.

[17] *Ibid.*, p. 216.

[18] *Ibid.*, p. 250.

by unease, the fifteen-year-old seems to be in the uncertain stage. He is more likely to express hostility and to be indrawn than are either fourteen- or sixteen-year-olds. Sixteen represents a period when everything seems to fall into place and a mature pre-adult appears.

The interpretation of such generalized statements in terms of the characteristics exhibited by specific senior-high-school students may give helpful direction for improving the curricular offerings available, and the methods used in the teaching and guidance of the students.

Gifted students do express concerns in senior high school. They are sensitive to problems of relationships with agemates and with adults, but they are better able to arrive at satisfactory ways of handling such problems than are average students. Gifted children have an increased awareness of social problems and their own responsibilities toward them. If they are as yet uncommitted to a certain field or profession, they may become anxious about careers; this problem differs from that of average students because many gifted boys and girls exhibit various competencies and interests that indicate probable success in many areas of work, and choices must be made.

Senior-high-school students as a whole appear to be settling into more consistent expressions of mature behavior than are shown by junior-high-school pupils. They exhibit greater control of emotions, and more adequate approaches to solutions for their own problems.

PROGRAM. The accepted program in most senior high schools over the country is composed of a series of required courses, the general education portion of the curriculum, and a variety of elective courses to satisfy the needs of specialized interests and abilities. The required courses ordinarily include three or four years of English, two or three years of social studies, one or two years each of mathematics and science, as well as physical and health education. The electives vary from school to school depending in large degree upon the competencies of the faculty and the expectations of the community.

When a program requires the collecting of certain credits for specific courses, a prescribed number of credits to insure graduation, the attitudes developed are apt to be somewhat different from those implied in the purposes of secondary education. The mere covering of content tends to receive greater emphasis than does the development of responsible citizens. The stated purposes of most secondary schools include the same basic philosophical considerations as are expressed by elementary-school and junior-high-school objectives; the very structure of the senior-high-school curriculum makes the attainment of these objectives much more difficult than it need be.

The differences appear as early as ninth grade. Even in schools that support a good general education program for grades seven and eight, grade nine often marks a significant change. Somehow, parents, students, and teachers are caught in a mass of regulations relating to high-school graduation and college entrance, and their very behavior is adversely affected. The implication is that playing around is all right for children, but adolescents are expected to work hard in school. Such an assumption is based on a false interpretation of elementary programs, as well as a misunderstanding of how people learn. The basic elements of learning continue to be operative within the teaching-learning situation regardless of a student's chronological age; the learner needs to see a problem clearly in order to define possible ways of meeting it, to gather pertinent information and apply it to the problem, and to evaluate his results. He needs to be personally concerned with whatever he may be studying; he grows to a greater degree on the basis of success than he does from continued failure experience; he needs to be praised, to experience satisfaction with his work; he needs a certain degree of readiness for each new problem situation.

Perhaps a confusion in the concept of discipline is another factor in the picture of this frequently surprising difference between elementary and secondary education. Perhaps the idea that anything that is good for a person must be difficult to accomplish, or even painful for him to achieve, is being revived. Perhaps it is the belief that the memorization of traditionally organized bodies of knowledge represents the best way of transmitting the cultural heritage to the young. Obviously people who are overly concerned about requirements for college entrance have not checked those recently; many colleges have changed their requirements from specific courses to be studied to a much broader base. Many factors may be involved. Whatever the reason, secondary education remains largely a collection of unrelated courses in which students are expected to cover certain content and to meet certain credit requirements in order that they may graduate.

Research of the proportions of the Eight-Year Study[19] has shown that accepted patterns of courses have little or no influence upon secondary students' future academic success; in fact one of the least publicized yet most outstanding findings of the Eight-Year Study indicated that the more radically the high-school curriculum deviated from the accepted pattern, the more successful the students were in academic achievement as well as desirable social qualities. Research on a smaller scale made by literally hundreds of people has borne out these kinds of results in many different schools. Yet most secondary schools continue to offer a series of courses much like those that have been offered for years and years to all comers, gifted, average, and slow learners. Courses have been added to the curriculum to meet certain demands, and a very few, such as Greek, have been removed from the curriculum. But little attention has been given to reorganizing the content and methods used in terms of the needs, problems, interests, and abilities of youth, of the ways in which youngsters learn best, and of methods that will serve to increase the values and usefulness of the content.

A growing interest in providing effective experiences for gifted secondary-school students has led to many experimental programs within the past decade. In one school, the gifted are offered seminars for investigation of specific in-

---

[19] Wilford Aiken, *The Story of the Eight-Year Study* (New York: Harper & Brothers, 1941).

terests, after school hours and sometimes on Saturdays. In another, the gifted are scheduled in classes composed of students of like intelligence, but average and slow learners may be included to fill out the classes so that the teacher's load will be consistent with that of other faculty members. In yet another school, the gifted may be guided into the "tough" academic courses and expected to achieve at peak performance in each. Some schools operate track plans whereby gifted students are segregated in all their classes. Others have developed "honors" classes, or schools within the school, which also are organized to help the gifted investigate advanced subjects not offered regularly to all students. Still others depend upon the ingenuity of each teacher to so personalize his instruction that all students in his classes, regardless of ability, are challenged and stimulated to their highest possible achievement.

The plans are many and varied. Each school shows successes and some inadequacies. The actual plan itself may not be so important as the fact that schools and communities are becoming aware of the need to improve the education of the gifted to the end that their abilities may be developed in socially useful ways. It is not feasible to lift a plan bodily from another school, transplant it into different ground, and expect it to flourish. Each school community must make its own decision as to what sort of program offers the best solution to educating the gifted in that locality.

The need for general education for integration and socialization is well established; so is the need for specialized education leading to differentiation. The problem lies in the choices involved in accomplishing these ends; the choices will be influenced by what the school and community believe about the function of education, psychology of learning, and the nature of the students and the society, all interwound with some system of values. Schools can profit from examinations of programs under way in other situations. For a program of senior-high-school education for the gifted to be most effective, it must be developed in terms of the specific situation in which it is to exist.

Recommendations for the high-school programs of gifted students are numerous. Conant[20] has suggested that ability grouping in required subjects would be helpful to the progress of all students in a comprehensive high school. Such grouping does not mean that a student would automatically be scheduled into the top group in every subject, but that he would be placed in each according to his demonstrated ability in that area. This might result in a student's being in a top group in American history, a middle group in English, and a lower group in chemistry. Such a recommendation presupposes the existence of a high school with a comparatively large enrollment; schools that normally graduate fifty or fewer seniors a year would obviously need to develop some other methods of working with the gifted.

Conant reported that his investigation led him to believe that the gifted were not electing a sufficiently wide range of academic subjects and that they were not working as hard as they should.[21] He offers his Recommendation 9 to help alleviate that situation, and to guide schools in developing programs for the gifted.

Recommendation 9: The Programs of the Academically Talented

A policy in regard to the elective programs of the academically talented boys and girls should be adopted by the school to serve as a guide to the counselors. In the type of school I am discussing the following program should be strongly recommended as a minimum:

Four years of mathematics, four years of one foreign language, three years of science, in addition to the required four years of English and three years of social studies; a total of eighteen courses with homework to be taken in four years. This program will require at least fifteen hours of homework each week.[22]

This basic pattern of courses is recommended for the academically talented who are by Conant's definition the top 15 to 20 per cent of all secondary-school students. A specific school may have more or less than that percentage, depending upon the typicality of its pupil population.

[20] James B. Conant, *The American High School Today* (New York: McGraw-Hill Book Co., 1959), p. 49.

[21] *Ibid.*, p. 40.

[22] *Ibid.*, p. 57.

The participants in the Invitational Conference for the Identification and Education of Academically Talented Students in American Secondary Schools[23] of the National Education Association supported these recommendations. They advise:

Four years of English with an emphasis on reading and writing should be made mandatory for all academically talented pupils. (p. 94)

In view of the increasingly scientific and symbolic nature of our civilization, *it is highly desirable that all academically talented youth pursue the study of mathematics for at least three years. Pupils with special talents in science and mathematics should continue for a fourth, or even the equivalent of a fifth year, at the high-school level.* (pp. 97-98)

In general, a four-year sequence of study in grades 9 to 12, or its equivalent in achievement, in one modern foreign language is the least to be expected of the talented. (p. 104)

Minimum requirements for students talented in science should be, in addition to ninth-grade general science, one good course in biology, and one in the physical sciences. (p. 111)

At least three years of advanced work, including a year of American history, a second year of history other than American, and a third year of work in the other social studies is recommended. (p. 117)

It is immediately noticeable that a minimum of seventeen or eighteen units of work is advised for the education of gifted secondary students. In a typical high school that schedules six or seven periods each day, and requires attendance in physical education classes, there would not be time after these minimums were met for the gifted student to engage in work in the fine and practical arts, in music, in a commercial or business subject. He would largely be confined to this minimum; the fifteen hours of homework each week would curtail to some degree his participation in extra-curricular activities, and the pursuance of personal hobbies. Each of these omitted areas has a great deal to offer in extending and broadening the gifted student's living and learning.

[23] Invitational Conference on the Academically Talented Secondary School Pupil, *The Identification and Education of the Academically Talented Student in the American Secondary School* (Washington, D.C.: National Education Association, 1958).

Such an insistence upon specific courses also minimizes the opportunities for a block-time or core program in which students would be working together to solve personal-social problems, to build necessary citizenship attitudes, understandings, and skills, and to learn by doing. Research indicates that students in core classes tend to acquire more subject matter content than do those enrolled in straight subject matter courses. The recommendations as listed effectively limit such desirable general education outcomes.

The recommendations given also seem based largely upon numbers of courses required. There is little to indicate that the content and methods of the suggested courses might be better organized and presented in order to provide for the best learning of the gifted. It is what happens within any course that makes it a meaningful learning experience for the students. The quality of the gifted student's learning is more significant to his development than the number of credits he amasses.

Passow[24] has written:

The role of the secondary school, then, is not to force youth to specialize in one area or another but rather to build a sound liberal foundation which will support the development of specialized competency at the higher education level. To undergird liberal learning, the comprehensive high school must: (1) re-examine its curriculum, not in terms of adding a course or a requirement but rather with a view toward developing an over-all framework which will emphasize concepts, understandings and appreciations, skills, and knowledge—all of which contribute to a liberal education; (2) restudy its teaching procedures, content, and materials so that these are based on what is known about the nature and needs of gifted youth; (3) develop flexibility in programming, teaching assignments, use of school resources, and requirements to make room for differentiated experiences; (4) involve other community resources in extending the range and depth of learning experiences.

There are some secondary schools that are working to strengthen their course offerings through such an examination of content and methods. Mathematics is undergoing a definite reorganization in many schools. It is known that junior-

<hr />

[24] A. Harry Passow, "The Comprehensive High School and Gifted Youth," *Teachers College Record*, LVIII (December, 1956), pp. 144-52.

high-school students as a whole are capable of tremendous gains in computation skills and in understanding number relationships. It is possible for them to explore meaningfully much of the geometric and algebraic content that has been traditionally reserved for grades nine and ten. Application of this knowledge leads the way not to entering more advanced traditional courses, but to further reorganization of those courses, and presentation and development of concepts at a much earlier grade level than was hitherto believed possible. Thus, the gifted student at the senior-high level may have opportunity to explore the field of mathematics in considerably greater depth.

Another area that is undergoing reorganization at the present time is that of science. Probably the work of the Forest Hills High School in Long Island is best known in this field. Students there learn science by developing and applying scientific concepts, methods, and principles to their projects; they are not limited to the study of the history of science and the reproduction of workbook experiments with results neatly presented and foreordained. There is nothing intrinsically bad about studying the history of science; it is unreal, however, and unfair, to have students learn history when they are under the impression that they are learning science.

Foreign languages, English, social studies—all are undergoing extensive study in forward-looking schools by forward-looking faculties. The best programs that develop are not based merely upon an all-out attempt to try to surpass the alleged educational achievements of other countries, but rather are planned to educate the boys and girls of this country as effectively as is possible in the light of the relevant knowledge at hand. It may be easier in some ways to continue with traditional content and method; it is hardly a fair approach to the education of boys and girls who are living in today's world. It is an accepted fact that provisions designed for the gifted have an upgrading effect upon the education of the other boys and girls in a school as teachers come into contact with enlarged understandings of the needs of youth, the social problems of the day, more adequate theories of learning, and more effective methods of teaching.

So long as the gifted secondary-school student lives in a society which values specific requirements for high-school graduation and for college entrance, he must be given opportunities to meet these. Better articulation between these two levels should improve the educational offerings of each. There is ample evidence to suggest that senior high schools and colleges alike can profit by cooperating toward the end of the best possible educational experiences for the students. One problem which requires further attention is that of forms for reporting student progress.

It is not the purpose of this book to discuss the various controversial questions on grading systems currently in use; they vary widely from percentages to letter grades to parent conferences. The fact that the same grade means different things to different teachers is well known. Students are graded in some fashion in every secondary school. These grades ordinarily form part of the transcript which is sent to the college they attend.

When gifted students are scheduled into classes organized heterogeneously, they can ordinarily earn superior grades. When the classes are composed of only gifted students, it is possible that some of them will be graded lower in a course in which they might have had an A, the highest grade, had they been in a heterogeneous group. Such a problem is perplexing to the faculty, and of high importance to the student and his parents, who realize that his recorded grades may affect his acceptance by one college or another.

Several general solutions have been suggested. One favors grading no gifted student who makes satisfactory progress lower than a B regardless of the composition of the class. Another suggests that segregated classes for gifted students be clearly indicated as such in the permanent record as an aid to accurate interpretation of marks. Sometimes a paragraph of explanation may be added to the student's record. None of these ideas is wholly satisfactory in the abstract.

However, the problem exists as long as so much importance is attached to final grades in each secondary-school course.

METHODS. Methods of teaching in the senior high schools are being examined in the schools that are also investigating and revising their curriculums. Method and content are so interrelated that the two should be considered together. The learning outcomes desired, whether they are skills, concepts, or factual information, help to determine the appropriateness of certain methods in teaching particular content.

It should be emphasized that there are no known methods of teaching that apply only to the education of gifted students. There are methods that seem to lead more directly to helping students exercise thought and reasoned judgment, to encouraging creative and original approaches to school tasks, to developing ability to relate knowledge gained in one area to problems involving many fields of knowledge, and to apply functionally what has been learned where it is found applicable in other situations. Such methods should be used as they are appropriate in the education of all youth; they lead to attaining the educational objectives recognized as valuable outcomes for all citizens of a democracy.

As in the elementary school the differences in the classroom procedures and learning outcomes depend largely on the quality of the teaching-learning situation, which can be greatly enhanced by the experiential background and knowledge the gifted student brings with him combined with the enthusiasm and interest the teacher shares with him. The very atmosphere of a classroom occupied by motivated students who have superior ability and a teacher who can be proud of their accomplishments as he guides their development is far different from that of the dull plodding repetition of the traditional classroom. Learning can be a very satisfying experience when teachers and students are able to make noticeable progress and to develop the valuable side issues that contribute to wider knowledge and understanding in every subject field.

When the methods chosen allow the students to experiment and to discover, learning takes place. When the methods lead primarily to the memorization of facts, it is doubtful that any students can derive the kind of learning that is most useful.

As concepts of teaching expand to include more appropriate class structures and organizations related to the kinds of learnings desired, method too must be altered. Lectures may be proper in some situations, memorization in others, personal investigation and experimentation in still others; the important point to stress is that the method used is inextricably related to the kinds of learnings that will result in the teaching-learning situation. Since "the education of the best thinkers should be an education for initiative and originality,"[25] methods that encourage such development must be used in the education of gifted students throughout their school careers.

Witty[26] has listed five ways which teachers have used to work toward creativity for their gifted students:

1. Modifying their program of studies to include more challenging subjects and more opportunity for creative work
2. Helping them to work on class projects that make a real contribution to the class, the school, the community
3. Providing a rich environment in which they may do independent work in science, art, music, and other fields
4. Forming informal groups in which they will learn the techniques of working happily with others toward a common goal
5. Giving them opportunity to learn how to use the human and physical resources of the community to enrich their daily program and also to gain real opportunities for service in the local community

Such suggestions are fully as applicable to the secondary-school classroom operation as they are to any level of education. Dealing with real-life situations and working on projects important to the community have value for secondary stu-

25 Hollingworth, op. cit., p. 290.
26 Paul Witty (ed.), The Gifted Child (Boston: D C. Heath & Company, 1951), p. 121.

dents whose wider experiences can help them realize the broader applications of their learning.

All aspects of the educational program must be correlated in order that gifted students may make optimal progress through school. The services related to guidance, curriculum, methods of teaching, use of community resources, administration—all must be involved in developing an effective program for educating gifted students. It has been recorded that not more than 5 per cent of the secondary schools of the country report organized programs for educating gifted students to their full potential. Interest, as shown by the numbers of articles being published in the area and the requests for materials from those schools wherein there are recognized programs for educating gifted students, is obviously increasing. That more attention must be given this problem is obvious; gifted students must be encouraged to achieve the fullest possible development of their potential lest society lose the immense possibility for good which they represent.

MATERIALS. When the gifted student reaches the secondary-school level he is ready for and capable of using profitably a wide variety of complex learning aids. His exploratory experiences with materials and equipment at the elementary- and junior-high-school levels have, in most cases, resulted in his centering his interest largely in one, or two, or perhaps three areas where complicated units of equipment will prove quite valuable to his learning progress. Such equipment will be found helpful not only in class work but particularly so in individual projects, seminars, and interest clubs.

Additions to the school library which are appropriate in this context include readers' guides and indexes in the specialized fields, adult-type biographies, educational films, comprehensive almanacs and atlases, and news magazines and current periodicals devoted to economics, government, labor, business, and similar fields. Classroom equipment and materials might well include tape recorders, television, projectors, electric computers, calculating machines, map-making materials, art materials, mathematical materials illustrating units of measurement and statistical concepts, and geometrical models illustrating forms and figures such as cubes, prisms, cones, and pyramids.

In laboratories and shops, desirable equipment includes telescopes for astral observation, barometers and anemometers for weather observation, photographic development equipment, and microchemistry equipment. Individual units such as hygrometers, electroscopes, fluoroscopes, galvanometers, light meters, high-powered microscopes, oscilloscopes, spirometers, and torsion apparatus, are useful to the young scientist. A few schools may be able to provide larger, more costly units of equipment which offer experimental opportunities in aviation, automation, electronics, and nuclear physics.

It is the gifted student whose interest and ability carry him well beyond the prescribed courses in the high school who will profit most from a wealth of material and equipment. He will use it most because he is likely to pursue his interests far beyond the classroom. He will welcome the chance to carry on individual projects after school hours and during vacant periods. Often, three or four students who share a particular interest will work together until the schoolhouse is closed for the day, if appropriate equipment is available to them.

Many gifted students will welcome the opportunity to care for a planetarium, a greenhouse, an aquarium, or even a foreign language laboratory with its tape recorder, complicated wiring, and earphones. Such responsibility carries with it a genuine opportunity to learn both subject matter and social responsibility.

Although the concept of learning which places the teacher in the key role is probably as true today as it ever was, the rise of technology in society has placed a premium upon instructional equipment. In science, perhaps to a greater extent than in any other field, the adequacy of laboratory facilities, equipment, and material influences the quality and effectiveness of the instructional program.

For the student who is willing and capable of going beyond the secondary program, of exploring depths and heights not touched upon in regular classroom and laboratory work, extensive equipment and materials offer learning experiences which can be rich and meaningful even though the teacher may also be the student.

COUNSELING IN THE SECONDARY SCHOOL

Guidance is a significant aspect of the best education of gifted children and youth. Counseling is by no means limited to senior-high-school programs, but it is discussed in this connection here because it is in the senior high school that trained guidance personnel are usually placed when they are hired for the school system. Guidance, in general, is treated in Chapter 5.

The key person in counseling will likely be the teacher who works closely with the youngster and has an opportunity to know all about him. It is the conscientious teacher who searches the cumulative files, holds parent conferences, talks with other teachers, and in general collects all the available information about the child, who is probably best qualified to guide his personal and educational development. The teacher has the opportunity to establish the friendly personal relationship necessary for effective counseling. The teacher who observes the youngster as he works and plays is in an excellent position to interpret his needs. Ideally, this person is the general education teacher who works with the youngster during a programmed block of time during the day.

Such a concept of counseling and guidance interwoven with the curriculum does not deny the need for professionally trained guidance workers at the secondary-school level. Necessary data concerning college programs and current requirements must be collected and classified. Information about opportunities in various fields of work and the skills required to perform specific jobs must be available and up-to-date. A professionally trained person should administer aptitude and other tests and help students interpret the results. A counselor whose entire time is devoted to guidance activities can supplement the personal guidance given by the general education teacher, and must be responsible for the entire guidance program where no such courses are provided. That guidance ought to be an integral part of the educational program is recognized; that it is not so handled in many schools increases the responsibilities of the guidance counselors themselves.

Recently, much stress has been placed upon the need for effective guidance to motivate the underachievers—those students whose intelligence quotients are superior, but whose achievement quotients are low. Havighurst, DeHaan, and Stivers[27] suggest the following means of motivating gifted students:

1. Giving information about the child's abilities
2. Guidance
3. Counseling
4. Program-building
5. Providing models
6. Giving rewards

For some reason the practice of withholding information about a gifted student's ability has become rather common practice. There are schools that pride themselves on never disclosing the results of intelligence tests to those most interested and able to profit from this information, the parents and the student himself. Families of some gifted students may develop the belief that everyone is as capable as their child—that their child is an average boy. Plans for college, for graduate work, for entering exacting professions, may be made upon receipt of such information, when such possibilities might have been ignored without it.

Students who are superior in dramatics, in musical performance, and in sports, are not only aware of their superiority but are encouraged to capitalize upon it. Information about superior intelligence may well lead to plans for its constructive uses.

When a student's needs, interests, and abilities are known, he can be guided into curricular and extracurricular activities

[27] Robert J. Havighurst, Eugene Stivers, and Robert F. DeHaan, *A Survey of the Education of Gifted Children* (Chicago: University of Chicago Press, 1955), pp. 15-17.

that will help him to develop and expand his knowledge and special ability. Counseling must be based on as full knowledge of each student as it is possible for the teachers and counselor to acquire.

Sometimes a quirk of personality is at the bottom of lack of achievement. This may respond favorably to personal interviews with a sympathetic, understanding counselor; it may require the help of a school psychologist or a psychotherapist in the community. The personal interest and attention given the student is often helpful in developing better response to satisfactory achievement.

A wide variety of activities, curricular and extracurricular, which help a gifted student follow interests, is important in motivation. The establishment of orchestra, bands, drama clubs, debating teams, and the like, provide experiences beneficial to gifted students with special abilities. The curricular offerings in the various fields of knowledge should offer acceptable growth experiences, and opportunities for participation in valuable creative activities.

Schools that are aware of the influence that outstanding people from various professions exercise over students can make opportunities to bring such personalities into the classrooms to meet students and discuss problems. A doctor from Brazil provided much inspiration for achievement in one class; a teacher from Bavaria not only supplied information, but also stimulated thinking in another.

Many schools participate in regular exhibitions which involve rewards of some kind for academic achievement. There are science fairs, art expositions, book and creative writing exhibits. Some encourage their students to enter contests. These rewards, whether they are actual prizes or honors, offer recognition to the gifted students, and may serve as motivating devices. There is some question about the value of such extrinsic forces as motivating factors; however, they are being used in many situations despite the controversy.

Underachievement remains a problem. It is only a part of the larger problem of providing proper educational programs for those gifted who are achieving at various levels, and should not be overemphasized to the extent that the pathetic underachiever is the only type of gifted student to receive special attention. There are many factors involved in underachievement; at the present stage of knowledge it is necessary to counsel with each individual separately to try to determine the causes operative for him. There are no specific patterns to follow to improve underachievement generally. Each case must be studied and treated according to its unique characteristics.

The development of the ability to appraise oneself accurately and realistically is of great significance in guidance. Strang[28] writes:

> At each stage of their school career, they should be helped to discover their potentialities, recognize their strengths and build on them, accept certain weaknesses. Bernard Shaw said that his happiness began when he discovered the things he could do and focused attention on them, ignoring the things in which he was not likely to succeed.

Guidance should begin early in the child's life and continue through both the elementary and the high school, and should be an integral part of the school program of the gifted student. Evaluation practices should be used so that the youngster can know his strengths and weaknesses, not merely because the teachers point them out for him, but because he has appraised his work himself, with the teacher's help.

Gifted secondary-school students, as they mature, may need help in solving personal and social problems. A friendly counselor or teacher to whom the student can go freely and know that his problems will be accepted seriously is essential to his development of mature emotional adjustment. A teacher or counselor should seldom attempt to tell the student exactly what he should do in a certain problem situation. A basic principle of guidance is that the counselor helps the student to see the whole situation, and to plan a course of action to meet it. He may make suggestions; he may skillfully draw suggestions from the student. He may give information that will be helpful in the student's attempts to

[28] Ruth Strang in National Society for the Study of Education, *Education for the Gifted, op. cit.,* p. 73.

work out the problem, but to achieve the most effective personality growth, it is necessary that the student work out the problem situation for himself.

This principle applies for educational and vocational problems, as well as for personal problems. In planning for advanced training, it is possible that students will desire help in making choices. The counselor's role is to point out the factors involved, but to let the student reach the final decision in terms of those factors. When a student is aware of his strengths and weaknesses, when he realizes the everyday kinds of performances required in various professions, when he knows about the openings available in a job or the opportunities it offers for regular advancement, when he is in full possession of the facts, then he can make an intelligent decision about choosing a profession for which to prepare. The choice may be a difficult one if the student is one of those fortunate gifted whose interests and abilities are widespread.

Another task of the guidance counselor is to secure information about scholarships currently available, and to bring the information to the attention of those students who can qualify and would profit from such aid. Since so many gifted students end their formal education with the secondary-school program because they cannot afford to attend college, and society thus loses what benefits their giftedness might have provided, such information is doubly important. It is a factor of prime importance in developing a satisfied individual as well: one who knows he is contributing what he is able to his society, and is happy in the usefulness of his work.

The discussion group concerned with the problem of guidance at the 1958 Invitational Conference on the Academically Talented Secondary School Pupil[29] embodied this statement in their final report:

Although the academically talented youth should have experiences in language arts, social studies, mathematics, science and foreign language areas, the nature and quality of these experiences need careful study and evaluation. Acting on the assumption that academically talented pupils will have an appropriate secondary education if they

[29] Invitational Conference on the Academically Talented Secondary School Pupil, *op. cit.*, pp. 66-67.

are scheduled into 'five solid subjects' will result in a somewhat naive oversimplification of the many problems involved in selecting and organizing learning experiences.

The statement also brings up the idea of "solid" subjects, an interesting concept in itself. Who is to say what is "solid" unless it be in terms of the needs of the pupils involved at a particular time? English is ordinarily accepted as a solid subject when such terminology is employed. Much of the time in the usual English class is spent in perfecting the skills needed in writing, despite the fact that studies indicate that a much larger proportion of people's time is devoted to speaking and listening. In view of this, would not training in listening and in speech be more solid? Apparently, training in speech is fully as necessary to a student's development of good usage. Another aspect of this problem is the excess stress on rules of grammar memorized so that they can be summoned up on demand, when studies have shown that rules learned by memorization have less effect upon usage than rules developed in functional settings.

An adequate case might be made for other skill areas that are often considered frills of educational programs, when they actually make basic contributions to the accepted objectives for educating gifted students.

Guidance must be based on intimate knowledge of the student and his capabilities. It must take into consideration his personal choices of profession and career. The function of guidance in the secondary school cannot be adequately met by scheduling students into difficult courses. Appropriateness for the student's future plans and optimum development must be considered. Effective guidance may even result in individual programming for students whose needs are not served by the usual class schedule. It is the student who is the center; his best interests must determine the process by which he attains social and individual growth.

EXTRACURRICULAR ACTIVITIES

Extracurricular activities, sometimes referred to as co-curricular, are another means by which the secondary school can provide opportunities for enrichment and for social participation. There are all kinds of possibilities for forming clubs and organizing student activities. As many as a hundred extracurricular activities are provided in some of the larger high schools.

Centers around which extracurricular activities can be organized include school subjects, hobbies, arts and crafts, music, dramatics, journalism, athletics, and student government. There are mathematics clubs and science clubs that permit students to explore areas not ordinarily considered in classwork, and encourage further development of ideas that are touched only briefly in the class. Creative writing clubs can offer extended opportunity for students gifted in that area and sufficiently interested to put more time into the development of the skills it demands. Any school subject offers possibilities for club activities. International relations clubs may be an outgrowth of the social studies program, and French and Spanish clubs allow students to pursue their investigation of the cultures behind the languages they study in class. Obviously, curricular materials form an important part of the program of these organizations. For those students who wish to study regular subject matter more fully, clubs can provide such opportunities.

The numbers and kinds of hobby clubs that may be established are limited only by the interests of the students and the ability of the faculty to supervise the activities. Hobbies too may be related to school subjects; radio and photography clubs may have their roots in the science program. No matter what the center of interest may be in any particular extracurricular activity, it should have some educative value if it is to be sponsored by the school.

The values of extracurricular activities should be definitely related to the values the school is attempting to develop through its curricular program. Opportunities for student leadership are worthwhile outcomes. All clubs are organized much less formally than classes and thus afford students the opportunity to practice leadership skills in functional settings. There is faculty supervision of activities, but it is usually far more permissive to the development of student leadership than the more formal classroom situation.

Students can learn from extracurricular activities. They can investigate new hobby areas and learn the skills involved; they can further develop established hobbies and perfect the skills already attained. This learning is of the most meaningful kind; the student is motivated intrinsically; he willingly performs tasks to increase his learning; he evaluates results and profits by his participation.

Not all activities are valuable for all students. No school should force participation in the extracurricular program; yet all students need to be encouraged to participate where there can be some valuable experiences for them. On the other hand, it is sometimes necessary that a school limit the activities of some students lest they schedule themselves too tightly, and lose the values the program attempts to provide. There can be no hard and fast rules on these points; each case must be judged on its merits, and the program adjusted accordingly. School authorities should not underestimate the energy and skills of gifted students; most of them are able to accomplish much more than the typical program allows.

While the students are learning and perfecting skills in fields of knowledge, and practicing skills of leadership, they are also having valuable experiences in establishing desirable relationships with their age-mates and adults. The extracurricular program can thus satisfy some of the needs of adolescents, and can help them in achieving some of their developmental tasks.

The faculty sponsors of extracurricular activities are very important to the success of any club or activity. Students need leadership, but not of the dominating kind. It should be democratic leadership in which the democratic values are stressed and in which students are encouraged and assisted to exert their own leadership abilities and qualities. Though the actual situation is usually much freer than that found in the secondary-school classroom, the need for responsible leadership in any school-sponsored activity cannot be denied.

Yet it must be the kind of leadership that encourages student participants to become increasingly self-directive and self-disciplined.

Many schools have developed schedules that include the extracurricular activities within the framework of the school day. This does not remove the necessity of having some of the activities take place during after-school hours; for example, athletic clubs that need to use the physical education area and equipment may have to wait until after school when these facilities are free from class schedules. Scheduling activities into the school day represents an attempt to recognize the educational values involved, to indicate that such activities are really not "extra" but an integral part of the school program.

Gifted students may enter into such of these activities as meet their particular needs, and profit by them. Activities, however, ought not to be used as a means of developing well-roundedness at the expense of curtailing the time and effort a gifted student may profitably give to an all-pervasive and valuable "interest-ability."

SELECTED READINGS

BRANDWEIN, PAUL F. *The Gifted Student as Future Scientist*. New York: Harcourt, Brace & Co., 1955. 107 pp.

    A description of the program developed in science at the Forest Hills High School is given, stressing the identification and development of those students likely to be gifted in science. Proposals are made for programs at local, state, and national levels for the identification and education of future scientists.

CONANT, JAMES B. *The American High School Today: A First Report to Interested Citizens*. New York: McGraw-Hill Book Co., 1959. 140 pp.

    This report of Conant's recent study of American secondary education includes full explanation of the comprehensive high school, and twenty-one recommendations for improving the education of American youth. Almost without exception, these recommended practices can be found in operation in some of the schools visited during the study, though no school was found to include all of the suggested practices.

GAVIAN, RUTH WOOD (ed.). *The Social Education of the Academically Talented*. (Curriculum Series No. 10.) Washington, D.C.: National Council for the Social Studies, 1958. 101 pp. Chapters 6 and 7.

    Chapter 6 describes several programs for social education at the junior-high-school level. Common characteristics possessed by these

programs include planning, emphasis on research skills, opportunity
for creative expression and leadership, attention to individual differences, and parental understanding of the programs.

Chapter 7 describes several programs at the high-school level
which involve acceleration, and enrichment in the regular classroom,
outside the classroom, through honors classes and seminars, and through
extracurricular activities.

HAVIGHURST, ROBERT J. *Developmental Tasks and Education.* New York:
Longmans, Green & Co., Inc., 1952. 100 pp. Chapter 5.

The principal developmental tasks of the age period are summarized and discussed in terms of their biological, psychological, and
cultural bases, and of the educational implications of each task. The
cultural bases are expanded to include discussion of the tasks as interpreted by American middle-, upper-, and lower-class families.

Invitational Conference on the Academically Talented Secondary School
Pupil. *The Identification and Education of the Academically Talented
Student in the American Secondary School.* Washington, D.C.: Na-
tional Education Association, 1958. 160 pp.

This conference report includes the addresses made under the
general title of identification, and the conclusions reached by the
study-discussion groups on the topic of education. The discussions deal
with the cultural attitudes affecting programs for the academically
talented, the ways of organizing programs, and the suggestions for
study in the various subject fields.

KLAUSMEIER, HERBERT J. *Teaching in the Secondary School.* New York:
Harper & Brothers, 1958. 499 pp. Chapters 1, 2, 5, and 13.

Chapter 1 discusses the changing patterns and goals of secondary
education, and Chapter 2 presents information concerning the nature
and needs of adolescents, explaining how this knowledge can be used
by the teacher in the classroom. Chapter 5 defines some terms commonly used in curriculum discussion, explains the historical development of the American secondary school, and describes some of the
recent experimentation with curriculum in order to help meet the needs
of the adolescents and the society as a whole. Chapter 13 points out the
variety of administrative and over-all curriculum provisions for educating the gifted. The author stresses the need for continuous and
systematic programs of identification as well as the necessity of enriched learning activities at all levels.

National Society for the Study of Education. *Education for the Gifted.* Chicago: University of Chicago Press, 1958. 420 pp. Chapters 8, 12, and
14.

Chapter 8 lists several characteristics and objectives of education for the gifted, each of which can be found in operation in some
active programs for the gifted. The goals have grown out of experience in teaching the gifted, and are based on accepted principles of
education. Chapter 12 presents programs in operation in secondary
schools concerned with education of the gifted student; the descriptions
are organized in terms of subject-matter fields. Chapter 14 points out
that counseling for the gifted is complex because of the many opportunities the gifted have, and because of their greater ability at self-

appraisal. Guidance is interpreted as a continuous process of gathering information and using it to arrive at logically based decisions.

NOAR, GERTRUDE. *The Junior High School, Today and Tomorrow.* Englewood Cliffs, N.J.: Prentice-Hall, Inc., 1953. 373 pp. Parts 1 and 3.

Part 1 discusses the unique functions of the junior high school and Part 3 deals with curriculum and methods. There is a detailed explanation of core curriculum and electives at the junior-high-school level; attention is given to dealing with individual differences in the classroom.

Philadelphia Suburban School Study Council. *Guiding Your Gifted: A Handbook for Teachers, Administrators, and Parents.* Philadelphia: Educational Service Bureau, School of Education, University of Pennsylvania, 1954. 89 pp.

This is a committee report describing how the nine districts of the Council developed their program for the gifted; it includes discussion on identification, organization of programs, ideas for helping the gifted in several subject areas, as well as suggestions for initiating special programs for educating the gifted.

TRUMP, J. LLOYD. *Images of the Future: A New Approach to the Secondary School.* Urbana, Illinois: Commission of the Experimental Study of the Utilization of the Staff in the Secondary School, 1959. 48 pp.

This publication looks at the secondary school of the future and projects a flexible program which will provide opportunity for every student to achieve to the limit of his ability. A brief section on the implications for the education of the gifted is included.

13

The College Program

There are in the United States more than 1,900 colleges and universities with enrollments totalling approximately three million. Over the next decade the growth in enrollment is expected to be substantial. These institutions of higher learning differ greatly in size, some being small private schools with rigorous entrance requirements and others large state universities which admit all or almost all high-school graduates who seek admission.

Only comparatively recently has the education of the gifted received much attention at the college level. It was generally held that when the gifted student reached college age he could pretty well take care of himself; at this level a wide choice of courses were open to him. As late as 1945 fewer than a dozen colleges and universities provided comprehensive special programs for the gifted. Fifteen years later the number had increased significantly but still represented a small fraction of the total.

EARLY PROGRAMS

The University of Chicago

The University of Chicago, a large privately endowed institution, may be credited with leadership in education of the gifted at the college level. Since the University contains not only a group of colleges but also a secondary and an elementary school, it was in a position to introduce flexibility into its program at all levels. In 1919 the precollege program at the University was organized into six years of elementary

442

training and five years of secondary schooling. Thus, the student was ready for college one year earlier than was ordinarily the case. If a student were considerably superior he was permitted to combine the senior high-school and freshman college year into one, thus gaining another year in his school progress.

Over a period of forty years the University of Chicago has experimented in organizing and reorganizing the curriculum in an effort to provide maximum learning opportunity through flexibility both in the program and in the student's progress. Duplication of high-school work in college was, as far as possible, eliminated. Standarized tests and comprehensive examinations took the place of college entrance units in determining student placement. Exemptions from courses and admission to advanced courses were obtainable through proficiency tests. The program was designed to avoid duplication of high-school courses in college as well as to make possible both enriched learning experiences and accelerated progress for the superior student.

Currently some of the early educational practices and organizational adjustments are being critically reviewed. Some will no doubt be modified in the light of changing times; others may be eliminated entirely. It is too early to predict the fate of many of the early innovations. However, regardless of what may be the outcome of the current readjustment, few will deny the impact which the institution has made upon educational practice with regard to superior students at the college level.

The University of Buffalo

In 1932 the University of Buffalo established a college-credit examination program with a twofold purpose; namely, (1) to eliminate duplication of work between the high school and college, and (2) to permit the more able students to accelerate their progress through the University. Proficiency examinations in college courses are given to students of superior ability either before or shortly following their admission to the University. Any prospective student or new enrollee is allowed to take these tests if his high-school record is outstanding and he is recommended for the program by his high-school principal. For every course examination which he passes the student is given "credit by examination" and is permitted to proceed with subsequent courses. Most "credit by examination" is secured in the freshman year and is in mathematics, foreign languages, and English. Although most freshmen who are eligible to participate in the program take only one or two proficiency examinations, a few take as many as a dozen examinations, and some earn as many as thirty semester hours, a year's work, in this fashion.

One of the important by-products of this program has been the close cooperative relationship developed with the contributing secondary schools. High school teachers and college faculty members have secured a better understanding of their respective roles in the education of the gifted. Each has the opportunity to learn more about the goals and achievements of the other.

CURRENT PRACTICE AND PROGRAMS

Current practice in meeting the educational needs of the gifted at the college level is far from uniform. This in itself may be promising inasmuch as it indicates experimentation or a willingness to try out different procedures. In fact, a major series of experimental projects, which are treated in a later section of this chapter, are now under way. There is considerable promise in such an experimental program.

Although the number of colleges and universities providing substantial programs for the gifted is quite small in relation to the total number, some of them are large institutions serving thousands of students and supported by large endowments or great tax resources. This, combined with foundation interest, enhances the prospects for improved programs through research and experimentation.

A second characteristic of present practice which goes hand-in-hand with the experimental attitude is closer cooperation with the secondary school. Any experimentation by the colleges in meeting the educational needs of the superior student brings them face to face with the high school. Education is a continuous process. Educational practice has over the years been fairly successful in closing the gap between the elementary school and the high school. This closure has been made possible by the prevailing type of district organization which places both types of schools under one administration. However, the break between the high school and college has been more or less accepted as fitting and proper. In most cases the only communication between the two has consisted of the forwarding of a certificate of graduation, a statement of the student's rank in class, and a transcript of credits.

In attempting to better meet the educational needs of the gifted, colleges and universities have become increasingly aware of the need for closer cooperation with the secondary schools. Early identification of the gifted was found in many cases to be dependent on getting accurate information from the high school. In making curricular adjustments or in counseling the student, the need for background information which only the high school could provide became quite evident. As a result the efforts of colleges and universities along this line have led to closer cooperation and an exchange of information which has been mutually helpful.

A third characteristic of present practice is the directed attempt to eliminate duplication in college of subject matter which has been covered in the high school. It is obvious that the cooperation referred to in preceding paragraphs is prerequisite to success in such endeavor. While in the case of the average student, repetition of some high-school work may be desirable or even necessary, it represents a waste of time for the gifted. Time thus saved may be used to accelerate the student's progress in college or to enrich his learning experiences there.

Fourth, in almost every case where programs have been established there is a realization of the need and desirability of guidance and counseling for the gifted in college. This need has long been recognized in connection with marginal students who are in danger of "flunking out of college." In fact, college guidance programs have been in a large measure directed toward this type of student. At present those who are responsible for college programs for the gifted are almost unanimous in pointing out the importance of giving guidance to the superior student as well. In most of these programs a serious attempt is made to understand the gifted student, his interests, his abilities, and his ambitions. Some institutions are asking the high school for more than just the graduate's academic record. They express interest in his extracurricular activities even though he may not be an athlete. They provide aptitude tests, personality rating scales, and interest inventories for use in counseling. The gifted student is provided with help in laying out a long-range program of academic achievement and is aided in selecting courses which will best fit into such a program. Despite the current awareness of the need for proper guidance of the gifted, few if any institutions of higher learning may be said to have a completely adequate program. There is much to be done in this connection if the realization of the need is to be translated into actual practice.

Finally, most if not all substantial college programs result in some acceleration of the gifted student, or some enrichment of his learning experiences, or both.

Curricular Adaptations

One major device used by colleges in their attempt to meet the needs of superior students is curricular adaptation. Such adaptation or flexibility has been largely a phenomenon of the 1950-60 decade. Although, as indicated earlier in the chapter, several institutions of higher learning had introduced a certain amount of flexibility into their programs in an attempt to accommodate superior students, the prevailing attitude in the first half of the century reflected little concern for the gifted student. It was generally felt that at the college level he was mature enough to make wise choices and that the regular program was broad enough to meet his needs. As a result many gifted students left college because they considered it a waste of time and effort to take courses and meet prerequisites which were geared to the typical student. Some dropped out because they did not find their regular college programs sufficiently challenging or rewarding. Others, although graduating, reported that they got much less out of their college work than they anticipated. The inflexibility of their college programs, lack of adequate counsel, and wasteful repetition of high-school work were often cited as reasons for this disappointment.

Following World War II, which helped to awaken the nation to the great importance of our intellectual resources, a wave of interest in the gifted student asserted itself in the colleges of the country. Stimulated by financial grants from the Ford Foundation, and other funds, a number of colleges and universities inaugurated experimental projects in curricular adaptations. The principal ways in which such flexibility is being provided are four in number:

1. Granting college admission to secondary students before they complete four years in high school
2. Granting advanced placement or credit for work done in the secondary school
3. Providing varied honors programs involving enrichment and intensified study opportunities
4. Offering a wide variety of options for independent study, often with tutorial assistance

Early Admission

Early admission is the name generally given to the practice of admitting students to college before their graduation from high school. This practice takes a number of forms, the most common being that of admitting students with three years of high-school work to freshman standing in college. Occasionally the transition is made at midyear after the secondary student has completed one semester's work of his senior year. Another practice which is gaining increasing acceptance is that of allowing the high-school junior to attend college summer school and then return to high school for his senior year. He then re-enters college the following summer or fall after his graduation from high school.

The practice of early admission is primarily an acceleration device. However, in some cases it serves principally to provide time for enrichment opportunities for the superior student. This is particularly true in the case of those who enter only one semester early or who attend a college summer session between the junior and senior year.

Although early admission has for many years had some acceptance in isolated cases involving a very limited number of students, it was not until World War II that it attained status as a curricular adaptation. The impetus provided by the desire of many young people to secure as much training as possible before entering military service resulted in many more colleges and universities opening their doors to high-school students who had not graduated. The purpose was plainly to accelerate progress and was customarily referred to as educational timesaving. President Lowell of Harvard stated the case for acceleration as follows:

With the long period of special training now required in every profession, there is a universal cry that men are beginning their careers in life too old, and that the period of education is too long. Disease and death are not postponed because a man starts upon the practice of his profession a year or two later than is necessary. His period of active life, his achievements and his usefulness are simply curtailed to that extent. . . . Much has been said about maturity, but that is the result less of age than of environment and responsibility. Maturity may easily become overripe.[1]

In 1951 further impetus was provided by the establishment of the Program for Early Admission to College supported by the Fund for the Advancement of Education. This program is briefly described in a later section of this chapter. Although in its early stages this program was described by some educators as most promising, there is currently little disposition among the participating schools to expand it. Among colleges not participating in the program a number have modified their entrance requirements so that nongraduates may enter, but there is little recruiting of eleventh-grade students.

[1] A. L. Lowell, *At War With Academic Traditions in America* (Cambridge, Mass.: Harvard University Press, 1934), p. 255.

It is yet too early to predict the future of early admission as a college policy in the United States. There is some evidence of social and emotional adjustment problems resulting from early admission. The male student in particular may feel a social inadequacy in his participation in nonacademic college life. He may feel that he is, by reason of his age, excluded from some college activities which provide valuable additions to his education. Certainly he will be handicapped with respect to participation in athletics if he enters a year early and spends only three years in college.

In skipping the senior year of high school the student misses some opportunities for leadership experiences which commonly accrue to senior students. As a senior in the typical high school the student has a number of extracurricular activities open to him. As a freshman in college he misses these and at the same time, because of his age, is at a disadvantage in engaging in comparable activities in college.

On the other hand there are to be considered the hazards involved in a secondary student marking time in a high school where his mind is unchallenged and where circumstances may even encourage him to adopt habits of carelessness and sloth. There is evidence that intellectual stagnation or even disability may be generated by retaining the bright student in an academic environment which he has outgrown.

It may be said that once it is agreed that moderate acceleration, up to one year, is desirable in the high-school–college span of eight years, the question then becomes, "Where shall this acceleration take place?" Early admission with the exception of college summer school experience to a greater or lesser degree assigns acceleration to the high school. The student's high-school career may be shortened by one semester or a year or even more.

On the whole it may be said that both the secondary schools and the colleges tend to favor advanced placement over early admission for the superior student. The breadth and quality of the high-school program should probably be given major consideration in determining the advisability of any student leaving for college early. In cases where the high-school program is of high quality and offers a sufficient variety of learning experiences to meet the needs and interests of the bright student, he will probably do best to remain in high school. There he can participate in school activities with his age-peers as well as work toward advanced placement in college. In such a situation the student has the opportunity to assume leadership roles and pursue extracurricular activities which would be unavailable in college.

In the small high school where the curriculum is limited and teachers commonly teach in two or three subject fields, the situation is quite different. It is under such circumstances that there are considerable grounds for concern with mental stagnation. There is a real possibility that the bright student may profit much more, at least academically, by moving from high school to college at the end of the eleventh year. However, it is in exactly this type of situation that the high-school student is likely to be least qualified academically for college work. The limited nature of the program in the small high school tends to circumscribe academic opportunity and unless the student has guidance from a teacher or some other adult in individual study he may have difficulty in qualifying for early college admission. Even when he has such guidance and even though the student has intellectual curiosity and drive, library and laboratory facilities are usually so limited in the small high school that he is seriously handicapped in preparing for college. For example, the aspiring young scientist will, in many small high schools, be without even the rudimentary science equipment necessary for experimentation. He will have difficulty in exploring the field of science without adequate equipment, and certainly he will be ill-prepared for college chemistry or physics.

In conclusion it might be said that in most cases advanced placement, honors programs and independent college study are preferable alternatives to early admission as curricular adaptations for the gifted student. However, this does not rule out individual cases in which circumstances might well dictate an early admission program. Each case should be considered in the light of the individual, his interests, his ability, his opportunities, and his achievement. There is undoubtedly no best way for everyone and there is every possibility that a combination of ways may be better than any one in many cases.

Advanced Placement

Advanced placement is the term used to describe the practice of placing superior high-school students at advanced levels in college or awarding college credit for courses taken in high school. Eligibility for advanced placement or college credit for high-school courses is usually determined by proficiency or achievement tests.

In some cases, the advanced placement allows superior high-school graduates to assume sophomore status upon entering. If they pursue their work successfully, they graduate from college in three years. In other cases, advanced placement is limited to the second semester level of the freshman year. In such cases, it is possible for the student to secure his degree in three years, but he usually attends one or two sessions of summer school.

The more common practice is to grant college credit for high-school work conducted on a comparable level with freshman college work in the subject field. The granting of such credit, usually based upon examination, permits the student to enrich his college program and at the same time avoid overlapping between high-school and college courses.

A formalized approach to advanced placement grew out of a study inaugurated in 1952 by a group of twelve colleges under the auspices of, and supported by, the Fund for the Advancement of Education. The study accomplished four things:

1. It assisted in the organization of new college-level courses in a group of cooperating high schools.
2. It conducted examinations for the pupils who took these courses.
3. It effected an agreement among the original twelve and later the fifteen colleges of the study to give credit and advanced placement to students who completed the work and passed the examinations in these courses.

4. It sponsored conferences for high-school and college teachers designed to help improve articulation between the two levels.

In 1955, the College Entrance Examination Board assumed sponsorship of the project, which became known as the Advanced Placement Program. The program provides full descriptions of college-level courses to be given in high schools and prepares examinations for these courses. On the basis of these courses and the attendant examinations, cooperating colleges grant advanced placement to students.

This program has been cited as one of the most promising, inasmuch as it provides framework in which curricular flexibility for the gifted may be achieved with the assurance that neither the student nor the school is being short-changed. The course descriptions and examinations are prepared by independent committees of specialists in the subject fields under the general policy direction of the Commission on Advanced Placement, a group of high-school and college teachers and administrators appointed by the College Board. These descriptions and examinations may be revised annually as a result of subject matter conferences with teachers and administrators.

The examinations are of such type as to allow for a considerable degree of difference in study patterns which may be developed in the various schools. Small classes are usually characteristic of the college-level courses. The courses demand the most highly developed teaching skills available on the high-school staff.

High-school and college teachers are encouraged to work together in special conferences for discussing and offering suggestions for the improvement of the program. Called by the Commission the "heart" of the program, these conferences enable the two groups to exchange ideas and learn about each other's work. This type of exchange is quite helpful in securing better articulation between the two levels, as well as promoting a common understanding of the objectives of the program. In a real sense, these conferences help to determine the scope and direction of the program.

The advantages claimed for the Advanced Placement Program as currently conducted by the College Board are as follows:

1. It offers opportunity for acceleration of the superior student.
2. It offers the opportunity for enrichment of both the secondary and college program.
3. It tends to avoid overlapping and duplication between high school and college.
4. It recognizes superior performance on the part of both student and teacher.
5. It encourages and stimulates the superior student in high school and in college.
6. It promotes a common understanding of instructional problems in connection with superior students among teachers at both levels, which results in a better coordinated and more effective program.

Reports from both high schools and colleges participating in the program indicate that teachers and students alike are pleased with the opportunities offered them. The program has stimulated some critical evaluation of curricula at both levels. Improved opportunities for superior teachers to exert their abilities are afforded. Communication between high school and college has been improved and expanded.

In general, students in the program have been successful in their college work. Harvard University reported that Advanced Placement students made higher marks in the last three years of college than did their classmates. In the first four years of this program at Harvard, more than 69 per cent of the Advanced Placement students had honor grades, compared with only 57 per cent of the regular class.

Although the practice of advanced placement existed before and exists now independent of the College Entrance Examination Board project, the sponsorship of the Board has formalized the practice by establishing standard procedures and providing services which greatly augment the practice. Membership in the program is growing at a rapid pace, which is one indication of the value of the program.

Honors Programs

Honors programs in general are designed not only to give superior students an opportunity to transcend regular course offerings, but also to stimulate them to satisfy their intellectual curiosity by intense and thorough inquiry. The Reverend Charles F. Donovan, S. J., Dean of the School of Education, Boston College, states the aims of the honors program as follows:

Among the outcomes desired from the use of this technique are habits of analysis and reflection, intellectual self-confidence, poise and tolerance in academic discussion, consistency in expressing and maintaining a point of view, and a habit of questioning, with appropriate humility, the generalizations of others, whether the generalizations are made by fellow students or famed philosophers.[2]

Honors programs in most cases include a series of special courses which require more intense work and higher quality achievement than are required in regular courses or sections. They lead to the bachelor's degree *cum laude*. In universities with honors programs a qualifying student usually has his choice of programs, since most if not all the colleges of the university offer special courses or sections in the areas of learning they represent. In small colleges the choice may be somewhat restricted due to the more limited curricula.

Usually a faculty committee in each college, called an Honors Council or Committee, is given responsibility for conducting the program. Each subject field, such as chemistry, mathematics, or psychology, often represented by departments in the universities, develops its own honors program. A student who qualifies for the honors program will ordinarily have the opportunity to pursue work in his major subject field from the freshman year until graduation.

In the larger institutions there is usually a director of honors programs who has over-all responsibility for the administration of the program. He has, in most cases, an advisory group made up of representatives from each department offering an honors program.

[2] "Notes and Comments," *The Superior Student,* Vol. II, No. 1 (February, 1959), p. 15.

Freshmen usually establish eligibility for the program on their high-school grades and scores on academic aptitude and achievement tests given by the college or university. Recommendations of the high-school principal, class rank, school activity record, and impressions made in personal interviews are also commonly given consideration in selection. Seldom does the number selected exceed 5 or 6 per cent of the total entering class. Occasionally sophomores and even juniors and seniors are selected for the program.

Honors programs, as the name implies, carry with them academic honor. To be selected for such a program is an honor for the student. It is also considered an honor for a faculty member to be chosen to teach a special course or section of the honors program. Special recognition is given the graduate who has successfully pursued an honors program. One of the incidental values of such programs is the development of an *esprit de corps* among students of exceptional ability. This leads to greater cooperation and more extensive exchange of ideas among members of the group. Often the instructors are included in the informal discussions which grow out of this group consciousness.

In general, honors programs are associated chiefly with departments of letters and science in the universities and with the liberal arts colleges. This is probably due to the fact that the programs had their origin in the fields of art and science where most of the fundamental disciplines are taught. However, honors programs are by no means excluded from the professional schools. Many educators are conscious of the fact that some of our most able students are in the professional schools. In this age of specialization the professional schools enroll some of the best minds among college youth, and their graduates assume leading roles and responsible positions in the American economy, society, and culture. Honors programs in these schools can render a real service in providing the student with a broad intellectual background which will enable him to see his profession in its proper social context as well as recognize its interdependence with other areas of knowledge.

Enrichment, largely in depth but also in breadth, is characteristic of the honors program. Few students are accelerated. A few graduate after three or three and one-half years of college work but the vast majority spend the full four years in college.

Cole,[3] writing in the College Board Review, says, "Of all the arrangements used to build greater flexibility into the curriculum for able students, honors programs appear to be most productive."

Independent Study

Independent study may be defined broadly as study which is not identified with or an integral part of organized courses. Most effective independent study is usually done with the guidance of one or more faculty members. It is almost invariably individual work with a one-to-one student-teacher relationship. A professor may serve as adviser to the student doing independent study, and as such makes himself available for consultation on the selection of a topic for study, the method of approach, and the evaluation of results.

E. E. Robinson[4] described the aim of independent study at Stanford as follows:

The primary aim of all independent study has been to stimulate the superior student to do more work and better work than he would ordinarily do without individual supervision. . . . And it has been the desire of those in charge of independent study to provide for the student of liberal studies such conditions that he will be led to work with the determination and the interest of the professional student at the program agreed upon as his own.

It has been the purpose of independent study not merely to lend flexibility to subject matter. It has been necessary also to bring students into contact with subject matter in fields where "abstractness" is essential. Through individual work, the student has learned, as in no other way, the "language" of the subject. Thus not only the facts in a particular field but also the reflections of men whose thoughts

[3] C. C. Cole, "Varying Patterns for Able College Students," *College Board Review*, No. 36 (Fall, 1958), p. 23.

[4] Edgar Eugene Robinson, *Independent Study in the Lower Division at Stanford University: 1931-1937* (Stanford, Calif.: Stanford University Press, 1937), p. 11.

about it are accepted, and the critical interpretation of contemporary scholars, have become realities to the student.

Independent study in some form or another has existed in American colleges since their establishment. However, until the 1920's provisions for such study were informal and largely an individual matter between student and professor. In the decade 1920-30 about seventy-five colleges adopted formal plans of independent study. By mid-twentieth century approximately one-fourth of the four-year institutions of higher learning had incorporated some type of independent study plan in their programs.

The independent study plan or program, as distinguished from informal and isolated cases of independent study, is defined by Bonthius, Davis, and Drushal as follows:

An independent study program is one which provides a formal opportunity on an institution-wide basis for the pursuit of special topics or projects by individual students, under the guidance of faculty advisers, apart from organized courses, for honors only or for credit toward graduation, available to students who meet certain requirements or required of all students.[5]

Most independent study programs offer credit or some type of recognition for independent study. They, like honors programs, may have an administrator with a faculty advisory committee who assumes responsibility for the coordination of the program on an institution-wide basis. In many of the plans not only the superior students but also average students are admitted to the program. Since each student may pursue independent study at his own pace, neither the gifted nor the general run of students suffer any handicap. By and large, however, the independent study plan is viewed as being more appropriate for the most able students.

Admission requirements vary widely. In some colleges all students must participate; in others, only those students who meet certain grade standards are admitted to the program; in still others participants are chosen on the basis of faculty recommendation and personal interviews.

[5] Robert H. Bonthius, F. J. Davis, and J. G. Drushal, *The Independent Study Program in the United States* (New York: Columbia University Press, 1957), p. 9.

In referring to the Stanford Independent Study Program, Lewis Terman said: "Perhaps it would be a good type of training for any student, bright, average, or dull, but for the gifted student at least, it is the only way that truly educates."[6]

The amount of academic credit given for independent study varies widely from one institution to another. The majority of colleges give some academic credit toward graduation but limit the amount which may be secured in this way. Independent study may be considered as a course in itself and appropriate credit given, or it may consist of work which parallels regular course work and adds to the credit value of the course.

Students who participate in independent study programs are given special consideration in such things as the arrangement of their course work, admission to graduate seminars, unlimited access to library facilities, and special privileges in the use of laboratories and laboratory equipment.

Independent study takes many forms. Probably the most popular form is that of library research on a selected topic which results in a written report. The topic is one which is of interest to the student and is ordinarily approved by a faculty adviser. From time to time during the research and production of the paper the student consults with his adviser. Upon its completion the report is evaluated by the faculty member, usually in conference with the student. If academic credit is to be given a comprehensive examination which covers the various topics of the student's study is prepared and given to the student.

A second form of independent study is laboratory research and experimentation. Again guidance is provided by an appropriate faculty member and laboratory space and equipment are made available, usually after school hours and on Saturdays. This type of project offers a real challenge to the gifted young scientist who is eager to explore the world of

[6] Lewis M. Terman, "The Independent Study Plan at Stanford University," *School and Society*, Vol. XXIV (July 24, 1926), p. 98.

nature. A report on the experiment or research, including methods used and results achieved, is customarily required.

A third form is field work which involves study in an extramural setting and usually a report on the project. Field projects include such things as making an analysis of tax income of a city, participation in a city planning project, development of a community resources manual, study of a slum clearance project, conducting a labor supply survey, making an area marketing study, conducting a survey of job opportunities in a specific area, or assisting in a public school survey.

A fourth form is the creation of some work of artistic merit such as a painting, a play, a poem, or a musical composition. Closely related is a fifth form of independent study which has as its purpose the achievement of excellence in a dramatic performance or in a ballet, or an opera or similar artistic performance. These forms of study usually involve no written reports since the results of the study are apparent in the product or performance.

In general students have wide latitude in which to choose not only the form but also the topic of their independent study. They must, however, secure the approval of their advisers before embarking on a study. Usually they present an outline of the proposed project indicating why it has been chosen, its value, its limitations, the method of attack, resources available, and results expected.

The values of independent study are many, as reported by both students and faculty. Chief among the values listed are the following:

1. The development of ability to work creatively and constructively on one's own
2. The opportunity to probe deeply and intensively into a topic of special interest
3. The opportunity to learn how to develop a research design and follow it through to secure research results
4. The opportunity to learn how and where to find sources of information
5. Development of ability to classify, organize and present material

6. Development of ability to analyze and criticize one's own work
7. Provision of closer student-teacher relationships which in turn stimulates student effort

The disadvantages usually ascribed to independent study are for the most part due to factors not indigenous to the plan. They include lack of sufficient guidance from professors, limited library and laboratory facilities, and insufficient academic credit allowances. Those which are indigenous to the program include temptation to procrastinate because of the lack of regular class meetings, overspecialization, and nervous strain involved in working alone. From the viewpoint of the faculty the major drawback of the plan seems to be the excessive load which is placed on the more capable and popular teachers. This is an objection which can, of course, be easily overcome by administrative action provided financial resources are adequate.

Personnel Adaptations

A second way of meeting the particular needs of gifted students in college is by personnel adaptations. In many cases, such adaptations are corollary to curricular adaptations. Often curricular flexibility is attained through adding personnel or revising duties and responsibilities of people already on the job. In fact, the key to the success or failure of most curricular innovations rests with the instructional staff involved. This section is devoted to a brief discussion of the major personnel adaptations which characterize the better college programs available to gifted students.

INSTRUCTIONAL STAFF. All curricular adaptations which are designed to improve learning opportunities for the gifted and upgrade the quality of their education rely upon superior instruction or extra effort on the part of the teacher. Particularly is this true of independent study and honors programs. It is also true of early admission and advanced placement, although to a lesser degree, since gifted students are channeled into regular classes. Nevertheless, the better teachers will see the need for individual attention for the student who is advanced into a class somewhat ahead of him in terms of academic experience.

The assignment of members of the college staff to teach special classes for superior students in the high school is reported in a number of instances where there is a close relationship between the college and the public school system of the city in which it is located. The practice of joint committees of secondary and college teachers studying the problems of articulation between the two levels and developing plans for curricular revisions is another example of personnel adaptation in the process of meeting the needs of gifted students.

Superior students need superior instructors if they are to profit most from their schooling. This is not to say that the average or typical student does not need them also. However, it is the superior teacher who is likely to have most success in a new program or in the introduction of factors of flexibility into the old. In practice, it is the better teachers, the stimulating, understanding, and dedicated members of the faculty, who assume the greatest responsibility in developing and maintaining special programs for the gifted. Their effectiveness is often limited because their work with the gifted is in the nature of an overload. They teach their regular courses, perform their share of committee work, carry on research, do some professional writing, and *in addition* work in the program for superior students. The best teachers are called upon most often to supervise independent study, to conduct seminars for honor students, and to counsel the accelerates.

Therefore, if the college program for the gifted is to be of maximum effectiveness, faculty members participating should have adjustments made in their teaching loads so that they may give the program adequate time and effort. Some institutions have offered extra pay for this type of work on the basis of the extra load. While this plan does give the staff member some recognition, it has undesirable features which militate against its use. First, it does not give the teacher any more time even though it rewards him for time spent. Second, it encourages teachers who have little or no interest in the gifted and who are not likely to challenge them, to participate in the program simply as a way to increase their salaries. Finally, the selecting of some teachers to receive extra pay while others are denied such an opportunity, may adversely affect staff morale. The adjustment of the teaching load where financial resources make this possible has proven to be the better solution.

GUIDANCE PERSONNEL. College guidance personnel have traditionally been concerned with the below-average student, the "flunkouts," the discipline problems, and health cases. It has been generally assumed that the superior student would find his own way in the college program. Since the premise to some extent has been found valid, neglect of the gifted has continued. However, when the question is raised as to whether he is finding his way as well as he should, whether his success is commensurate with his ability to succeed, the answers are not reassuring. The gifted student will probably achieve as high a level of adjustment by himself as the general run of students do with the help of guidance workers, but this level may well be far below that which he could attain.

Adequate attention to the identification and counseling of superior students is essential at the college level, as well as in the high school. Comprehensive testing programs, adequate counseling, and the maintenance of informative student records require training and skilled personnel. Such personnel add to the cost of education, but the increased effectiveness which they can bring to the education of the gifted is difficult to overestimate.

In a few institutions, guidance services especially for the gifted are maintained in conjunction with advanced placement and honors programs. In at least one state university, such services are extended to cooperating high schools. University psychologists prepare and administer tests in the high schools, conduct interviews and use other diagnostic techniques in an effort to identify gifted pupils early in their school careers. This service supplements the high-school guidance programs and in the case of many small high schools represents a major part of their guidance programs. Many gifted high-school students who would otherwise go unnoticed are identified and encouraged to go on to college. Specialized counselors from the university staff can provide guidance which for the most part is unavailable on the high-school level. Thus, a university, by extending its services to the gifted to the high-school level, may improve its effectiveness in discharging its responsibility for leadership of education in the state.

TUTORIAL PERSONNEL. Tutoring or coaching of superior students is characterized by detailed direction and frequent consultation at regular intervals over a comparatively long period of time, usually a semester or a year. The usual one-to-one relationship of tutoring makes close supervision possible. In some cases, tutoring may be employed with small groups having a common objective. Definite study goals are usually set up and plans for their achievement carefully laid.

Most tutoring is in connection with regular courses and is designed to help the student master the course content. In the case of the gifted student, the aim may be to excel or to win honors or in the case of early admission or advanced placement students, to supplement the course instruction. Often early admission students require some help in background development in order to do their best in college courses. Likewise, the advanced placement student may profit from tutoring since he may need help in orienting himself to advanced work.

Tutoring is also practiced as a device for preparing students for proficiency examinations and College Board Examinations in connection with advanced placement and early admission. Occasionally, tutoring is employed in independent study when the student is working on a project or experiment which requires rather continuous supervision or direction. In such cases, the tutor supplements the work of the instructional adviser.

Tutoring personnel are largely drawn from three sources: college instructors, high-school teachers, and advanced college students who in most cases are superior students themselves, often in honors programs. Retired but mentally alert professors and high-school teachers are a largely overlooked source of tutors. Few colleges support tutorial programs involving either college or high-school teachers, since tutoring is obviously far too expensive for general use. Most tutoring done by teachers is arranged for on a private basis and the student pays for the service. In the case of tutoring by advanced students, such is not so often the case. These tutors may assume tutorial responsibilities as a part of their program. Often fraternities and honor societies provide tutors as a service to their members or prospective members.

While the practice of tutoring gifted students is not widespread, it is a personnel adaptation which has value in helping these students succeed in developing their abilities to the maximum in college. It is of greatest help to early admission and advanced placement students, since it is an effective way of orienting them to college work and filling in any gaps that may exist in their knowledge of prerequisite subject matter. Junior and senior students, who themselves are superior or honors students, make very effective tutors. The college which recognizes the need for special attention to the gifted student should not overlook the possibilities of a well-organized tutoring program.

Materials and Equipment

If the college is to be most effective in the education of gifted as well as typical students, it must provide adequate materials of instruction and equipment. This is particularly true in the case of the gifted student pursuing honors programs and doing independent study.

Adequate library facilities are of paramount importance. The superior student who has an inquiring mind requires not only a library with a large collection of volumes in his major area, but also a library service which will enable him to borrow books from the great libraries of the country. Most independent study involves major library research, and limited library facilities seriously handicap the student.

Laboratories and laboratory facilities are of the utmost importance in meeting the educational needs of the gifted. The experimental approach is at the heart of most programs for the gifted. If the superior student is to pursue his interests above and beyond the regular course work, he must have the equipment to do so. Today, many of the large universities are equipped with the most up-to-date scientific devices and machines. Well-equipped laboratories for research in electronics, nuclear physics, astrophysics, aeronautics, biophysics, chemistry, and many other sciences are available for use in special programs for the gifted. Data-processing laboratories are equipped with electronic computers and the most complex data-sorting and -classifying machines. The future scientist has in such universities the materials and equipment he needs to make the most of his college training, provided the administration has set up programs or plans for their use by superior students above and beyond class work.

The possibilities of "teaching machines" as aids to independent study are just beginning to be explored. Such machines include tape recorders, slide projectors, movie projectors, and closed-circuit television. Language laboratories in which students may record their words and hear them repeated later as often as they wish offer examples of the use of teaching machines. Scoring machines make it possible for students to take examinations themselves and have them scored by machine. The use of "teaching machines" is consistent with the conceptual framework of the technological world in which we live and offers considerable promise in programs of independent study for the gifted and in general educational practice as well.

Experimental Programs

The beginning of the second half of the twentieth century marked the inauguration of a period of experimentation in college adjustment and treatment of gifted students. Chief among the experiments were those sponsored by the Ford Foundation's Fund for the Advancement of Education.[7]

[7] Fund for the Advancement of Education, *Bridging the Gap Between High School and College* (Evaluation Report No. 1 [New York: Fund for the Advancement of Education, 1953]); *They Went to College Early* (Evaluation Report No. 2 [New York: Fund for the Advancement of Education, 1957]).

Those in charge of the Fund clearly recognized the importance of the full development of exceptional ability at the college level as well as in the earlier stages of the educational process. The five major experimental programs which have been underwritten by the Fund are briefly described here. Brief descriptions of four other types of experimental projects follow those of the Fund.

THE STUDY OF GENERAL EDUCATION. This study[8] was launched in 1951 in three colleges and three preparatory schools. The colleges were Harvard, Princeton, and Yale; the secondary schools were Andover, Exeter, and Lawrenceville. Selected faculty members of each of the schools formed a study committee to appraise the individual programs and progress of 344 students who had attended these institutions from the eleventh grade through college. Chief among the committee's findings were:

1. A general lack of coordination between the preparatory and college programs
2. Useless repetition of learning experiences and frequent overlapping of course materials
3. Omission in many programs of study of areas of learning deemed important to a good general education
4. Failure to capitalize on basic courses in such fields as mathematics and languages due to abandonment of the field at the conclusion of the first course
5. Failure to give the student a well-balanced program in terms of his abilities and interests
6. Frequent emphasis on minor areas of study to the exclusion of a major area
7. Lack of adequate guidance and counseling at both secondary and college levels
8. Lack of coordination between secondary school and college in such guidance programs as did exist

Recognizing that these findings represented a rather severe indictment of the educational process with regard to the gifted, combined committees worked out integrated course plans in the standard subject fields for the last two years of

[8] For a full report, see *General Education in School and College* (Cambridge, Mass.: Harvard University Press, 1953).

high school and the first two years of college. A series of examinations were developed by the instructional staff members in cooperation with the College Entrance Board. These examinations help to identify students with superior achievement in the various subject fields and provide a basis for enrichment of their programs as well as acceleration of their progress.

The study has served to point out the great need for coordination of secondary and college programs and has provided some leads on how the two may be better integrated. It has also called attention to the need not only for more adequate guidance for the gifted, but also for greater cooperation between the two educational levels in the counseling of gifted students.

THE PORTLAND–REED COLLEGE PROGRAM. Also supported by Ford Foundation funds, this program features a cooperative effort by the Portland, Oregon, Public Schools, and Reed College, located in Portland. Included in the program are not only the intellectually gifted, but also those who are talented in art, music, dramatics, and mechanics, as well as those who possess such desirable characteristics as drive, social sensitivity, originality, and self-direction.

The program is designed to enrich the learning experiences of these superior students rather than to accelerate their progress. They are identified while in high school and divided into a number of groups in terms of their particular interests and abilities. Seminars are then organized for each group; many of them include college instructors as well as high-school teachers as participating members. Enrichment inaugurated in high school is continued through college so that students participating encounter no breaks in their program.

A unique feature of the Portland–Reed College Program is the special attention given to public relations. The public was not only acquainted with the goals and objectives of the program, but is kept informed of its procedures and progress. Since the future of the program may well depend on the public support, this aspect of the experiment assumes major importance. Another feature which is worthy of note is the close and continuous cooperation made possible by the location of Reed College and its close ties with the Portland school system.

THE ATLANTA EXPERIMENT IN ARTICULATION AND ENRICHMENT. This experiment in articulation and enrichment in school and college is designed to improve the integration of the high school and college programs and the enrichment of both for the particular benefit of gifted students. Participants are Agnes Scott College, Emory University, Oglethorpe University and the Westminster Schools. Encouraging progress in the elimination of repetition and wasted effort in grades eleven through fourteen and the significant improvement in opportunity for superior students to broaden and intensify their learning experiences has been reported.

ADMISSION TO COLLEGE WITH ADVANCED STANDING. Another experimental program supported by the Ford Fund was inaugurated in 1952 by Bowdoin, Brown, Carleton, Haverford, Kenyon, Massachusetts Institute of Technology, Middlebury, Oberlin, Swarthmore, Wabash, Wesleyan, and Williams, in cooperation with twenty-two secondary schools. It was designed to stimulate the identification and intensive preparation of gifted students while they were in high school so that they might enter college with advanced standing. In this program the student spends the regulation four years in high school, but by virtue of concentrated study achieves advanced college standing. Such standing is determined by subject examinations. In this way he may complete his undergraduate training and start on graduate work in the four years typically spent in undergraduate study.

In 1955, the program was taken over by the College Entrance Examination Board and continued as the "Advanced Standing Program." In the first year, more than 400 high-school graduates took tests for advanced standing. Almost one-half of this number won placement in advanced courses or credit for college courses, or both. The majority of these students went to colleges other than the colleges originally participating in the program. The program has grown steadily since the College Entrance Examination Board assumed sponsorship, and by 1960 over 300 colleges and more than 700 preparatory schools were participating.

EARLY ADMISSION TO COLLEGE. A fifth Ford Foundation project, known as the "Early Admission to College" program, was specifically designed to accelerate the progress of intellectually gifted students. One of the announced purposes was to give superior men students the opportunity to obtain their general education before entering required military service at age eighteen. In this way, they would be able to enter specialized fields and professional schools upon their return from military service. However, the program was open to all who could qualify and many who did not anticipate being drafted into military service did participate.

Twelve collegiate institutions participated. They were Chicago, Columbia, Fisk, Goucher, Lafayette, Louisville, Morehouse, Oberlin, Shimer, Utah, Wisconsin, and Yale. Most students qualifying for early admission to these institutions were between sixteen and seventeen years of age and had completed only the tenth or eleventh grade. They were known as "Fund Scholars," since each, upon qualifying for the program, received a two-year financial grant. Although the majority of participants were men, a significant number of women qualified for Goucher College and the co-educational institutions in the group.

Qualification for entrance in the program was largely determined by basic tests such as the College Entrance Examination Board tests, Ohio State Psychological Examinations, and those of the American Council on Education, and achievement tests in the subject fields. The majority of the twelve institutions also took into consideration high-school records as well as the maturity and emotional stability of the applicants. Isolated factors considered by one or more of the institutions included financial need, geographical representation, extracurricular activities, leadership ability, and even height and weight.

Once the Fund Scholars entered the college of their choice, they were confronted with varied types of educational services and programs. Each institution provided for these exceptional students according to its own policies and program procedures. However, in all except two of the colleges, the greatest emphasis has been placed on the liberal arts. Educational guidance has been quite general among the colleges, but personal and vocational guidance in some of the schools leaves much to be desired.

In order to gain some idea of the effectiveness of the program, three types of evaluation were undertaken. The first was a comparison of the Fund Scholars with matched groups of regular students and with the total college enrollment as to academic records in college and achievement tests in subject areas. In general, it was reported that the Fund Scholars compared favorably with both groups on both achievement tests and academic records. A second evaluation consisted of an analysis of long essays on the program written by 184 Fund Scholars and essays on acceleration by a comparable group of selected students. The latter group was older, but on the same academic level. In general, the Scholars did not suffer in comparison with the older group, except in the area of personal and social problems where their youth proved somewhat of a handicap, although not a serious one. A third evaluation was centered on the problem of social and emotional adjustment. It was reported that the proportion of Scholars with neuroses, psychoses, and similar difficulties did not exceed that among college students in general.

In 1957, the results of the "Early Admission to College" experiment were reported in full in *They Went to College Early*.[9] They are summarized in the first chapter as follows:

1. Although the program has operated more smoothly at some colleges than others, all of the participating colleges consider it to have been successful.
2. In a few cases, some of the colleges made mistakes in the selection of their first group of Scholars, and some were over-protective in their handling of the Scholars during

[9] The Fund for the Advancement of Education, *They Went to College Early, op. cit.*, pp. 9-10.

the first year of the experiment, but, by and large, these difficulties were overcome in the selection and handling of subsequent Scholar groups.

3. Academically, all four groups of Scholars have out-performed their classes as a whole and their Comparison students.

4. The rate of failure among the first two groups of Scholars was somewhat higher than that among their Comparison students, but, at most of the colleges where comparable data were available, it was lower than that among their classmates as a whole. When the reasons for failure were examined, they were found to be no different for the Scholars than for college students in general.

5. The Scholars encountered more initial difficulties in adjusting to campus life than their older Comparison students, but most of these difficulties were minor and were soon overcome.

6. There is some evidence that in many cases early admission to college freed Scholars from the boredom and frustration of an unchallenging high-school environment, gave them new intellectual momentum, and enhanced their social and emotional maturation.

7. Among the first two groups of Scholars who graduated, the proportion planning to go on to graduate school was substantially higher than that among their Comparison students.

8. Although the period of Fund support has ended, eleven of the twelve participating colleges and universities have incorporated the early admission idea into their regular admissions policy. The twelfth, Wisconsin, which has three Scholar groups still to graduate, has not yet taken any action on the matter.

9. In all but a few cases where such data are available, the parents of the Scholars and the principals of the high schools from which they came have expressed themselves as favorably disposed toward the results of the experiment.

10. The evidence gathered thus far clearly suggests that high academic aptitude and the ability to handle the responsibilities of college life are the *sine qua non* of early admission, and that colleges should not be over-protective in the handling of early admission students.

Despite the generally favorable evaluation of the early admission program, it is by no means without critics. Many secondary and some college teachers agree with a statement in the evaluation report of the University of Wisconsin which reads as follows: "With all these restrictions, intellectual, moral, and financial, it is clear that early admission is only advisable for a tiny proportion of high school students, and that it accents more problems than it answers."[10]

THE LOCATION OF TALENTED STUDENTS PROGRAM. This program, established at Indiana University by the University administration in 1958 and known as the LOTS program, is designed to aid high schools in the location and counseling of talented secondary students. The two primary purposes of the program, as indicated by the name, are (1) to help the high school locate its gifted students at all grade levels, and (2) to aid in giving them educational, personal, and vocational counseling.

In helping to locate talented students, Indiana University provides help in testing, interviewing, and in other diagnostic techniques. The talented student is defined as one "who is truly superior to his peers" in general intelligence and whose "talent for work" in science, music, art, or any other useful area of learning, is appreciably superior to that of his fellow students. The program does not include those whose academic work is above average, but whose I.Q. is only average or slightly above average.

Usually a high-school teacher or guidance worker acts as a liaison officer between the high school and the University. He arranges for the testing and interviewing of students by the University staff members. Counseling often involves the parents as well as the University and high-school representatives. The gifted students are advised regarding their college programs and the subject fields which seem appropriate in terms of their interests and abilities. By 1960, more than one hundred secondary schools were participating in the LOTS program.

10 *Ibid.*, p. 87.

THE HONORS COLLEGE PROJECT AT MICHIGAN STATE UNIVERSITY. The Honors College program was established at Michigan State University in 1956. The Honors College acts as an agency working with the regular colleges of the University in providing gifted college students with special enriching educational experiences. There is no set program, but rather the needs and interests of the student dictate his program. The project may be said to have three guiding principles of operation. They are:

1. Restrictions and requirements with regard to courses and programs are waived for gifted students, so that they may have unimpeded opportunity for intellectual adventure.
2. The gifted student must have adequate guidance and counseling at all times so that he may obtain maximum values from his educational experiences.
3. The program must be kept simple in organization and operation so that the needs of the student are never lost in administrative detail.

Students are granted admission to the program at the freshman or sophomore level by invitation. A minimum of B+ or a 3.5 average in course work is required. Once a student is admitted to the program, he is assigned an adviser who helps him develop his program, after which it is submitted to the honors committee of the college in which the student will do his major work. If his program is approved, the student is then free to pursue his work in the Honors College as long as he maintains a 3.2 average (slightly above a B). His program may include credit by proficiency tests, independent study, individual research, graduate courses, and seminars. Adjustments in program may be made if approved by the adviser and the honors committee. When the total required hours of his program are completed, the student receives the bachelor's degree upon recommendation of the adviser and approval of the honors committee.

THE UNIVERSITY OF ILLINOIS HONORS PROGRAMS. For many years honors programs have been in existence at the University of Illinois, operating in a more or less informal, uncoordinated fashion. However, in 1958, the programs were officially recognized by the board of trustees. Since then they have been expanded and coordinated through a Director of University Honors Programs.

The Director of University Honors Programs and the Faculty Honors Council, an advisory group, are charged with selecting and providing guidance to a group of superior students from each freshman class beginning with the 1959-60 entering class. These students will be known as the Edmund J. James Scholars in honor of one of the distinguished presidents of the University. These selected scholars will major in the field of their choice and will participate in specific departmental honors programs. They will be provided with an enriched program of studies suited to their needs. The program will be such as to qualify these scholars for graduate work in their chosen fields and stimulate them to pursue such advanced work. No monetary award is connected with the James Scholars, although many of them, no doubt, will receive scholarships from various sources.

Eligibility for the program will be determined by the students' grades during the first three and one-half years of their high-school careers. They must rank in the upper 30 per cent of their class at the end of the seventh semester of their schoolwork. Grades, recommendation of the high-school principal, and tests of aptitude and achievement will all be given consideration in the selection. The aptitude and achievement tests are given to all incoming freshmen, so no extra testing is required. It is anticipated that between 3 per cent and 5 per cent of each entering freshman class will qualify for the James Scholars Program. Some students who are not initially selected for the program may qualify in their sophomore and junior years if their work in college proves outstanding. On the other hand, poor performance on the part of selected students will result in their elimination from the program.

EXPERIMENTAL COURSES. A number of colleges and college-high school combinations offer special courses for the gifted. Ohio State University, for example, offers a course known as "Arts Survey 402." To be eligible for this course, which is open to freshmen only, a student must have a superior high-school record and score high on certain psychometric and proficiency tests. A quarter's work on the college level in which all grades are satisfactory is prerequisite to enrollment in the course. The course aims to give bright students the "broad background in history, natural science, political science, and sociology which potential leaders should have."

MacMurray College and Jacksonville (Illinois) High School cooperate in offering a course in philosophy to superior students at the high-school level. It is designed to give the student some concept of, and concern for, the basic ideas of mankind, so that when he enters college he will have a background which will facilitate his understanding of the significance of the educational experiences which the college offers. The course is planned by the college and taught by a member of its faculty. Only high-school seniors of superior ability are eligible to enroll in the course. Specific aims of the course include (1) the motivation of the student to formulate a philosophy of life, (2) the development of conceptual thinking and creativity, (3) the presentation of moral and ethical values, and (4) acquainting the student with the vital issues of Western civilization.

A number of other institutions over the country are experimenting with similar types of courses. All are attempting to discover better ways of meeting the educational needs of the gifted student as he moves through the high school and the college or university of his choice. The courses represent one means of adjusting the program to the interests and abilities of the gifted and as such merit continued experimentation and evaluation.

SELECTED READINGS

Bonthius, Robert H., Davis, F. James, and Drushal, J. Garber. *The Independent Study Program in the United States.* New York: Columbia University Press, 1957. 259 pp.

This is the report of a survey of twenty representative independent study programs in a like number of colleges and universities of the United States. The authors define independent study, trace its development, and indicate its extent preliminary to reporting on the nature and costs of independent study programs in the twenty selected institutions.

College Entrance Examination Board. *Advanced Placement Program.* New York: College Entrance Examination Board, 1956. 136 pp.

This publication of the College Entrance Examination Board gives an authoritative history and detailed description of the Advanced Placement Program, including course outlines and sample examination questions.

CONANT, JAMES B. *The American High School Today: A First Report to Interested Citizens.* New York: McGraw-Hill Book Co., 1959. 140 pp.

This report of Conant's recent study of American secondary education includes full explanation of the comprehensive high school, and twenty-one recommendations for improving the education of American youth. Almost without exception, these recommended practices can be found in operation in some of the schools visited during the study, though no school was found to include all of the suggested practices.

Fund for the Advancement of Education. *Bridging the Gap Between School and College,* (Evaluation Report No. 1.) New York: Fund for the Advancement of Education, 1953. 127 pp.

This publication was the first of the evaluation reports on programs sponsored by the Fund for the Advancement of Education. It discusses the nature and progress of four projects specifically directed at improving articulation between school and college and increasing the efficiency of general education at this level.

Fund for the Advancement of Education. *They Went to College Early.* (Evaluation Report No. 2.) New York: Fund for the Advancement of Education, 1957. 117 pp.

This publication provides a complete account of an experiment in early admission of high-school students to college. The experimental program, established in 1951, was financed by the Fund for the Advancement of Education. A major portion of the volume is devoted to reporting on the results of the evaluation of the program.

Fund for the Advancement of Education. *Better Utilization of College Teaching Resources.* (A report by the Committee on Utilization of College Teaching Resources.) New York: Fund for the Advancement of Education, 1959. 63 pp.

This booklet reports on the second year of the program of grants inaugurated by the Fund for the Advancement of Education in an attempt to secure better utilization of college teaching resources. Brief descriptions are given of the individual programs for which grants were made in twenty-seven colleges and universities throughout the United States.

Name Index

Aiken, Wilford, 420
Alberty, Elsie J., 409
American Association for Gifted Children, 288
Ames, Louise Bates, 416–17
Ausubel, David Paul, 80–82
Ayres, Eugene, 259

Bentley, John Edward, 26, 29, 31, 377
Blow, Susan, 326
Bole, Mrs. Benjamin Patterson, 278
Bonthius, Robert H., 457
Bossing, Nelson, 408
Brandwein, Paul, 15, 118, 121

Caesar, Irving, 314
Carroll, Herbert A., 212
Carson, Rachel, 298
Cole, Charles C., Jr., 126, 456
Conant, Dr. James B., 38, 136, 422
Cox, Catharine, 70
Cronbach, Lee, 139 n, 151 n
Cutts, Norma E., 407

Davis, F. J., 457
DeHaan, Robert F., 367, 432
Donovan, Charles F., S. J., 454
Douglass, Harl R., 401
Drushal, J. G., 457

Frampton, Merle Elbert, 69 n

Gesell, Arnold, 416–17
Gilmer, B. Von Haller, 302
Gowan, John, 128–29
Gruhn, William T., 401

Guilford, J. P., 13

Harris, William T., 26, 187
Havighurst, Robert J., 5, 265 n, 293, 335 n, 390
Heck, Arch O., 32, 146–47, 230
Herbart, Johann F., 23–24
Hildreth, Gertrude H., 296, 376
Hollingworth, Leta S., 4, 66, 70, 74, 75, 76, 85–86, 92, 93, 296, 391, 428 n
Hughes, Raymond M., 258–59
Hymes, James L., Jr., 331

Ilg, Frances L., 416–17

Kelvin, Lord, 23
Kennedy, Dr. John, 27
Keys, Noel 83–85, 89, 99,
Klausmeier, Herbert J., 396, 415
Kough, Jack, 367

Lamson, Edna E., 69, 78, 84, 88,
Lancelot, Willim H., 258–59
Larrick, Nancy, 311–12
Lehman Harvey, 129 n
Lightfoot, Georgia Frances, 79, 92
Locke, John, 24
Lowell, A. L. 448
Lurry, Lucile L., 409

McDonald, Robert Alexander Fyfe, 28
Martens, Elise H., 340
Mead, Margaret, 125–26
Meier, Norman, 17
Moore, Margaret Whiteside, 90

477

Moseley, Nicholas, 407

Newland, T. Ernest, 65, 280
Norris, Mrs. Dorothy, 278

Oden, Melita H., 12, 73–74, 81, 92, 100, 197
Orwell, George, 186–87

Passow, A. Harry, 338–39, 392 n, 395, 424
Pressey, Sidney L., 100, 197, 202

Robinson, E. E., 456
Rothney, J. W. M., 154

Scheifele, Marian, 363–67
Stendler, Celia B., 338–39
Stivers, Eugene, 432
Strang, Ruth, 434
Sumption, Merle R., 85

Terman, Lewis, 4, 12, 73–74, 76–77, 81, 92, 100, 141–42, 197

Genetic Studies of Genius, 66
    Vol. I, Mental and Physical traits of a Thousand Gifted Children, 1926, 66, 77, 87, 95
    Vol. II, The Early Mental Traits of Three Hundred Geniuses, 1926, 66, 70
    Vol. III, The Promise of Youth, 1930, 66, 83, 95, 97
    Vol. IV, The Gifted Child Grows Up, 1947, 66, 84, 90, 97, 100–101
    Vol. V, The Gifted Group at Mid-Life, 1959, 66, 70, 74, 77, 91–92, 98–99, 100–102
    summary of his research, 103–5

Wallas, G., 12
Watson, John, 24
Wilson, Dr. Frank T., 69, 377
Witte, Karl, 23
Witty, Paul, 5, 7, 13, 129 n, 428
Wright, Grace, 408

Subject Index

A

Abilities
  academic, 11–12
  artistic, 16–17
  creative, 12–13
  leadership, 13–15
  mechanical, 17
  scientific, 15–16
Abstract thinking, mental characteristic of the gifted, 121
Academic ability, 11–12
Academic achievement
  differences due to personality, 113
  individual differences, 111
Acceleration
  accelerated students superior to nonaccelerated, 104
  advantages, 195–98
  colleges, 192–94
  definition, 163, 187–88
  disadvantages, 198–201
  early admission, 164–67, 188–89
  favorable to social and educational adjustment, 85
  forms of, 188–92
  gifted need to begin careers early, 202–3
  historical developments, 28–29
  New York City plans, 28
  present organization and practice, 187–203
  rapid progress programs, 167–71, 190–92
  research studies, 195, 201, 230
  secondary schools, 192–94
  skipping, 167, 189–90
  summer school, 192–93
  types of programs, 163

Achieve, desire to, 100
Achievement (*see also* Scholastic achievement)
  individual motivation affects, 100, 130–32
  quotients, 103
  research studies, 86–92
  stimulating, 127
  tests, 57–58, 87, 148–49
  well-balanced temperament important, 100
Activities
  leisure, 92–96 (*see also* Leisure activities)
  outdoor, 114
  solitary, 95
Activity interest, 87
Administration of education for the gifted, 157
  acceleration, 162–71
    early admission, 164–67
    rapid progress, 167–71
    skipping, 167
  criteria for, 178–80
  enrichment programs, 162–63, 171–78
    individual programs, 175–76
    in seminars, 174–75
    in special classes, 173–75
    in special schools, 172–73
    through the regular classroom teacher plan, 176–77
    through the special teacher plan, 177–78
  financing, 180–82
  in the individual school, 160–62
  number of gifted pupils, 157–58

Administration of education (*Cont.*)
  orienting teachers to the program, 179
  practices, 162–78
  school system, 159–60
  screening program, 179
  selecting teachers for the program, 179
  staff advisory committees, 161–62
  system-wide programs, 160–61, 178
Administrators
  assist teacher of the gifted, 245
  relationship with teachers, 253
Adolescence
  age limits, 387
  characteristics of, 388–89
  dating, 144
  desire for economic independence, 389
  developmental tasks, 390
  fifteen-year olds, 417
  fourteen-year olds, 417
  gangs and clubs, 389
  gifted, 391–92
  growth and development, 387–92
  need for counseling, 144
  reading interests of, 95
  reliance on peer group, 388
  senior high school pupils, 416–18
  social activity, 387
Advanced Placement Program, 36, 451–56
  advantages, 453
  attendance at summer school, 451
  definition, 451
  examinations, 452
  sponsored by the College Entrance Examination Board, 452
Advanced Standing Program, 468–69
Affection, need for, 42
Age, as a factor in identifying gifted students, 50
Amusements, enjoyed by the gifted, 94
Andover Academy, 466
Approbation, desire for, 127
Aptitude tests, 58–59, 138–39
  types of, 139
  used for guidance, 58–59
Arithmetical reasoning ability, 15

Arlington County (Virginia) public schools, 357
Art activities, offered by the community, 269, 272
Art expositions, 433
Artistic ability, 16–17
  characteristic traits, 17
  preschool child, 45–46
Artistic interests, 117
Attention, span of, 124
Attitude and interest tests, 139
Attitudes
  negative, 112
  toward education of the gifted, 343–44
Audio-visual materials, 208, 244

B

Backgrounds of the gifted, socio-economic, 134
Baltimore (Maryland) schools, 28, 36
Batavia (New York) schools, 27
Behavior, junior high pupils, 401–4
Belgium, education of the gifted, 33
Belonging, need for, 337
Bernreuter Inventory of Personality, 76, 84, 139
Block scheduling of gifted students, 406–8
Board of education, 159
Boasting, 120
Book and creative writing exhibits, 433
Books, literature for young children, 309–13 (*see also* Reading)
Boredom with school tasks, 195, 198
Boston College, 454
Boston University, 36
Boy Scouts, 283
Brockton (Massachusetts) schools, 35
Budgets, program for the gifted, 180–82
Buffalo, University of, 443–44
Buildings, school, 342, 397–99
Businessmen, aid seminar program, 274

C

California, University of, 89

California Achievement Tests, 149
Cambridge plan, 27
Carnegie Corporation of New York, 38
Character traits, 104
  gifted superior to control group in, 77–78
  research studies on, 77–82
Characteristics of giftedness, 10
  cultural and social, 109–10
  general, 108–11
  mental, 121–24
  physical, 109
Cheating, 75
Chicago, University of, 164
  Committee on Human Development, 284, 286
  programs for the gifted, 442–43
Child study courses, 240
Civic responsibility, research studies, 102–3
Clark University, 287
Classes
  enrichment in regular, 205–12
  optimum size, 254
    kindergarten and nursery school, 330–31
  special, 218–20
    enrichment in, 173–75
Clay, playing with, 308
Cleveland (Ohio) schools, 29, 31, 32, 36
  Major Work program, 85, 173, 218, 229, 278
Collections and collecting, 94, 95, 114–15
  interest in making, 50
  scientific, 94
College Entrance Examination Board
  Advanced Placement Program sponsored by, 452
  Advanced Standing Program, 468–69
College programs, 442–75
  academic superiority of gifted students, 86–92
  acceleration, 192–94
  achievement of gifted, 89
  admission program, 159, 442–75
    early programs, 442–44

admission with advanced standing, 194
advanced placement, 451–56
current practice and programs, 444–75
curricular adaptations, 446–47
early admission, 164–66, 193, 447–51, 469–72
  evaluation of the program, 470
  qualification for entrance, 469
  They Went to College Early, 470–72
enrichment programs, 176
experimental projects, 444–46, 465–75
  admission to college with advanced standing, 468–69
  Atlanta Experiment in Articulation and Enrichment, 468
  early admission to college, 469–72
  experimental courses, 474–75
  Honors College Project, 473
  Location of Talented Students Program, 472
  Portland-Reed College Program, 467–68
  Study of General Education, 466–67
  University of Illinois Honors Programs, 473–74
failure of superior pupils to go to, 150
grades of gifted students, 91
guidance program for the gifted, 445
honors programs, 454–56, 473–74
income of graduates, 98–99
independent study, 456–60
materials and equipment, 464–65
need for cooperation between secondary schools and, 444–45, 467
percentage of gifted who attend, 90–91
personnel adaptations, 460–64
  adjustments in teaching load, 461–62
  guidance personnel, 462–63
  instructional staff, 460–62
  tutorial personnel, 463–64

College programs (*Cont.*)
rapid progress programs, 169–71
underage students, 90, 99
Columbia University, 36, 164
Committees, staff advisory, 161–62
Community, role of, 258–88
action taken by, 278–85
agencies serving the gifted, 266–77
recreational programs, 267
American, 261–88
attitude toward education of the gifted, 343–44
concern for program for the gifted, 262–63
general programs, 283–84
local control of education, 261–62
motivation of the gifted, 277–78
musical activities, 271–72
opportunity centers, 281–82
programs for identifying the gifted, 279–81
self-survey, 280
provisions for the gifted, 263–66
factors influencing, 265
related state and national programs, 287–88
research center, 282
responsible for searching out talent, 259–61, 273
special programs, 284–85
supplementing the school, 282–83
theaters, 271, 272
use of resources as a teaching method, 374–76
Conceit, grouping the gifted does not cause, 227, 229
Concept of giftedness, 108
Concepts, ability of gifted to form, 121–22
Conferences, parent-teacher (*see* Parent-teacher conferences)
Conformity, 112, 378
social pressures and, 125–26
Conscientiousness of gifted child, 120
Consultant, program, 161
Cooperation, 120
Cooperative Tests, 149
Coordinator, program, 161
Core program
characteristics of, 409–10

junior high schools, 408–9
senior high schools, 424
Corporations, scholarships provided by, 262, 281, 284, 288
Correspondence courses, 176
Cost of educational programs, 229, 263–65
Counseling the gifted, 141–45 (*see also* Guidance of the gifted)
adolescents, 144–45
definition, 142
in educational guidance, 149–50
in elementary schools, 143
gifted have multiple potentials, 154
group, 142
in secondary schools, 143–44
vocational guidance and, 152–55
Courtesy, 120
Creative abilities, 12–13
definition, 12
measuring, 13
preschool child, 44–45
teacher must stimulate, 234–35
Creative imagination, 121, 122
Creative thinking, 13
Creativity
stimulating, 234–35, 297
in elementary school, 376–83
research studies, 377
Criticism of American education, 38–39
Cultural characteristics of the gifted, 109–10
Cumulative records
educational guidance based on, 149
importance of, 252
interpretation of, 60–62
used in the guidance of the gifted, 139–41
vocational guidance based on, 151–52
what it should include, 140
Curiosity of the gifted, 114, 118, 297
keeping spark alive, 376–77
Curriculum
bulletins, 357
core, 409–10
junior high schools, 408–9
senior high schools, 424

determines structure and equipment, 398
effect of limited, on the gifted, 134
elementary schools, 347–68
  geared to individual needs and interests, 349–52, 380
  general content, 349–52
  guides to language art activities, 357–68
  other language arts, 355–57
  play, 348–49
  reading, 352–55
guides, 350
junior high school, 404–12
secondary schools, 396, 420
senior high school, 416, 420, 424
state requirements, 349

D

Dallas Public Library, 285
Dalton, Massachusetts, 32
Dating, 144
Dayton (Ohio) Boys' Choir, 285
Definition of giftedness, 4–10
  comparative, 5–6
  descriptive, 5
  objective, 4–5
  superior intellectual ability, 6
Democracy
  confused idea concerning, 258–59
  in education, 259
  education for the gifted and, 205
  grouping the gifted called undemocratic, 226
  teacher must understand principles of, 238
Denver, Colorado, 35
Dependability, 111
Dependence as a personality trait, 120
Description of the gifted child, 92
Development (see also Growth and development)
  adolescent, 387–92
  developmental tasks, 294, 335–36
  elementary school pupils, 333–37
    developmental tasks, 335–36
  preschool child, 290–95
  senior high pupils, 416–18

Developmental aspects of giftedness, 4
Developmental tasks
  adolescence, 390
  elementary school pupils, 335–36
Discipline
  elementary schools, 380
  preschool child, 291
  reactions of child to, 51
  resentment toward physical punishment, 51
Discussion method of teaching, 242–43, 372–73
Divorce rate, 101
Docility, not indicative of giftedness, 49
Drill procedures, 371–72
  overemphasis on, 379
Drives, to achieve, 131
Drop-out rate for superior pupils, 150

E

Early admission to college, 447–51, 469–72
  advantages and disadvantages, 448–49
  attendance at summer school, 447
  preferable alternatives, 450–51
Early admission to elementary schools, 164–67
East Meadow (New York) schools, 35
Education
  democracy in, 259
  effect of Russian-made satellite on, 38–39
  goals and objectives
    elementary schools, 337–41
    secondary schools, 392–97
  historical background, 21–39
  local control, 261–62
  preschool child, 295–98
  of teachers, 239–48
Education for the gifted
  administration of, 157–82
  criticism of, 39
  effect of Russian-made satellite on, 38–39
  not undemocratic, 39, 93–94

Education for the gifted (*Cont.*)
  policies concerning the gifted,
    159–60
  present organization and practice,
    184–230
Educational achievement of the
  gifted, 68
Educational Policies Commission, 37,
  393 *n*, 410, 415
Eight-Year Study, 420
Elementary schools
  couseling services in, 143
  curriculum, 347–68
    general content, 349–52
    guides to language art activities,
      357–68
    other language arts, 355–57
    play, 348–49
    reading, 352–55
  developing creativity, 376–83
  discipline, 380
  early admission, 164–65, 167
  educational goals and objectives,
    337–41
    individual responsibility, 340–41
    social responsibility, 338–40
  enrichment classes, 174
    individual programs, 176
  environment, 341–44
    attitudinal climate, 343–44
    physical plant, 342–43
  individual adjustment, 382
  instructional program, 344–83
    curriculum, 347–68
    objectives, 344–47
  materials and equipment, 381
  methods of teaching the gifted,
    368
    community approach, 374–76
    discussion, 372–73
    group work, 371
    influence of personality, 369
    problem approach, 369–71
    routine drill, 371–72
    work units, 373–74
  number of gifted, 158
  optimum class size, 254
  outcomes, 381–82
  program, 333–83
  pupil growth and development,
    333–37

common needs, 336–37
  continuity of growth, 334–35
  developmental tasks, 335–36
  rapid progress, 168–70
  social responsibility, 382
Elizabeth (New Jersey) schools, 26
Emotional behavior, adolescents, 391
Emotional characteristics, 75–77
  research studies, 75–77
Emotional development, 146–47
Emotional health, of teachers, 237–
  38
Emotional maladjustments, due to
  acceleration, 199–200
Emotional reactions, junior high
  pupils, 401–4
Emotional stability, parents are responsible for building, 302
English courses, 436
Enrichment, 171–78
  definition, 171
  function of, 203–4
  goals of the program, 209–10
  group, 215–24
    special classes, 218–20
    special schools, 172–73, 215–18
  historical development, 29–32
  individual programs, 175–76, 185,
    205–15
  junior high schools, 412
  materials and equipment required,
    206–8
  number of, 32
  present organization and practice,
    203–24
  program must be carefully plan-
    ned, 204–5
  publications giving specific sugges-
    tions, 210
  in regular classes, 205–12
    advantages, 211
    disadvantages, 212
  research studies, 230
  in seminars, 174–75, 220–24
  in special classes, 173–75, 218–20
    purpose of, 219
    selecting pupils for, 218
  in special schools, 215–18
    require talented teachers, 217

special teachers, 177–78, 212–15
 involves staff cooperation, 213–
 14
 through the regular classroom
 teacher plan, 176–77
Environment, 302–20
 achievement stimulated by, 16
 elementary schools, 341–44
 for preschool child, 302–20
 literature for young children,
 309–13
 love and security, 302–3
 music, 313–16
 rich vital experiences, 303–5
 toys, 305–9
 secondary schools, 397–99
Equality of opportunity
 faulty conception, 186–87, 205
 grouping the gifted and, 226
Equipment, 180
 for colleges, 464–65
 elementary schools, 342–43, 381
 for enrichment program, 208–9
 secondary schools, 397–99
 for senior high schools, 430
 special classes, 220
Europe, education of the gifted,
 33–34
Evaluation of program for the gifted,
 157
 periodic, 180
 practices, 434
 secondary schools, 392
Evanston (Illinois) schools, 35
Excel, desire to, 119
Exeter Academy, 466
Experiences
 for developing social responsibility, 340
 for preschool child, 303–5
 with living things, 316–17
 provided by nursery and kindergarten programs, 327–28
 teaching-learning
 secondary schools, 395–96, 398
 senior high school, 427–28
Experimental programs for the
 gifted in college, 465–76
Extension services, 246
Extracurricular activities, 173, 433
 faculty supervision, 437–38

opportunities for leadership, 438–
 39
 participation in, 83–84, 438
 purpose of, 437–38
 role of teacher, 255–56
 scheduling, 439
 secondary schools, 436–39
 types of, 437
 value of, 256, 437

F

Failure
 ability to accept, 119
 in academic achievement, 111–12
 fear of, 131–32
 social, 146
Family background
 college attendance and, 150
 effects choice of vocation, 152
Family relationships, preschool chil-
 dren, 317–18
Federal aid for education, 262
Field projects, 459
Field trips, 374–75
Films and film strips
 foreign, 272–73
 home movies, 300
Financing program for the gifted,
 180–82, 229, 263–65
Finger paints, use of, 308
First grade, early entrance, 188
Ford Foundation, 89
Fund for the Advancement of Ed-
 ucation (*see* Fund for the Ad-
 vancement of Education)
Foreign languages
 in junior high schools, 412
 in senior high schools, 425
Forest Hills High School, New York
 City, 425
Foundations, scholarships provided
 by, 262
4-H program, 275–76
France, education of the gifted, 33
Free association tests, 87
Free-choice period, 348
Friends, ability of gifted to make,
 92–93
Fund for the Advancement of Edu-
 cation, 89, 201–2

Fund for the Advancement (*Cont.*)
  advance placement program, 451
  experimental programs sponsored
    by, 465–75
  admission to college with ad-
    vanced standing, 468–69
  Atlanta Experiment in Articula-
    tion and Enrichment, 468
  in curricular adaptations, 447
  early admission to college, 469–
    72
  experimental courses, 474–75
  Honors College Project, 473
  Location of Talented Students
    Program, 472
  Portland-Reed College Program,
    467
  Study of General Education,
    466–67
  University of Illinois Honors
    Programs, 473–74
  Program for Early Admission to
    College, 448
  They Went to College Early, 470–
    72
Fund scholars, 469

G

Games preferred by gifted, 94, 115
Gangs and clubs, 389
Gardening experiences, 317
Gates Basic Reading Test, 149
General characteristics of the gifted,
  108–11
General intelligence, 121
Generalize, power to, 122
Geniuses, 10
  emotional characteristics, 75
  number of, 10
George Peabody College, 36
Germany, education of the gifted, 33
Giftedness
  characteristics of, 10
  concept, 4, 108
  definition, 3
    types, 4–10
  developmental aspects, 4
  manifestations of, 11–19
    academic ability, 11–12
    artistic ability, 16

creative ability, 12–13
leadership ability, 13–15
mechanical ability, 17–19
scientific ability, 15–16
nature of, 3–19
potential and performance, 10–11
specific characteristics, 10
Girl Scouts, 283
Goals, educational
  elementary schools, 337–41
  preschool, 295–98
  secondary schools, 392–97
Government and politics, stimulating
  interest in, 276–77
Grades and grading
  achieved by gifted students, 89–
    90
  of gifted students in college, 91
  scholastic achievement and, 88
  senior high schools, 426
  used to identify the gifted, 52–53
Great Britain, education of the
  gifted, 33
Greece, education of the gifted, 21–
  22
Group work, as a teaching method,
  371
Grouping of gifted pupils, 185–86,
  224–29
  ability, 205
  advantages, 224–26
  basis for, 186
  disadvantages, 226–29
  for instruction in reading, 353–54
Growing things, experiences with,
  317
Growth and development
  adolescent, 387–92
  developmental tasks and, 294–95
  elementary school pupils, 333–37
    continuity of growth, 334–35
    developmental tasks, 335–36
  fifteen-year olds, 417–18
  fourteen-year olds, 417
  junior high pupils, 401–4
  norms, 293–94
  plateaus, 293
  preschool child, 290–95
  rate of, 292
  senior high pupils, 416–18
  understanding patterns of, 293

Guidance of the gifted, 108–46
  aptitude tests used for, 58–59
  college programs, 445–46, 462–63
  concerning available scholarships, 435
  counseling, 135, 136
  counselors, 135, 431
    number needed, 136
    professionally trained, 431
    role of, 435
  educational, 145–50
    counseling, 149–50
    cumulative records, 149
    observation and tests, 147–49
    overachievement, 146
    underachievement, 145
  evaluation practices, 434
  function of, 436
  general characteristics, 108–11
  individual differences among the gifted, 111–13
  intelligence tests used in, 56
  interests, 113–17
  junior high school, 401, 406
  knowledge of handicaps and limitations, 137
  mental characteristics, 121–24
  mental hygiene, 132–35
  motivation, 124–32
    individual, 130–32
    social, 125–30
  observation and tests, 147–49
  by parents, 135–36
  personal, 137, 434
    counseling, 141–45
    cumulative records, 139–41
    observation and tests, 137–39
  personality traits, 117–21
  principles of, 434–35
  problem of underachievement, 432–34
  program, 180
  purpose of, 135
  secondary schools, 431–39
  in social problems, 434
  teacher training for, 136, 242
  by teachers, 136
  types of, 135–37
  vocational, 150–55
    counseling, 152–55

  cumulative record, 151–52
  observation and tests, 151
Guides, curriculum, 350

H

Handicapped children, state aid, 182
Handicaps, as a spur to greater achievement, 16–17
Handwriting, 355–56
Harvard University, 448, 466
  Advance Placement Program, 453
Health, 103, 108–9
  gifted and average children compared, 71–75
Health record
  effects choice of vocation, 152
  used to identify the gifted, 53–54
Height, gifted and average children compared, 71–75
Highly gifted children (I.Q. over 170), 104
Historical development in education of the gifted child, 21–39
  beginning of a new era, 38–39
  differences in mental ability, 24–26
  early attempts to accommodate the gifted, 26–29
    acceleration, 28–29
    enrichment, 29–32
    flexible promotion, 26
  early history in western culture, 21–24
  at mid-twentieth century, 33–38
    in Europe, 33–34
    in the United States, 34–38
Hobby clubs, 437
Homework, 95
Honesty, 111
Honors College Project, 473
Honors earned by gifted students, 89, 90
Honors programs, 254, 421
  college, 454–56, 473–74
    administration of, 454–55
    teachers, 455, 460
Honors Programs, University of Illinois, 473–74
Horace Mann–Lincoln Institute of School Experimentation, New York City, 35

Houston (Texas) schools, 36
Human relations, ability in, 19
    preschool children, 317–18
Human resources, development of, 260
Humor, sense of, 120
Hunter College Elementary School, New York City, 36, 69, 75, 172, 215, 376

I

Ideas
    fluency of, 123
    "joy of ideas," 121–22
Identification and Education of the Academically Talented Student in the American Secondary School, The, 38
Identification of the gifted child, 41–62, 228
    community programs for, 279–81
    community self-survey, 280
    formal methods, 52–62
    health records, 53–54
    informal methods, 42–52
    parental observations, 43–47
    preschool children, 324–26
    standardized tests, 55–62
    teacher observations, 48–52
    teachers' marks, 52–53
    test scores, 54–55
Illinois, University of, 36
    Honors Programs, 473–74
    research program on the gifted, 36
Imaginary playmates, 94, 115
    some gifted children develop, 93
Improvise, ability to, 123
Income
    of the gifted, 98–99
    related to amount of education, 98–99
Independence
    achieving personal, 336
    child's need for, 302
    desire for, 131
    gifted child has sense of, 120
Independent study programs, 456–60
    academic credit for, 458

admission requirements, 457
    aims of, 456
    forms of, 458–59
    teachers for, 460
    values of, 459–60
Indiana University, 472
Indianapolis (Indiana) schools, 36
Individual differences among the gifted, 111–13
    academic achievement, 111–12
    personality traits, 113
    physical development, 113
Individual responsibility, goal of elementary education, 340–41
Individualized instruction, 243–44
    elementary schools, 382
    junior high schools, 405
    secondary schools, 397
Initiative of gifted children, 377
    education for, 296–97
Innate capacity, definition, 3
Insight, extraordinary, 122
Insight learning, 52
Instructional program, 397
    junior high school, 415–31
    senior high school, 415–31
Intellectual interests, 87
Intellectual status of the gifted, maintained through life, 67–71, 104
Intellectual traits, 121–24
Intellectually gifted, definition, 67
Intelligence
    nervous system, foundation of, 109
    of teachers, 233–34
    world places high premium on, 260
I.Q. (Intelligence quotient)
    indicates potential ability, 57
    individual differences, 111–13
    offspring of gifted parents, 101–2
    140 used as lower limit of gifted group, 3, 4
    stability of, as children grow, 68–70
Intelligence tests
    constancy of I.Q., 68–70
    help to predict academic success, 56
    historical development, 25–26
    range of abilities tested, 56

used in guidance counseling, 138–39
used to identify giftedness, 55–57
when given, 55
Interest Blanks, 83
Interest inventories, 60
Interests of the gifted, 94, 113–17
  artistic, 117
  individual differences in, 113
  intellectual, 87
  junior high school students, 403–4
  leisure, 92–96
  reading, 94–95, 114
  scientific, 116–17
  teachers should have diversified personal, 236–37
  tests, 139
  variety of, 113–14
Interviewing people, as a method of learning, 374–76
Invitational Conference for the Identification and Education of Academically Talented Students, 423, 435–36
Iowa High-School Content Examination, 88
Iowa Silent Reading Tests, 149
Iowa Tests of Educational Development, 149

J

Jacksonville (Illinois) High School, 475
James Scholars Program, 474
Jealous reactions, handling, 238
Jewish Youth League, 283
Jews, motivation toward intellectual achievement, 128
Junior Achievement, 275–77, 283
Junior high schools, 401–4
  block scheduling for the gifted, 406–8
  core program, 408–9
  curriculum, 404–12
  departmentalized organization, 405
  educational experiences for gifted students, 410–11
  electives, 406
  enrichment, 412
  first established, 400

goals and objectives, 399–401
guidance program, 401
individualized instruction, 405
instructional program, 399–431
interests of students, 403–4
materials, 414–15
methods of teaching, 412–14
organization of, 405
preparation of teachers, 407
problems of adolescence, 390
program, 404–12
pupils, 401–4
purposes, 399–401
rapid progress classes, 191, 406–7
school environment, 397–99
seminar programs, 220–24
subjects commonly offered, 406
use of special projects, 411
Junior Red Cross, 283

K

Kent State University, 36
Kindergarten
  early entrance, 188
  entrance requirements, 188, 328–29
  historical development, 326
  provide experiences children need, 327–28
  size of classes, 330
  tests used by teachers, 325
  value of education, 326–27
Kuhlman-Anderson Tests, 138

L

Laboratories
  facilities in colleges, 464–65
  research and experimentation, 458–59
  secondary schools, 397–99
Language ability
  babies, 43–44
  preschool child, 43–44
Language arts
  elementary school, 355–57
  guides to activities in, 357–68
Lawrence (Kansas) Children's Summer Studio, 286
Lawrenceville, 466

Leadership, 13–15
    among the gifted, 227
    definition, 13–14
    motivation and, 124–25
    personality traits, 14, 86
    political and social, 116
    potential of the gifted, 110
    relationship between the intelligence of the group and the leader, 86
    research studies, 83–86
    social sensitivity, 19
    social studies, 83–86
Learning
    insight, 52
    theories of, 241
    through play, 331
Leisure activities, 267–77
    of adults, 95
    of children, 92–95
    research studies, 92–96
Libraries, 265, 398
    community sponsored, 267–68
    creative writing clubs, 285
    junior high school, 414
    librarian offers guidance, 268
    program, 283
    research, 458
    senior high schools, 429
    story hours, 312
Listeners, gifted children are good, 118
Listening, instruction in, 355–56
Living things, experiences with, 316–17
Long Beach (California) schools, 36
Los Angeles (California) schools, 29–30, 32, 36
Love, child's need for security and, 42, 302–3

M

MacMurray College, 475
Maller Self-Marking Test, 81
Manifestation of giftedness, 11–19
Manual ability, preschool child, 44
Marital adjustment, research studies, 100–102
Marks, school, aid in vocational guidance, 151

Marriage of gifted people, 100–102
    divorce rate, 101
    I.Q. of offspring, 101–2
    research studies, 100–102
Materials, instructional
    in colleges, 464–65
    in elementary schools, 381
    for junior high schools, 414–15
    reading, 207–8
    for senior high schools, 429–31
    special classes, 220
    teacher education in, 244
    variety of, 206–7
Mathematics, 424–25
Mechanical ability, 17–18
    mechanical skill differs from, 18
Mechanical aptitude tests, 18
Mechanical ingenuity, 78
Memory of the gifted child, 123
Mental ability, differences in, 24–26
Mental characteristics, 121–24
    abstract thinking, 121
    power to generalize, 122
    power to reason inductively, 122–23
    rapid memorizing, 123–24
    research studies on, 67–71
    span of attention, 124
    vocabulary, 123
Mental health, 75, 132–35
    characteristics of good, 132
    gifted children as a group are superior in, 132–33
    problems of the gifted, 133
Mentally retarded children
    classes for, 25
    education of, 259
Metropolitan Achievement Tests, 149
Metropolitan Association for the Study of the Gifted, 288
Michigan State University, 473
Minnesota Occupational Scale, 99
Minority groups, motivation toward intellectual achievement, 128
Modern School Achievement Tests, 149
Moral development, preschool child, 303
Moral issues, interest in, 116
Mortality rate, 73–74, 103, 109

Motion pictures, used to record growth and development, 300
Motivation, 124–32
  by the community, 277–78
  individual, 130–32
    desire for independence, 131
    desire to achieve, 130–131
    fear of failure, 131
    social level affects, 130
    monetary reward a primary force, 129
  problems of, 124–25
  social, 125–30
Motor ability, 19
Muscle coordination, 44
Museums, 265, 266
  programs, 269
  of science, 269–70
Music, interest in, 117
Musical ability, preschool child, 45
Musical activities
  lessons, 315
  offered by the community, 271–72
  for preschool children, 45, 313–16

N

National Association for Gifted Children, 288
National Education Association, 38, 254, 423
National programs for the gifted, 288
National Youth Conference on the Atom, 277–78
Nationality, has no effect on giftedness, 109
Nearsightedness, 148
Needs, common needs of elementary school children, 336–37
Negroes, motivation toward intellectual achievement, 128
Nervous disorders, gifted less prone than average to, 77
Nervous system of superior quality, 109
New York City schools, 36
  accelerated programs, 28
  enrichment programs, 32
  intellectually gifted classes. 218

rapid progress classes, 191, 218, 406–7
  special-progress classes, 28
  special schools, 215
New York State, research program on the gifted, 36
Nonconformity, 112
  social pressures and, 125–26
Norfolk County, Virginia, 35
North Carolina, research program on the gifted, 36
Northwestern University, 36
Nursery schools, 320
  entrance requirements, 328–29
  provide experiences children need, 327–28
  size of classes, 330
  tests used by, 325
  value of, 326
Nutrition, gifted and average children compared, 73–75

O

Observations of gifted children
  educational guidance, 147–49
  of parents, 43–47
  of teachers, 48–52
  used by guidance counselor, 137–39
  vocational guidance and, 151
Occupational adjustment, research studies, 97–100
Ohio, research program on the gifted, 36
Ohio State University, 99–100, 474
One-sidedness, 104
Opportunity Centers, agencies providing opportunities for self-development, 281
Opposition to programs for the gifted, 39, 83, 93–94
Organizations dealing with the gifted, 288
Originality of thought and expression, 52, 118–19, 376–77
  education for, 296–97
Otis Quick-Scoring Mental Ability Test, 138
Otis Self-Administering Test of Mental Ability, 138

Overachievement, 146
    causes of, 124
Overpermissive parents, 303
Overprotective parents, 303
Overwork, gifted as a group do not,
    228–29

                        P

Parent-teacher conferences
    aid in counseling the child, 143
    aid in educational guidance, 150
    importance of, 180
Parents
    counseling by, 142
    exploitation of the gifted by, 133
    identifying the gifted, 43–47
    observations of, 43–47
    overpermissive, 303
    overprotective, 303
    responsibilities of, 298–320
        keeping records, 140–41, 299–
            300
        baby books, 299–300
        home movies, 300
        pictures, 300
        suggested record content,
            301–2
        tape recordings, 301
        providing a favorable environ-
            ment, 302–20
        love and security, 302–3
        rich vital experiences, 303–
            5
Peer group, adolescents relate with,
    388
Pennsylvania State University, 36
Peoria (Illinois) schools, 173–74
Performance
    individual motivation effects, 130–
        32
    physiological factors affecting, 130
    potential and, 10–11
Perseverance, gifted child has, 119
Persistence, 15
Personality tests, 139 (see also Tests
    and testing)
Personality traits, 104
    individual differences, 113
    not possessed by the gifted, 120–
        21
    possessed by the gifted, 117–21

research studies, 77–82
    sometimes militate against achieve-
        ment, 130
    used in counseling, 137
Pets provide good experiences, 316
Phi Beta Kappa, 89, 90, 91
Philosophical interests of gifted,
    115–16
Physical characteristics, 74–75
    individual differences, 113
    research studies, 71–75
Physical development, 42–43, 108–
    9, 146–47 (see also Growth and
    development)
    gifted child superior to average,
        70–75
    gifted children, 70–75
    research studies, 70–75
Physical growth, preschool child,
    290–95
Physical health, of teachers, 237–
    38
Physical traits, research studies on,
    74
Physique of gifted students, 103
Pictures
    for preschool children, 309
    used to record growth and devel-
        opment, 300
Pittsburgh (Pennsylvania) schools,
    36, 221
Plato's plan for the education of
    gifted children, 21–22
Play, 115
    children learn through, 331
    excellent source of learning, 348
    imaginary playmates, 93, 318–19
    toys for, 305–9
Play areas, for preschool children,
    320
Play groups, 319–20
    supervising, 320
Poetry, for preschool children, 311
Political leadership, 116
Portland (Oregon) Public Schools,
    35, 467
Potentials of the gifted, 154
    identifying, 11
    parents help child to develop, 41
    performance and, 10–11
Preschool child
    artistic ability, 45–46

creative ability, 44–45
identifying the gifted, 279
imaginary playmates, 93
language ability, 43–44
manual ability, 44
musical ability, 45
observing, 43
parental records of, 140–41
questions asked by, 44, 305
reading ability, 46, 313
reading aloud to, 46
Preschool program, 290–332
child growth and development, 290–95
educational goals, 295–98
environment, 302–20
experience with living things, 316–17
liaison between school and parents, 321–24
literature for young children, 309–13
musical activities, 313–16
need for rich vital experiences, 303–5
nursery and kindergarten, 326–31
parental responsibilities, 298–320
keeping records, 299–302
baby books, 299–300
home movies, 300
pictures, 300
suggested record content, 301–2
tape recordings, 301
providing a favorable environment, 302–20
experience with living things, 316–17
literature, 309–13
love and security, 302–3
music, 313–16
play areas, 320
play groups, 319–20
playmates, 318–19
relationships with other people, 317–18
rich vital experiences, 303–5
toys, 305–9
reading readiness, 46, 313
relationships with other people, 317–18

school responsibilities, 321–31
liaison with home, 321–24
testing service, 324–26
toys, 305–9
Pressures, social, 125
working against outstanding achievement, 126, 129–30
Prestige motivation, 80–82, 127
Princeton University, 466
Principal, education of the gifted and, 160–62
Problem-centered teaching, 52, 243, 369–71
Procreation rate of the gifted, 101–2, 105
Professional education of teachers, 240–44
Professional people, aid seminar program, 274
Proficiency examinations, 189, 194
used by colleges to determine early admissions, 443
Programs, educational
acceleration, 28–29, 163–71
administration, 157–82 (see also Administration of education for the gifted)
community, 285–87
cost of, 229
enrichment, 29–32
evaluation of, 157
gifted child sometimes frustrated by, 133–34
need for a balanced, 147
objectives, 187
opposition to, 83
orienting teachers for, 179
research, 35
secondary school, 386–441
selecting teachers for, 179
state and national, 287–88
supervisor or consultant, 161
system-wide, 160–61, 178
usually geared to the average child, 145
Promotions
double, 189, 190
double-track plan, 27
flexible, 26–28, 187
Santa Barbara plan, 27
"social," 190

Psychology, educational, 241
Psychometrists, 325
Public Schools, few extremely gifted
    children in, 93
Publicity program of schools, 322
Puppetry and marionettes, 271

Q

"Questing," 15, 118
Questions, of preschool child, 305
Quincy (Illinois) Youth Develop-
    ment Commission, 284, 286–87

R

Race
    effect on intellectual achievement,
        127–28
    has no effect on giftedness, 109
Radio and television
    educational, 323
    story hours on, 312–13
Rapid progress programs, 167–71,
    190–92
    junior high schools, 406–7
Ratio of gifted children in schools,
    157–58
Readiness, concept of, 41–42, 313
Reading
    aloud to children, 46, 310
    elementary-school program, 352–
        55
    gifted children learn to read be-
        fore entering school, 114, 313
    grouping for instruction, 353
    guides for stimulating gifted chil-
        dren, 357–68
    individualized program, 353
    literature for young children, 309–
        13
    materials, 207–8
    need for differentiating instruction
        in, 352
    to the preschool child, 309–13
    primers and preprimers, 352
    program for teachers, 247
    readiness programs, 313
    story hours, 312
    use of library and, 268, 352

Reading ability
    preschool children, 46
    research studies on, 68
Reading interests, 114
    research studies, 94–95
Records
    baby book, 299
    color slides, 300
    cumulative (see also Cumulative
        records)
        factual items on, 61
        interpretation of, 60–62
        used in the guidance of the
            gifted, 139–41
    home movies, 300
    kept by parents, 299–302
    medical, 301
    parental record of the preschool
        child, 140–41
    pictures, 300
    tape recordings, 301
Recreational programs, 267
    play areas, 320
Red Cross courses, 270
Reed College, 467–68
Religion, effect on intellectual
    achievement, 129
Research
    community research center, 282
    definition, 64
    developing skills in, 243
    marital adjustment, 100–102
    occupational adjustment, 97–100
Research on the gifted, 35, 64–103
    character and personality traits,
        77–82
    civic responsibility, 102–3
    descriptions of educational pro-
        grams not research, 64–65
    emotional characteristics, 75–77
    enrichment and acceleration, 230
    high school curriculum, 420
    leisure activities, 92–96
    by Leta S. Hollingworth, 66–67
    mental characteristics, 67–71
    physical characteristics, 71–75
    scholastic achievement, 86–92
    social adjustment and leadership,
        83–86
    studies based on acceptable pro-
        cedures, 66

summary of Terman's research,
103–5
Resource units, 350
Responsibility
individual, 340–41
social, 338–40
willingness to assume, 120
Rewards, in community programs,
277
Rewards for scholastic achievement,
433
Rochester (New York) schools, 29–
31
Rome, education of gifted children,
22–23
Routine drill, 371–72
overemphasis on, 379

S

Safety measures, preschool child,
303
St. Louis Public Schools, 187, 326
San Francisco schools, 36
education of gifted children, 27–
28
San Francisco State College, 36
Santa Barbara (California) schools,
27
Scholarships
counselor advises concerning, 435
sources, 262
state programs, 288
student loan service and, 281
won by young entrants to college,
90
Scholastic achievement
college students, entering under
sixteen and a half, 90
grades received and, 88
honors earned by the students, 89
inferior, 91
research studies, 86–92
school subjects preferred by
gifted, 87
School retardation of the gifted, 104
Schools
compulsory attendance, 387
elementary (*see* Elementary
schools)

high schools *see* Senior high
schools)
open house or parents' nights, 322
periodical newsletters, 322
preschool (*see* Preschool program)
publicity program, 322
radio and television programs, 323
responsibilities for preschool program, 321–31
secondary (*see* Secondary schools)
special, 215–18
group enrichment in, 172–73
Science
courses, 425
fairs, 433
laboratory equipment, 430–31
laboratory research, 458–59
Scientific ability, 15–16
definition, 15
personality traits, 16
value and importance of, 15
Scientific interests, 116–17
Screening program for the discovery
of the gifted, 179
Secondary schools, 386–441
acceleration, 192–94
administrative organization, 386
adolescent growth and development, 387–92
adolescent period, 387
characteristics of adolescence,
388–89
gifted adolescents, 391–92
problems of adolescence, 390–
91
college-level courses for gifted
seniors, 193–94
counseling services, 143
early admission, 164, 166
educational goals and objectives,
392–97
ten imperative needs of youth,
393–94
enrichment classes, 174
environment, 397–99
extracurricular activities, 436–39
guidance program, 143, 431–39
instructional program, 399–431
individual, 397
junior high school, 399–415
senior high school, 415–31

Secondary schools (*Cont.*)
  junior high schools (*see* Junior
    high schools)
  need for cooperation between col-
    leges and, 444–45, 467
  number attending, 393
  number having organized pro-
    grams for the gifted, 429
  optimum class size, 254
  program, 386–441
  rapid progress programs, 169–70
  ratio of gifted, 158
  seminar programs, 220–24
  senior high schools (*see* Senior
    high schools)
  special schools, 215–18
  teaching-learning experiences,
    395–96, 398
Security, child's need for love and,
  302–3, 334, 337
Self-confidence, 119–20
Self-diagnosis, tests aid in, 139
Self-expression, 378
Self-sufficiency, 131
Seminar programs for the gifted,
  174–75, 220–24, 254
  advantages, 222–23
  hours for, 221
  use of business and professional
    people, 274
Senior high schools
  academic superiority of gifted stu-
    dents, 86–92
  college entrance requirements, 420
  college preparation, 415
  core program, 424
  courses recommended for gifted,
    422–23
  curriculum, 416, 418–19
  grading systems, 426
  honors classes, 421
  materials for instruction, 429–31
  problems of adolescence, 390–91
  program, 418–27
  pupils, 416–18
  purposes, 415–31
  school environment, 397–99
  superiority of gifted children in,
    88
  teaching-learning experiences,
    420–21

teaching methods, 427–29
Sexes
  effect on intellectual achievement,
    128–29
  gifted evenly distributed between,
    109
Sexual adjustment, 100–102, 104,
  389
Sharing, by preschool children, 318–
  19
Skipping, 167
  disadvantages, 198
  present organization and practice,
    189–90
Skokie (Illinois) schools, 175
Slow learners, 24–25
Snobbery, grouping the gifted does
  not cause, 227, 229
Social activity, adolescence, 387
Social adjustment
  of gifted men, 100
  research studies, 83–86
Social competence, 19
Social development, 109–11, 146–47
Social interest, 87
Social issues, interest in, 116
Social leadership, 14–15, 116
Social maladjustment, due to accel-
    eration, 199–200
Social motivation, 125–30
  desire for prestige, 127
  social pressures, 125
  social status, 125
Social pressure, 125–26
Social problems, junior high pupils,
  401–4
Social promotion, 190
Social responsibility, goal of ele-
    mentary school education, 338–
    40, 382
Social sensitivity, 19, 110, 217, 341
  senior high students, 418
Socioeconomic backgrounds, gifted
    affected by, 134
Sociometric tests, 60, 81
Special classes, 218–20
  enrichment in, 173–74
Special schools
  enrichment by means of, 215–18
  group enrichment in, 172–73
Speech, training in, 355–56, 436

Speed tests, 74
Spelling, elementary school, 355
Speyer School, 79
Sports, 95–96
Standardized tests, 55–62
Stanford Achievement Tests, 87, 149
Stanford-Binet scale, 67
  Terman-Merrill revision of, 138
Stanford University, 36
  independent study program, 456,
  458
State programs for the gifted, 180–
  82, 287–88
  curriculum supervised by, 349
  teacher institutes, 246–47
Status
  monetary rewards contribute to,
  125
  social, 125
  socioeconomic, 127
Stereotype of the gifted child, 75
Strength of gifted children, 74
Strong Vocational Interest Test, 97
Study habits, 176
Stuttering, 76
Stuyvesant High School, New York
  City, 28
Success, 97–100
  ability to accept failure and, 144–
  45
  definition, 154
Suleiman the Magnificent, 23
Summer schools, 264
  rapid progress programs and, 170
  used in acceleration procedures,
  192–93
Superintendent of schools, 159–60
Superiority, superior children who
  parade their, 133
Supervisors, 159
  assistance given to teachers, 245
  relationship with teachers, 253
Switzerland, education of the gifted,
  33

T

Talent
  aptitude tests may indicate, 59
  motivation of person affects development of, 59

  nature of, 35
"Talented Youth Project," 35
Tape recordings, 301
Teachers, 233–56
  certification, 240
  colleges, 460–64
    instructional staff, 360–62
  comments written on records, 61
  conferences with parents (*see*
    Parent-teacher conferences)
  as counselors, 431
  docility not indicative of gifted-
    ness, 49
  education of, 239–48
    administrative aid, 245
    general, 239
    in-service, 245–48
      classes and study groups, 246
      informal methods, 247–48
      institutes, 246
      reading, 247
      workshops, 245–46
    practice teaching, 244–45
    preservice, 239–45
    professional, 240–44
    specialized, 239–40
    workshops for, 245–46
  enrichment programs, 167–78
  extracurricular services, 255–56
  honors program, 455
  influence of personality, 369
  institutes, 246
  interest in working with superior
    students, 248, 249–50
  junior high school, 407
  load, 253–55
    size of classes, 254
  marks given by, 52–53
  observations of the gifted child,
    48–52
  orienting teachers, 179
  preparation of, 239–48
    in-service education, 245–48
    preservice education, 239–45
    qualifications, 233–39
      broad knowledge, 236
      creativity, 234–35
      diversified personal interests,
        236–37
      good physical and emotional
        health, 237–38

Teachers (*Cont.*)
  qualifications (*Cont.*)
    interest in students, 234
    personal, 238–39
    resourcefulness in method, 235–36
    superior intelligence, 233–34
    understanding of democracy, 238
    relationships with other teachers, 250–53
    selection of, 179, 248–50
Teachers College (Columbia University), 36
Teaching
  discussion methods, 242–43
  hours of preparation required, 206
  individual instruction, 243–44
  methods and techniques, 242
  practice, 244–45
  underteaching as a cause of underachievement, 145
Teaching-learning experiences
  secondary schools, 395–96, 398
  senior high schools, 427–28
Teaching machines, 465
Teaching methods
  community approach, 374–76
  discussion, 372–73
  elementary schools, 368–76
  group work, 371
  guidance type of training, 376
  influence of personality, 369
  junior high schools, 412–14
  problem approach, 369–71
  routine drills, 371–72
  senior high schools, 427–29
  teacher must be resourceful in, 235–36
  work units, 373–74
Tests and testing
  achievement, 57–58, 87, 148–49
  aptitude, 58–59, 138–39, 151
  Bernreuter Personality Inventory, 139
  diagnostic, 149, 189–90
  early admission to college program, 469
  educational guidance, 147–49
  free association, 87
  group, 325
  intelligence, 55–57
  interest inventories, 60
  interpretation of cumulative records, 60–62
  Kuhlman-Anderson Tests, 138
  Maller Self-Marking Test, 81
  Otis Quick-Scoring Mental Ability Test, 138
  Otis Self-Administering Test of Mental Ability, 138
  personality, 139
  preschool children, 324–26
  proficiency examinations, 189
  scores, used to identify giftedness, 54–55
  sociometric, 60
  standardized, 55–62, 148–49
  Stanford Achievement, 87
  Strong Vocational Interest, 97
  teacher training in use of, 242
  Terman-Merrill revision of the Stanford-Binet scale, 138
  vocational aptitude, 151
  vocational guidance, 151
  Wechsler Intelligence Test, 138
Textbooks, elementary schools, 349
Theaters
  children's, 271
  summer, 271, 272
Thinking, creative, 13
Three-year olds, 330
Toys for the preschool child, 305–9
  craft supplies, 307
  for creative play, 307
  finger paints, 308
  musical, 314–15
Trustworthiness, 111
Truthfulness, 120
Tutoring college students, 463–64
Two-year olds, 330
Typewriting, 367–68

U

Underachievement
  causes of, 91, 124, 145, 433
  problem of, 433–34
Underachievers, 91, 111, 145, 228, 229, 432
U.S.S.R.
  educational program, 172

effect of Sputnik on U.S. education, 38–39

Union of Soviet Socialist States, education of the gifted, 33–34

United Nations Assemblies, 276

United States, education of the gifted, 34–38

Upjohn Institute for Community Research, 282

V

Versatility of gifted children, 104

Vocabulary of the gifted, 123

Vocational achievement of the gifted, 97–101, 104

Vocational guidance, 150–55
counseling, 152–55
gifted have multiple potentials, 154
observation and tests, 151
social welfare affects the selection of a career, 154–55

Vocations
income related to amount of education, 98–99
number of gifted entering the professions, 97–98
research studies, 97–100

Voting in national elections by the gifted, 102–3

W

Wechsler Intelligence Test, 138

Weight, gifted and average children compared, 71–75

White House Conference Report of 1931, 32

Who's Who in America, 92

Wife, role of, 129

Winnetka (Illinois) schools, 32

Wisconsin, University of, 164, 472

Wisconsin Counseling Study, 154

Women
career, 129
role of, 128–29
working outside their homes, 99

Worcester Girls' Club, 287

Worcester (Massachusetts) Art Museum, 287

Worcester (Massachusetts) schools, 28, 32

Work units, as a method of teaching, 373–74

Workshop groups, 221
for teachers, 245–46

World War II, gifted men and women in, 102–3

Writing, creative, 51–52, 355–57, 378

Y

Yale University, 164, 466

YMCA and YWCA organizations, 270–71, 283

Z

Zoos, learning values of, 270